Additional Praise for *Law on Trial*

"*Law on Trial* is an incisive, surprising, and deeply insightful account of how lawyers play a key role in sustaining inequality and injustice. Shaun Ossei-Owusu begins with this counterintuitive claim and then takes readers on an unforgettable journey through the training and practice of lawyers from his vantage point as an 'unlikely insider'—a young Black Ivy League law professor. He is one of the most important legal scholars of his generation, and the book is both brilliant and highly readable. You'll never think of law the same way again after reading it."
—Imani Perry, author of *South to America: A Journey Below the Mason-Dixon to Understand the Soul of a Nation*

"*Law on Trial* is a bold indictment of an American legal system that betrays its own ideals—and a rare insider's view of the lawyers complicit in its inequities. At once personal testimony and systemic critique, *Law on Trial* dismantles the myths of legal neutrality and delivers an essential call to imagine—and demand—a more equitable order."
—Dorothy Roberts, author of *Torn Apart: How the Child Welfare System Destroys Black Families—and How Abolition Can Build a Safer World*

"A generation-defining critique and roadmap for transformation, *Law on Trial* challenges all of us to critically examine our role in the system and what we can do to make real law's promise of equal justice for all. A call to radically reimagine how we understand and teach law in a deeply flawed democracy, this book could not be more urgent and timely. It should be required reading for all first-year law students."
—Scott L. Cummings, author of *An Equal Place: Lawyers in the Struggle for Los Angeles*

"Beautifully written, exhaustively researched, and cogently argued, this wonderfully accessible book meets the moment in every possible way. It takes you on a remarkably textured journey inside law school classrooms, the chambers of judges, and the offices of lawyers—prosecutors and defense attorneys, corporate lawyers and public interest advocates—to unmask the normality and ordinariness with which the legal profession produces inequality across every dimension of social life. *Law on Trial* is a book not only for lawyers and law students. It is a book for all of us."

—Devon W. Carbado, author of *Unreasonable: Black Lives, Police Power, and the Fourth Amendment*

"Have you ever had the uneasy feeling that the American 'justice' system is operated by and for the haves at the expense of the have-nots? If so, *Law on Trial* is the book for you. Shaun Ossei-Owusu takes us on a brutal, but accurate, tour of a broken American legal system from law school to Wall Street to public defenders and every stop in between. Ossei-Owusu keeps it raw like sushi and uses his own unique journey from the Bronx to teaching in the Ivy League to shine a piercing light in the darkness. Bracing and brave, we are lucky to have this book."

—Benjamin H. Barton, author of *The Credentialed Court: Inside the Cloistered, Elite World of American Justice*

"*Law on Trial* is a brilliant socio-legal analysis of the relationship between law and systems of inequality. Shaun Ossei-Owusu's monumental achievement is his capacity to draw on his own lived experiences coming from the communities that law most often neglects. The writing is as lyrical as it is percussive. *Law on Trial* is a once-in-a generation accomplishment that echoes the most beautiful but devastating hip-hop ballad. Scholars, students, and the public will be captivated by this masterful book."

—Laura Beth Nielsen, coauthor of *Rights on Trial: How Workplace Discrimination Law Perpetuates Inequality*

"This book pulls back the curtain on the legal profession to expose the myths we cling to and the deeper injustices that are often overlooked or willfully ignored. Shaun Ossei-Owusu executes the rare feat of offering a book that blends personal narrative with scholarly rigor and arresting humor. This is the book I wish I had before law school and the one I'd hand to anyone who wants an accessible primer on how our legal system fails."

—Bernadette Atuahene, author of *Plundered: How Racist Policies Undermine Black Homeownership in America*

"*Law on Trial* lays bare how law professors, law firms, government lawyers, and even public interest attorneys routinely take steps—intentionally and unconsciously—to ignore and promote inequalities and unfairness in the law.... Nuanced and rigorous while also being conversational and even humorous, this book is a must read for every law student, professor, lawyer, and person who cares about inequality and injustice in the legal system."

—Eve Primus, Yale Kamisar Collegiate Professor of Law at the University of Michigan and the director of MDefenders and the Public Defender Training Institute

"Shaun Ossei-Owusu has produced a revelatory study of how the American legal profession mirrors and magnifies social inequalities. *Law on Trial* dissects the myriad ways in which lawyers protect powerful interests, obscure inconvenient truths, and normalize injustice—all while telling the public, and themselves, that they are fighting the good fight. Panoramic in scope yet rich in detail, unsparing in its criticisms yet never self-righteous, this book deserves to be read by every law student."

—David Pozen, author of *The Constitution of the War on Drugs*

"*Law on Trial* is both an insider's treasure house of information and an outsider's tell-all of the inner workings of the US legal system. Shaun Ossei-Owusu thoroughly explores and exposes how legal education, law firms, and the regulatory state skew toward maintaining the status quo while seeming to the untrained outside eye as neutral arbiters of justice. This book is essential reading for anyone interested in understanding how the law perpetuates inequality."

—Mehrsa Baradaran, author of *The Racial Wealth Gap: A Brief History*

"*Law on Trial* is required reading for every dreamer going to law school to change the world—and for anyone who wants to understand the divides that fracture our society. Shaun Ossei-Owusu's tell-all tale is a sobering account of the legal system's shortcomings as could only be told by an insider working in the belly of the beast."

—Nicole Gonzalez Van Cleve, author of *Crime Fictions: How Racist Lies Built a System of Mass Wrongful Conviction*

"In this sharp and engaging work, Shaun Ossei-Owusu—one of the nation's leading scholars of the legal profession—delivers a bold critique of lawyers and the law schools that shape them."

—James Forman Jr., author of *Locking Up Our Own: Crime and Punishment in Black America*

LAW ON TRIAL

AN UNLIKELY INSIDER RECKONS WITH OUR LEGAL SYSTEM

Shaun Ossei-Owusu

W. W. NORTON & COMPANY
Independent Publishers Since 1923

Copyright © 2026 by Shaun Ossei-Owusu

All rights reserved
Printed in the United States of America
First Edition

For information about permission to reproduce selections from this book, write to Permissions, W. W. Norton & Company, Inc., 500 Fifth Avenue, New York, NY 10110

For information about special discounts for bulk purchases, please contact W. W. Norton Special Sales at specialsales@wwnorton.com or 800-233-4830

Manufacturing by Lake Book Manufacturing
Book design by Chrissy Kurpeski
Production manager: Louise Mattareliano

Library of Congress Cataloging-in-Publication Data

Names: Ossei-Owusu, Shaun author
Title: Law on trial : an unlikely insider reckons with our legal system / Shaun Ossei-Owusu.
Description: First edition. | New York : W.W. Norton & Company, 2026. | Includes bibliographical references and index.
Identifiers: LCCN 2026001677 | ISBN 9781324091264 hardcover | ISBN 9781324091271 ebook
Subjects: LCSH: Discrimination in justice administration—United States | Equality before the law—United States | Equity—United States | Fairness
Classification: LCC KF384 .O87 2026
LC record available at https://lccn.loc.gov/2026001677

W. W. Norton & Company, Inc.
500 Fifth Avenue, New York, NY 10110
www.wwnorton.com

W. W. Norton & Company Ltd.
15 Carlisle Street, London W1D 3BS

Authorized EU representative:
EAS, Mustamäe tee 50, 10621 Tallinn, Estonia

1 2 3 4 5 6 7 8 9 0

CONTENTS

Introduction: *Notes From the Margins* 1

PART I: LAW SCHOOL

Chapter 1 | Legal Bootcamp 27

Assembly #1: Untold Tales in Contract, Tort, and Property Law 51

Chapter 2 | Manufactured Consent and Contractual Inequality 54

Chapter 3 | Injurious Matters: *Tort Law and the Narrow Construction of Harm* 72

Chapter 4 | Property, Ownership, and Injustice 89

Assembly #2: The Written and Unwritten Rules in Criminal Law, Constitutional Law, and Civil Procedure 107

Chapter 5 | Textbook Injustice: *Criminal Law and the Unspoken Politics of Punishment* 109

Chapter 6 | The Ultimate Con Job? *Constitutional Law and the Effacement of History and Politics* 127

Chapter 7 | Civil Procedure and the Architecture of Inequality 149

PART II: GOVERNMENT LAWYERING

Preliminary Hearing 169

Chapter 8 | The Power to Choose: *Prosecutors and the Criminal Justice Machinery* 174

Chapter 9 | Municipal Matters: *The Hidden Civil Power of County Counsel and City Hall Attorneys* 195

PART III: BIG LAW

A Sober View of Big Law — 223

Chapter 10 | Transactional Violence: *Healthcare and the Afterlives of Mergers and Acquisitions* — 229

Chapter 11 | Environmental Degradation in the Regulatory Wild West — 247

Chapter 12 | Litigating Labor: *Class Action Killers, Wage Theft Accomplices, and Union Busters* — 268

PART IV: PUBLIC INTEREST LAWYERING

Intake: *Public Disservice and the Paradox of Good Intentions* — 291

Chapter 13 | How We Got Here: *The Political and Economic Straitjacketing of Public Interest Law* — 296

Chapter 14 | Power, Prejudice, and Paternalism in the Pink Ghetto — 310

Chapter 15 | High-Level Impact Litigation and Inequality — 323

Conclusion: *For the Record* — 343

Acknowledgments — 359

Notes — 363

Index — 409

LAW ON TRIAL

Introduction

Notes from the Margins

"Equal Justice Under Law" is emblazoned on the United States Supreme Court building. Lawyers invoke it, textbooks proclaim it, and it circulates throughout society. This powerful aspiration is echoed so often that it can feel less like a goal and more like a given. Unfortunately, the phrase belongs to America's collection of beautiful fictions, nestled somewhere between Huckleberry Finn, the Tooth Fairy, and trickle-down economics.[1]

"Equal Justice Under Law" mocks the brutal, lived reality of many Americans. It tells us little about a legal system that distributes pain and privilege unevenly. There's an obscene catalog of legal inequalities that we've been conditioned to either digest or ignore. Countless others remain hidden from view entirely. Let us confront only a few places where the law betrays its rhetoric and fails to live up to its own hype.

The child welfare system scrutinizes motherhood through the watchful lens of class. In poor neighborhoods, mothers face the threat of losing their children because their poverty is mistaken for neglect. The mom who works two shifts and leaves her young teenage daughter in charge can be accused of negligent supervision, whereas wealthy parents who entrust their children to foreign au pairs earning poverty wages do not have to worry about a social worker pounding on their door.

Or picture this. A dozen migrant children are sitting in a room. They are swiveling in chairs and sitting in front of a computer for a virtual immigration court hearing. Visualize that four-year-old girl in a tie-dye shirt or the seven-year-old boy wearing a shirt with a pizza on it. The judge tells them, "The reason we're here is because the government of the United States wants you to leave the United States. . . . It's my job to figure out if you have to leave" and "it's also my job to figure out if you should stay." No parents or lawyers are present. Just shelter workers who helped the children log on for the hearing.[2] The same government that insists on booster seats in cars for children's safety somehow believes that they can navigate court proceedings without legal help.

On the other end of the age spectrum, complicated Medicare denial letters come in English-only paperwork to Dominican grandfathers who cannot navigate the layers of appeals. Vietnamese grandmothers seeking benefits they earned through decades of work get lost in administrative hearings where no one speaks their language. Meanwhile, Black elders are uniquely vulnerable to predatory loans at a time when the Feds have purposely gutted the agency that regulates these instruments.

"Equal Justice Under Law" is a bad joke for poor rural white people, too. Try explaining that lofty phrase to a woman in rural Arkansas, a state where women experience the highest rates of domestic violence.[3] She needs help with an emergency protective order but lives in a legal desert where the closest legal aid office is eighty miles away. On the other hand, a team of corporate lawyers can easily parachute into Little Rock for a court hearing when big money is on the line.

Read in even the most favorable light, "Equal Justice Under the Law" merits an asterisk. A nation premised on democracy has a longer history of racialized voter suppression and gender exclusion than equal access to the ballot. We have some statutes that prohibit discrimination on the basis of sex, disability, religion, and age. But they are so new that if they were people, they wouldn't be eligible for Social Security.

In a world of normalized injustice, many struggle to understand a simple question that is the starting point for this book: Why does a legal system that purports to represent ideals like justice, equality, and fairness consistently fail to meet these ideals? The often-highlighted culprits of legal inequality are the various -isms and -phobias of the world: racism, sexism, capitalism, and homophobia, to name a few. Less discussed, and much less well understood, is the role lawyers play in perpetuating inequality. Yet we need not look far.

Lawyers are embroiled in scandals that have become flashpoints of national debate and drawn criticism from all sides—whether at Republican town halls, in libertarian media, or across progressive grassroots movements. Attorneys have justified immigration officers' detention of US citizens. They have chipped away at protections meant to shield consumers from scams. Others have helped engineer nearly a trillion dollars in domestic healthcare cuts to the poor. Those efforts came alongside foreign aid rollbacks projected to cause 14 million deaths globally (including 4.5 million children). They even endorsed freezes on funding for life-saving research into diseases and conditions that may affect the life of someone you know: cancer, Alzheimer's, Parkinson's, PTSD therapies for veterans, and suicide prevention. These aren't isolated recent events but part of a longer history of how legal professionals—the people entrusted with justice—become central actors in its betrayal.

Law on Trial examines how the socialization of lawyers and the structure of legal practice perpetuates inequality.

This is not a story about mustache-twirling villains. What I want you to understand most deeply in this book is this: Law schools cultivate a dangerous but tragically necessary talent—the ability to extract legal questions from their moral weight and social implications. This separation becomes a habit that follows lawyers into the law firms, government offices, and public interest organizations that impact everyday Americans. Even those who resist this training and hold onto their moral clarity face pressure in their work environments, which can reward technical skill over societal concern.

Here's the quandary: Lawyers *must* take human problems and repackage them for legal usage, much like doctors must translate a patient's imprecise description of pain into specialized diagnostic codes. But the legal profession sometimes takes this necessary process and stretches it until the human element fades faintly into the background.

I've observed the legal machinery from uncomfortably close range: as a scholar wrestling with the demons of inequality, then as a nontraditional law student bearing the weight of this socialization, as an attorney who had to confront the contradictions of practice, and now as a professor responsible for training the next generation of lawyers. These pages are an attempt to reflect parts of the profession to itself and the public.

Lawyers are behind many of the political scandals of our times, but the inequality that flows from them doesn't follow neat ideological lines. If your political compass leans right, a host of issues probably grind your gears. Government theft of property, infringements on the right to bear arms, invasions of privacy, and insensitivity to religious liberty have lawyers lurking in the background. If you lean left, the fingerprints of attorneys can be found on issues tied to anti-Black racism, reproductive rights, consumer protection, and climate change.

More generally, if you give me any other pressing social issue—housing insecurity, economic inequality, disability rights, Indigenous Peoples' rights, or free speech—I'll pinpoint with ease how lawyers exacerbate these problems. And I do that in these pages. But before we proceed any deeper into the legal wilderness, I have to pause to say something about myself.

I'd much rather keep moving forward and keep my focus on the legal system. But those who have read these pages in their early form—especially women friends and colleagues—have reminded me gently, but firmly, that readers need to know who I am before they can decide whether they want to go down this road. This is wisdom that I initially resisted, but they were right. They're often right. The message is not the only thing that matters; the messenger is important too.

A long line of thinkers has argued that individual knowledge comes from specific people with experience, histories, and encounters with power. This is not about rejecting some kind of unachievable objectivity or embracing loose subjectivity. It's about trying to be more transparent and thorough when explaining from where this critique emerges. And so, recognizing its necessity, I reluctantly offer some background. Not to exceptionalize my background—the statistics on Black men from the Bronx who become Ivy League professors speak for themselves. I provide this context to anchor my observations and help you decide whether my voice merits your attention among the many people trying to explain American law.

How I Got Here and How I Got Over

I was never destined to be an academic. You should know upfront that I'm Black Black. I'm a dark-skinned, sneaker-wearing, hip-hop referencing, first-generation everything with an unmaskable New York accent. I look like a rapper. I have a pandemic afro that occasionally transforms into cornrows. Few people have this bundle of characteristics in the legal profession.

My students sometimes remind me of my distinctiveness when they stare in awe at a Black man who can explain how a constitutional provision works. I have a law degree and a PhD. Sometimes I get interdisciplinary and traverse legal history or urban sociology. Some of my colleagues also look at me in awe, as though I'm a trapeze artist performing a daring stunt. I read the same story in the eyes of students—white, Black, international, first-generation, or privileged—a disbelief that I might be able to offer some knowledge they lack. I'm basically Bigfoot in these academic streets.

I was born and raised in the Bronx. For much of my life, this part of New York City has been one of the poorest, if not the poorest, congressional districts in the country.

A gauntlet of halfway houses and drug rehabilitation programs populate my childhood block. The rent-controlled apartment I grew up in and still call home when I visit family abuts the Cross Bronx Expressway. Scholars uniformly agree that this highway—which was unnecessarily rammed through the borough by urban planners in the mid-twentieth century—produced some of the poverty that defines the Bronx. Spiraling home values transformed landlords into slumlords who burned their properties for the insurance payouts. White people skedaddled. The depressed economic conditions created spaces for people like my parents—immigrants from Ghana—to set up shop in the 1970s and secure cheap rent in what was culturally, sociologically, and colloquially a ghetto.[4]

Everybody in my neighborhood was from some part of the African Diaspora—Black America, Puerto Rico, the Caribbean, West Africa—most were law-abiding neighbors weaving through social disadvantage. But they weren't alone. Squatters posted up in abandoned buildings—their numbers were estimated to be as high as fifty thousand in a portion of the city that barely cracked five hundred thousand people in total.[5] Drug dealers hung out in front of semi-solvent bodegas that peddled calorically empty food packed with salt, sugar, and fat. Stickup kids were so common that there is an academic book about them set in the neighborhood where I went to school.[6]

By the time I reached adolescent awareness, the dust from the crack epidemic had settled (though it never fully disappeared). Broken windows policing was in vogue, and the country entered a new phase of anti-immigrant welfare reform. Even without the precise vocabulary to describe it, I understood that the legal system treated my neighborhood differently.

My local public school, William Howard Taft High School, was not great. Some years only half of the enrolled students made it to class, and 40 percent of students dropped out. My parents said, "We'll pass." They sent me and my older brother to Catholic schools from first to twelfth grade. Maybe this is why I'm sometimes sympathetic to conservative arguments about school choice and supportive of, but not fanatical about, public education.

At the turn of the century, New York City Catholic schools were typically spaces where poor and working-class parents sent their kids when they could not afford $30,000 for private school but could scrap together $2,000–$3,000 a year in an effort to forgo underfunded public-school options.[7] My schools were modest; they weren't magnet schools or academic powerhouses, but they weren't failing either. I learned the basics, a sense of discipline that still stays with me, and plenty about heaven, even though outside sometimes felt like purgatory.

By high school, I studied as if my life depended on it. I had a sense that my parents were making trades in real time: tuition over homeownership, school uniforms over equity, and educational access over asset-building. It got even clearer when I spoke to my mom as an adult. On the precipice of purchasing my own home, I asked her why she and my father opted to rent in perpetuity and didn't buy a co-op or a house like some working-class families with some savings did. She said, without hesitation, "Your education is my house. That's my investment." I didn't fully grasp the labor behind the sacrifices in real time, but I still treated those high-stakes exams like they were being paid for in overtime work.

I graduated near the top of my class, and my standardized test scores put me within striking distance of elite schools, but I only ended up at Northwestern because of an unlikely break: a counselor doing the rounds at fancy Manhattan schools made an unscheduled stop in the Bronx. (Northwestern had no recent history of recruiting at my school before, and I still don't know why they did that day.) In any event, the school by Lake Michigan and I discovered each other. Sadly, in today's post-affirmative action world—where a Black student's acceptance is *still* treated as per se evidence of a university cheating—I doubt I'd get in, even with strong credentials.

That full ride to Northwestern was more than money; it stretched the fence line of my imagination. But within weeks of getting to campus, I was bum-rushed by unfamiliarity. The offhand talk of my classmates about SAT tutors, personal-statement coaches, vacation homes, family lawyers, and gap years caught me off guard. Check this out: I'm barely forty, and for almost *half* my life, I had no white friends. Segregation deprived me of that possibility. The only white people I saw were teachers and cops.

Many of the white people that eventually became friends in college grew up less than ten miles away from where I had—in downtown Manhattan, Westchester County, or some New Jersey suburb. We bonded as diehard New York sports fans, but their lives were otherwise completely different from mine. I developed friendships with them, with solidly middle- to upper-class Black students (whose worlds were foreign in a different way), and with the few other working-class minorities like me. Those bonds helped me manage the cultural whiplash and hold my own academically. I was fortunate to encounter a cadre of professors—two of whom are literal Black MacArthur geniuses—who put me on an academic conveyor belt and planted the dangerous idea in my head that I could be a lawyer, an academic, or both.

This may sound like a neo–Horatio Alger feel-good tale, but it was still very clear to me then and now that the legal system was not designed for people like me to be training up-and-coming attorneys. In hindsight, I'm often amazed that I gathered the magical code-switching capabilities necessary to navigate this world, let alone become a lawyer.

When I move through legal spaces—classrooms, conferences, and courthouses—I can't unsee this past. Not sharing it would be like a tour guide not mentioning that they grew up in the place they're showing. This background informs my understanding and blends with all the formal education, practice, and teaching to shape how I view the legal system.

With some knowledge of environmental law, it's clearer why asthma pumps dangled from my friends' necks like dog tags and why labored breathing was a common sound. The borough referred to as "Asthma Alley" doesn't have the highest rates of this condition for no reason. Environmental impact statements and legal frameworks that undervalue poor people's lungs play a role.

The Medicaid recipients I knew who had to wait months for appointments for conditions needing immediate attention? That was just regular poverty to me. I thought the same about landlords who shut out Section 8 tenants with flimsy excuses. Now I know that's part of a field called poverty law.

With a better understanding of how law intersects with the economy, I know now that the paucity of supermarkets with fresh produce and the flood of bodegas weren't natural market distributions. These were the result of legal incentives, subsidies, and business regulations that shape the geography of food inequality.[8]

Before becoming an attorney, I thought disability law was niche. Now, it feels deeply personal. All it takes is a flashback: teachers who treated learning differences as misbehavior; bus drivers and passengers who sighed when accessibility ramps had to be deployed; and broken elevators that were dismissed as routine inconveniences instead of the civil rights violations they often were.

I'm in the strange position of being a legal insider who comes from communities the system often disregards. Why this position is so unusual becomes clearer when you have a better sense of the legal profession that governs all of us.

An Elite Industry

Now it might be painful for some to admit, and obvious for others, but the law is a white man's game. The Supreme Court has sadly been a two-hundred-year-old frat house. Out of 120 justices, only 6 women have been able to join Lamda Alpha Bro. That's 5 percent. As political scientists Adam Bonica and Maya Sen note, "for much of the nation's history, the bar—the Men of Letters—exclusively represented the interests of the well-educated, moneyed elite."[9]

Look at the alumni portraits that line the walls of law school hallways, or at who staffs the leadership of powerful American law firms, or at the demographics of Congress (which has a sizeable number of lawyers). They all skew toward white men. I'm not asking you to draw any inferences from that; I'm just trying to set the scene.

After generations of outright exclusion and a few decades of half-hearted inclusion, the legal profession is only 21 percent non-white. Five percent of America's lawyers are Black, and 6 percent of the professoriate is Black. The numbers for other minority groups are similar.[10] Nevertheless, some think the slow-motion tanning of the legal profession is *too much*. As I write, plaintiffs in a pending lawsuit against Northwestern Law School argue that the school—which has more than 80 percent white faculty—viciously discriminates against white men.

The legal aversion to racial inclusion is rarely stated in explicit terms. Sometimes it occurs through the new conservative dog whistle—DEI—or through the polite racism of white liberals. This is the type that Martin Luther King Jr. criticized late in his cut-short life—the kind that is okay with some people of color, but certainly not beyond tokenistic thresholds. This is a world I didn't *expect* to break into.[11]

A fish rots from the head down. If you look at the composition of the Supreme Court, eight of the nine justices went to Harvard or Yale and all of them are millionaires. They all spent more time as judges in lower federal courts than any other cohort in American history—meaning they've had lifetime appointments where they've likely had minimal substantive contact with the public.[12]

The justices are really accomplished people who amassed some of their wealth before getting on the court. Chief Justice John Roberts left practice thirteen years before I joined the bar, but people still talk about his legend in DC. He was one of the best litigators of his generation. All of this probably explains why he's the richest justice with assets reported somewhere between $9 and $27 million.[13]

But maybe, just maybe, there is some connection between the court's overall wealth—estimated to be as high as $68 million—and its reputation as one of the most business-friendly courts in American history?[14] Is this background part of the reason why they've unfurled the red carpet for corporate spending in politics, seemingly hate unions, appear to be agnostic about the idea of consumer protection, and rarely hear challenges brought by low-income litigants?[15] Yes, Justices Clarence Thomas and Sonia Sotomayor are from the trenches. But I'm still willing to bet that no five-member majority of the Court has ever had to time their showers around when the hot water might work or bob and weave through rooms lined with buckets catching leaks from the ceiling.

And it's not just their likely insulation from poverty, but their probable estrangement from the realities that working-class and middle-class

Americans face. Have they—or anyone they intimately know—put up with a dehumanizing job because losing health insurance would mean gambling with a family member's health? Postponed divorce because neither person could afford to move out? Finished a full-time shift only to put on a second hat as a DoorDash driver, Taskrabbit cleaner, Instacart shopper? Lived experience is not a prerequisite for the job, but how much trust can the public place in a court so removed from the day-to-day realities of the millions it affects?

Things are not much better in the lower federal courts. In his first full year on the job, Chief Justice Roberts advocated for judicial pay raises. He complained that the salaries of lower-court federal judges, which ranged from $165,000 to $175,000 at the time, was a "constitutional crisis"—a complaint that would probably ring hollow to the average American who lived in a household that made a third of that amount.[16] A *Wall Street Journal* investigation found that half of the federal judges examined disclosed minimum assets of at least $775,000; the same survey also found that 131 had violated ethical rules by hearing cases involving companies in which they or their family-owned stock.[17]

The professoriate that trains the future lawyers often comes from financial comfort as well.[18] One study of new law professors found that they attended colleges that served the wealthiest strata of society—where two-thirds of the students came from the richest 20 percent of families.[19] The overwhelming majority of professors at "top-ten" ranked law schools went to other top-ten law schools (94 percent). Outside of the top law schools, an estimated 68 percent of schools hire faculty who graduated from these highly ranked institutions.[20]

Law professors are in the top 15 percent of income earners in the US, with an average salary of $142,000; if they have practice experience, which is hit or miss, it probably did not involve providing legal services to poor or working-class Americans. Economic security likely shapes their understanding of the legal system and leaves them with "little incentive to buck this paradigm" and bring low-income perspectives into their teaching and scholarship.[21]

These dynamics trickle down to law students, a large percentage of whom come from elite backgrounds. Individuals from families in the top 10 percent of income are ten times more likely to attend law school than students whose families are in the bottom half.[22]

I outline the race and class makeup of the bar not to point a finger at white legal professionals. Some are brilliant students, colleagues, and principled allies. I dwell on the composition of the profession because it reveals who runs the show. This is about power: who teaches, applies, and interprets law, and in doing so, determines which problems deserve attention. I also offer this background to provide context for the institutional landscape we'll be traversing in these pages. These demographic realities point toward some of the tensions that animate this book—tensions between institutional narratives and lived realities.

The Book's Design and My Standpoint

Law on Trial is based on ten years of observations and reflections on the legal field, first as a scholar of race, then as a law student, then as a practicing lawyer, and now as a law professor.

While completing my PhD at Berkeley, I decided to attend law school. Every snowflake is unique, but I was different from most for a few reasons. Some of the distinctions were demographically obvious; I was one of a few Black men in a state school that banned race-based affirmative action. I held a particular view of the world, as just described. Unlike the typical student who goes straight to law school from college or works for a few years, I spent three years as a research fellow at the American Bar Foundation and had five years of doctoral training under my belt. I knew that the widespread veneration of our legal system was often misguided. I also knew I wanted to be a law professor—a statistically rare outcome for law students.

So, I set off to acquire an arsenal of legal knowledge and some practice experience. I would be dishonest if I claimed there were no practical or material considerations—I come from a working-class family and I'm human. But I was and still am consumed by issues of inequality, many of which are central to this book.

In the following pages, I'll walk you through the classrooms where attorneys are conditioned and the law offices where they subsequently work to chronicle the underreported dimensions of inequality. This is not the kind of empirical study involving formal data analysis, surveys, and regressions; it's a view from the inside, based on experiences, stories, cases, and scholarship that seldom make it out of the legal world.

This insider-outsider status informs this unflattering view of America's legal system. Some will consider it sacrilegious. My takes will almost certainly generate negative reactions from legal establishment types. IDGAF. Their comfort is not my concern and my sleep schedule remains unaffected. This book challenges self-serving and popular accounts of attorneys as stalwarts of justice.

During the ten-year period at the center of this writing—in my years as a law student, attorney, and professor—I took notes on matters of inequality that were important to me but that were too controversial or tangential to raise in my classes or with my professional peers. Even though these settings screamed for more real-world context, many of my colleagues seemed uninterested. And so, I kept up a conversation with myself.

As my colleague and mentor Regina Austin mused, "Naturally, I talk to myself. Who else is there to talk to?" What else is there to do when "being a token is like being in solitary confinement," and the jailers are a legal profession with no time for serious, dissident views?[23] In this book, I take some of those reflective notes from the margins, which at times served as my sanity check. I bring them to the fore with a clear recognition that I'm one of the few people in the privileged position to disclose.

But I'm an imperfect vehicle for the arguments this book makes.

I work at a fantastic institution—the University of Pennsylvania—a fortress in a city marked by poverty. I'm a begrudging gatekeeper to the high-paying profession that I am critiquing. No matter how uncomfortable I am when lawyers and academics regale me with stories about golf, investment portfolios, and upscale things I couldn't care less about, I am technically part of this club. One of the reasons I started this form of journaling, all the way back in 2013, was that I knew that if I got a job as a professor, "my experiences with poverty were only going to be a part of my memory, not my life going forward."[24] The deep connections I keep with family and friends who live in economic uncertainty are no substitute for living in it. I could have worked forever in public interest law (where I did a short stint) or chosen to remain a K–12 teacher (my first job out of college). Instead, I opted for the legal world, knowing it would put space—though not a wall—between me and where I come from.

What I Mean by Legal Inequality: The Six-Headed Hydra

This is a book about lawyers, but it is hard to write about them without writing about the law. They are different but connected, like music and musicians, and it's important to say something about that relationship.

Law, most simply, is a system of rules, institutions, and processes that order social life. *Lawyers* are the flesh-and-blood people who give law meaning. Part of their training as law students involves processing human problems into technical questions that can strip away social context. Practice settings reinforce this separation through resource constraints, incentives, and office cultures. That is what this book is focused on—how legal education and practice can teach lawyers to disconnect legal questions from their social implications. The consequences of this disconnection go beyond classrooms, courtrooms, and legal offices; they have a spillover effect that lands on people who are often least equipped to absorb them.

When I talk about *legal inequality*, I typically refer to historically marginalized groups that empirical evidence has consistently shown to face social disadvantage—racial minorities, women, the poor, people with disabilities, and immigrants. But I'm also talking about the subtler ways the law shapes the lives of those we don't always picture when we talk about inequality. The middle class. Elderly people on fixed incomes. Working single parents. Rust Belt whites. People in places America has forgotten on purpose. Legal inequality stretches wider than most people think.

So I can tell this story more clearly and avoid slipping into empty phrases, we need some kind of structure. What I offer here isn't a grand theory. It's a rough map. It's not something you'll be quizzed on; it's just a way to stay oriented as the story unfolds. Without it, what comes next risks reading like a series of disconnected tragedies. But they're not disconnected. That's the point. What I'm tracing are six shapes legal inequality tends to take—six heads of the same hydra. They remind us that Lady Justice's blindfold sometimes does what it's supposed to do—offering fairness without fear or favor—and sometimes, it's a fashionable accessory she lifts for the right person.

Legal inequality as a reflection of society. Social hierarchies can exist outside of law, and the legal system maintains or exacerbates them—often through the agenda-setting power of specific groups. Wealthy school districts get more funding and resources for their children than poorer districts do. The legal system greenlights these disparities; they reflect the reality that American society values children differently based on their zip codes.

In some instances, the law is like a funhouse mirror that grotesquely reflects hierarchies that are normalized as fair. Peaceful protestors who violate minor rules get serious felony charges. But when police break laws and bodies, they get paid administrative leave. They also get qualified immunity—a legal forcefield that limits their ability to be personally sued for misconduct. These protections reflect the deference society has toward police, which can be justified as necessary because of their unique role. But these protections also limit police accountability vis-à-vis the poor and minority groups they often "serve." That limited accountability might have to be a burden those race- and class-disadvantaged communities must endure. This is part of a broader pattern I highlight in this book; I show how law takes existing social hierarchies, puts them on legal letterhead, and tells you to respect them.

Legal inequality as discursive power. The second head of inequality speaks in tongues that are indecipherable to the general public. This is actually a twofold problem. On the one hand, law schools are where students get their linguistic baptism; this is part of the reason why legal education gets so much real estate in this book. In the required first-year civil procedure course, a question like "Was this coal mining community poisoned?" can easily mutate into "Did residents of that community file their poisoning complaint correctly and in a timely fashion?" The same restyling of harm happens in the legal system. Whether medical debt should lead to financial ruin gets lost in the weeds of bankruptcy exemptions and statutes of limitations.

But on the other hand, this kind of inequality is not just about lingo. Whose story gets told and whose omitted is crucial. Depending on the class and instructor, law-created human suffering can be missing or peripheral, while business interests are the marquee headliner. The same privileging of certain narratives occurs in real-world disputes; poor people's experiences get the "anecdotal" label, whereas corporate insights get the "data-driven" designation. Large slices of this book show how "the language of law" and the elevation of certain voices play a role in exacerbating inequalities.[25]

Legal inequality as selective enforcement. The third feature focuses on the referees who apply rules differently depending on players. In the context of criminal law, AR-15-owning white supremacist shooters like Dylann Roof and Payton Gendron can kill scores of Black people and be arrested alive, but if you're a large Black man selling loose cigarettes on the street, then you are a threat requiring maximum force. As for prosecutors, the multinational bank HSBC can be accused of terrorist financing and laundering money for Central American drug lords, but SWAT is not kicking down their doors, and you will certainly see no perp walks. How the law gets applied sometimes depends on its focus.[26]

Legal inequality by design. A fourth component concerns the rigged rulebook itself. When this head hisses, we see inequality encoded into the law. For example, government-funded lawyers help low-income people with civil issues such as evictions, consumer debt, and public benefits. The law limits their services to those below the federal poverty line, leaving many working people without help by design. And even among those who qualify, chronic underfunding means most are still turned away. The intentional constraints don't stop there: These lawyers can't take on class actions involving groups of plaintiffs challenging systemic problems. Representing prisoners and undocumented immigrants is generally off the table. Fee-generating cases that win money are even against the rules. Because of federal regulations, these attorneys are legal emergency doctors who treat gunshot wounds while not having the time to address why people in the neighborhood keep getting shot.

Legal inequality as a structural imperative. A fifth organ of legal inequality is tied to the professional mandates of being a lawyer. In this context, no one has to be evil, they just have to do their jobs. When corporations do bad things they are still entitled to a zealous legal defense. This is where things get funky. Large law firms are the offensive line for corporate malfeasance; they are the 6'8", 330-pound, gallon-of-milk drinking athlete who is there to protect the client. So when women bring sexual harassment claims against these large employers, it is considered fair game to throw procedural obstacles in the way, exhaust their resources, and extort confidentiality as a price of compensation. The tragedy here, and in many other legal settings, is that this may be morally problematic, but it is legally permissible irrespective of who bears the social costs.

Legal inequality as contested advocacy. The last dimension of inequality involves people and organizations that hold themselves out as challenging inequality while arguably reinforcing it. Consider the conservative weaponization of civil rights language to undermine civil rights protections. Groups challenge affirmative action and "reverse discrimination" while working to preserve racial advantage. Meanwhile, corporations' ability to pour money into politics was strengthened by an unlikely ally: the liberal American Civil Liberties Union (ACLU), whose commitment to speech rights extended to political spending. The truth is that many of the hot-button issues that make it to courts are fueled by the American mythology that legal actors are applying neutral principles to produce fair outcomes. Such a mythology not only fails to keep a true tally of who is winning and who is losing, but it neglects an important reality: Inequality is a contested concept that is filtered through ideology, experience, and power. Justice has subjective qualities, and equality is, more often than we admit, in the eye of the beholder.

A BASIC TYPOLOGY OF LEGAL INEQUALITY

Type	Definition
Legal inequality as reflection of society	How legal systems mirror and reinforce existing social hierarchies and power dynamics
Legal inequality as discursive power	How legal language frames disparities, transforms moral questions into technical legal issues, and excludes certain narratives
Legal inequality as selective enforcement	How laws are differently applied across social groups and contexts
Legal inequality by design	How law (e.g., statutes, regulations, constitutional provisions, and precedents) encodes and institutionalizes inequality
Legal inequality as a structural imperative	How professional roles and norms channel attorneys' work in directions that perpetuate disparities
Legal inequality as contested advocacy	How equality becomes subjectively defined in legal advocacy, with competing claims that sometimes entrench existing hierarchies

This rough taxonomy isn't airtight because inequality is leaky. Sometimes the injustice is loud and proud, written into the very text. Other times, it hides in rituals and silences. You don't need to memorize this list. If you keep reading, these themes will reappear. Inequality travels with the law, and this book is built to trace that path.

Audiences and Caveats

This project began as a conversation with my pre-law self. I had an urgent desire to understand legal inequality that bordered on desperation. As I got to law school, I realized that the place wasn't going to answer many of my questions. It could, however, provide me with invaluable technical expertise to get closer to explanations.

As I moved through law school and practice, I realized that the questions that drove me weren't unique to people like me—first-generation college graduates, racial minorities, or those from low-income communities. Other people had frustrations with the legal system: people with disabilities whose access needs are framed as "special treatment" by institutions who spend millions on cosmetic upgrades; LGBTQ individuals facing workplace discrimination because of how they identify and who they are attracted to; and working-class whites who found that their faith in legal institutions was misplaced. These are different coordinates on America's demographic map, but they share a similar predicament: trying to reconcile law's lofty rhetoric with its earthbound practice.

Though this book remains a time-capsuled field guide for my younger self, its reach extends to anyone asking fundamental questions: Why does the legal system work this way? Who really benefits, and who loses?

These questions may emerge for the approximately 38,000 people entering law school each year and the 117,000 students enrolled across all three years. They may come up for the approximately 1.3 million lawyers in the United States—some of whom may be questioning their role in the system.

But these questions may come from complete outsiders—people who have no interest in becoming lawyers but are trying to make sense of a system that impacts their lives. One that claims to care about equality but sometimes produces the opposite. The desire to understand how lawyers and our legal institutions actually function transcends background and circumstance.

What follows is necessarily incomplete. I do not discuss every aspect of legal education or the legal profession.[27] I cannot and do not claim to know what happens in every classroom, government office, law firm, or public interest organization across this vast legal landscape. No single narrative, not even the most sophisticated empirical study, could capture that totality. The legal profession contains a remarkable diversity of practice and perspective. There are classrooms where professors illuminate rather than obscure inequality, firms where lawyers prioritize justice, and government offices where public servants resist institutional pressures to reproduce inequality. Instead of comprehensiveness, I offer situated knowledge—insights gleaned from my experiences as a student, practitioner, and professor. My hope is to spur different kinds of conversations at a time when our legal system is embattled and its future is unclear.

Three final warning shots. First, unlike some of my national colleagues, I don't idealize law, its institutions, and norms. I know legal doctrine like the back of my hand; I got tenured at Penn in three years. But I don't obsess over legal niceties at the cost of eclipsing real-world suffering. I don't fetishize American-style democracy, though I understand its principles as an important source of inspiration, at the very least. Accordingly, this isn't the typical book that criticizes the Supreme Court, focuses on a single legal problem, or laments our undemocratic culture. It is, rather, a no-frills tour through sectors of the legal profession.

Second, though this book was drafted across presidential regimes—Trump 1, Biden, and the early months of MAGA 2.0—don't mistake this for another book about Trump. The arguments here are about enduring structures of the legal profession that long predate Trump and will likely outlast him. Don't forget that lawyers have helped engineer rights erosion—from their defense of slavery to their enforcement of women's second-class status under the law. But they've also played crucial roles in democratic expansion—from crafting labor protections to opening the ballot box to people that the Founding Fathers never intended to include. The deeper story I want to tell is about structural tensions that stretch across time: how lawyers sometimes act as guardians of justice and at other times as its pallbearers. This project takes the present seriously but refuses to mistake it for the whole story.

Third, if you read closely, you'll see that I'm hard to place politically. I've been mentored by foundational figures in racial justice scholarship, but I also think an appreciable amount of crime can't be tied to structural racism or entrenched poverty. Some people are sick individuals and need to be contained. I'm not an abolitionist, but I respect the courage it takes to imagine a world without militarized police and cages. I have the predictable problems with certain conservative claims, but I also have so much heat for the liberals who surround me. I play footsie with strands of libertarianism, but I also believe in a robust, muscular welfare state. I'm ideologically homeless.

Ultimately, I care more about power than I do red/blue, left/right, Democrat/Republican. This is not because I think those categories are irrelevant; political identity shapes how we see the world. But focusing on power relations reveals the deeper architecture of inequality: It unmasks whose interests are prioritized, who benefits from the status quo, and whose lives are deemed sacrificial by our legal system. Those issues are more important to me than the gaudy theater of partisan performance.

The Game Plan

The book is organized into four parts. It is modular; you can jump around if linear reading is not your jam. My modest suggestion if you choose your own adventure is to read each part's introduction first—it'll help you see what each section is doing before you dive in.

Part I, the book's longest section, consists of seven chapters that provide a glimpse into the law school experience. The first chapter offers a broad overview of legal education, the first year, and how law students are socialized; it lays the foundation for what follows in this part. The remaining chapters cover the six courses that are commonly taught in the first year of law school—two of which are always in the news (criminal law and constitutional law), three of which pervade our everyday life but get less popular attention (contracts, torts, property law), and one that is technical but determines the all-important question of who can have access to the law (civil procedure). The chapters are presented in groups of three, each punctuated by an interlude—Assembly 1 and Assembly 2—that frames these triads and provides light orientation along the way.

Of course, the other two years of law school matter, but Part I hones in on the first year because it is a foundational and shared rite of passage for lawyers. In these chapters, you'll see how legal education often misses easy opportunities to surface some of society's biggest issues: poverty, language rights, corporate wrongdoing, domestic violence, and childcare policy. Instead, schools offer narrow understandings of the law that may make students better technicians but susceptible to detachment from the real world.

Part II is comprised of two chapters that focus on government lawyers. The first type, prosecutors, are the subjects of Chapter 8. I show how these lawyers contribute to a criminal justice system that some conservatives say is too bloated, that liberals want to reform, and that abolitionists hope to extinguish. Chapter 9 focuses on a lesser-known type of lawyer: city and county attorneys. These lawyers represent municipalities. When these localities are sued for civil rights violations, their job is to provide representation. This means their job sometimes requires undermining legitimate claims brought by some of society's most vulnerable members.

Part III focuses on where some students go after school: large law firms or what is commonly referred to as Big Law. These three chapters examine three different types of lawyering in firms: *transactional work*, which involves facilitating business deals; *regulatory work*, which is concerned with ensuring that clients comply with relevant laws; and *litigation,* which focuses on resolving disputes through courts.

The transactional work chapter shows how these lawyers play a role in various kinds of industry consolidation that harm everyday consumers and limit their options. My focus is on healthcare, but the discussion also speaks to why a town might only have a handful of retailers, banks, and grocery chains: mergers and acquisitions. The second chapter in this trio focuses on the regulatory tricks and clever math lawyers engage in to slow walk meaningful approaches to climate change. The third chapter focuses on how law firms crush class actions brought by workers and undermine union efforts.

Part IV turns our attention to public interest attorneys—an unlikely bunch to appear in a book about the reproduction of inequality. Chapter 13 provides a brief history of how law and politics constrained the working conditions of these lawyers in the late twentieth century. Chapter 14 focuses on lawyers in the trenches: the legal aid attorneys and public defenders who don't get due credit for fighting in a cosmic battle on behalf of the poor against a powerful state or better-resourced private parties. But these lawyers are not immune from critique. A strange combination of being under-resourced and susceptible to implicit bias, among other causes, means some of these attorneys can be additional agents of inequality. Chapter 15 looks at appellate advocacy and the use of courts to enact social change. In this context, various liberal and conservative nonprofit organizations have advanced arguments that some people argue exacerbate the plight of marginalized groups.

The Conclusion offers some practical strategies and tactics any concerned citizen, lawyer or not, can use to try to change the status quo.

Buckle up.

PART I

LAW SCHOOL

CHAPTER 1

Legal Bootcamp

WELCOME!
It's the end of August or the beginning of September. Excitement and uncertainty are in the air. Depending on the institution, anywhere from 150 to 500 students have descended on a law school with a mix of social justice dreams and six-figure salary ambitions.

Some students are confident—maybe because of their personalities, the strong academic record that many law schools require, or because they are among the 20 percent of students with a parent who has a professional/doctoral degree. In half of such cases, the degree (or one of the degrees) is a JD.[1]

I remember sitting in a room with fellow law students when we were asked how many of our parents were lawyers. Hands shot up like a stadium wave. I wasn't prepared to sit in that sea of inherited familiarity. To be sure, no one in that room was unwelcoming. This was Berkeley and most people were naturally friendly. But the room spoke a language I was still learning. It felt like being a visitor in someone else's country—grateful for entry but touching your pocket every few minutes to make sure your passport is still safe in case the authorities come.

Some new students do not have inherited confidence or cultural fluency. Maybe they are first-generation law students for whom high school, let alone college, is a novelty.[2] Their apprehension could be the standard impostor syndrome that comes with being around other high-performing students. Or they could be a racial minority, LGBTQ, or a person with a disability. When people from historically marginalized groups enter law school buildings replete with portraits of able-bodied straight white male alums and see few people who look like them, implicit messages about belonging can be communicated, and forms of social isolation can ensue.[3]

When I started at Berkeley Law, I was somewhere in the middle. I was wrapping up a PhD, so I was confident in my intellect. I knew the research on stereotype threat, so I wouldn't let any sense of belittlement set in, extrinsic or self-imposed. I listened to way too much Black nationalist hip-hop for that. But I was one of 5 percent of Black students, very few of whom were men. Even though affirmative action was illegal in California, I still received looks and comments that suggested that I was some meritless token.

In any event, some students do not feel such isolation or they disregard it amid this new opportunity. Too much potential for increased status and upward mobility is on the line.

Things pop off with an orientation that ranges in its formality. There may be tours of the campus or events hosted by upperclass students and professors (e.g., dinners or bar crawls). Or a student may have a multiday experience that involves being introduced to faculty and the various staff who help the law school run, such as career services, academic support, librarians, tech staff, and the folks in financial aid. This is where, unsurprisingly, you find more women and minorities.

Some orientations might be more educational and provide students with a basic legal background that will help them when classes commence. Here, professors might explain the difference between federal and state constitutions, how a dispute comes to court, how it is appealed, and how to read a case.

During orientation, students are introduced to the high-school-like aura of legal education. They buy their casebooks, which are heavy, thousand-page, $250 textbooks stocked with legal cases, rules, and commentary. When they are not using them, they keep them in assigned lockers. Most notably, first-year students are divided into smaller sections. For example, a class of two hundred new students might be divided into four sections of fifty (e.g., Sections A, B, C, and D). Students take most of their classes with that cohort. Some classmates become lifelong friends. Others are objects of the inevitable gossip and drama that comes from being in the same space with new people for a year.

Festivities might begin with or be capped off by an address from the law school dean. Sometimes, a dean will lead students in taking an "Oath of Professionalism" that involves commitments to academic honesty, civility, and ethical practice. The oath also includes a promise to abstain from prejudice.[4] More commonly, the dean gives a speech that contains thoughts on the journey students will embark on and genuine attempts to ease new student jitters.

Now that I'm on the faculty side, orientation has a different weight. I watch these students—full of principle and adrenaline—and I know the kind of rewiring that lies ahead.

These public rituals begin to train students to think about morality in abstract, professionalized terms that can be disconnected from real-world consequences. Students pledge to avoid bias in theory while entering a system that routinely produces biased outcomes. They promise to act ethically without yet realizing that in law, ethics is often about following professional rules, not confronting what is just or humane. The orientation represents the beginning of an education that can lead one to meaningfully examine, outright disregard, and/or implicitly justify social inequalities.

This part of the book is about law school, but it touches on much more. You don't have to be a lawyer to feel the implications of the training I describe in the following pages. Legal education shapes the people who draft laws, defend powerful interests, and interpret the Constitution. If you care about housing, speech, immigration, criminal justice, or democracy, then you already live with the consequences of how lawyers are trained.

This chapter examines the learning environment law students enter. It is a setting that socializes students into particular ways of thinking. Legal education encourages students to approach problems with an analytic distance that prioritizes technical reasoning over moral or social consequence. That orientation isn't accidental. It emerges from the structure of the classroom, the deep ambiguity about the purpose of law school, and the professional norms embedded in the curriculum—all of which we'll explore in the pages ahead. This foundation sets the stage for a deeper reflection the book invites: What kind of justice system are we producing when lawyers are trained to reason this way?

The dynamics I describe play out differently across law schools. At places like Northeastern or the University of Denver—institutions that serve economically diverse student bodies and emphasize practical training—students may face financial constraints, less predictable job outcomes, and heightened anxiety about the bar exam. These conditions influence how legal education is supplied and absorbed. At more well-resourced schools, like Michigan or NYU—those challenges may be less visible, but teaching and learning are shaped by other factors—ideas about prestige, competition, and long-term career signaling. Nevertheless, across many law schools, a common process unfolds: Students are taught to approach legal problems with a distance that can push human suffering to the margins.

This Ain't Undergrad

At some point before classes begin, students are hopefully alerted to the fact that law school is unlike undergrad or any other educational setting they've occupied. These differences are not trivial.

The reading is different. High school and undergraduate textbooks often try to make complex ideas accessible. Legal casebooks have dense legal language. A professor might assign fifteen to twenty pages of reading for each class. That page count can easily take ninety minutes to read, and students are always advised to read more than once. Some professors care about minute details, and others care about the big picture. This means what a student needs to retain and comprehend can vary wildly across classes. Research shows that first-year students spend about half of the average work week—twenty-one hours—*just reading*.⁵

Classroom engagement can be a roller coaster. In many first-year courses, professors *cold-call*. This means the professor does not rely on volunteers to answer questions. Instead, they select students who sometimes get no advance notice. They may pick students randomly, based on where they are sitting, because they came late, in alphabetical order, or through some other method. It's basically an intense, oral pop quiz about the day's reading in front of anywhere from 40 to 120 people.

Cold calling is supplemented by the *Socratic method*. This 150-year-old approach to legal education involves a professor asking a student questions about underlying assumptions, facts, legal details, and in some instances, broader policy issues. In an hour-long class, this exchange can be five minutes or fifteen minutes. It can be with one student or with a series of students. The idea behind this approach is that it fosters active engagement, critical thinking, and mental agility, especially when a whole class is looking at *you*.

Socratic cold calling has its benefits. It pushes students to stay on top of the reading. It can prevent a few dominant voices—often overly confident, extroverted men—from hogging the mic and dominating the discussion. It also simulates the unpredictability and pressure that legal practice can involve. But these advantages can mask deeper problems. The same threat of public embarrassment that motivates some students can create debilitating anxiety for others. This approach also reinforces classroom hierarchy and centers the professor's authority. And because the questions tend to focus on narrow legal issues—often out of necessity because students are still learning the basics—cold calling trains students to prioritize technical application over human nuance. A sample dialogue might look something like this.

Professor: *Today, we'll be discussing the landmark case of* Brown v. Board of Education. *Mr. Smith, could you tell us about the background of the case?*

Student: *Sure. This was actually one consolidated case that arose from several out of Delaware, Kansas, South Carolina, Virginia, and Washington, DC. They all involved segregation in public schools based on race.*

Professor (interrupts): *Right but tell us about the lead case.*

Student: *Sure. Oliver Brown is a Black parent in Topeka, Kansas, and he wants to enroll his daughter in a school close to their home but can't, so she has to go to a segregated school that's farther away. He and several other families file a class action against the Board of Education. They are challenging the separate but equal doctrine from* Plessy v. Ferguson, *which said such segregation was okay as long as public facilities were equal.*

Professor: *Okay, what is the legal basis for the claim?*

Student: *The Fourteenth Amendment's Equal Protection Clause.*

Professor: *What did the court conclude?*

Student: *It ruled unanimously that separate but equal facilities were, in fact, unconstitutional.*

Professor: *Why? The court acknowledged that the segregated schools were about equal when it comes to the facilities, salaries of the teachers, etc. What's the problem?*

Student: *The court relied on some social science data that showed segregation has a detrimental impact on Black children, and so it says segregation in public education itself is "inherently unequal."*

Professor: *What are some possible objections to the decision?*

Student: *(Nervously recognizing he's asked to defend race-based segregation). This is obviously NOT my opinion, but some might say it wasn't* *based on legal precedent but on judicial activism. They might also say that there is a state rights problem. Education is in the domain of the states, and here, the federal government is telling states what to do.*

Professor: *Are those arguments availing to you?*

Student: *They make sense, but I don't think they justify a system of state-based segregation. I think it is morally wrong for the government to provide access to resources based on race.*

Professor: *Thank you. I want to move on to the next student. Ms. Anderson, tell us about your reactions to the case.*

This is a simplified, gentle version. No vignette can capture the fraught power dynamics and the theater-like nature of the classroom. Imagine your last or current boss asking you detailed questions about everything you've worked on in the past week in front of one hundred colleagues. Also, note that this exchange is probably being recorded. Most law schools now capture classes by default—a holdover from the pandemic era. And layered onto that is the ambient fear that a classmate might be *secretly* recording, waiting for a moment that could go viral.

In this specific example, like many others, students may be anxious about being wrong on a legal issue or making frowned-upon comments that are circulated on X or TikTok (e.g., someone complaining that John, a white student, said *Brown* was decided incorrectly, or that Tamara, a Black student, doesn't believe in integration). Some students are asked more pointedly to defend positions they do not hold.[6] A sexual assault survivor might be asked to make an argument for the accused rapist in criminal law. A Jewish or Muslim student might be asked to justify when religious discrimination by the state is permissible.[7]

This kind of engagement—cold calling, challenging hypotheticals, asking students to argue positions they don't believe—has its pedagogical uses. Like most professors, I encourage my students to separate legal analysis from personal belief; it's part of learning the craft. But this kind of engagement can normalize moral dissociation and encourage students to develop the ability to argue any position irrespective of personal conviction or social consequence. That kind of moral flexibility is sometimes described as professional competence, but it can be an important step toward treating clear injustices as legally contestable.

Law school grading is different from undergrad too. College courses may have periodic assignments, midterms, quizzes, presentations, and a final exam. Some law professors try to mimic this structure, but it is common for first-year courses to have one evaluation: a final exam. This test could be three, eight, or twenty-four hours, and it constitutes the bulk of a student's grade (e.g., 85 percent). Students feel tremendous pressure because so much hinges on one exam.

Since most law students across the country are taking the same bundle of courses across law schools, first-year grades are paramount. These grades dictate who gets a summer internship at a law firm—the going rate for which is approximately $4,000 a week for ten weeks at the highest paying firms. Yes, a $40,000 salary can be earned over the summer, which leads to a $225,000 salary that waits for them post-graduation should they receive an offer, which many do. (First-year salaries can range from $135,000 to $225,000, depending on the firm's profitability and location.) Competition for these jobs is especially fierce, thanks to rising tuition, the crushing debt that follows, and the reality that the highest-paying gigs grow scarcer outside the most elite programs.

Relatedly, first-year grades can determine who gets to keep their scholarship or who gets one in the following years. These evaluations also determine who obtains the fancy clerkships with judges and prestigious public interest gigs. With all this money on the line, things get *Hunger Games*-like quickly.

Considering this cocktail of heavy reading, intense intellectual engagement, and high-stakes, one-shot-deal grading, it's unsurprising that people have been writing about first-year anxiety and depression for half a century.[8] But we're just getting started.

The Vague Purpose of Law School
(and the First Year in Particular)

In theory, law schools are designed to endow students with the skills necessary to be lawyers. But if one went beyond this generality and double-clicked on the purpose(s) of law school, they would find a scandalous lack of clarity. There are several explanations for this vagueness. Some of these reasons are better than others, but on balance, this vagueness is consequential for the future lawyers who exert influence on society.

Law schools vary a lot, which means each place's goals differ. Yale is known for producing students who become professors. As part of its mission, the City University of New York School of Law seeks to "graduate outstanding public interest attorneys and enhance the diversity of the legal profession."[9] Meanwhile, schools like Cornell and Columbia are known for producing the most graduates who go on to work for large law firms. Most law schools, however, prepare students for small-firm or government practice in their regions. One would expect legal education to vary based on such different orientations and occupational pathways.

Even within the same school and course, students can encounter big differences in *how* a professor teaches and understands their job. Some core concepts will be covered in any course, but the fundamentals and the nonessentials can be very contingent on who is in front of the classroom.

At my institution, criminal law is taught by an economist, a former public defender, a few philosophers, and me, a sociolegal scholar. We all teach in ways that accord with our expertise (e.g., a focus on data-driven studies, legal practice, deep philosophical issues, and sociolegal studies, respectively). I teach stuff they don't teach and vice versa. And that's our prerogative as tenured professors. But these differences aren't stylistic. They reflect deeper disagreements about what should happen in a core course. And it's not just at my school. Across subjects and institutions, academic freedom, combined with deep uncertainty about the purpose of law school, means students receive very different messages about what matters—and what it even means to learn the law.

Some of the imprecision around what law professors are peddling is purposeful. Lawyers like specificity, but we also thrive in gray areas and have a knack for strategic ambiguity, which preserves potential deniability. "I didn't mean x, I meant xy!" According to one scholar, such doublespeak is a "political necessity" that allows people to apply different interpretations to a message.[10] Strategic ambiguity is most on display with the American Bar Association (ABA), which houses the accrediting agency for law schools. The ABA's Council outlines the criteria for schools to get the stamp of approval and keep their operations running.

Let's look at the rules like lawyers do.

According to Rule 301, "Objectives of Program of Legal Education," law schools must provide "a rigorous program of legal education that prepares its students, upon graduation, for admission to the bar and for *effective, ethical,* and *responsible* participation as members of the legal profession."[11]

Let's try to decipher this mumbo jumbo by putting those three terms under a microscope. These vague ideals start to come into focus when we connect them to some of the real-world paths most law students take: public interest work, government lawyering, and law firms—the same areas explored in the last three parts of this book.

Effectiveness: This is such a context-dependent, subjective, and squishy term. Consider public defenders. Victory rates for public defenders are notoriously hard to obtain. Should they decide to go to court and not take a plea, their success rates in trials are far from impeccable.[12] That would be impossible. They are typically under resourced, and because they are unable to hand-pick their cases, they sometimes get clients who are guilty. What is effectiveness in this context?

Effectiveness might be specific to the organization—maybe public defenders in Mobile County, Alabama, think about it differently than those in Los Angeles, California, but that doesn't tell us what effectiveness means in preparing young lawyers.[13] In the larger world of indigent defense, what counts as "effective" bears little resemblance to justice.[14] Lawyers have slept through trials, failed to meet with their clients, and even appeared in court visibly drunk—yet courts have still ruled their performance "effective."[15] Georgia executed a death row inmate whose lawyer was chugging a quart of vodka each evening (about twenty-one shots). That might sound like an ineffective lawyer, but Georgia courts found no problem.[16]

Effective is a linguistic placeholder that floats through legal education, bar exams, and accreditation standards with an assumed clarity. In many cases, it describes outcomes we'd never accept in any other profession. Could you imagine an "effective" building inspector who signs off on unsafe structures because they meet the eyeball test? Or an "effective" paramedic who is often late? In criminal court, that term somehow includes catastrophic failures.

So the question remains: What does it mean to train future lawyers about effective representation in educational contexts that may not sufficiently show them how that idea falls apart in the real world? This kind of failure is not just about criminal law; it stretches out to other areas where people with the fewest resources and the most at stake sometimes bear the brunt of underspecified and poorly actualized ideas about effectiveness. If legal education normalizes hollow standards, we shouldn't be surprised when the system does the same.

Ethics: I used to think *ethics* and *morality* were basically the same thing. And I'm not alone; a lot of people use the terms interchangeably. Finding out they were different was like discovering that butter and margarine are not identical. (Blame it on growing up in a food desert.) In fact, legal ethics and morality are as far apart as gas station chicken tenders and a farm-to-table dinner.

Morality is about personal beliefs—what we think is right or wrong in everyday life. One textbook defines *legal ethics* as the "principles of conduct that members of the profession are expected to observe in the practice of law." These two frameworks can diverge with ease.[17]

A lawyer can act in ways some would find deeply immoral and

still be considered ethical under professional rules. Nonviolent possession of a small amount of drugs? Legal ethics permit a prosecutor to threaten a multiyear prison term, even though some would find this wildly disproportionate. District attorneys can also rely on plea deals that pressure people to give up their right to a trial. In that case, a defendant may plead guilty not because they are actually guilty, but because the two-year deal is far less terrifying than taking a twenty-year gamble on a trial. That's considered ethical, even if it offends basic moral sensibilities.

That's one kind of problem: when following the rules *still* leads to injustice. The other side is harder to swallow: when prosecutors *ignore* ethical rules and lives are ruined anyway.

During the half century of what some call "mass incarceration," there have been *thousands* of cases that have been reversed due to prosecutorial misconduct, and this is almost certainly an underestimate.[18] The unethical prosecutors behind these kinds of cases do awful things. They conceal information they *know* would exonerate the defendant. They lie and present false evidence. And they exclude potential jurors on the basis of race and gender. Such conduct violates professional norms and, in some instances, constitutional law. Why would they do such dastardly things? There is a grab bag of reasons: a narcotic addiction to winning, revenge on behalf of the victim, some kind of bias, case overload (#prosecutorsmatter), tunnel-vision, and immunity from professional consequences, to name a few.[19]

The law schools that students stampede to are not at fault for lawyers' ethical shortcomings, but whether they are providing the ethical training those who write the rules say they should is an open question. What does preparing students for ethical practice mean in a world where ethics is defined so narrowly?

Legal ethics is typically treated as its own subject and is taught during the second and third years of law school. I teach the course and I understand the reasons for the separation. Teaching doctrine is demanding, and many believe ethics is easier to grasp once students have some legal knowledge under their belts. But when we take the already narrow category of legal ethics and tuck it away in a separate course, we send the message that questions of harm, justice, and human consequence are extra credit and not part of the daily work of legal reasoning.

To be sure, the point isn't that law schools deliberately train students to ignore justice. But they do cultivate habits of thinking that can make it easier to do so. And when ethics is framed as rule-following and neglects to sufficiently reckon with social harms, it prepares students for a version of the profession in which procedural correctness is enough. Legal education may not cause prosecutorial misconduct, but it helps shape the kinds of lawyers who can explain it away, rationalize it, or engage in it without blinking.

Responsible: Finally, what is *responsible* participation in the legal profession? An easy answer starts with the Watergate scandal, when the Nixon administration had goons break into Democrats' offices in 1972 and then tried to cover it up. The scandal involved more than twenty of the country's most powerful lawyers (attorneys general, White House counsel, the chair of the Securities and Exchange Commission [SEC], and the president himself).[20] The ABA scrambled to restore public trust and two innovations followed.[21]

Professional Responsibility (PR) is the legal ethics course I just described, and it covers the rules of conduct that govern lawyers. Knowledge of the rules is then tested on the Multistate Professional Responsibility Examination (MPRE), one of the few multiple-choice exams students must pass to become attorneys. These requirements are a huge leap from the 1960s. Back then, a prospective lawyer might be simplistically asked to explain, in a paragraph, "what the Code of Professional Responsibility mean[s] to me."[22] In other words, the ethical foundation of a career that might defend or prosecute a criminal case began with vibes.

In the grand scheme of things, professional responsibility is a curricular afterthought and this is reflected by the fact that many law schools often hire an adjunct to teach the course and pay them meagerly.[23] Students are often disengaged in the course and consider it a "public relations digression" from their coursework.[24] The MPRE is equally reviled, and students often forget what they learned within weeks of taking the exam.[25] The next time you meet a practicing lawyer, use the Socratic method you learned earlier and ask them to recite five rules from the Model Rules of Professional Conduct. Then you'll get my drift about "responsibility."

The problem sharpens when we turn to attorneys at large law firms. They help big-money clients do things that are quite innocent, like drafting contracts, or represent them in disputes with other big companies. No problemo. But in some instances, they help clients do bad stuff that is perfectly legal, but that some would call irresponsible.[26]

Fossil fuels—coal, oil, and gas—contribute to climate change and all types of public health problems (e.g., air and water pollution, food insecurity, various diseases). Still, between 2017 and 2021, law firms helped facilitate $1.62 *trillion* in transactions for these industries.[27] When a client wants to engage in environmentally harmful but legal conduct, a crunchy attorney could warn them about the consequences. The client might say, "I have listened to your advice and would still like to proceed with these perfectly legal, environmental harm-causing activities."[28] The ethical rules would consider continued representation of this client permissible and *responsible*. Why? Because the rules think of lawyers as neutral robots who pursue their clients' lawful interests while being exempt from any moral accountability.[29]

"I'm just doing my job" is the easy refrain for lawyers who represent actors who engage in "awful but lawful" behavior. Screw the Indigenous Peoples whose land is exploited by these companies and the poor white communities who live near coal mines and develop respiratory problems. The larger societal consequences of "awful but lawful" behavior extend to fields like banking, employment, securities, healthcare, privacy law, and other areas students go into for practice. The ethical frameworks students are furnished with can lead to ambiguous ideas about responsibility that harm marginalized third parties.

This isn't theory for me—it's personal, professional, and lived. I've seen firsthand how legal education struggles with competing visions of its purpose.[30] I've been a faculty candidate offered jobs by dozens of schools across the rankings hierarchy, which gave me a rare chance to press students, professors, and administrators on their thoughts about what legal education is supposed to accomplish. As an implicated professor, I'm still trying to unlearn some of the habits I critique. And as an observer, I've watched the questions I've carried for more than a decade about the ends of legal training sharpen in 2025. That was when bipartisan groups of lawyers, law school deans, and the ABA issued statements about "threats to the rule of law."[31] As those warnings were voiced, some professors stayed relatively quiet in the classroom about those challenges—even when directly relevant—out of fear, indifference, or concern that describing the legal world in front of them might appear politically partial. This is the lived ambiguity of legal education.

I'm pleading with anyone who will listen: The uncertainty at the heart of legal education shapes more than just students. It shapes the society they enter after law school. These graduates end up being the people responsible for laws that govern us and make their way into political, business, and nonprofit worlds that impact daily life. What they learn or don't learn about professional responsibility matters for all of us.

What the Best Law Professors Say

We've examined orientation, the intense social environment of the first year, and the broader ambiguity surrounding law school. But what about the people standing at the front of the classroom? Professors, after all, have no shortage of theories and frameworks for everything. If you asked one about the purpose of the first year, I suspect you would hear some variant of one of the following answers: "thinking like a lawyer," skills development, socialization, or bar preparation.[32] These various rationales help explain what is going on in law schools, but there are problems with them, too.

Thinking like a lawyer is commonly said to be the goal of a legal education. The term is somewhat misleading since lawyers are diverse, and it's hard to homogenize their thinking.[33] In any event, identifying relevant legal issues is central to thinking like a lawyer because clients sometimes come to lawyers with complex problems. A woman on a tight budget might be filing for divorce and trying to save her home from foreclosure. Counseling her means parsing through bankruptcy, property, and family law issues.

But thinking like a lawyer can also mean sifting through nonlegal issues to reach the right legal conclusion. A client might have a straightforward legal problem but not recognize the simplicity. This is the new homeowner who is complaining about the lack of heat in her home and offers too much factual fluff. "I understand that you dealt with a lousy seller when you bought the condo and that you made several fruitless phone calls to a home insurance policy that, in my experience, probably doesn't cover your problem. To get things on track, we'll figure out whether the utility company or the condo board is responsible for this problem and then send a clear letter asking them to fix it." Lawyers have to spot both the relevant facts and legal issues.

Thinking like a lawyer can also involve learning how to evaluate evidence dispassionately and go beyond one's ideological assumptions. The 1930 words of legal scholar Karl Llewellyn still ring loudly almost a century later: "The hardest job of the first year is to lop off your common sense, to knock your ethics into temporary anesthesia. Your view of social policy, your sense of justice—to knock these out of you along with woozy thinking."[34] The skill of dispassion is important because students may have to represent a client that they are not simpatico with or actually disdain (e.g., violent offenders or unapologetic white-collar criminals).

Relatedly, students also develop the skill of being better devil's advocates. Satan hardly needs any more spokespersons, but lawyers in training can develop the valuable disposition of seeing different legal sides of an argument. In the future, that inclination can help them anticipate what opposing counsel will do and strategize accordingly.

Socialization, in this context, means developing certain norms of professionalism—things like email etiquette, dress code, and punctuality. These can be particularly important considering the high number of students coming straight out of college who have never been in the full-time workforce. It also means developing seemingly basic but actually technical skills—learning a new way of reading, writing, researching, and advocacy—all of which are qualitatively different in the legal context. Because of the intensity of first-year law—lots of reading, writing, and analysis in a short period of time—students become acculturated to work-life tradeoffs and the long hours that characterize some areas of practice.

This socialization process—with its shared experiences, expectations, and knowledge base—loosely bonds future lawyers to one another and allows them to share war stories about law school and practice for decades. There may be little that I, a Black guy from the Bronx, share with my sixty-something-year-old, white, Phillips Exeter Academy–attending colleague besides being professors and going through this socialization process.

Finally, there's *bar readiness*. You have to pass the bar exam to be licensed to practice, and most first-year courses are tested on this exam. Some law professors are instrumental and want to provide a foundation for the exam that students will take roughly two years later. Other professors care less about bar exam preparation because they do not want to teach to a test, believe other themes are important, or do not believe this is their duty (which can especially be true at schools where bar passage rates are high).

Thinking like a lawyer, socialization, and bar readiness all sound like reasonable things to focus on, right? I think so. But there is another side to these goals that bears some connection to existing social inequalities out in the world.

Thinking like a lawyer can strip away the sociopolitical, economic, psychological, and moral factors that shape lawmaking and legal inequality.[35] I'll offer a few examples.

Politics: One would be kidding themselves if they believed criminal law was insulated from politics, but it has long been taught in a manner that conceives of politics as separate from law.[36] When it comes to what we categorize as "criminal," the role of special interest groups like police unions or race-baiting, tough-on-crime politicians like Bill

Clinton is barely touched on. I suspect most professors won't touch January 6 with a ten-foot pole, even though, depending on who you believe, the prosecutions tell us *something* about politics (e.g., either the prosecutions of nearly 1,500 people were partisan hit jobs *or* their subsequent pardons were ideologically motivated).

And let us not forget the corruption charges that were brought against New York City mayor Eric Adams and subsequently dropped. His supporters described the prosecution as the byproduct of a "weaponized" Department of Justice. His critics—including a Trump-appointed prosecutor who clerked for conservative Justice Antonin Scalia—called the dropped charges "a quid pro quo" that would ensure Adams would help President Trump with his agenda.[37] Of course, politics might matter less in a straightforward carjacking where the defendant is guilty. But in a world where elected judges might feel the need to sentence defendants punitively or where there is strong public opinion around *not* harshly punishing users of certain illegal drugs (i.e., opioids), political considerations can be part of thinking like a lawyer.[38] But good luck getting that lesson as a first-year. Thinking like a lawyer often means parsing legal doctrines without fully addressing how politics shape who those doctrines target, protect, or ignore.

Psychology: Psychologists have shown for decades that bias can shape the decisions of judges and juries in trials.[39] Still, these insights are outside the scope of civil procedure—the core course that describes to students how litigation happens. Outside of slivers of (other) first-year courses, students will be hard-pressed to find a meaningful discussion of the large body of laws that prohibit discrimination in housing, credit, voting, employment, and education. The first year's inattention to bias was so pathetic that the ABA had to slap on a mandatory first-year bias requirement after George Floyd was killed in 2020. This requirement is typically satisfied through bias training, coursework, or programming that focuses primarily on race and sex, and as opposed to categories like religion.

Could this inattention to bias be relevant to claims that law schools are insensitive to Islamophobia and antisemitism?[40] As an educational matter, maybe, just maybe, some conversations about antisemitism and Islamophobia would be more informed if legal education took a more proactive approach to these forms of bias as opposed to pretending like they didn't exist until October 2023 and then responding in ways that were defensive and unsatisfactory to many? As a matter of legal training, if various legal actors can be impacted by bias, might it be important for an up-and-coming attorney to develop a toolkit for strategizing around this issue? In the world of thinking like a lawyer, bias is a background noise as opposed to a recurring force that influences how legal systems see, sort, and decide.

Economics: One doesn't have to be a raging, Bernie Sanders–like socialist to admit that slavery and the theft of Native American land played some role in American economic development.[41] But American legal education has sidestepped these facts for decades. "Though conquest and enslavement were key to producing property for centuries," K-Sue Park writes, the teaching of property law has been "largely devoid of these histories."[42] Property law casebooks didn't confront these realities until the 1970s, and even since then, the treatment has been patchy. Without this engagement, it's easy for students to get an incomplete picture of a legal regime that valorizes the importance of private property rights to free market capitalism.

In the PG version of property, students are taught that the law allows people to own tangible assets like land and intangible assets like stocks. The law allows such ownership to happen with security and certainty; people can sell, buy, lease, and give away property and know that they have legal entitlements and protections should things hit the fan. But the NC-17 version—the ways wealth concentration coupled with property law impacts gentrification, homelessness, and zoning rules that keep poor people out of certain communities—is more likely to be ignored or footnoted in ways that silently endorse the economic status quo. Thinking like a lawyer tends to emphasize rule mastery without interrogating whose economic interests legal rules protect and whose they suppress.

Morality: Abortion has been one of the controversial issues in constitutional law for the last half-century. It's a morally weighty topic. Pro-life arguments focus on the idea of the fetus as a person, the sanctity of human life, and abortion as infanticide. Pro-choice arguments focus on bodily autonomy and the various forms of harm that come with forcing a person to carry a fetus to term (especially in cases involving threats to maternal health, rape, or incest). But the legal discourse on this topic filters these debates into legal terms like "privacy," "states' rights," and "due process." Morality may get some airtime, but it's subordinate to the legal issues, even though a self-described Christian law firm helped bring the case that overturned *Roe v. Wade*. Thinking like a lawyer often means translating moral questions into legal frameworks and reducing urgent human dilemmas to technical disputes.

As part of *professional skills development,* law students are often taught to maintain an emotional distance on sensitive legal matters. Some students never arrive at such emotional regulation; others come to law school knowing how to desensitize. But this emotional work is a common complaint about law school. Writes one student, "It is no wonder that my soul is so often a battlefield. To acknowledge emotion in law school is to invite pain. The refusal to become an amoral technician is dangerous."[43]

According to law professor James Elkins, emotional detachment, though useful, can be one of the many "hazards of legalistic thinking."[44] There's a reason why being lawyerly can be understood as being rigorously detailed, overly technical, or borderline chilly. The former president of my university, a lawyer, publicly resigned in 2023 after answering a hypothetical question in front of Congress. When asked whether calls for Jewish genocide would violate university policies against harassment, she said it would be context dependent. Some thought her answer was technically and legally correct. But many across the political spectrum considered her answer unacceptable and an example of less-than-ideal emotional intelligence (to put it nicely). A year and a half later she admitted, "I just didn't seem like a person with common sense and humanity, and I am."[45]

Now imagine when the stakes are not a televised, political hit job. Instead, we're in low-profile housing courts where insensitive judges oversee eviction mills. Or the Social Security hearings where people with disabilities are routinely denied benefits by cold-blooded, "rule-abiding" judges. Fear and disgust have influenced the creation of laws from criminal justice to welfare to national security. Broken contracts tick people off. People can sue for emotional distress![46] Law is bound up in all kinds of emotions, but future lawyers must typically check them at the door or pretend as if emotion is the enemy of rationality.

"*Socialization*" does some of the problematic work of nudging students into understanding law as a science that is superordinate to social, political, economic, moral, psychological, and emotional concerns. My sensei, Elizabeth Mertz, explores this process in her study of eight law schools. She finds that legal education endows students with distinctive analytical abilities—some really good stuff. But it also precludes important discussions that could serve the public. Mertz calls this the "detached mastery" of legal education. Legal scholars Lani Guinier and Susan Sturm have argued that this model communicates that understanding of issues like racism, sexism, poverty, ableism, or religious bias "can be developed on their own, easily picked up in practice, or are simply not as demanding or significant in the development of foundational expertise for lawyers."[47]

Students can easily leave the first year not understanding the specific ways various -isms and -phobias shape our legal system. This can be troubling for students disinclined to believe bias exists despite decades of empirical research. But it can also impact those students who *believe* in the power of bias. These students sometimes overassign value to categories like race and sex, or find bias everywhere. Because they have been socialized in an educational environment where such discussions are peripheral, their ideas go untested. This is a disservice to the communities they care about and gives their ideological opponents more ammunition.[48]

Since the bar exam includes most of the first-year curriculum, some professors imagine themselves as taking a first stab at ensuring that their students are "*bar-ready*." At schools that send a large percentage of their students to law firms, extensive bar-oriented instruction may be less necessary. These future employers will pay thousands of dollars for private prep courses after graduation that will teach students what they need to pass. They want to protect their six-figure investment.

At schools that don't send people to firms and for students who can't afford the approximately $3000 to pay for a prep course, bar-ready instruction is sensible. People need to pass the exam to get jobs, and society needs lawyers with some baseline of competence. If your home is being foreclosed on, or your kid's facing jail time, you want a lawyer who knows what to do.

Bar-focused education takes all the familiar problems of teaching to the test—surface-level learning and narrow instruction—and builds an entire professional gateway around them. In some classes and exams, students are told implicitly and sometimes explicitly that questions about politics or power are off-topic. Bar-focused teaching, like some of the first year, is less concerned about who bleeds and more concerned about getting the right box checked.

The limits of bar-focused education mirror a broader pattern in the first year: a curriculum that treats a narrow set of issues as foundational while setting others aside as leftovers, irrespective of their importance. Many of the most pressing legal challenges of our time—voting rights, workplace inequality, consumer exploitation, environmental collapse—are simply hard to find.

Some might say these issues belong in electives. But that misses the point. These aren't niche interests. They are the legal emergencies of the day. The exam tests little housing law despite millions of people facing housing insecurity. It does not test environmental law: No questions about the Clean Air Act, the Clean Water Act, or legal remedies for poor communities who live in the shadow of pollution are covered. Immigration law is a ghost, even though detention, asylum, and due process tragedies have unfolded at the border and in courts across the country for the last few decades. Disability law has no place on the exam, even though forty-two million Americans live within its scope.[49] These are more than oversights. They are choices that communicate to future lawyers who and what matters.

I offer all of this with a clear awareness of the constraints that make a more grounded, justice-conscious legal education difficult. Some of the challenges are institutional. At many schools, bar passage rates and employment statistics loom like creditors. Time can also be an enemy: We have thirteen or fourteen weeks to cover much material. Large class sizes in these first-year courses can discourage deep conversation. And depending on the school, teaching innovation gets less credit than citation counts. Going against the grain can feel like a professional liability.

Then there are the interpersonal challenges.

Professors live with the prospect of student judgment going viral. In this climate of scrutiny, some try to watch every word and avoid veering too far from the script in case a truncated set of comments ends up on social media. Speaking about inequality might earn a standing ovation—or a scathing evaluation—especially if you're a woman, minority, and/or pre-tenure.[50] But that tightrope extends to white faculty and men, too. I've had white friends describe a reasonable calculus of caution when it comes to discussing race, gender, or religion in the classroom: better to be faulted for saying nothing than punished for trying and getting it wrong. Others get it from all sides—too radical or not radical enough. (I've been dinged in my evaluations for assigning too much Cato Institute and Heritage Foundation and for not assigning enough.) Then there are the students who believe they are getting a lower return on investment because a professor is daring to raise issues that feel off topic to those still getting their bearings in the field.

I know these pressures. I've felt them in my gut. But constraints can't be confused with absolution. Law professors are entrusted with training people who will wield the law in ways that alter lives and shape history. And when something matters this much, courage is not optional. It's the baseline. If the teachers don't model what it means to wrestle with power, responsibility, and moral complexity, students may come to believe that comfort matters more than conscience. And it won't just be an academic loss—the public will bear the cost.

By now, I hope I've given you a sense of the strangeness that defines the first year of law school. We've sat through orientation, tried to breathe under the pressure of the first year, and seen the unclear purpose that shadows legal education. Along the way, we've encountered some of the rationales professors offer for what they teach and why, even as the meaning of the job itself remains up for debate.

The first year is a setting where students are endowed with a range of skills and dispositions—some of which are socially beneficial, while others can be used to perpetuate silences and social harms. It is a space that treats emotional detachment like a professional imperative. These conditions make it possible for blatant wrongs to become legally contestable or nonissues. And this is all despite some law schools' chest-pounding about social justice.

Much of my discussion so far has been rather high-level. Now we'll turn to the classes themselves. The rest of this part focuses on the core courses taught in the first year, which is where things get more interesting.

Assembly #1

*Untold Tales in Contract,
Tort, and Property Law*

IN THE NEXT THREE CHAPTERS, we explore three of the core subjects students typically confront in the first year of law school. Think of it as akin to a semester. *Contract law* concerns when and how the legal system enforces promises. *Tort law* focuses on harm caused by one party against another, with the solution usually being monetary compensation. *Property law* governs ownership rights that one entity has vis-a-vis another.

All three fall under the larger category of *private law*, which focuses on legal rights and relationships between private entities, whether they be individuals or organizations. Some argue that this "private" aspect makes them different from *public law*, which focuses on rights and relationships entities have with the government. The distinctions between the private and the public are not tidy and legal writers have spent decades debating the separation.[1] We need not concern ourselves with those debates for now; what's most relevant is that contracts, torts, and property are often bundled together conceptually.

Before diving into first year and its relationship to social inequalities, a few things must be said. Consider them themes and caveats.[2]

First, a good chunk of what I'll be describing is the product of *omission*—the failure to do something. On a cognitive level, people tend to think that an act that leads to negative consequences is worse than an omission that leads to the same consequences.[3] Susan's vehicular assault of Jack is bad and criminal. But when Katie, a stranger, drives by a dying Jack thirty minutes later and fails to provide life-saving treatment, her omission is not considered as bad or criminal.

Some omissions do not allow people to escape being blameworthy. Our legal system punishes people for a range of omissions. Some states have "duty to rescue" laws that would punish Katie for her failure to provide reasonable assistance. People can get locked up for failing to provide food to their kids (child neglect), failure to register a gun, or failure to register as a sex offender. Morally, we may think it's bad if a government actively kills its people, but as the philosopher Peter Singer observed, "Many people die because of insufficient food or poor medical facilities." Some might say a state's failure to provide life-saving aid is different than a state actively killing many and others would say they are one in the same.[4]

In the legal education context, many problems emerge from the *failure* to engage or substantively approach certain discussions. Most law professors are not raging racist, sexist, trans/homophobic, et cetera. In fact, if you buy what some researchers are selling, most law professors identify as liberal—whatever value you want to attach to that.[5] Issues of identity and inequality may not rank as first-, second-, or third-order priorities for many of these teachers. And they don't have to be. There are other important things in the world. But when you think about these omissions alongside the vague goals of first-year law, real-time constraints in a forty-hour semester, and the different competencies of law professors, it can be clearer how inequality often becomes a footnote in law students' education.

A second point of emphasis is the nature of the omissions. Fault finding is an easy exercise for many, especially for lawyers and scholars, myself included. Critique is what we do. You could give me a bag of french fries, and I can find some problems. But the omissions I identify are not obscure or pedantic. They involve tectonic social problems that impact large swaths of the population.

The omissions I focus on in this part of the book aren't random complaints about curriculum coverage. They share certain characteristics that help distinguish between miscellaneous gaps and integral oversights.

First is doctrinal relevance. The issues I discuss are immediately relevant to each area of law and core assumptions about how legal doctrine operates.

Second, some of the omitted topics represent issues that lawyers who practice in the field regularly encounter and shape the lives of millions daily. These topics are not theoretical curiosities.

Third is inequality revelation. These aren't social issues grafted onto legal doctrine. They represent important topics that show us how doctrine functions in different communities. Without engaging these issues, students risk developing a one-dimensional understanding of legal rules that flattens how they work in practice.

Finally, many of these issues involve areas of broad agreement. Many would say homelessness or domestic violence are bad; the difference tends to come with what legal solutions should follow. Rather than avoiding these topics because they might seem ideologically charged, schools should include them to actually promote critical thinking and genuine viewpoint diversity that they say—and are increasingly saying—they value. These issues force students to grapple with hard questions about law as opposed to accepting simplistic, default conclusions.

The specific issues I examine in this part aren't the *only* possible examples. The bigger issue is what avoidance teaches students about who and what legally matters. In failing to engage some of the issues discussed in the following three chapters—language barriers, government misconduct, housing insecurity, and more—law students, I worry, are not engaging with the broader world around them and are not deliberating about legally relevant injustices.

I'm reminded here of a comment uttered in *A Bronx Tale* and restated by the rapper Pusha T: "The worst waste is talent." The discussions in these chapters are not universal, but they have broad applicability and will likely resonate with former, current, and future law students. They will also probably be startling to the non-lawyer reader.

CHAPTER 2

Manufactured Consent and Contractual Inequality

I HAVE A RUNNING JOKE with a few first-generation lawyer friends about learning how to be an attorney as a teenager. Readers who are the first in their families to be white-collar professionals, have immigrant parents, and/or grew up working class may feel me on this. But anyone who's ever tried to decode bureaucratic language for a loved one likely knows what I'm talking about too.

A rental agreement arrives. A medical bill needs explaining. A credit card application requires interpretation. We'd play lawyer-translator, trying to break down legalese for parents who thought in another language—Spanish, Twi, Creole, Vietnamese, or Arabic. They knew English, but they were in a daze when it came to American contract law. As unpaid interns we were lost too.

We watched them sign lease after lease, barely understanding the fine print, nodding along as landlords rattled off terms for apartments where heat and hot water were unpredictable. Fathers squinted at credit card contracts, running their fingers under words like *variable APR* and other terms they couldn't quite parse. Mothers stared at health insurance forms, trying to understand why "covered services" seemed to exclude things a sick child needed.

And then there was the Bronx, where predatory contracting seemed like a working business model.

Furniture stores lined the major avenues and peddled "no credit, no problem" financing designed to keep people in debt longer than the furniture would last. Cell phone storefronts were wedged between bodegas and narrower than subway cars. Their contracts were full of hidden fees and early termination penalties. Used car dealers provided financing agreements with conditions that made it impossible to eventually own the car—more hidden terms, high interest rates, and balloon payments. Meanwhile, those vehicles were held together by whatever makeshift solutions would hold until the ink on the contract dried.

These vendors knew people needed furniture, phones, and cars, so they priced desperation accordingly.

When I got to law school, I thought contract law would teach me how to protect people from these elaborate cruelties. That didn't quite happen. I did receive much of the vocabulary I'd been missing. But the class taught me and others to see systemic predation through a different lens. There were several legal fictions in the course, but we pretended like they were true. Getting through the course really required suspending basic human psychology.[1]

We had to act like signatures meant comprehension regardless of literacy or language barriers.

Economic desperation was, for the most part, irrelevant to whether a contract was truly voluntary. Someone staring at the prospect of homelessness apparently possessed all the freedom in the world when signing the only lease they could afford.

And in law school—the place manufacturing tomorrow's legal minds—we learned to accept that surrendering your right to sue in court was just the price of getting basic services, as normal as voting on Tuesdays or saying "bless you" when someone sneezes.

I remember sending a picture of my contract notes to a friend from undergrad who was already a practicing attorney. With a tongue firmly in cheek but an edge of concern, I asked her: "Is contract law a course in advanced oppression techniques? WTF is going on?" Her reply was brutally pragmatic. "You're thinking like a human being instead of a law student. Cut it out with the PhD stuff and turn off your conscience. Give them what they want to hear and keep it moving."

If it had been anybody else, I would have thought they were telling me to "stop seeing exploitation as exploitation." But this was my homegirl, and I trusted her. What I realized was that mastering legal doctrine sometimes required a numbness to human consequences. I became fluent enough in legal doublespeak to pass the final exam, but something deep in my spirit kept telling me we were just putting bow ties on oppression.

IF YOU'RE LIKE MOST AMERICANS, parsing through legalese is not a high priority. Consider the findings of one famous study. The researchers created a fake social networking site that included terms users had to agree to before signing up. One of the terms included an agreement that users would give up their firstborn child as payment for access. Ninety-eight percent of users "consented."[2] Not 30 or 50 percent. Ninety-eight percent of people agreed to surrender their children for access, which shows you how common it is to breeze through these so-called agreements.

Contracts are ubiquitous in our lives. Most employed people signed a contract detailing the terms of employment. On the housing front, we have lease agreements for renters, real estate contracts for homeowners, and underlying mortgages for people who don't have enough to buy a house with straight cash. Then there is the mundane stuff. Agreements for utilities, warranties, insurance policies, credit cards, and subscription services (think DoorDash or Netflix).

If the contract is written, minute but legally consequential details might appear in fine print so small it would be difficult to mimic in handwriting. Or vital details might come up virtually via the gauntlet of boxes and "I agree" buttons. Never mind that by checking that box, you're typically consenting to behavior that might ordinarily give you pause. Because you want to use that new app you downloaded from the Apple Store or watch a video clip your friend sent, you are now allowing a website to track your location, send you boatloads of shitty promotional emails, and sell your data to third-party businesses. Is that really consent?

Depending on the contract, you may have forfeited the right to sue altogether and be forced to take any legal beef you have to a corporate-friendly arbitrator. In a five-year span, Google, which had more than 150,000 employees, only had to deal with eleven arbitration claims from their workers.[3] Former chairwoman of the Federal Trade Commission Lina Khan and her coauthor Deepak Gupta argue that arbitration is a "transfer of wealth upwards."[4] In their view, it tends to make it harder for atomized consumers and workers to get their money back. At the same time, it gives big companies repeat advantages that let them hold on to money that should go back to the people who paid it or earned it—leaving more in the hands of the powerful.

Do you think those Google employees understood they were signing away their constitutional right to trial by jury when they accepted their job offers? If you worked at Google and had a wage dispute, would you be okay with it being resolved by a process designed by Google's lawyers to favor Google? Arbitration, Khan and Gupta argue, is an "outcome of and contributor to economic inequality."[5] Contract law is one of the pillars of this inequality, but law students are rarely exposed to this reality in depth. And this is only one slice of the problem.

Contract law is replete with fictions. Among the most significant is the idea that one who signs a written agreement is presumed to know its contents. They are legally bound irrespective of whether they actually read or understand the agreement.[6] There are good reasons for this rule—mainly the concern that people will try to back out of promises by saying, "I didn't understand." That's how legal fictions work—they simplify complex realities to make law more workable. But there are problems with this assumption. In academic terms, comprehension and signing are distinct cognitive activities. In street terms, the assumption is BS.

Omri Ben-Shahar, one of the country's most cited scholars of contract law, puts it nicely: "Real people don't read standard-form contracts. Reading is boring, incomprehensible, alienating, time-consuming, but most of all, pointless. We want the product, not the contract."[7] And yet contract law, he argues, refuses to come to grips with this reality and instead puts forth a bunch of "myths, fictions, and presumptions" designed to preserve an imaginary conceptual apparatus that doesn't accord with how people contract in the real world.

That is my beef with this course and what I take aim at in this chapter. Contract law can easily train students to divorce legal analysis from social consequences. It does this by proceeding with doctrine built on acknowledged fictions while frequently sidelining the everyday contexts where contracts cause harm.

Some of this narrowing is necessary—law school can't cover everything. The fictions aren't hidden either; many professors acknowledge that people don't really read agreements and that bargaining power is rarely equal. But these admissions are treated as side notes and unfortunate facts of life rather than fundamental challenges to the field's core assumptions. We proceed with analyses that assume informed consent, voluntary agreement, and equal negotiation while knowing none of these things are true.

The sidelining of relevant contract issues is subtle but equally problematic. Problems affecting vulnerable populations get reassigned to specialized fields—consumer protection, employment law, elder law—while the foundational contract course focuses on a narrower conception of the field's scope and relationship to inequality. By treating these as someone else's specialty, the core curriculum remains detached from the contexts where contract law's impact has deep significance.

The standard contract curriculum is organized around some foundational questions that sound neutral and technical. Is there really an agreement? How do we interpret problematic or vague terms? When is not adhering to the contract okay? What happens when one party does not perform their duties according to the contract? Underneath these big questions are various historical, cultural, and social issues that are unlikely to surface throughout the semester. If such topics appear, it's likely to be tokenistic relative to how our diverse population transacts. Such an approach risks teaching students to see contracts as abstract legal puzzles while missing how they can be tools that can protect vulnerable people or systematically exploit them. This chapter examines how contract laws can obscure the relationship between law and inequality.

Manufactured Consent and Contractual Inequality | 59

Freedom of Contract and the Art of Forgetting

As we dive into the weeds, I want to pull a standard contract law professor move and a more subversive one: provide a quick course overview and excavate a buried history.

Picture yourself in your first semester of law school, sitting in a Contracts class. There may be anywhere from 40 to 120 other students, all stacked in tiered rows that are meant to keep you in view, not at ease. Casebooks are open, highlighters are working overtime, and laptops glow across the room (except in no-laptop classes, where students scribble furiously in notebooks).

The professor walks in and, after an introduction and some pleasantries, starts mapping out the semester like they're planning a military invasion. Maybe you all review the syllabus, which outlines the major topics and key concepts. Things likely begin with *contract formation*, which is how promises turn into something the law actually cares about. Part of making a contract involves an *offer* (someone puts terms on the table), an *acceptance* (the other side says "cool, I'm down"), and *consideration* (both sides put something up—even a dollar counts).

Then you've got the *defenses* to contract enforceability—basically your legal way of saying, "nah, this deal doesn't fly." Maybe one of the parties couldn't legally agree because of *incapacity* (e.g., they were drunk or a minor), they were under *duress* (i.e., pressured), subject to *fraud* (lied to), or the agreement was so unfair that it is deemed *unconscionable*.

After that, it's about *performance*—whether each side actually does what they promised to do under the contract. When that doesn't happen, it's called a *breach*—one party shows up late, does the wrong thing, or walks away completely. That's when *remedies* come in: the court's way of trying to make things right.

Three-ish months of learning who owes what to whom. Sounds reasonable right? Maybe interesting? These are definitely the kind of things future lawyers should know. But what gets lost in this polite vocabulary is that contract law evolved alongside—and helped legitimize—systems of inequality. What follows isn't a full history, just a brief sketch. But even a glimpse can cast the field in a different light; it reveals the stories contract law tells about itself by leaving them untold to its initiates.

Lochner v. New York (1905) is a notorious Supreme Court case that invoked the concept of *liberty of contract* to strike down laws limiting working hours. According to the Court, the Constitution protected the rights of both workers and employers to enter into agreements— even exploitative ones—without government interference. The decision and the four-decade period of Lochnerism (1897–1937) are prime examples of how courts used freedom of contract principles to protect corporate interests over people and invalidate basic labor protections (e.g., minimum wage and workplace safety). This NC-17 version of freedom of contract doesn't appear in many casebooks and is rarely shown to students.[8]

In contract law, you get the stripped-down, domesticated version. This kind says freedom of contract is a presumption; courts will generally enforce agreements unless something has gone sideways (e.g., there is fraud or coercion). This classroom version can create space to talk about inequality, but it has problems accommodating more troubling dimensions of contract law's relationship to power. Importantly, the gap between these two ideas of contracting is not accidental; it reflects a choice to focus on the mechanics of contract enforcement. The uncomfortable aspects of freedom of contract get excised and relocated to other courses, departments, and disciplines altogether.

If the legal enforceability of a promise is central to contracts, it feels necessary to begin with treaties. These are the formal agreements between the United States and Native Nations that looked like contracts: negotiated terms, authorized signatures, and binding obligations between parties.[9]

In the late eighteenth and early nineteenth century, the Cherokee Nation signed multiple treaties with the US government (some of which occurred under the threat of violence). These agreements promised peace, recognized the Cherokee as a sovereign nation, and guaranteed their territorial boundaries. In other words, the US government gave its word that Cherokee land was Cherokee land. But the state of Georgia wanted the Cherokee land and Andrew Jackson wanted the Cherokee people gone. So the Cherokee went to court and pointed to the agreements they signed with the US government.

In *Cherokee Nation v. Georgia* (1831), the Supreme Court said the Cherokee weren't a foreign country, but a "domestic dependent nation"—a newly invented category that let the US break its promises while pretending it wasn't.[10] In doing so, the court turned what looked like mutual agreements into paternalism. The decision didn't erase those treaties, but it drained them of contractual meaning. The federal government could now ignore or reinterpret them under the guise of "protection."

The Cherokee saga, and the many others like it, align with one of the many themes in American contracting. On paper, the field is about equality: Two parties freely agree to strike a deal. But in practice, when one party has the power, formal equality is a farce. Like those Cherokee treaties, contracts involving vulnerable parties often maintain the appearance of consent but enable control and exploitation. The Cherokee Nation decision reminds us that the law doesn't just enforce agreements but sometimes reinterprets them to serve the interests of the powerful.

Before the Civil War, Black people were not able to fully exercise the freedom of contract. There were legal limitations on their ability to buy property, claim wages owed to them, or hold anyone to a promise. Section 1981 of the Civil Rights Act of 1866 banned racial discrimination in contracting. The law is older than many seminal contract cases and is actively litigated. But it is absent from many casebooks and often goes undiscussed.[11] Instead, it's ghettoized and shipped off to civil rights courses despite definitionally being about contracts. Section 1981 disrupts the apolitical, race-minimized version of contract law. It reminds us that contract law is not just about promises; it's also about who gets to make them, who gets to enforce them, and who the law was written to protect.

Around the same time, white women were getting exploited by

contract law. In the late 1800s, the sewing machine was revolutionary. One historian of credit called it the "first durable, technologically complex household appliance to find a national market."[12] It offered working-class white women a way to earn income from home—one of the few economic openings available to them. The machines were expensive, so companies revolutionized the business model by selling them through installment plans: Take it home now and pay in monthly chunks, like we do today with car payments.[13]

These were some of the first widespread consumer credit contracts. On the surface, they looked like a path to economic freedom—but in reality, they were traps. They were often take-it-or-leave-it contracts signed by women who were not legally literate, couldn't afford legal help, and had no power to negotiate the terms. Repossession of these machines was tragically common. Why? Because of basic contract law principles students learn in the first year.

Take *modification*, which refers to changing the terms after a deal is signed. If a woman missed a payment, the company could revise the agreement, add penalties, or shorten the repayment timeline—and contract law said, "Sure, no problem." Or consider *remedies for breach*, which refers to what happens when someone breaks a contract. If a woman missed a payment, she had breached, and the company could repossess everything she had ever bought from them, not just the sewing machine she was behind on.

This form of white, gendered, working-class entrapment matters because it widens the lens: It shows how contract law has structured inequality not only along racial lines, but wherever power could exploit vulnerability, including among those not typically cast as its victims. These arrangements—installment plans, repossession, and debt dressed up as freedom—don't just involve contract law. They challenge an assumption that floats above the first-year course: that agreement means fairness.

Asian Americans faced waves of contractual exploitation and exclusion during this period and thereafter.

In the second half of the nineteenth century, Chinese immigrants faced widespread discrimination and limited job opportunities, which led to them "accepting" one-sided, exploitative contracts in the agricultural, railroad, and mining industries. In one noteworthy case, a company employed 216 Chinese laborers at a site where the "sulfur smell and condition of the mines were reportedly so opprobrious that no white men would consent to work there." But corporate lawyers successfully reframed this exploitative arrangement as mutual contractual freedom, arguing that "a corporation possesses the same right to employ whom it pleases as a natural person has, and the friendly alien coming here is entitled to exercise his vocation in a lawful manner." Under freedom of contract principles, the legal system transformed what was essentially economic coercion—where desperate workers had no real choice but to accept dangerous conditions—into a story of voluntary agreement between equals.[14]

The curricular cleansing of these histories represents several forms of inequality this book examines. It demonstrates discursive power: the ability to control which stories get told and what counts as legitimate legal knowledge. This narrower framing makes certain questions about justice unaskable to students still learning the law. The choice to teach dehistoricized contract doctrine also shows how legal education can reflect hierarchy and reinforce existing power relations. By relegating the historically relevant contractual experiences of marginalized groups to footnotes and specialized courses, the course teaches students to see certain vulnerabilities as exceptional rather than systematic.

Some might reasonably claim that students, especially those in their first semester, need doctrinal clarity and not this messy history. That may be right, but it involves a consequential tradeoff: teaching law as if it rained down from the sky as opposed to emerging from human struggles over resources. This is especially true in common law courses like contracts, which are propped up by hundred-year-old cases that claim to show how the law "developed"—but only by spotlighting the parts of history the field chooses to remember. When professors say, "I'm here to teach law, not history," they are offering what looks like professional neutrality masked behind a political choice—the teaching of a tragically curated version of law. The question is not whether law schools should abandon doctrine for history; that wouldn't be wise or realistic. No one is asking professors to turn into Ken Burns.

Contract law loses something meaningful when it is taught without the relevant history that illuminates questions of power, consent, and exploitation. Training competent lawyers means teaching students to understand not just how law works, but how it has failed, and how it might work better. Legal education that acknowledges its own history can produce lawyers who understand that the law they're learning to practice is still being written and can be improved.

Speaking in Tongues: Legal English and the Presumption of Understanding

The historical omissions that define contract law education create the perfect conditions for contemporary linguistic forgetting. I'm talking here about a specific group of people who make spotty appearances in the course: people with limited English proficiency (LEP). This group constitutes about 8 percent of the American population (about twenty-five million people) and many of them are immigrants. Thirty years ago, Steven Bender observed that American law tends to have "little patience" for people who are unable to understand English.[15] The same is true in an era of increased immigration enforcement; these language barriers carry heightened consequences that make contractual vulnerability even more acute.

A study by political scientist Álvaro José Corral involved 367 Latin American migrant and immigrant workers in Ohio. He found that language barriers and the fear of deportation prevent many LEP workers from asserting their contractual rights. As one undocumented worker explained after recent ICE raids in her community: "I don't know how to defend myself because I don't speak English."[16]

Even those *with* legal status face similar vulnerabilities. One worker who had achieved legal permanent resident status described how "Getting a job is really hard if your English isn't perfect.... Once they told me to go and sign some papers that said that if we fall it was our fault and there was no discussion about it."[17] His experience and others' show how LEP creates contractual vulnerability that persists even after gaining legal status, as language barriers continue to undermine workers' ability to understand, negotiate, or challenge unfavorable contract terms.

This isn't just a documented/undocumented immigration issue—language barriers affect a wider group of people that include long-term US residents. Americans encounter these folks regularly—eight out of ten adults say they often or sometimes interact with immigrants who speak little or no English.[18] This is the grandmother who thinks she's protecting her computer but "agrees" to a scam that drains her account. The father at the DMV trying to piece together the clerk's explanation of registration requirements. Or the Uber driver holding up his phone with Google Translate on.

People with LEP enter into contractual relationships across the country daily. They sign employment agreements that waive basic workplace protections. They sign residential leases loaded with unenforceable terms. They accept purchase agreements for goods and services they barely understand. They enter into commercial contracts for their small businesses. They agree to credit terms that lock them in cycles of debt. They consent to medical treatment through forms written in impenetrable legalese. A menu of federal laws prohibits language discrimination in all these areas and many more.[19] But the basic contract law course has little to say about this.

A defender of this omission might say that these issues are not about contract law and are better covered in specialized courses on consumer law, housing, and employment. Maybe. But some schools do not offer such classes regularly, and only a slice of the student population will take them. But there is a bigger problem. Sometimes such courses *do not* have the answers, and contract law might.

In finance, the federal government has found that people with LEP "face challenges completing account applications, *understanding contracts*, and resolving problems, such as erroneous bills."[20] When they are targeted for and sign predatory loans, as the feds have also shown is the case, they have contract claims tied to fraud.[21]

In the housing context, researchers have shown that landlords routinely include unenforceable terms in residential leases. These are terms that a court would not enforce if they were challenged by a tenant.[22] If a person with LEP is fortunate enough to recognize the legal problem, get a lawyer, and/or get to court, they are likely relying on contract remedies.

Wage theft is the withholding of compensation and other benefits from employees. The amount of stolen money has been estimated in the billions, and immigrants with LEP are particularly vulnerable.[23] In the industries where they work (restaurants, agriculture, domestic service), there may or may not be a written contract. In these contexts, courts sometimes view these disputes through a "breach of contract lens" instead of labor/employment law.[24]

Regulatory priorities ebb and flow; in periods when the federal agencies that police these issues scale back on enforcement—as is the case at the time of this writing under Trump's Consumer Financial Protection Bureau and Department of Labor—contract law may be one of the few avenues left for addressing these harms. Gaps in regulatory protection make it all the more striking that the course cordons off these interpretive contractual problems as "something else," and as a result, reinforces staid ideas about the field's boundaries. It also marginalizes live legal issues that are costly to a vulnerable population. In a multilingual society, students learn to think of English-speaking, legally literate, economically secure people as the default parties in contractual disputes.[25] The stories of these relatively absent linguistic minorities could provide crucial human context for understanding how legal doctrine operates and would raise fundamental questions about consent and fairness.

Policing Contracts?

This is not to say that the standard contract course is silent on questions of inequality. Most casebooks have a chapter that focuses on "policing the bargain." This chapter usually focuses on what happens when an agreement is in place, but a court needs to intervene "because of an abuse in bargaining or a defect in the substance of the bargain."[26] This part of the semester offers what appears to be the curriculum's saving grace—a space where inequality arguably gets the most acknowledgment.

Undue influence is one of the simpler contract doctrines and involves instances where one person unfairly persuades another into entering a contract. It tends to focus on relationships of trust. Examples might include the spiritual leader who convinces an adherent to hand over assets, the son who convinces his elderly mother to transfer property, or the lawyer who selfishly makes himself the primary beneficiary of a will. Some casebooks only offer a short commentary on undue influence. When it does get airtime, the focus tends to be on extracting legal rules from individual cases while understating the power dynamics that make contractual abuse possible.[27]

Undue influence gets relegated to specialized courses on family law or trust, wills, and estates. This marginalizes discussions about how elders face systematic financial exploitation through contracts and represents a meaningful oversight. Most relevantly, an alphabet soup of federal agencies care about this issue, and a substantial chunk of law faculty would be defined as "elderly."[28] By 2030, 20 percent of the population will be sixty-five or older.[29]

Cognitive decline, technological illiteracy, social isolation, and health problems make elders prime targets for financial abuse, which is estimated to cost older victims approximately $28 billion annually.[30] Undue influence is one of the tools some people subjected to contract-based exploitation might have at their disposal.[31] But the average law student likely leaves the class not able to recognize the contractual dimensions of this systematic targeting of a fifth of the population. This boomer cohort will be wealthier and live longer than previous generations, but will also face new forms of algorithmic exploitation that capture far more victims than decades prior.[32] This represents a missed opportunity for discussions about age and inequality that are less salient in legal education than conversations about race or gender.[33]

Duress is the cousin of undue influence; it deals less with manipulation and concerns instances where people are coerced into agreements. So many examples fall into this category.

Cities across the country have a long history of making people sign "release-dismissal agreements" that involve prosecutors dismissing criminal charges in exchange for a defendant agreeing not to sue the city for violating their civil rights.[34] Translation: We won't prosecute and railroad you if you agree not to sue us. I'm thinking here of Jose Mendoza. He was shot in the jaw in a drug raid that produced no drugs. The prosecutorial geniuses in Salem, Oregon, responded by charging *him* with attempted murder. This case must have been remarkably unconvincing, since they were willing to make it vanish the moment Mendoza signed away his right to sue the city for his medical bills.[35] These kinds of agreements, which the Supreme Court has okayed, don't show up in contracts casebook discussions about duress—even though scholars have spent decades drawing connections between contract law and the coercive power of the state in dealmaking.[36]

Under duress-like conditions, workers routinely sign "covenants not to sue" that waive legal claims against the employer. So if they are discriminated against because of their religion or disability, tough luck. An Illinois court had to step in after UPS driver John Reliford signed one of these agreements. Reliford waived his right to bring an age discrimination claim for a measly $200 after his employer allegedly threatened to withhold his ill wife's health insurance benefits.[37]

The prospect of duress is so real that the Equal Employment Opportunity Commission (EEOC) and dozens of law firms specifically offer guidance on how employers can legally break ties with employees without being coercive.

Individual coercion gets varying treatment in contract law—ranging from minor coverage to inclusion. But you know what can take up much of the space in conversations about duress? Duress against *businesses*.

As illustrated in one of the leading cases students learn, here's how *business compulsion* works: A restaurant chain has a deal with their food supplier. The latter is supposed to deliver fresh meat every week.

One day the supplier says, "We want double the money or we're not delivering anything." Now the restaurant is screwed because they can't serve customers without food, and finding a new supplier takes weeks. So they pay up, even though the supplier is basically holding them hostage.[38]

Now, it makes sense that law students learn about this. Some will be transactional lawyers who might encounter a version of this problem. But some will not. And for any lawyer, it might be easy to miss the plight of the average person who is coerced into a contract, likely uncounseled, and has unequal bargaining power. The pattern across casebooks—variable treatment of individual coercion but consistent, detailed coverage of business duress—reflects ideas about which kind of economic pressures deserve study.

Finally, the *unconscionability doctrine* allows courts to invalidate unreasonably one-sided contracts. Such contracts "shock the conscience." When I was in law school and we reached this point in the semester, I said to myself, "Finally, something I actually care about." One of the staple cases on this issue, *Williams v. Walker-Thomas Furniture Co.*, is a sixty-year-old decision where a court pumped the brakes on a fine-print provision that allowed a furniture company to repossess a slew of items from a single Black mother of seven on welfare. It's somewhat of a feel-good story, but it poses a bunch of problems.

First, since *Walker-Thomas Furniture* is one of the few canonical cases that invites conversations about race, class, and gender, it can dangerously reinforce stereotypes about irresponsible poor people, racial minorities, and women of color if left in the hands of an uncareful professor.[39] Second, some versions of the contracts curriculum undermine unconscionability doctrine by suggesting—paradoxically—that refusing to enforce exploitative contracts would harm poor consumers. The claim is that companies would either stop selling to poor consumers or raise prices, arguments that are empirically complex and well beyond what contract courses are equipped to evaluate.[40] Finally, the value of this doctrine is minimized by the squadron of professors who mistakenly suggest that it is obsolete.[41]

Ultimately, the narrow terms in which contract law approaches inequality-related doctrines all set the stage for limiting and underwhelming discussions. The doctrines meant to protect vulnerable people from exploitation either get sidelined entirely or watered down. This pattern reflects something deeper about some approaches to contract law and the first year more generally: Even when courses address inequality, they do so at arm's length and with a comfortable distance from human consequences.

BY THE END OF THE SEMESTER, something shifts in how some students talk about contracts. What might have struck them as obviously unfair becomes more technical and abstract. Efficient breach becomes about rational promise-breaking as opposed to moral wrong.[42] Fine print trickery becomes standard form contracts. Desperation-driven agreements get swallowed by an "objective theory of assent." In some ways, the contract classroom becomes a training ground for rationalizing lopsided economic arrangements.

But everyone doesn't go through a metamorphosis.

In many contract classrooms, some resist this new vocabulary and way of looking at the world. I wasn't one of them—I was too disoriented by the newness of it all, too focused on survival to mount any meaningful resistance. But I watched others try. There was that classmate whose mother was an attorney—which probably gave her the confidence to push back. She asked the uncomfortable questions. She pointed out that some of our hypotheticals looked like what was happening to families in East Oakland. Her questions disrupted the flow of conversation and made students uncomfortable. But they also led some of us pause and consider the human cost of what we were learning.

Unfortunately, some students will go on to be what the Duke law professor Paul Carrington called "unconscionable lawyers." These are the people who will help draft rights-stripping contracts designed to prevent people from having a jury trial, an impartial judge, or the ability to participate in a class action.[43] Some of them will litigate disputes and gleefully point to contract provisions in attempts to protect their clients. "Never mind those millions who are illiterate, uneducated, disabled, or to whom English is a foreign language," Carrington explained, "none of whom can possibly be said to have assented to any terms disadvantageous to themselves."[44] And some lawyers will do this work while believing themselves to be engaged in neutral professional practice rather than the active construction of an unjust world. Those are the lawyers I worry about: the ones who follow the structural imperatives of zealous advocacy and go scorched earth on everyone else.

CHAPTER 3

Injurious Matters: Tort Law and the Narrow Construction of Harm

TORT LAW IS one of the most alien yet most familiar legal topics in the first year of law school.

Most simply, a *tort* is when someone injures or harms you. It's different from contract law, which deals with the wrong of broken promises. Tort law is focused on injuries that stem from carelessness or misconduct. Torts are usually handled in civil court, where the goal is compensation, as opposed to criminal court, where the focus is punishment. The person who caused the harm is called a *tortfeasor*.

Tort law, or what is sometimes called *torts*, is unfamiliar because it's a term most people do not use. You don't hear it at the barbecue or in the group chat. It's not on banners at protests and it's not a word wounded people would use as a default. You won't hear the word *torts* in a song, at a religious service, or on a podcast, unless the person responsible for the content went to law school. It sounds like something you nod at and pretend to understand when the waiter says it's the chef's special.

But torts involve one of the most ordinary human experiences: being hurt by somebody. That injury might be physical, like getting hit by a distracted driver. It could be emotional, like enduring psychological abuse by a supervisor. Or it could be financial, like having your name besmirched in ways that cause you to lose out on money and job opportunities.

Thought of this way, tort law is everywhere.

This is the personal injury commercial where an attorney insists that "accidents in life are inevitable, but I'm here to fight to the death for the compensation that you deserve." This promise might be followed by a group of former clients who say, in succession and concert, "When I was hurt, Shaun Ossei-Owusu was there for me!" You see torts in the auto insurance policies that states compel drivers to get in case of an accident. Tort law shapes the recalls that one might see in the course of a year because of a defective product (e.g., malfunctioning airbags in cars, home appliances that present a fire hazard).

I lived on the South Side of Chicago and Southwest Philadelphia as an adult. During my first year of law school, I commuted from East Oakland. Harm wasn't theoretical to me—I'd seen it, smelled it, and lived next to it. So when I walked into that torts classroom, I thought we'd be talking about the kinds of injuries that filled the trauma centers, marked the sidewalks, and got whispered about on the front stoops of all of those neighborhoods.

I was shocked by what didn't make it into our discussions. This wasn't about what I *wanted* to see covered—I didn't know enough to have strong preferences. This was about forms of violence and injury that were statistically significant and so clearly connected to the legal principles we were studying that their absence raised questions about the curriculum.

I noticed more patterns as I moved through the course and my career. I realized that the doctrines typically covered were often framed in ways that brushed aside their relationships to inequality or relegated them to literal footnotes. The professor in me recognized the dilemma. Torts is often taught in the fall. Students are being hit with an avalanche of new concepts. Foregrounding inequality isn't feasible; it would overwhelm students still learning basic legal reasoning. But avoidance and cursory coverage are problems, too.

In any event, I worry that there is a fundamental problem with how the curriculum treats this balancing act of foundational learning and contextual understanding, especially when we're talking about something as grave as harm and suffering. What I'm going to show you in this chapter is how tort education conceals some of the field's most politically charged applications. Intentional harms, such as domestic violence (DV) and police brutality, typically get rushed through, skipped over, or quarantined in specialty electives.

Doctrines that do get taught are framed in ways that obscure power relations. *Negligence*—the part of the course that focuses on accidental injuries—is presented as neutral risk allocation. Insurance coverage is discussed without mentioning systematic racial discrimination. *Damages* are how people are compensated for harm. Depending on the state, two people can suffer the same injury and get different awards based on race and gender—a reality that also gets uneven attention in the course. And the increasing restrictions on people's ability to sue for harm, called *tort reform*, is sometimes presented as an abstract policy debate about frivolous litigation without fully exploring its impact on access to justice.

Sadly, the tort curriculum constructs an incomplete picture of the harms faced by vulnerable groups and the legal remedies available to them. Importantly, understanding how future lawyers are taught to recognize harm affects all of us. It shapes whose pain gets validated, whose is overlooked, and how justice is ultimately distributed.

The Invisible Harm of Intimate Partner Violence

Let's start at the margins with *intentional torts*. These are injuries that are caused on purpose. Examples include *battery* (unwanted physical contact like punching or spitting), *defamation* (harming a person's reputation), and *false imprisonment* (restricting someone's freedom). Despite being the simplest subcategory of torts, it typically gets less attention in the curriculum. Besides the common explanation of limited time and trade-offs, some professors subscribe to the view that accidental injuries—described in more detail in a moment—are the primary domain of torts.[1] Such sidelining of intentional torts comes with significant costs, one of which is inattention to issues of gender-based violence.

How could a course concerned with harm pay little attention to intimate partner violence? In many ways, this neglect normalizes one of the most common forms of battery and renders it invisible. Approximately 41 percent of women and 26 percent of men reported experiencing intimate partner violence during their lifetime (e.g., sexual violence, physical violence, and/or stalking).[2] These are harms that fit into some of the previously mentioned categories like battery as well as a host of other tort categories, such as invasion of privacy, trespass, and intentional infliction of emotional distress.

I initially didn't question the absence. Like most first-year students, I assumed what we learned represented the boundaries of the field. Then I spoke to an upper-level student at Berkeley Law taking a domestic violence law course with one of the pioneers in the field. She told me about *Thompson v. Thompson*, a 1910 Supreme Court tort decision that provides an excellent window into the discussion of tort law, injury, gender, and power.

The dispute was tragically simple: A wife wanted to sue her husband for beating her. She filed a lawsuit seeking $70,000 in damages for multiple assaults, some committed while she was pregnant. The husband's defense wasn't "I didn't do it." Instead, he argued that because they were married, she legally couldn't sue him at all. The Supreme Court agreed.

A relatively progressive District of Columbia statute was at the heart of the case. The law gave married women the right to own property, conduct business, and, for our purposes, "sue separately for torts committed against them, as fully and freely as if they were unmarried." Even though the law historically treated married women as having no distinct legal identity from their husbands, this law allowed them to sue without needing their husbands' blessing.

Despite the clear language that again, wives can sue "for torts committed against them," the court used some pretzel logic. They ruled that the statute couldn't possibly allow wives to sue their husbands, just other people. The court worried that such lawsuits would "open the doors of the courts to accusations of all sorts" between spouses and threaten "domestic harmony." Translation: If one survivor were allowed to seek justice through tort law, courts would be clogged with complaints about being assaulted, slandered, and harmed. Having domestic violence aired out in public was undesirable to them.

Three justices dissented and pointed out the perverse reasoning. The same statute that allowed women to sue husbands for stealing their property did not allow them to sue for physical assault. The dissent basically asked: Was a woman's furniture or jewelry more legally sacred than her physical person?

The majority's proposed remedy to women like Thompson makes the case especially instructive to tort education. First, it pointed women to family law. It concluded that women subject to domestic violence "had adequate grounds for relief under the statutes of divorce and alimony." The court minces words here in ways I cannot. It told Thompson that her husband's assault against her pregnant body was not a tort worthy of legal consideration, just grounds for dissolving her marriage.

The *Thompson* court also pointed to criminal law and said such women could "resort to the criminal courts, which, it is to be presumed, will inflict punishment commensurate with the offense committed."[3] This was peak judicial fantasy. Note again that this was in 1910, when DV was considered a private matter, police had reservations about arresting perpetrators, prosecutors were hesitant to charge, and bias could lead to male jurors siding with men who "disciplined" insufficiently submissive wives.[4] Prosecution and punishment did occur, but it was subject to these biases and limitations.[5]

The Supreme Court's channeling of DV away from tort law toward divorce and criminal remedies maps onto how legal education treats these harms. Just as the court insisted that battering belonged in other legal categories—despite fitting perfectly within tort doctrine—modern curricula shuttle domestic violence off to criminal law courses and family law courses, as if intimate partner violence were not a tort issue.

Thompson is not an obscure case. This Supreme Court decision is missing from most mainstream casebooks despite being written about by scholars and appearing in specialized DV casebooks. Maybe this is a sincere oversight, which raises troubling questions about how the field constructs its canon. Or maybe keeping DV cabined in specialty courses is an active choice. Either way, the absence of this case and the larger issue show how legal categorization decides which stories get told in which rooms. It also reflects a reality we see in larger society: DV is often not considered worthy of being a main conversation. Martha Chamallas and Jennifer Wriggins are two pioneering scholars working at the intersection of tort and DV, and they rightfully observe that the absence of DV from these discussions communicates that these "are not to be regarded as core personal injuries."[6]

These days, there are several obstacles to bringing these claims to court—some of which grow out of the historical hostility courts have had toward claims of injury brought by women.[7] But survivors persist and sometimes prevail in court on DV issues. Some states, such as New Jersey, Illinois, Washington, and California, have even gone so far as to create new legal rules to deal with tort law's inattention to gender-based violence.[8] And that is alongside traditional torts like assault and intentional infliction of emotional distress. In other words, the doctrine is there; the issue is about pedagogical will. Without that commitment, torts instruction risks fostering a professional identity that regards gendered harm as beyond the scope of civil accountability and legal concern.

The State Terror Exception

State violence gets the same treatment as gender-based harm—systematic exile from the mainstream torts curriculum.

If torts are about holding people accountable for harm, constitutional torts are about holding government officials liable for harm that stems from violations of constitutional rights. Constitutional torts are related to but separate from the first-year constitutional law course, which is more big-picture and focuses on the structure and limits of government power. In many law schools, constitutional torts are taught in the second year, sometimes in a civil rights course or a class on federal courts.

Constitutional torts are a relatively new legal category. The relevant laws have existed since Reconstruction but were relatively dormant until the 1960s when the Supreme Court exhumed the idea. Since then, plaintiffs have used constitutional torts to sue government officers accused of causing physical, dignitarian, and economic harms. This might include killer cops—the typical subjects of constitutional torts—as well as a wide range of other government employees: correctional officials, public housing authorities, school district employees, social workers, and many more. All of them are capable of harming people, but few, if any, are likely to appear in the course.[9]

If you audited a torts class, you'd likely find that most of the parties causing harm are private parties. *Consumer v. Corporation. Employer v. Employee. Guest v. Landowner. Individual v. Individual.* The government shows up in some cases as a defendant, but in this course it primarily serves as the arbiter of disputes.

Students are nudged toward being concerned about the wet floor that might cause an accident, the defective product, or the careless driver. They do not learn to fear the officer who lies in a warrant affidavit or turns off their body camera before administering a beating. The prison guard who deliberately ignores an inmate's urgent medical emergency is nowhere to be found. The social worker who unlawfully removes a child from the home without a warrant is of no concern. Powerful government actors who have the ability to separate families as well as surveil, detain, and use force—things that would qualify as harms in most people's book—are rendered invisible in the required course on how law deals with harm. These actors live in another legal universe during the first year.

Some genuinely unique rules and standards are tied to holding government officials liable for harm. These, again, might be hard to teach early in students' careers. But tort professors are no intellectual slouches. They spend weeks translating the law of nineteenth-century railroad accidents for twenty-something-year-olds. Law and economics is a dominant paradigm in the field, and professors must deploy cost-benefit math for parts of the course ("the Learned Hand formula"). If it is taught, insurance has complex rules about indemnification and subrogation (akin to reimbursement). Those issues are difficult too; this is about which complexities we choose to prioritize.

And it's worth saying that engaging with constitutional torts need not be driven by an ideology. Organizations across the political spectrum get in on the action, too, whether they be the conservative Pacific Legal Foundation or the left-leaning American Civil Liberties Union. The libertarian Institute for Justice goes as far as to grade each state based on its constitutional tort law rules.[10] These kinds of claims proliferate so much that the Department of Justice has a special division—the Constitutional and Specialized Tort Litigation Section—which defends federal employees accused of harming people. This isn't a sideshow.

Ultimately, all kinds of losses come with treating government-caused harm as some kind of exotic constitutional specialty. Intellectually, there are a bunch of justifications for tort law—namely deterring people from engaging in injurious behavior, compensating people for harm, and enforcing social norms. Slicing up legal harms in this way prevents students from really examining whether tort law achieves those goals.

The liability rules for government officials are different, but that reflects political choices rather than legal necessities. They represent another place where students could see how power shapes doctrine. But perhaps most importantly, minimizing constitutional torts obscures students' understanding of where legal danger emanates from. To call constitutional torts "state terror" is to name the government's monopoly on force, which arguably makes it the most fearsome source of harm. Recognizing this reality pushes students to consider what obligations should bind the state if we took its power to injure as seriously as that of private wrongdoers. Omitting government harm from the curriculum can leave students with the innocent impression that the state does not engage in tortious conduct worthy of examination.

Most generally, the same pedagogical choice that pushes domestic violence in family law and constitutional torts in civil rights sends a clear message: DV and state violence aren't "real" tort problems worthy of mainstream legal attention. They are specialty concerns for activists, not the serious business of learning how law and harm actually operate in American society.

Neglecting History and Context in Negligence Law

Now that we've seen what tort education pushes to the margins, we can examine what it puts at the center. Negligence and accidental harm are the main events of the typical torts course. The way negligence doctrine gets presented tends to ignore how deeply political its development was.

Let's travel back in time to the late nineteenth century, which was a period of unintentional mayhem. Accidental deaths and injuries skyrocketed. Americans experienced what Yale historian John Fabian Witt called an "accident crisis like none the world had ever seen," and one no 'Western nation has witnessed since."[11] The growth of mechanical power (e.g., elevators, cranes, belts) and the proliferation of different forms of transportation (e.g., cars and trains) occurred amid mushrooming urban populations. That combination was a breeding ground for disasters. Accidents included explosions, fires, people being struck by vehicles, falling objects at construction sites, and electrocution, to name a few. And the consequences could be the loss of limbs or life.

Some injuries came from the workplace. "By the turn of the century," Witt explains, "one worker in fifty was killed or disabled for at least four weeks each year because of a work-related accident."[12] People didn't stand by idly or apolitically. Labor unions challenged restrictive understandings of negligence that shielded employers from legal liability.[13] Focusing often on wounded male breadwinners unable to support their families, the growing population of personal injury lawyers "politicized the interruption of wages" that came with these injuries.[14] Insurance companies and employers were additional players.

They pushed tort law in different directions and helped shape the development of workers' compensation laws.[15]

Negligence, historian Barbara Welke observes, "developed into a distinct, concrete body of law only in the last third of the nineteenth century, and the vehicle which powered its rise was the railroad."[16] Railroad companies make guest appearances in the typical torts course. I remember being in the middle of torts class as a student and remarking, "Another train company; you gotta be kidding me." Nevertheless, the *political* context of this industry's influence on tort law tends to be evacuated. Negligence cases between passengers and the companies are present, but the legitimate concerns and underhanded tactics of railroad lawyers are less visible.

Railroad attorneys and their bigwig clients worried—quite reasonably—about biased local juries who viewed these "large, impersonal organizations" with "skeptical disdain," especially when presented with a maimed plaintiff.[17] These lawyers frustrated tort law's goal of compensating people for civil wrongs. Their playbook was deep and ranged in ethical propriety. Pressuring injured passengers into taking paltry settlements before they could file a lawsuit was not beyond the pale.[18] They also relied on "friendly judges, stacked juries, powerful attorneys, special agents, and sympathetic expert witnesses." If those options failed, they used procedural wizardry to remove their cases from local courts to favorable federal venues.[19]

Why is this background relevant to the law of negligence?

Understanding this history matters because it restores the human suffering that legal education systematically drains from negligence doctrine. In torts, students may learn technical elements but not see the blood and struggle that produced them—the labor organizers who demanded accountability, the families bankrupted by medical bills, and the political fights over who would bear the costs of industrialization: humans or corporations. Without this context, students may understand negligence abstractly and miss how it can be a system that distributes pain and protection in a variety of directions.

Knowing how corporate lawyers historically frustrated tort law's compensation goals may give students a sneak peek of what is to come. Some of the strategies railroad lawyers used to deny compensation to injured people—manipulating procedure, venue shopping, and expert witness cultivation—remain standard corporate defense tactics today. Students entering the profession would likely benefit from knowing what they will be asked to do (should they go on the defense side) or fight against (should they work for plaintiffs).

Finally, not teaching this history may leave students unable to meaningfully engage with contemporary tort debates. A longstanding debate about reform in this area—discussed in detail in the last section—seeks to limit people's ability to sue for harm and receive damages. Absent this history, it becomes harder to determine whether current reform efforts represent genuine improvement or if they are repackaged arguments designed to limit corporate liability. Students, in turn, learn technical rules without understanding the ongoing political projects those rules serve or resist.

Unequal Remedies:
Insurance Coverage and Damage Calculation

Having discussed intentional harms and accidents, let's follow tort law to its logical conclusion: how injured people actually get paid.

One option is what my colleague Tom Baker calls "blood money"—money paid out of the defendant's pockets. But most individuals don't have deep enough pockets to compensate for harms, which is where insurance enters the picture. Insurance is the primary mechanism by which injured plaintiffs often get paid. Some personal injury attorneys won't even take a case if they think insurance is not in the picture (e.g., auto, premises liability, and medical malpractice insurance).[20] This makes insurance fundamental to understanding tort law's goal of compensation for harm.

Here is where we see tort law jostling with the realities of American inequality. Insurance markets introduce biases that subvert the goal of compensation for people who suffer comparable injuries. Casebooks range in their treatment of insurance, with some giving the topic a full chapter, a subsection, or scattered discussions. In each of these versions, there are two tendencies.

One is to pretend that demographic categories like race, gender, or age are irrelevant to insurance. But this is belied by reality: Women paid more for health insurance until the passage of the Affordable Care Act and racial minorities have long struggled to get insurers to pay after accidents (and when they do, the payments have been lower than for whites).

Some casebooks acknowledge these disparities. One of the few books that does engage these issues notes that differential premiums based on identity might be justified in some instances, as there is "sound empirical evidence that a higher percentage of teenage boys drive recklessly than other groups."[21] But even when the issue surfaces, a deeper challenge is frequently left unexamined—namely how structural inequalities in insurance undermine tort principles. Can the field retain full legitimacy when discrimination in compensation is encoded into the system?

Insurance companies use classification criteria—such as age, sex, marital status, occupation, and residence—to assess risk and determine policy coverage. These criteria reflect and reinforce broader patterns in American society. As tort scholar Regina Austin explains, this classification process is inherently tied to social stratification and hierarchy.[22]

Racial discrimination in auto insurance is almost an unspoken norm that is sanitized through actuarial language. In 2017, investigators found that Allstate, Liberty Mutual, Progressive, and Geico charged 10 to 30 percent more on average in risky minority neighborhoods than in similarly risky majority-white neighborhoods.[23] In other words, when the actuarial tables said the risks were identical, the insurance companies seemed to say, "Yeah, but look who lives here. Let's add a surcharge." Alternatively, their complex mathematical models mysteriously kept generating higher premiums for minority neighborhoods despite identical risk profiles.

Antidiscrimination scholar Deborah Hellman explains that

insurers justify their pricing practices based on the principle of *actuarial fairness*. A scheme is actuarially fair if an insured person "pays a price for coverage that is equivalent to the risk she poses of drawing from the insurance pool, given available information."[24] So if you're more likely to make a claim, you pay more. But actuarial fairness becomes something more complicated and can creep into legal inequality by design when you examine what's being measured.

When insurance companies use zip codes as risk factors, they're not just pricing individual behavior but larger historical and sociological factors. I'm talking about the residual effects of housing segregation and all kinds of disparities in public resources: unrepaired potholes that increase the likelihood of accidents; broken or nonexistent streetlights that increase the chance of theft; inadequate snow and ice removal that can lead to more weather-related accidents; and poor public transportation options that increase reliance on driving and overall risk exposure.

This kind of structural inequality isn't random or some natural market variation; it's the result of political choices that filter into insurance schemes. This raises challenges for tort law's goal of compensation for injury. If insurance coverage is more expensive or less accessible to racial minorities, that means tort remedies are less available to people who might need them. Students who learn tort doctrine without understanding this backdrop are trained to see legal remedies as more universal than they are, when they are in fact contingent on social, economic, and demographic factors that sometimes have very little to do with tort law.

Beyond insurance coverage, there's the question of *damages*—how much money injured people receive for their harm.

For decades, the torts curriculum had little to say about how identity shaped compensation. This silence occurred notwithstanding experts' use of identity-based actuarial tables to make such calculations. Two people who experienced the same injury might get vastly different awards because these experts would look at things like the victim's life expectancy, anticipated years of work, and expected wages. All of these categories can be influenced by race and gender (among other classifications), which can lead to lower awards for minorities, women, and women of color—all of whom occupy the lower rungs of the labor force.

But there has been pushback to this approach. In 2003, James McMillan Jr. suffered a disabling injury while on a New York City ferryboat. In an effort to decrease the amount of money it would have to cough up, the city tried to introduce evidence that suggested that Black people with injured spinal cords lived shorter lives than people of other races with similar injuries. The judge in *McMillan v. the City of New York* (2008) rejected the use of race-based computations of life expectancy.[25]

Or consider the time Niki Hernandez-Adams sued her landlord on behalf of her son, who suffered injuries to his central nervous system because of lead paint. A jury awarded the child $2,000,000 and the defense brought in an expert who used race and gender-based actuarial tables to testify, I kid you not, that since "Hispanic males" were less likely to obtain college and graduate degrees, the child's award should have been reduced.[26] Fortunately, the court rejected this contention, but the fact that it was raised by an attorney with sincerity illustrates how inequality can seep into tort practice.

A similarly egalitarian approach to damages was deployed on the September 11th Victim Compensation Fund. The federal government created this reserve of money to compensate the victims of the 9/11 attacks and their families. In exchange, the families agreed not to sue American and United Airlines; if they had done so, it would have crushed the airline industry. Ken Feinberg, who administered the fund, made the critical decision not to rely on race and gender in determining lifetime earnings. The fact that treating people equally demanded explanation illustrates how deeply tort law can normalize and accept inequality.

These days, some casebooks discuss these high-profile developments and highlight scholarship on this issue. But many casebooks still avoid this background entirely, and some that do cover it treat it as resolved rather than ongoing. Some states like Oregon, California, and New Jersey prohibit race-based calculations; others like Georgia,

Kansas, and North Carolina affirmatively green light the practice; and most other states appear to allow it by default since there is no prohibition.[27] Students who learn damage formulas without understanding that many states permit race-based disparities in compensation are trained to normalize systematic discrimination. This represents a troubling feature of what tort education accomplishes: an emphasis on technical competence while concealing systemic inequality.

Tort Reform and the Battle Between "Ambulance Chasers" and Stingy Harm-Doers

Tort reform is a constellation of ideas that focus on making it harder for plaintiffs to file lawsuits when they are injured and reducing their awards should they prevail in court. Supporters of tort reform point to a host of problems: money-hungry plaintiffs who are quick to file lawsuits over papercuts; "sleazy" personal injury attorneys who get a large percentage of recoveries; and biased juries who are duped by the melodramas of these so-called victims and give away millions in award damages.

The less heavy-handed, and more sympathetic version of their concerns focuses on how tort litigation can detrimentally impact various sectors of society, such as a health profession that is burdened by high malpractice insurance and practices medicine with a certain kind of timidity (out of a fear of being sued); small businesses that are uniquely exposed to risk and could be decimated by one big tort award; and an insurance industry that is forced to issue big payouts that subsequently raise costs for everyone else. Some states have heard tort reformers' cries and have put caps on certain kinds of damages. Others imposed statutes of limitations on certain kinds of harm. And with the passage of the Class Action Fairness Act of 2005, the feds have made it harder for attorneys to file lawsuits in state courts that might be more favorable to plaintiffs.

Others see something more pernicious in tort reform. The *Bronx effect* was a term used in the 1980s and 1990s to describe the pro-plaintiff sensibilities of people in my hood who served on juries. The late Temple law professor Frank McClellan described tort reformers' ideas about urban jurors gone wild as racially coded complaints about distributive justice. When reformers grumbled about urban juries being too generous to plaintiffs, McClellan understood this as resistance to Black and Brown people having a form of economic power. Juries, he noted, are one of the few "institutions in America where people of color have the power to make immediate wealth redistribution decisions"—in this instance, taking money from "corporations" and giving it to injured community members.[28]

Now consider this: The American Tort Reform Foundation publishes *Judicial Hellholes*, an annual report of plaintiff-friendly jurisdictions that furnish excessive awards. Anti-tort reformers have pointed out how many of these hellholes seem to have a lot of minorities.[29]

Meanwhile, legal scholar Carl Bogus suggests that the use of *reform*, which has a progressive connotation, does important discursive work. He argues that the word reframes the debate and camouflages the "regressive agenda" of the group, whose membership includes powerful, harm-causing industries (e.g., gas, pharmaceutical, gun, and for-profit healthcare companies).[30] Tort reform has traditionally been a Republican issue, but because it is tied to big business, some Democrats have also supported the movement, whereas libertarians have registered skepticism—all of which are realities that upset what might appear to be a typical partisan story.[31]

The debate over tort reform turns less on mystery than on perspective. Tort reformers frame restrictions as protecting fairness, while critics believe these limitations are attacks on minority communities' rare access to power. For these reasons and others, some sidestep the issue altogether, whereas others try in earnest to be more diplomatic.[32]

Regardless of what side of the debate one is on, tort reform is actively shaping this body of law and merits meaningful engagement. By definition, tort reform presumes that bringing cases to court is too easy, and so it is focused on making civil litigation *harder*. This is an access to justice problem that conflicts with tort law's goal of remedying wrong. This means an evolving body of law is impacting everyday people's ability to sue for harm, but this issue receives uneven attention in the required curriculum.

OVERALL, MY PROBLEM WITH the torts curriculum is this: It strips away some of the social, political, and moral context that can reveal the field's broader workings. Tort law is supposed to deal with civil wrongs, but it is insensitive to some profound harms that are legally relevant.

Domestic violence and constitutional torts get exiled to family law and civil rights courses despite representing some of the most consequential and pervasive forms of harm in American society. Students learn negligence theory without being fully exposed to its contested origins. Insurance discrimination and race-based damage calculations get treated as technical side issues as opposed to contradictions of tort law's promises. Meanwhile, tort reform—which reshapes remedies—gets presented through sterile policy language that distances readers from its human impact (if it is discussed at all).

This approach risks producing a form of legal education that limits a broader understanding of the social world. The curriculum's selective presentation of tort doctrine—doctrinally sophisticated but drenched in ideas of neutrality—teaches students to be good legal technicians while remaining disconnected from what that technique actually means for real people's lives.

CHAPTER 4

Property, Ownership, and Injustice

THE SAN FRANCISCO BAY AREA was one of the most honest but brutal teachers I ever had. While in law school, I fellowshipped with allies in San Francisco, called Oakland home, and studied property in Berkeley.

Tech money hit San Francisco like a Mack truck, flattening many things in its path and remaking the city into a curated playground for the ultra-rich.

In the Mission, Mexican American families were pushed out by hoodie-wearing professionals in search of "authenticity." Property law offered some protections—rent control and eviction defenses—but they were corner-store umbrellas: thin, temporary, and no match for the monsoon of market pressure.

Generations ago, officials and private parties used property law to corral Chinese immigrants into Chinatown, denying them access to the generational wealth-building activity that is homeownership. By the 2010s, their descendants watched as rising prices displaced people and unraveled the social fabric.

The Fillmore neighborhood was once known as the Harlem of the West, but six decades of urban renewal, market speculation, and gentrification displaced Black residents and left behind a neighborhood where a few strips of "Millionaire's Bacon" go for $28. San Francisco now has one of the smallest Black populations of any major US city at just 5 percent.

The people who kept San Francisco alive—teachers, nurses, and other essential workers—were driven out because rent outstripped their salaries. They now endure ninety-minute-plus treks to get to work. These folks, now referred to as "extreme commuters," ended up in places like Stockton or Sacramento—the equivalent of working in Atlanta but living in Chattanooga, or commuting from Brooklyn to Scranton.

Oakland was its own heartbreak. Black families fled the Jim Crow South only to be subject to redlining and disinvestment. Despite generations of organizing and deep-rooted investment—social, cultural, and even infrastructural—they were displaced by markets that recognized only titles and deeds. To make matters worse, and to show just how deeply property and capitalism collude, the culture of resistance was repackaged as an aesthetic and sold to the highest bidder: people who wanted the look of struggle without living through it. Down in East Oakland, Latino families watched in disbelief as real estate agents rebranded their neighborhoods as "emerging markets." It seemed like decades of community meant nothing until outsiders suspected profit.

Then there was homelessness. The unhoused could be found next to freeways, in train stations, on sidewalks, in parks, you name it. This was all over the Bay Area, but it felt stark in Berkeley. Could you imagine walking past people sleeping in doorways on your way to learn about "property rights"? What does it mean to spend days learning about real estate when living people couldn't find places to sleep?

The Bay Area was still teaching me about property law long after I'd finished the formal course.

In May 2016, just as I was graduating, the ACLU in San Francisco published a report showing how law enforcement across the state was systematically extracting wealth from racial minorities. The report revealed that 85 percent of federal property seizures in California went to agencies policing majority communities of color, while half of all seizures involved people with Latino surnames. This was a massive taking of property—the kind one would expect to learn about in property law, but it remained relatively invisible.[1]

That same year, I was exposed to the work of the Child Care Law Center—a legal advocacy group located just three miles from Berkeley Law that focused on how discriminatory zoning affects families.[2] Zoning is basically the government telling you what you can and can't do on your own property, like keeping gas stations away from schools or factories out of neighborhoods. The Center's research showed how these same rules systematically prevented women from running childcare businesses in their homes. This created a vicious cycle: Property law restricted women's ability to use their property economically, which reduced childcare options for other working mothers, and caused some women to leave the workforce entirely. All of this reinforced broader patterns of gender inequality across the economy.

These issues captured problems far beyond my personal experience. I was never homeless nor had I lost a home to gentrification. Police had never seized my property. I was childless at the time.

And this was bigger than my property law course; my instructor, like most during my first year, cared about injustice.

But here were widespread property problems affecting hundreds of thousands of Californians. All of this was happening within miles of where I had learned property law. Yet they weren't in the casebooks, on the bar exam, or part of the curriculum that was supposed to prepare lawyers to understand how property law actually operates.

Here's the skinny for this chapter. Property law demonstrates a pattern of selective attention that shapes future lawyers' education. This happens in several distinct ways. Sometimes it's straight *omission*. Contemporary housing crises like homelessness and gentrification receive minimal attention despite their connections to property law.

Other times it's *fixation*—dwelling on doctrines with limited contemporary application while overlooking present-day analogs. Students master archaic rules tied to aristocratic property control but spend little to no attention on how contemporary billionaires use lawyers to concentrate property and wealth across generations.

Then there's *selectivity*—teaching some problems in depth while barely mentioning others. Property law casebooks provide extensive coverage of government taking of homes for public use but devote far less attention to civil asset forfeiture, in which police seize cars, cash, and personal property from ordinary citizens.

Finally, there's *underdevelopment*. Zoning is a prime example of this tendency and receives mixed treatment. Zoning has been a tool of race and class exclusion, and instructors vary in how deeply they engage that history, but other dimensions of inequality—like gender—often go unexamined.

These patterns—only a few of many—matter because the lawyers trained in property classes today will draft the zoning codes to determine where your kids can access childcare. They will represent the police departments that might seize your property. And they will advise the governments that decide how homelessness gets addressed in your community. The selective attention of legal education doesn't stay in the classroom—it shapes how power operates in the real world.

Invisible Housing Markets, Homelessness, and Gentrification

Property law concerns owners' right to do as they please with their stuff. They can freely use, sell, rent, gift, dispose, transfer, or exclude others from using their property.

Property generally falls into one of two big categories.[3] The first is *real property*, which refers generally to land as well as things that are above, below, or permanently attached to land. Sometimes referred to as *real estate*, you might think of this as a plot of land that holds a house, the groundwater underneath it, and the trees that are above it. The second category is *personal property*, which refers to tangible items like vehicles, jewelry, or artwork, as well as to intangible items that one might own, such as stocks or cryptocurrency. Real property tends to be the focus of your typical property course, but some professors spice things up.

Property law courses vary in how they're taught, and, unlike some first-year courses, tend to be more modular and less anchored by a stable arc. Still, they typically cover a few core areas. *Interests in land* are about the different ways you can own property. You might own that house forever and pass it down to your kids, or you may hand it over with strings attached and say, "this land can only be used for farming; no alcohol can ever be sold on this property." *Concurrent ownership* is when multiple people own the same spot—think siblings who inherit grandma's house. *Landlord-tenant relationships* cover rental drama like landlords' obligations to fix things and eviction procedures.

Contracts for sale of land involve the legal requirements for buying and selling property. Everything must be documented properly, the land has to be described accurately, and the seller actually has to own the property. That leads to *title*, which is legal proof of ownership. *Mortgages* explain how real estate loans work legally. *Land use* covers how the government controls what you can do with your property through zoning laws, like whether you can run a business or build apartments in a residential neighborhood.

At the heart of all this lies the home, and rightfully so. It is hard to understate the social significance of a home in American life—whether it is a house, an apartment, or a trailer. Homes are culturally significant markers of identity and receive all kinds of favorable legal protection. Constitutionally, the government is limited in its ability to run up in your home willy-nilly looking for wrongdoing. The tax code lavishes benefits on homeowners via the mortgage interest deduction. In certain criminal contexts, you could shoot someone with impunity just because you're at home.[4] Property law scholar Lee Fennell is spot on when she notes that homes are not just about "shelter, privacy, and storage" but also help facilitate "childrearing, pet care, meal production and consumption, personal hygiene and clothing maintenance, recreation and exercise, education and work, guest accommodation, event hosting, and more."[5]

Considering the importance of the home, one would think that property law would have a fair bit to say about the inverse: people who are literally homeless and/or face housing insecurity. The feds tell us that on a single night in 2023, 653,000 people lacked "a fixed, regular, and adequate nighttime residence."[6] This is greater than the populations of Atlanta, Miami, and New Orleans. Those people are parents, children, veterans, and/or disabled. Yet unhoused people remain absent from many property law casebooks. This means students can learn the technical vocabulary of property while remaining unprepared to ask moral questions about why property is distributed as it is.

One might say that homelessness is not a property law issue but a problem of housing policy. Au contraire! Property law is about ownership and the ability to exclude. In the context of private property, you can legally prohibit someone from entering your home. The doctrine of trespass allows private property owners to prevent homeless people from sleeping or using a bathroom in their home or their business.

In the context of public property, the government can regulate when and how these spaces are used. Cities have passed all types of anti-camping and anti-loitering ordinances that prohibit the kinds of things unhoused people must do somewhere: sleep, sit down, and urinate.[7] There are some good reasons for these regulations: to promote public health and safety as well as fair use of these spaces. But this is law doing three things: defining how property can be used, who can be excluded from property, and who can be punished for not abiding by these rules. These are already core topics for any property course. In 2024, the Supreme Court greenlighted laws designed to exclude homeless people from public places and to criminalize them, so expect a belated rush of new casebook editions with "Now includes landmark 2024 SCOTUS decision!" on the cover.[8]

Some property law courses explore the financial aspects of purchasing homes (e.g., mortgage markets). They may also discuss the 2008 foreclosure crisis. This is another place where homelessness could be discussed that is sometimes squandered. Even though experts and the public often focus on mental health, poverty, and meager incomes as causes of homelessness, compelling evidence suggests that housing market conditions are equally, if not more, important than these explanations.[9] And as much as people want to think markets are "free," they are not independent of the law, which creates the conditions in which markets operate.[10] The inclusion of housing insecurity in this portion of the course should be an obvious decision.

Besides the reasons for omissions provided in previous chapters—interest, time constraints, expertise, and a narrow definition of the field—I'm really left with two explanations for why homelessness is curved.

The good-faith explanation is offered by Temple law professor Jane Baron. She notes the "difficult-to-fathom state" of what might be called "no property" and the challenges of describing "a negative or lack."[11] Figuring out how people who do not own land figure into a course about land ownership is counterintuitive, though it is not impossible.

The more troubling explanation is gestured to by philosopher Jeremy Waldron, who suggests that housing insecurity is an unflattering reminder of how capitalism works. "People do not want to be confronted with the sight of the homeless—it is uncomfortable for the well-off to be reminded of the human price that is paid for a social structure like theirs."[12] Property law looks uglier when its rules must justify the wretched worlds inhabited by some people who are unhoused. Add to that the reality that six-figure-earning property law professors probably can't relate to the experience of being homeless, and you have a recipe for serious omissions.

Do you know what issue is similarly underplayed that professors are more likely to be familiar with? Gentrification. A few apologists and critics of the process have acknowledged as much. Georgetown law professor J. Peter Byrne proudly proclaims, "I am a gentrifier," whereas scholars in other disciplines have tried to be more introspective about the academics' role in gentrification.[13] But despite this occasional self-awareness, gentrification is still hard to find in most property law curricula. Geographer Tom Slater thinks the lack of attention to gentrification is a byproduct of professors' class position. He argues that their proximity to gentrifiers (e.g., friends and colleagues) and their distance from those impacted by the process produce a kind of "epistemic ignorance."[14] I think there is some there there.

This reluctance to engage with gentrification may also stem from universities' own complicity in the process. Universities have been major actors in the gentrification of adjacent neighborhoods (e.g.,

Columbia, the University of Chicago, and my employer, Penn). Their professors, students, and recent graduates—some of whom are increasingly unable to afford living close to campus—often disperse to poorer parts of the city.[15] They bring their preferences for matcha, yoga, and bike shops with them, and boom: Neighborhood "revitalization" happens. Gentrification involves a range of property law issues and is a process students are impacted by, and implicated in; it could affect some future clients—individual and corporate. Property law courses should be all over this.

Part of the crickets surrounding gentrification in property law may stem from definitional disputes. Some see the infusion of moneyed people in poor neighborhoods as free markets simply doing their thing. More critical takes on the issue focus on displacement. This perspective says that revitalization, at least, is fine. Who doesn't want fresher fruit? The problem is when long-term residents of historically disinvested neighborhoods are pushed out.[16]

Several property issues become immediately relevant when gentrification is understood through the lens of displacement. This might include landlord-tenant issues. Landlords sometimes illegally harass their tenants and kick them to the curb in search of the larger profits that might come from leasing to richer tenants.[17] On the zoning front, neighborhood organizations have challenged zoning commissions' approvals of development projects on the grounds that these initiatives would spur gentrification and displacement.[18] And then there is foreclosure, the process by which one's home is taken by another (e.g., a lender or the state). Places with higher rates of foreclosure can also be singled out by speculative investors eager to make a quick flip.[19] The increase in property values can lead to new tax burdens for low-income and elderly homeowners and thus to more foreclosure.

This doesn't have to be about partisan politics either. From the far left, gentrification is a particularly useful topic if one is trying to upset liberal dogma on inequality, property, and housing. As a demographic matter, craft-brew-loving, vinyl record–collecting white hipsters are the stereotypical villains of gentrification—a representation that ignores the unflattering reality of Black-on-Black gentrification.[20] On the other end of the spectrum, conservatives and center-left skeptics see homelessness as a problem of housing affordability that has been partly spawned by antigrowth liberals—homeowners, environmentalists, tenants' rights activists, and "rock-ribbed socialists." This loose constituency has used a variety of property law tools to prevent the development of more housing, particularly in California.[21] It's no coincidence the cities struggling with homelessness are invariably run by Democrats.

Irrespective of one's views on homelessness and gentrification, their relative absence in property law curricula reflects how comfortable American society is with displacement and dispossession. Students can graduate understanding complex property doctrine while not fully understanding why the American Dream of homeownership is becoming increasingly elusive for average Americans as well as the generation of debt-burdened students sitting in law school seats right now.[22]

Ancient Rules vs. Modern Wealth

Fixation is what happens when legal education becomes absorbed in dissecting one doctrine while giving less attention to a parallel issue with significant, real-world stakes. The rule against perpetuities (RAP) is a pedagogical hazing like no other. I'll spare you the minutiae by quickly describing the rule and the historical justification.

RAP is an old legal rule from seventeenth-century England that basically says this: You can't control what happens to your property forever after you die. Sure, you can leave property to people in your will—that's normal. But RAP kicks in when someone tries to make rules that stretch too far into the future. If I own a piece of land next to my house and I say in my will, "This has to stay a park, and only my descendants can use it," the law says no to this. RAP is there to stop people from running the show from their graves; it reflects a legal discomfort with people dictating the use of property for eons.

During its heyday, RAP targeted concerns about concentrated wealth and inequality. Two eminent property law scholars explain that "the rule is sometimes associated with the objective of breaking up large, potentially overly aristocratic estates."[23] Students learn this history, master the technical requirements, and the conversation often ends there since many states have abandoned the rule. Meanwhile, the uber wealthy now use dynasty trusts, family limited partnerships, shell companies, and offshore structures—all of which are legal vehicles that ensure vast fortunes stay in the family forever. Watching this unfold from the sidelines and seeing real-estate-focused RAP instruction on a yearly basis feels like watching someone log into Zoom on a flip phone.

As Cornell professor James Grimmelmann argues, this "misdirection" encourages students to "think that property law is only about houses and land." Meanwhile, it whispers to them, "please pay no attention to the vast amounts of abstract wealth sloshing through the financial system."[24] This fixation on land and houses is peculiar, he notes, because most lawyers don't practice real estate. Some do, but they are more likely to deal with other kinds of property—think bank accounts, stocks, bonds, retirement accounts, trusts, hedge funds, and venture capital.[25] When property law shifts its gaze from land to the financial instruments the wealthy use to move money around, the picture gets more complicated: You see how the dynastic wealth concentration RAP tried to mitigate is flourishing and stronger than ever.[26]

We are now witnessing one of the greatest wealth transfers in American history. Financial researchers estimate that $105 trillion ($105,000,000,000,000) in assets will be transferred to heirs through 2048.[27] This transfer of concentrated wealth is alarming for many across the ideological spectrum. Welfare-loving socialists might be worried about the tax avoidance strategies that inevitably come with wealth transfers. Such dodging can reduce funding for public services like education and healthcare, and/or increase taxes on everybody else.[28] Capitalism-championing economists might worry about inherited wealth that doesn't circulate freely in the market, is shielded from creditors, and raises the cost of business for everybody else. Others might fear that concentrated wealth undermines meritocracy and democracy if aristocrats can wave their checkbooks and sway an admissions counselor or an elected official.

This matters practically because some students will go to law firms and work in the "politics of wealth defense." Such work involves lawyers "drawing upon skilled and motivated professional advice to defend their [clients'] fortunes against public policies that curtail dynastic wealth across generations."[29] Law firms are not shy about this work.

Holland and Knight's Private Wealth Services Group is the self-proclaimed "largest private wealth practice in the United States," and it does work in the areas of real property and estate planning. It warns international investor clients that "vacation property ownership must be carefully structured to reduce tax and legal exposure."[30]

Proskauer Rose's Private Client Services group has as its motto: "Expertise, experience, discretion—generation to generation." Their counterparts at White and Case state unabashedly, "We assist high net worth individuals and families worldwide with the accumulation, management, transfer, and protection of personal wealth."[31]

Of course, some students go into this work consciously. No judgment from me, and kudos to them for picking a well-paying, client-oriented job. These lawyers will likely understand themselves as people simply doing their jobs, not necessarily as people who help shape wealth distribution patterns. And some budding lawyers may be unwittingly conscripted into wealth defense. Either way, if time is going to be spent in a property law course examining governmental restrictions on how people can transfer their property, shouldn't the discussion focus on things that approximate practice and impact society rather than some half-abolished rule?

Shakedowns and Police Theft

Property law education demonstrates selective vision when it comes to government power over private property. Students usually spend time learning about eminent domain—the process by which the government can take your home to build a highway, shopping mall, or some other public project.[32] Such takings are replete with constitutional protections because, recall, Americans cherish the home. But civil asset forfeiture, which allows police to seize property and affects hundreds of thousands of Americans annually, barely registers in most curricula.

Forfeiture comes in different flavors. *Criminal forfeiture* happens after a person is convicted of something. This is when the state takes the defendant's property—let's say, his money-counting machine, laundered money, or guns. Criminal forfeiture is not without problems, but it at least requires a conviction, so we'll put it to the side. *Civil forfeiture*, our concern here, is different.[33] In these cases, your property can be confiscated even though you broke no law. Police just need to believe it's connected to illegal drug activity. To illustrate the problem, let's use an example offered by the conservative Heritage Foundation:

> Drivers—usually those with out-of-state license plates—are stopped on some pretext. The officer then engages the driver in conversation and asks whether he is carrying any cash, and whether it is all right if the officer searches the car. If large amounts of currency are found, the officer claims it is somehow drug-related, even if no drugs or traces of drugs are present, and then seizes it.[34]

Let's add a little more texture. Maybe it's nighttime, and you're in your ten-year-old Toyota Camry. (And yes, I mean you, the reader, whoever you are, whatever your background). You're driving down Martin Luther King Drive/Blvd/St., a thoroughfare in many major cities that not only passes through poor minority neighborhoods but also connects drivers to freeways or important parts of the city (e.g., Chicago, New York City, Oakland). You're carrying $1,300 in cash (the median amount seized).[35]

Before someone says something like, "Why would I carry that much in bills?" or touts the superiority of credit cards or mobile payment apps, please know that many people still use paper money. This includes those who are underbanked and often come from disabled, Black, Hispanic, and American Indian/Alaska Native households.[36]

The same is true for various merchants, such as barbers, farmers market vendors, convenience store owners, and repair professionals (e.g., locksmiths). Most importantly, as Trump-appointed federal judge Julius Richardson reminds us, it's not illegal to carry large amounts of cash.[37]

In this scenario, police can institute legal proceedings that allow them to seize your cash and your car, and things can go south from there. A *civil* case is brought against the property, not you. The idea behind this legal fiction is that the property is suspected of wrongdoing, not the owner. As one government report put it, "The innocence of the property's owner is legally irrelevant. If the taint in the property exists, the rights of the property holder are extinguished."[38] Absurd, right? But it doesn't stop there. Because the case is against the property, you get case names like *US v. 1948 South Martin Luther King Drive* or *US v. Range Rover on 24-Inch Rims*.

Since these are civil proceedings, some of the standard criminal trial protections do not apply. You have no right to an attorney to help you navigate the complicated process of getting your stuff back. Civil forfeiture can involve motions, petitions, and funny-looking legal symbols like §§ that would make a non-lawyer dizzy.[39] Inevitably, many people lose their property, especially when the value of the seized property is worth less than the cost of an attorney.[40] A conservative estimate of legal services for such a case is $3,000.[41] Would you spend that much to get back $1,300 or a car worth a little more? No wonder researchers found that owners fight back in court only about 20 percent of the time.[42]

Besides other personal property like cell phones, jewelry, and legally registered firearms, governments have no problems confiscating homes.[43] Philadelphia mastered the practice. In addition to $50 million in cash and 3,000 vehicles, the city seized 1,200 homes from 2002 to 2014.[44] Sometimes, the money went to the city, and in some instances, the homes were auctioned to cops.[45] The most notable case involved seventy-seven-year-old Margaret Davis, a homeowner who suffered from end-stage renal disease and used paratransit to go to dialysis treatment three times a week. Davis was bedridden and left her doors unlocked so neighbors could check in on her. A drug dealer in the neighborhood knew this and ran into her house during a police chase. Although she was charged with no crime (because she was innocent), the city tried to seize her home under the idea that it was connected to criminal conduct. It took almost two years for Philadelphia to drop the case. My Penn Law colleagues have been waging war against cases like this for more than twenty-five years.[46]

Business owners and the wealthy can have their stuff taken, too. This was the case for Maryland farmers who were falsely accused of breaking banking laws and had $30,000 wiped from their accounts.[47] Another egregious example: the unconstitutional 2021 raid of a Beverly Hills storage facility accused of money laundering. After going through approximately 1,400 safe deposit boxes, the government tried to keep $86 million and millions more in personal property—even from the people who were not accused of criminal conduct. Other items included $100,000 in gold, luxury watches, family heirlooms, and things you'd find at Zales or Jared.[48]

There are many problems with property law's inattention to civil asset forfeiture. First, students are being trained to overlook a major legal problem that directly implicates property rights. Recall that these proceedings literally have the piece of property as the defendant! Such cases are also replete with technical property law issues such as title, ownership interests, and the rights of third parties, to name a few.[49] Asset forfeiture is also a timely issue. In 2024, the Supreme Court decided another case in this area, and a majority of the court signaled a willingness to rein in abusive state practices.[50]

Forfeiture sometimes involves bare theft.[51] In the context of revenue generation, the late Justice Antonin Scalia noted that it makes sense to "scrutinize governmental action more closely when the State stands to benefit."[52] Justice Clarence Thomas sees the unequal deprivation of property rights that comes with civil forfeiture. He notes that "the poor and other groups [are] least able to defend their interests in forfeiture proceedings" and "more likely to suffer in their daily lives while they litigate for the return of a critical item of property, such as a car or a home."⁵³ Such travesties undermine the due process and fairness principles touted by our legal system.

Finally, there is practice relevance. Students might go on to work in city, county, state, and federal prosecutors' offices that have dedicated asset forfeiture divisions. Maybe students go to work at one of the many federal agencies that use forfeiture as an enforcement tool (e.g., the Department of Homeland Security [DHS], the Internal Revenue Service [IRS], the Securities and Exchange Commission [SEC]). Some go to law firms that specialize in helping property owners recover assets. And let's not forget the range of ideologically diverse public interest organizations denouncing the practice (e.g., the ACLU, the Institute for Justice, the Pacific Legal Foundation, the NAACP). This selective attention to property rights violations shows how legal education trains students to protect certain kinds of property while remaining largely unaware of other forms of government theft that can disproportionately impact marginalized groups.⁵⁴

Day Care Dilemmas and Zoning's Gender Problem

Underdevelopment shows up in how property law handles zoning. This is a potent governmental power that affects how and where we live, work, shop, and play. In the most basic example, a local government might say, "We want businesses only on Main Street and residential properties on Maple Street." Or it might designate a part of the city for sports facilities like stadiums and another for pollution-generating industrial activity.

Some professors may discuss how zoning historically excluded minorities and poor people from certain neighborhoods, which represents real pedagogical progress.⁵⁵ But even this expanded analysis tends to stop at race and class, missing other dimensions of how zoning continues to organize exclusion in contemporary America. I'll focus specifically on gender and childcare here.

Crisis is a word that is lobbed around too easily these days, but if you Google the term *child care crisis*, you'd be inundated with results from most major news outlets. Childcare costs more than college tuition in thirty-eight states and Washington, DC.[56] The infant-child care crisis costs Americans a whopping $122 BILLION in lost earnings, productivity, and revenue *annually*.[57] In 2018, researchers found that about half of Americans live in so-called childcare deserts. These are places where the supply of licensed childcare is absent or demand outstrips supply.[58]

The federal government pumped billions of dollars into the industry during the Covid pandemic once people realized that daycare workers were "essential," but that wasn't enough to stem the tide of closures to such facilities—sixteen thousand between December 2019 and March 2021.[59] Some of the reasons for the supply problem have little to do with property law: paltry wages for workers in this field; employers' general opposition to including childcare as part of the suite of employee benefits; and President Nixon's veto of a national daycare program in 1971, to name a few. But zoning has also been offered as one explanation for the crisis.

Planners, feminists, and writers have drawn attention to zoning and childcare since I was a toddler with a flattop.[60] Part of the problem is tied to restrictions on home-based childcare.[61] These are spaces where people care for children in a home as opposed to in a traditional, institutional setting. Depending on the city, home-based childcare might be limited to commercial zones (even though these childcare sites are also residences) or permitted in residential areas but subject to complicated exemption processes that can be expensive and/or require a lawyer. This is to say nothing about landlords, homeowner associations, and neighbors who oppose home-based childcare.[62]

It makes sense that governments and affected parties would be wary of home-based childcare. Noise, traffic, and parking problems are potential nuisances that could accompany these spaces and potentially decrease property values.[63] But strict zoning can lead to bizarre results. One prospective provider complained: "You're telling us that we cannot operate a day-care facility in a residentially zoned, middle-class neighborhood with a large number of working mothers, but we can operate a center in a commercial zone between two topless bars."[64]

Beyond such absurdity, there are deeper consequences. On the supply side, seemingly gender-neutral zoning regulations can discourage the creation of new centers or force existing ones underground.[65] Such regulations also impacts workers, particularly women of color who see these types of daycares as a "significant entrepreneurship opportunity."[66] On the demand side, mothers who desperately need affordable, flexible care find their options artificially restricted. When care becomes scarce and expensive, gender norms tell us who will have to either leave the workforce or accept part-time positions to caretake: mothers.

The absence of this issue from property law curricula represents a missed educational opportunity on multiple levels.

First, examining childcare zoning would crack open a gendered dimension of property law that gets systematically ignored despite its seismic effects on American society. This isn't academic feminism—it's about how legal rules shape who gets to work, how families organize their economic lives, and which communities receive essential services.

Second, this is a live legal issue affecting millions of Americans right now. Governments from Hawaii to Connecticut are recognizing that this corner of property law has created artificial scarcity in services that families desperately need. As a result, they are increasingly passing laws that prevent zoning departments from placing restrictions on home-based childcare.[67] These reforms garner support from both liberals concerned about gender and economic inequality and small government conservatives who champion property rights.

Third, there is a clear practice relevance for future lawyers who will encounter these issues across multiple professional contexts: public interest attorneys advocating for childcare providers, government lawyers defending zoning board decisions, attorneys helping developers create childcare facilities through development incentives, and lawyers providing pro bono assistance to providers navigating regulatory compliance.

Perhaps most importantly, many of these students will become parents who are directly affected by childcare shortages that property law exacerbates—a reminder that these aren't abstract legal problems but fundamental questions about how we organize human care and community.

PROPERTY LAW ADDRESSES fundamental aspects of American life, but the course often overlooks the inequalities the field helps sustain. The issues in this chapter aren't personal obsessions or marginal concerns. We're talking about billion-dollar problems affecting millions of Americans—issues that have prompted Supreme Court decisions, bipartisan state legislation, and national policy debates.

This selective attention shapes what future lawyers learn to see and not see about how property law operates in people's lives. These topics aren't exhaustive, but they show how legal education's selective attention reflects existing hierarchies and silences certain stories about how property law operates. These issues could easily foster the critical thinking and problem-solving skills that law schools want to inculcate while connecting students to the real-world impact of the doctrines they're mastering. The question is simple: Will these gaps be filled, or will the profession continue producing lawyers who know property doctrine but are less attuned to property's human toll?

Assembly #2

The Written and Unwritten Rules in Criminal Law, Constitutional Law, and Civil Procedure

THE FIRST THREE COURSES we've covered concern mostly private relationships—private agreements in contracts, interpersonal and corporate harms in torts, and property rights between private parties. As I've shown, government looms in the background of all these areas, but the next three courses—criminal law, constitutional law, and civil procedure—put the state at the center. These courses from the architecture of state authority in the first year show how the government exercises control.

In a nutshell, *crim* (criminal law) focuses on how the state regulates undesirable conduct; *con law* (constitutional law) focuses on the structure of government and its relationship to individual rights; and *civ pro* (civil procedure) concerns the process by which civil disputes get resolved by courts. These are the rules that determine who gets caged, whose rights matter, and who gets heard in court. In these chapters, I'll show you how these courses confer undue legitimacy on the American legal system in part by pushing questions about money, politics, power, and history to the side.

Yale law professor Justin Driver clerked for two Supreme Court justices and captures the pedagogical challenge perfectly. He notes that one of the major challenges of teaching "is to impress upon the students" that there is internal integrity to legal doctrine and that this is "not simply politics by other means."[1] Driver is pointing to a semi-structural problem. It's borderline irresponsible to provide students with a critique before teaching them the rules. How can the radical left or the radical right make compelling arguments about abolishing the police or the Department of Education without understanding the legal justifications for their existence?

But an orientation around teaching the rules, even when one is thoughtful and critical, can serve as a silent endorsement of those rules and the system that they undergird, especially when we're talking about impressionable first-year students.

Criminal law, which I teach, is arguably the worst offender. (No pun intended.) It focuses on the mechanics of punishment but obscures who gets punished, who doesn't, and why that is the case.

Constitutional law invites students to respect branches of government that have never reflected this country's rich diversity and have historically trampled over the interests of minorities, women, immigrants, and the impoverished, to name a few. All of this while focusing on the document that begins with "We, the people."

Civil procedure centers on elite federal courts that ordinary Americans rarely access. It is essentially a course about complex litigation involving the elite echelons of the bar and clients who often have more money than me, you, and our entire bloodlines combined; the litigation travails of low-income and ordinary Americans are peripheral concerns.

These problems help produce lawyers who can operate in systems of inequality and see them as legally inevitable as opposed to contingent byproducts of money, power, and social hierarchies. The implications of this training spread far beyond the classroom. Law students become the attorneys, legislators, civic leaders, and business executives who carry these assumptions into every corner of American society.

CHAPTER 5

Textbook Injustice: Criminal Law and the Unspoken Politics of Punishment

THE FIRST TIME I CRIED in public as a teenager wasn't for the usual reasons—not over physical pain, a romantic heartbreak, or any of the casual cruelties that mark adolescence. It was at a funeral, watching a neighbor grieve his father while wearing handcuffs.

I never knew the exact charge—only that it was a nonviolent drug offense that was serious enough to send him upstate. His father's death didn't pause that sentence; it just made space for a brief, shackled visit.

Two corrections officers flanked him as he approached the casket. I expected them to eventually unlock the cuffs, but they didn't. It was a reminder that he wasn't allowed to mourn freely. He was a prisoner under escort first, and a grieving son second. I watched him struggle to wipe his own tears without the full use of his arms.

I had seen police beat people in the street. Saw people disappear from my neighborhood for crimes they didn't commit. I could even give you a walking tour of the Bronx and point out the exact streets where I was stopped and frisked on nothing but suspicion. But this was one of the clearest moments of criminal justice cruelty I've personally witnessed. The criminal legal system denied someone the dignity of mourning like a human being.

That image—a son saying goodbye to his father while bound in chains—has stayed with me. It returns every semester I teach first-year criminal law, a course I have been highly critical of in scholarly and mainstream publications.[1] The class tends to focus on the mechanics of state power—the what, when, and why of punishment. But deeper questions sometimes get sidelined: which groups are more likely to be punished, how law enforcement priorities are politically determined, and what constitutes the core/periphery of criminal law.

What we teach is clean—rules, doctrines, and carefully selected cases. The structure has some rationality. Outside the classroom, the system tells a different story. I've seen wealthy, well-connected, and undeniably guilty defendants avoid prison entirely. No cell. No chains. And certainly no cuffs while grieving a parent.

But I've also seen people arrested for trespassing, unlawful assembly, and low-level drug possession. Maybe they were technically breaking the law, but it often felt arbitrary—less about rule-breaking and more about control. Peter Moskos, a sociologist who spent twenty months working as a beat cop in Baltimore and wrote a book about it, pulls back the curtain. "Although it is legally questionable, police officers almost always have something they can use to lock up somebody, 'just because.'" He notes the ready supply of these go-to charges. "New York City police use disorderly conduct. In Baltimore, it is loitering."[2] Criminal law isn't always about public safety; it can be a toolkit for enforcing social boundaries and deciding when someone's existence is a crime.

These contrasting realities—the impunity often granted to the powerful and the harsh scrutiny imposed on the marginalized—are underthematized in criminal law. The common cases tend to involve clear harms and tidy legal questions. But that apparent clarity is misleading. Moreover, there's a strange irony here: Students are exposed to graphic accounts of violence but remain largely sheltered from the cruelties that the system inflicts—like forcing a grieving son to mourn his father while shackled.

Let me be clear about what this chapter is arguing: Criminal law education creates a distorted portrait of American punishment by obsessing over exceptional violence while ignoring the misdemeanor offenses that actually drive incarceration and elite corporate harm. This distortion teaches future lawyers to see our system of punishment as rational and necessary while obscuring how it actually functions: as a mechanism that protects some, criminalizes others, and makes inequality appear normal.

This matters for all of us. The students sitting in lecture halls today will become the people who will control American justice tomorrow. They are the prosecutors who determine whether your college-bound kid is treated as a "child who needs guidance" or a "threat to society." They are the corporate lawyers who help companies avoid accountability when they poison our air and water. And they become the legislators who amend old laws and write new ones, creating novel forms of criminal liability that will govern how we live, work, and exist. We can't afford to ignore this.

What Criminal Law Is and Is Not

Because many Americans learn about crime from the news, popular culture, and occasionally firsthand experience, I typically begin each semester by letting students know what the class is and is not about. This helps manage expectations and provides more context for the course's narrowness. In law school, a few classes cover criminal justice issues.

Criminal law is the system of laws that specifies what kind of behavior is unlawful. It includes offenses like murder, theft, and assault, to name a few. This field also concerns the kinds of defenses that might be available to a person that could excuse criminal behavior. For example, a person can bring a self-defense claim if they can show that their use of violence was necessary to protect themselves from an unlawful attack. Most generally, criminal law is about what kind of behavior we penalize and under what circumstances we punish. It also focuses on *why* we punish, which I'll complain about in a bit.

People often think of *criminal procedure* when they think about the criminal justice system. Criminal procedure refers to the rules government officials must follow to enforce criminal law. Some of these rules are derived from the Constitution. The Fourth Amendment generally prohibits unreasonable searches and seizures unless they fall under several exceptions.

Criminal procedure also includes post-arrest issues, such as the Fifth Amendment Miranda rights cops must read once people are detained and in custody, as well as plea bargaining and jury selection. All of this made-for-TV stuff is typically absent in a first-year criminal law course, often to the chagrin of students.[3]

You know that dramatic "Objection!" moment in courtroom dramas? That is usually a lawyer complaining about *evidence law*—the system of rules that governs what kind of information can be considered in a trial and the weight that should be attached to it. Evidence issues include expert testimony, hearsay information, and whether a defendant's prior convictions should be considered. Does this so-called expert have the credentials to be weighing in on forensics? How should we credit information that a person heard about but did not personally witness? Should the fact that John was convicted ten years ago for jaywalking be relevant to a case about theft today? With rare exceptions, few of these issues show up meaningfully in a criminal law course.

Legal education's division of criminal justice issues makes sense conceptually and pedagogically. Each area contains a wealth of information that would be hard to bundle into one class. But in some ways, the division is impractical and does not coincide with the more integrated ways students are tested on the bar exam. It also doesn't line up with how lawyers practice.[4] This super subcategorization easily shunts discussions about race and inequality to the side.

Georgetown's Gary Peller called this out more than three decades ago when he noted that "a common assumption is that significant racial issues all involve questions of *criminal procedure* rather than substantive criminal law."[5] It's easier to talk about racial discrimination in the context of stop-and-frisk or immigration officers than in conversations about whether someone should be punished. The modern right to counsel is inextricably tied to indigence and lends itself to discussions about class, but in criminal law, poverty is typically considered irrelevant.[6] When we divvy up the criminal justice system into digestible academic products, the human costs of our penal system are more easily shuffled off to other professors, courses, and semesters. Not here and not now, please.

Until quite recently, people decried the criminal law curriculum's inattention to mass incarceration.[7] This civil rights issue was often reserved for the end of a casebook at best or ignored at worst. But in the current climate, DEI commitments have been abandoned, and words like "race," "the state," or "gender" can land in the classroom like live grenades. Mere description of the social world can feel dangerous, pushing students and professors toward the safety of neutral language—even when the issues at stake are anything but neutral. Avoidance, in some ways, becomes its own curriculum.

The Practical Irrelevance of Criminal Law

Besides superficial attention to race and class, the carving up of criminal justice issues also underscores a strange theory/practice divide that permeates legal education. Criminal law is where you get the theory. Criminal procedure, the optional course, is where you're likely to get more of the nitty-gritty practice issues.

While mass incarceration was tearing through American communities, law students were trained to argue over convoluted hypotheticals about "transferred intent" that sounded like stoned philosophy majors theorizing in a dorm room: "If A shoots at B, but the bullet bounces off a fire hydrant and hits C while she's making a sandwich in her kitchen—can we say that A intentionally murdered C?" Legal education has evolved somewhat since then, but this kind of abstract detachment still has a firm foothold in many classrooms today. It's part of the reason why you have prosecutors telling interviewers things like, "Practically speaking, my law degree ... was worth about as much as ballet lessons ... when I started out."[8]

Scholars have lamented students' lack of exposure to the "structural concerns" that plague our criminal legal system and the curriculum's failure to "take a hard look at empirical data about crime rates, incarceration rates, and the intersections of race, poverty, and crime."[9]

The professors who do try to center these issues, like the thoughtful instructor I had at Berkeley, sometimes encounter resistance from students who are more focused on the rules and what's going to be on the final exam than a structural critique. In her study of law schools, sociologist Kathryne Young reminds students that policy issues "are not a waste of time" and "make you a wiser lawyer," but she also warns them that "nine times out of ten they won't help you on the exam." She encourages them to assume that, come grading time, professors will care mostly about the rules.[10] Accordingly, policy concerns take a predictable backseat if they come up at all.

For some law schools, making sure students can pass the bar and get jobs is undeniably more important than understanding sociopolitical issues. These economic pressures can lead some schools to emphasize skills development, sometimes at the expense of knowledge acquisition and public policy deliberation.[11] Consequentially, some leave their first year of law school and legal education unable to "describe and critique the political and economic theories underlying various legal arrangements."[12] They are more likely to get idealized accounts than accurate descriptions of how the system actually works.

Criminal law often begins with the *purposes of punishment*—four rationales for why we penalize people who commit crimes. They help the system appear principled, even when its outcomes suggest otherwise.

Retribution is the first. You hurt somebody, then the state hurts you back. "Society," one court explained, "stands with victims and exacts punishment in rough approximation to the detriment caused by the defendant."[13] That is why the punishment for premeditated murder can be the death penalty or life in prison.

We use prisons and jails to effectuate a second purpose, *incapacitation*. This is about physically removing people from society to prevent them from committing more crimes.

Deterrence is another rationale, and it is two-fold. *General deterrence* is concerned with discouraging the public from committing an offense by making an example out of someone. If you rob, like Lisa, you will get five years, like Lisa. *Specific deterrence* is singularly focused on deterring sticky-finger Lisa from committing more robberies.

Rehabilitation is focused on providing people with the tools necessary to avoid reoffending (e.g., mental health services, education, job training).

Depending on the context, I'm on board with these rationales. Methodical serial killers need to be incapacitated and taken off the streets. If the threat of consequences keeps people from driving drunk, that's not a bad thing.

But the rationales for why we punish can also be incomplete and unserious. Consider rehabilitation. The United States is no Sweden or Norway—places where education, vocational training, and community ties are prioritized.[14] It is somewhat settled that the rehabilitative ideal in the US began to fall by the wayside in the late the twentieth century due to three-strikes laws, more punitive sentencing reforms, and changes in parole.[15]

Incapacitation sounds good, but as Robert Blecker noted in his study of a Virginia prison, we're not eliminating violence when we haul people off to correctional facilities. We're just making it invisible to the world and transferring it to spaces where it might be inflicted on other inmates and staff.[16] Moreover, incapacitation is applied selectively; it is rarely on the table for CEOs whose business choices lead to mass harm or police officers who brutalize civilians with impunity.

Blecker also notes that deterrence can fail because it assumes that everyone weighs the costs and benefits of wrongdoing. Repeat offenders who commit the same crimes suggest otherwise. Moreover, do we think people pulling off a bank heist are thinking about the time that the other guy got?

Retribution can be problematic because punishment is sometimes disproportionate to the offense. The fact that Maryland recently pardoned an estimated one hundred thousand people convicted of possessing cannabis and cannabis-related paraphernalia is telling. (Yes, one hundred thousand.) Maryland's governor and attorney general claimed that this mass pardon was a move to address the disproportionate harm the state's marijuana laws wreaked on minority communities. As one beneficiary of the pardon mentioned, "You can't hold people accountable for possession of marijuana when you've got a dispensary on almost every corner."[17]

Notwithstanding all the problems with these theories of punishment, they serve an important function. They cast punishment as a neutral and principled response to wrongdoing. Sometimes it is. But too often, punishment is coated in a layer of moral necessity it hasn't fully earned. These justifications work as discursive tools that transform the messy realities of American punishment and repackage them into clean, respectable theory. They shape how many students are taught to think about punishment and sometimes leave less room to confront other explanations for why we punish.

Almost a century ago, a Jewish lawyer and a social scientist fled Nazi Germany and wrote an influential, Marxist-inspired book explaining how punishment practices are inextricably tied to the economy and existing class structures.[18] Some have offered a current version of this argument by describing how the loss of jobs via late-twentieth-century deindustrialization, automation, and globalization has produced a "surplus population" of workers that needs to be controlled.[19] Local officials, especially in rural areas that have experienced economic and reputational decline, responded by building more correctional facilities.[20] Other prominent social scientists have argued more straightforwardly that the criminalization of poverty has coincided with a stingier welfare state. For them, the criminal justice system is a simple form of poverty management.[21]

Others point to a long history of criminalizing race—whether it be vagrancy laws that targeted free Black people and tried to conscript them into slavery or the late nineteenth-century development of an anti-Chinese immigration regime that increasingly criminalized being foreign. Around the same time, people of Mexican ancestry were increasingly treated as inherently criminal—a racial association that would only deepen in the decades to come.[22]

Fast forward to today and immigration enforcement functions as its own rationale for punishment: a system of boundary-keeping and exclusion. ICE raids resemble urban policing. Immigration detention deprives people of their liberty like prisons. And deportation certainly feels like a punishment—much more than the fines and days in jail some people face for certain kinds of offending. But first-year criminal law treats immigration as a sideshow—notwithstanding the two-decade existence of "crimmigration" scholarship.

The One Big Beautiful Bill Act of 2025 directed approximately $150 billion to ICE to carry out core criminal law functions—arrest, detention, and punishment. Some of these future detainees/deportees will have broken no law, have no criminal record, and pose no public safety threat but will be swept up by this growing enforcement regime with the help of local and state officials. However, it remains unclear whether this massive system of punishment will receive serious attention in the classroom or whether one of its central functions—limiting access to citizenship for outsiders—will be acknowledged.

Beyond poverty, race, and citizenship, scholars have highlighted other forces at work. Feminist scholars have focused on how the legal system uniquely criminalizes women's bodies by regulating sex work and punishing women who seek abortions; the post-*Dobbs* world is accelerating the prosecution of the latter.[23] They've also lobbed separate critiques about the criminalization of poor and/or minority moms who are punished for behavior that is categorized as "child neglect" but is overlooked when committed by better-resourced, white counterparts.[24]

Police and prison abolitionists have focused on the ineffectiveness of the criminal legal system, the ways it profits and preys on vulnerable communities, and how resources would be better spent on social welfare services that might address the root causes of some crime (e.g., education, mental health services, housing assistance).[25]

These alternative explanations and critiques are imperfect, too. The poverty management thesis tells us little about white-collar crime. Race-based discussions cannot explain why 78 percent of white murder victims were killed by white offenders.[26] Abolitionism—which 13 percent of surveyed professors identify with—has struggled with how to talk about and manage the "dangerous few."[27] Feminists have had internal debates about the appropriate role of the state when women are harmed.[28] These shortcomings are not fatal. No singular account of punishment can do the job. These explanations, and others, can widen the aperture for students and better orient them to how our legal system does not live up to its equality imperatives. Notwithstanding the viewpoint diversity they offer, they remain at the periphery.

Kill, Kill, Kill, Murder, Murder, Murder

I have my suspicions about why alternative perspectives have not fully penetrated the criminal law curriculum. Besides some of the explanations I've already discussed (the racial homogeneity of the professoriate, their social distance from economic inequality, and path-dependent ideas about what is relevant), I think it's because the course sometimes focuses on a subset of criminal behavior. Homicide, rape, and theft tend to be the primary crimes discussed in this course. These are some of the most serious offenses, but they only capture a narrow range of criminal behavior.

Brooklyn Law School professor Alice Ristroph has examined the history and content of criminal law casebooks and captures the problem with what she calls the "homicide/rape/and maybe-theft model" of teaching. She argues that the last fifty years of American legal education have only covered a "tiny slice of the vast range of conduct defined as criminal," and that that slice is far from representative.[29] It's not unusual to spend two weeks in a thirteen-week course discussing homicide, the "paradigm" topic, and that does not count other parts of the course than can easily overlap with homicide.

Here's a quick outline of the big units in a criminal law course (though the order can vary by professor or casebook).

After discussing the purposes of punishment and the general contours of the legal system, a course might move on to discuss the *criminal act* (e.g., the killing or physical contact) and the different *mental states* tied to criminal behavior (e.g., intentional vs. negligent homicide).

From there, the course might spend a few weeks delving into different kinds of homicide (e.g., first and second-degree murder, voluntary and involuntary manslaughter). Afterward the class might discuss other crimes against people (rape) and/or property offenses (e.g., burglary or robbery).

Self-defense in cases involving assault or attempted murder is another staple of the course. *Incomplete offenses* are next, and these will be things like solicitation to kill or conspiracy to commit murder. *Accomplice liability* involves helping another person commit a crime (e.g., being the getaway driver in a robbery or a murder).

See how dispersed conversations about murder can be?

Homicide prosecutions only capture "a tiny fragment of criminal law concerns," Ristroph notes. "By the numbers, criminal law is used much more often to manage petty disorder and low-level disruption than to respond to physical violence of any type."[30] When we look at the misdemeanors and nonviolent felonies that bring people into the legal system—offenses like drug possession, gun possession, disorderly conduct—some of the stated rationales of punishment don't work as well. If we look at the criminalization of homelessness and prohibitions on money-making sex between consenting adults, the tidy character of criminal law becomes much less convincing. "The relative inattention to low-level offenses," Ristroph argues, "prunes from students' views much of the arbitrariness and discrimination that characterizes actual enforcement."[31]

Rape presents a different though still distortive set of problems. Some professors teach the topic, and there has been a longstanding concern in legal academia about whether they are sensitive when they do since it is likely that there are survivors in the classroom. Accordingly, some professors do not teach sexual assault out of a concern for their students. This is understandable, though some have argued that it sidelines a grave social problem and remarginalizes topics that feminists fought to have included in the curriculum less than forty years ago.[32] When professors do not cover sexual assault, they are unlikely to replace it with other sex crimes, in part because rape is the primary and sometimes the only sex offense present in the casebook.

It is difficult to be definitive about the prevalence of rape because of underreporting, but more people are arrested for sex work than for sexual assault.[33] This of course, does not suggest that they involve the same kind of harms, but it does suggest that sex work merits attention in a criminal law course, *especially* if a professor opts to not teach sexual assault. Arrests for sex work are not just about sex for cash, but include solicitation, maintaining an establishment where prostitution occurs, and promoting sex work. Prostitution-related charges fall disproportionately on women. In the field of criminal law, it's almost as if women are selling sex to themselves; pimps and Johns are just Santa Claus–like fictions.

Sex work also seeps into other substantive offenses. In one survey of sex workers in Philadelphia, half of the respondents reported being arrested and charged for minor offenses like loitering and obstructing traffic.[34] Sometimes, police officers pose as gay men and conduct sting operations on gay men, entrap them, and charge them with things like public lewdness and solicitation. (There is a long history of this.)[35] "Walking while trans" refers to the profiling of transgender people, especially trans women of color. The DOJ and Human Rights Watch have noted how transgender individuals are profiled and have their condoms confiscated as evidence of intent to commit prostitution-related offenses.[36] Despite being well-documented by scholars, nonprofits, and the feds, these forms of sexual regulation tend to be marginalized in the first-year criminal law course—as if they're too inconvenient or messy to merit inclusion.

Theft is another category given distorted treatment in the typical criminal law course. As it appears in casebooks and is tested on the bar exam, theft usually includes a few subcategories, the primary of which includes theft itself (sometimes called larceny); robbery, which is theft plus the use of force; and burglary, which refers to the breaking and entering of a home to commit a crime (usually theft). If they are lucky, students may cover embezzlement, which is theft by a person entrusted with property, such as a cashier or bank teller.

Embezzlement is sometimes the closest first-year criminal law students will get to white-collar crime. This area might be relegated to the end of a course if time permits or sprinkled into a discussion here or there throughout the semester, but it is typically not a major unit of the course despite its relevance to some of the core issues students learn and professors obsess over. For example, white-collar crime raises interesting questions about mental states, what constitutes an act, and the availability of certain defenses. The siloing of white-collar crime as something different does the simultaneous work of overemphasizing a narrow band of conduct committed by a particular group while neglecting other types of criminal behavior.

Elite Violence:
The Whitewashing of White-Collar Crime

If first-year criminal law moved from the street corners and private residences where blue-collar crime happens to the corporate offices, political backrooms, and difficult-to-monitor professional interactions where white-collar crime occurs, students would see all types of unseemly behavior. I'm talking money laundering, insider trading, public corruption (bribing government officials), bid rigging for government contracts, Ponzi schemes, kickbacks, campaign finance crimes, and tons of fraud (mail, wire, bank, accounting, mortgage, and securities). In other words, crimes that many former members of Congress have been convicted of in recent years.[37] With this broader version of wrongdoing, the conjured image of a criminal would no longer be a gangbanging ese with tattoos, Black dudes with locs, or scruffy white meth dealers from trailer parks; it would also include people in business attire who hail from the same places as many students and professors.

The general exclusion of white-collar crime is bizarre. Many students will go on to litigate on behalf of corporate defendants. Some will provide regulatory counsel to keep their clients from being hit with criminal sanctions. Others will become transactional lawyers who draft agreements that, if not worded carefully, could easily veer into the land of fraud and misrepresentation. White-collar crime is much more relevant to their future practice than the difference between first and second-degree murder.

White collar crime is economically and socially costly. Doctors and healthcare organizations engage in fraud by overbilling the federal government for Medicare and Medicaid, estimated at $100 billion annually.[38] Employers who purposely misclassify employees to reduce workers compensation premiums fit into the larger category of insurance fraud—a practice that can carry civil or criminal penalties and costs another $300 billion a year.[39]

You might think that the nonviolent nature of these offenses makes them completely different from, and still less of a problem than, murder, rape, and theft. Yet instances of corporate misconduct have led to death and warranted criminal prosecution.

For over a decade, General Motors knew about a defect in its ignition switches that would shut cars off while they were still in motion and prevent airbags from deploying. In the words of one of its engineers, the company made a "business decision not to fix this problem."[40] That "business decision" was linked to 124 deaths and 275 injuries and involved more than 2.6 million vehicles. This was wire fraud, criminal concealment of a deadly defect from regulators, and criminal negligence. Behind those legal terms are real people: lives cut short, others derailed by permanent trauma, and families left to grieve—all because some business leaders decided fixing a deadly defect wasn't worth the cost.

No one from GM went to jail, notwithstanding the availability of federal fraud statutes and DOJ guidance encouraging prosecutors to focus on individuals in cases of corporate wrongdoing.[41] I can imagine the GM folks' quiet relief in the conference room when they learned they wouldn't face prison time. Duke law professor Brandon Garrett captures another travesty of this scandal when he notes how some people were "wrongly convicted of vehicular manslaughter" for deadly crashes caused by GM's own negligence.[42]

I think here of a mugshot of Candice Anderson, a young white woman whose face doesn't fit our usual scripts for criminality. In 2004, she lost control of her car in an unexplained crash that killed her boyfriend. Her parents drained their 401(k) to hire a lawyer and she pleaded guilty to negligent homicide. In addition to paying $10,000 in fines and restitution, Anderson spent a decade believing she was responsible for her boyfriend's death. She also carried the mark of a conviction that closed off her dream of a nursing career. Ten years after the accident, the GM scandal revealed that the car, not Candice, had failed. But her conviction for negligence—set against GM's impunity for *mass* negligence—reveals just how hollow our theories of punishment can be. Cases like hers, which involve large-scale corporate criminality, are too often treated as outside the core of legal analysis.[43]

When 346 people died in two 737 Max crashes in 2018 and 2019, Boeing was charged with conspiracy to defraud the United States. One of the federal prosecutors on the case claimed that the company chose "profit over candor by concealing material information" about the planes' flight control systems.[44] The DOJ squeezed $2.5 billion out of Boeing and got them to accept a "deferred prosecution agreement," which is basically corporate probation.

Two days before that deal was set to expire in 2024, a door ripped out of a plane during a flight carrying 171 passengers. A government report found that four critical bolts were missing. Alaska and United Airlines also discovered loose bolts in their grounded Boeing jets, as though they were Ikea furniture. Boeing was magically unable to find any document related to that door plug that blew off the Alaska Airlines flight. (There was also the strange death of a whistleblower who complained about quality control practices at the company.) Prosecutors accused Boeing of violating the 2021 settlement, but settled again with the company in 2025. Under this new deal, Boeing agreed to another $1.1 billion in tribute. It also admitted to conspiracy to avoid being branded as a convicted felon; that label would be ruinous for business and could lead to loss of government contracts, plummeting stock prices, and exposure to even more lawsuits (e.g., from shareholders).

Some have speculated that prosecutors treat Boeing with kid gloves because of its cozy relationship with the American government as a military contractor. This relationship has been openly acknowledged for years. Back in 2013, President Obama joked, "I'm expecting a gold watch from Boeing at the end of my presidency because I know that I'm on the list of top salesmen at Boeing."[45] Boeing's privileged status meant it could negotiate repeat deals and a payment plan for killing 346 people.

Then there is the opioid crisis.

As the Supreme Court has noted, "between 1999 and 2019, approximately 247,000 people in the United States died from prescription-opioid overdoses," and "Purdue Pharma sits at the center of that crisis."[46] These were white-collar drug dealers. Shortly after the company introduced OxyContin to the market in 1996, the company knew that it "was being crushed and snorted for its powerful narcotic." Prosecutors found that Purdue sales representatives used the words *street value*, *crush*, or *snort* in more than one hundred internal notes during visits to medical professionals between 1997 and 1999. Still, the company misrepresented the risk of addiction, which led to a 2007 guilty plea of felony misbranding for the company and misdemeanor misbranding for a few executives who got away with fines and community service.[47] In total, the company and the executives paid $634 million in fines.

In 2020, Purdue was convicted of various conspiracy offenses. The company lied to the Drug Enforcement Administration when it claimed to have an effective program that would prevent prescription drugs being redirected to illegal channels. In reality, Purdue continued to market its opioid products to more than one hundred healthcare providers who, it had good reason to know, were diverting opioids for illegitimate nonmedical use.[48] This conviction came with $8.3 billion in penalties and, again, no jail time for Purdue officials.

Executives from Insys Therapeutics were imprisoned for their role in bribing doctors to prescribe its addictive fentanyl spray Subsys. The bribery included the payment of bogus speakers' fees, expensive dinners, and frozen filet mignons for grilling. More salaciously, it also entailed the hiring of sales reps based on their sex appeal (including one former stripper-turned-sales director who gave a doctor a lap dance). There were also subsidized freak-offs at strip clubs that included private "champagne room sessions." One doctor-participant subsequently texted, "Thank you for the best weekend in years!!!" and wrote seventeen prescriptions of the drug over three days.[49] The longest sentence was given to CEO John Kapoor, who received 5.5 years and was released after two in a minimum-security federal prison. One inmate described the facility as "dorm-like." It had a "fully equipped prison gym," a movie theater, and good food that included "a salad bar and at times fresh cinnamon rolls for breakfast."[50] Nine hundred people overdosed on Subsys. John Kapoor got amenities and artisanal pastries.

The impunity secured by GM, Boeing, and various drug companies reflects legal inequality in its dual form. In these instances, criminal law mirrors society's deference to corporate power and operates selectively by reserving cages for those who lack the capital to demand leniency. Homicide is understood as the most serious personal harm in criminal law but when death can be traced to white-collar professionals, our legal system abandons its punitive instincts. Meanwhile, the offenses that typically bring people into the justice system often receive less emphasis in criminal law courses. This can shape how future lawyers understand which conduct warrants the harshest punishment—and which deserves sophisticated legal maneuvering.

CRIMINAL LAW FOCUSES ON some of the most exceptional forms of interpersonal violence—murder and sometimes sexual assault. These harms are undoubtedly serious. But they paint a picture of the legal system as a legitimate evaluator of moral wrongs while obscuring how the system actually operates. Students rarely encounter the misdemeanor prosecutions and nonviolent felonies that actually fill courtrooms and correctional facilities. They don't see the assembly-line processing of poor people through plea bargains, the criminalization of mental illness, or the routine dehumanization of daily practice.

All future lawyers must take criminal law, irrespective of whether they want to work in the criminal justice system. Some will become politicians, judges, and civic leaders, and law school is where they develop some shared assumptions about what constitutes criminal conduct and who deserves punishment. During this formative experience, students spend time digesting philosophical puzzles while remaining underexposed to the systematic inequalities that characterize actual enforcement.

These academic exercises can actively distance students from the human consequences of the legal machinery they're learning to operate. For some students, this process may gradually erode the moral outrage that brought them to law school and replace urgent questions about justice with competence in legal doctrine. This professional conditioning makes it possible for some future lawyers to look at the cruelties of the criminal justice system and see technical issues as opposed to moral failures.

CHAPTER 6

The Ultimate Con Job? Constitutional Law and the Effacement of History and Politics

LIKE CRIMINAL LAW, constitutional law (con law) is an area that many people have preconceived notions about.

Many Americans develop a decent—though far from comprehensive—understanding of the Constitution through a mix of formal education and media. From civics classes and AP Government courses to cable news and popular podcasts, constitutional knowledge is shaped by schools, screens, and soundbites alike.

Cultural rituals also shape constitutional consciousness. The Pledge of Allegiance—recited in schools and at civic events—reflects constitutional values from the preamble. Recital doesn't mean agreement with its content (the "under God language" might be a lot for people of different faiths), but it suggests symbolic respect for underlying constitutional principles.

Then there is the "faith" people have in the Constitution.[1] I know some old-school professors who carry around pocket-size versions of the Constitution. Sometimes people display a cult-like adherence to the document that borders on misguided and uninformed veneration.[2] I've seen conservatives wrongfully complain about their First Amendment speech rights being infringed upon by private actors that the clause doesn't apply to and I've watched dope boys complain about being unconstitutionally searched when there was definitely probable cause to believe they had crack in their socks.

Students bring some of this background into the classroom, so a lot of unlearning needs to happen.

A demographic challenge arises for women and students of color, as well as the men and white students who support them. The class is organized by a document that, in legal analyst Elie Mystal's words, "was written by a collection of wealthy slavers, wealthy colonizers, and wealthy antislavery white men who were nonetheless willing to compromise and profit together with slavers and colonizers." Things have gotten better, but still: "At no point have people of color or women been given a real say in how it was written, interpreted, or amended."[3]

Reconstruction makes the point plain: The court gutted the Fourteenth and Fifteenth Amendments and paved the way for six decades of Jim Crow, a blip of remediation, and five more continuing decades of backlash to civil rights for minorities, women, and other marginalized groups. In casebooks, relevant rulings show up as technical waypoints instead of what they were—judicial betrayals of equality that leave our historical scorecard both corrupted and unreconciled.

This tension between the Constitution's exclusionary origins and its contemporary claims of equality hovers over many constitutional law classrooms. Can we say with confidence that the Constitution has been purged of its racial and gendered taint? Having observed these conversations in constitutional law classrooms and participated in them as both a student and a teacher, I can attest that the arguments do not fully persuade. A common defense usually claims "this is what we've got" or offers unhelpful comparisons to other constitutional orders that sidestep critique. Maybe that's selection bias, or I'm just a tough audience.

The best case for constitutional redemption tends to focus on roominess and capacity—from abolitionists' leverage of the Constitution as an antislavery document to its eventual utility for other historically marginalized groups.[4] These historical facts are hard to deny, but they risk overdetermining triumph. War, violent protest, government theft, incarceration, and death paved the way for democratic *semi*-inclusion. Marginalized groups scrap for legal recognition in a world where the Supreme Court has closed numerous doors on them.[5] Some of the biggest boosters of the Constitution's majesty look like and descend from the people who framed it, which raises the question of whether their reverence reflects a universal ideal or a loyalty to a legacy that has served them more reliably than others.

This is not to say that the document and its principles should be discarded, but rather that we should acknowledge that constitutional law education is capable of replicating the hierarchies and exclusions that shaped the document. The course typically teaches predominantly from a narrow band of elite perspectives—constitutional convention debates, Supreme Court opinions, and legal scholarship. This makes it easier to marginalize the voices that experienced constitutional law's limitations, which can lead to the production of lawyers who mistake elite consensus for constitutional reasoning.

With this tension between constitutional promises and exclusions as our backdrop, here are the patterns I want to unpack for you in this chapter. Constitutional law courses often reduce the nation's most pressing inequalities to technical legal questions. This approach is necessary and appropriate. However, it can also eclipse the sociohistorical reality that constitutional interpretation has been a series of ongoing struggles over power. Who gets saved. Who gets stepped on. Who gets counted.

The course sanitizes the document's ugly colonial history.

For legitimate efficiency reasons, it outsources constitutional issues to other courses in ways that fragment students' understanding of who the document has consistently served.

Con law also privileges certain kinds of formal legal reasoning over other ways of thinking about constitutional meaning. Originalism and living constitutionalism—the two dominant modes of interpretation that shape judicial reasoning and increasingly dominate the cases students must study—serve a similar function: They make political choices look like legal inevitabilities. Both approaches allow judges and lawyers to present their preferred outcomes as legally required, as opposed to acknowledging that they're making contested (and sometimes self-serving) political judgments. This teaches students to treat legal analysis as if it were objective, even when these interpretive approaches are used for partisan purposes. Such training makes it easier for attorneys to work within unjust legal systems while believing that proper technique can justify certain legal results.

Lawyers play a role in who gets what in society. How they learn to approach constitutional questions of power, rights, and justice can shape their future work and reverberate outside the classroom. This makes their legal education a public concern, not just an academic one.

Con Law 101: How Power Gets Scattered

Constitutional law touches so many areas of American life that it is hard to discipline it into a three-month course. This sprawl means many of the most consequential legal issues are left on the cutting room floor.

Most of the constitutional provisions that concern the state's unevenly deployed monopoly on violence—the Fourth, Fifth, Sixth, and Eighth Amendments—go missing in con law and are typically reserved for criminal procedure courses. In this sense, state violence is generally understood as specialized knowledge for future criminal lawyers as opposed to foundational for all.

Con law typically covers some classic cases involving race and gender-based discrimination at the ballot or the manipulation of electoral boundaries for political advantage (gerrymandering). But the range of pressing issues facing our democracy—such as voting rights, campaign finance, and electoral disputes—are more customarily assigned to Election Law courses.

First Amendment law is typically an elective in law schools. This means live social issues—book bans, freedom of the press, hate speech, online communications, and the Gaza/Israel campus protests should a professor be so brave—are unlikely to be broached.[6] Some casebooks dedicate a chapter or two to First Amendment issues, and some professors give the topic some airtime. In this context, the focus on Supreme Court cases means students encounter only a narrow slice of First Amendment complexities and likely bypass contemporary controversies that haven't made it to the court.[7]

National security, legal scholar Sahar Aziz notes, touches many aspects of American life, but for many decades, it has been "exploited for ulterior commercial or political purposes to increase profits, obtain more government funding, and expand government authorities in areas that historically were not related to national security."[8] This area is saturated with constitutional issues, but students typically get bite-sized morsels. They probably discuss that time the feds lied about possible espionage and imprisoned Japanese American citizens in barbed-wire detention camps.[9] And they may cover the more recent episode where the Supreme Court ignored explicit Islamophobia and upheld the so-called "Muslim ban."[10] But there is less space to interrogate how national security has been commandeered as a constitutional rationale for a disparate range of issues: trade wars, climate change, TikTok, transgender military bans, and the separation of migrant families. Better luck in a National Security Law course.

Instead, a typical constitutional law course looks something like this (with the order depending on the casebook and instructor):

Students are first introduced to the document's main features—its preamble, articles, and various amendments.

Then they learn about *judicial review*. This is the power of courts to examine the constitutionality of government action and strike down a law if necessary.

Judicial review sets the stage for examining separation of powers (what it has been and/or what's left of it).[11] This is where students focus on the division of authority between the courts, the legislative branch (Congress), and the executive branch (the President, Cabinet officials, and federal agencies). Judicial review can also tee up an exploration into federalism, which focuses on the allocation of power between federal and subnational governments.

Next the class examines the other branches more closely. This includes Congress's powers to tax, spend, and control commerce and different aspects of executive power, such as the commander-in-chief's authority to implement national priorities, handle aspects of foreign policy, and lead armed forces.

The next major topic might be many of the rights that the public associates with the Constitution. These include due process, equal protection, and maybe a smidgen of the First Amendment, if the instructor is so inclined. This is often the liveliest part of the course because it touches on controversies over abortion, affirmative action, guns, and LGBTQ rights. At some point during this ride, instructors may delve into interpretive methods (e.g., originalism) as well as "justiciability" doctrines that focus on whether a court is permitted to hear a case.

Each of these stages can take anywhere from one to three weeks. The concepts are dense, and some of them are close calls, which can make conversations weightier and crowd out engagement with other issues. Beyond the breadth of material that must be covered, the course faces a deeper challenge: It assumes a functional democracy. Things like free and fair elections where losers accept results; credible checks and balances among institutions like Congress and the courts; and a legal system where officials are bound by law rather than partisanship. But contemporary constitutional controversies—presidential immunity, the use of the pardon power, challenges to electoral legitimacy, defiance of congressional oversight, and pressure on the Justice Department's independence—test those assumptions.

Trump 1.0 and 2.0 first brought these constitutional vulnerabilities into sharp relief, but many of the issues are bipartisan and long predate him. As University of Chicago scholars Aziz Huq and Tom Ginsburg note, "the problem of democratic decline is general in nature and not linked to a particular presidency."[12] Examples can be found in the forty-year politicization of judicial appointments, Democratic presidents' use of executive orders as a policymaking tool, the 2013 elimination of the Senate filibuster for nominations, and a Congress that is more dysfunctional than airport baggage claim.

Against this backdrop, it is no surprise that the standard first-year con law course, which centers on Supreme Court cases often far removed from these issues, is limited in its ability to equip students for unfolding constitutional emergencies. The breadth of issues deserving attention creates a circumstance in which the typical course—through no fault of the instructor—is bound to have critical omissions.

Herein lies one of many tensions. Con law trains budding lawyers—some of whom will go on to defend or challenge unconstitutional arrangements. But it does so with analytical tools that may be inadequate for contemporary constitutional problems that are rooted in exercises of raw power as opposed to legal principle. The course's struggle with current events points to design flaws that extend far beyond current democratic breakdowns.

The Inconvenient Truth of Colonialism

Even if we stipulate that con law professors have to cover immense ground just to get through the basics, one omission is so bold that it demands calling out: how the Constitution has enabled colonialism in the past and into the present.

The Constitution has been one of the tools America used to build and defend its empire. The document provided legal cover for territorial expansion. At the same time, Congress and the courts contorted it to deny protections to Native Nations, overseas colonies, and others the US ruled without equality. But these constitutional realities seldom appear in the way the Constitution is taught. In fact, a con law classroom is one place to learn how to hide an empire.[13] This kind of selective version of history can foreclose forms of critical thinking about the document that I suspect professors want to encourage. Regrettably, lawyers are dispatched into the next stage of their careers with a cribbed understanding of the legal system's foundational text.

As Federal Indian Law scholar Phil Frickey notes, Americans are governed by a Constitution that "became possible only by virtue of colonization," notwithstanding its promotion of rights to liberty and property.[14] This is not an outrageous claim. Yes, the country would have likely had a constitution even if the continent had not already been populated. But it would not have had *this* one.[15] The federal Constitution contains an explicit reference to Congress's ability to "regulate commerce" with "Indian tribes;"[16] the Treaty Clause that gives the President the power to negotiate treaties with Native Americans;[17] and the Supremacy Clause that says treaties trump federal laws and state laws.[18] The Constitution's explicit and implied references to Native Americans coincide with the big-ticket items in the typical con law course, but constitutional issues facing them get short shrift in many casebooks.

The relative nonexistence of Native Americans in con law is the culmination of educational malpractice. According to the National Congress of American Indians, most Americans "likely have attended or currently attend a school where information about Native Americans is either completely absent from the classroom or relegated to brief mentions, negative information, or inaccurate stereotypes."[19] Scholars of American K–12 education have found that more than half of states make no mention of a single Native American in their curriculum. To make matters worse, 87 percent of state history standards do not mention Indigenous history after 1900—as if Native people stopped existing and the textbook industry signed a pact of silence.[20]

As for higher education, an analysis of college textbooks found that they often portray North America as unoccupied, misrepresent the complicated boundaries of land owned by Tribal Nations that predate the US, and understate how violence supported colonial expansion. The creation of the United States is naturalized as white people simply "showing up," pulling a rabbit out of a hat, and saying "ta-da."[21] Considering the lack of knowledge students have about the history of US–tribal relations, devoting a small amount of time to related constitutional issues could be a "modest measure to address that deficiency," legal scholar James Grijalva argues. Such correction could be "the last chance for students to receive any formal education in that history." But every year, droves of students leave law schools with this "significant hole" in their education.[22]

A predictable defense of the status quo might suggest that these issues are better suited to coverage in the standard Federal Indian Law course. That doesn't quite work. Such a course is only available in a quarter of ABA-accredited law schools. In California, which hosts the fourth biggest Native American population, only four of the eleven law schools offer the course. And if you go to school in Alabama, Kentucky, Maryland, Ohio, North Carolina, New Jersey, or Virginia, there's no course for you.[23] Professors' lack of familiarity with constitutional issues impacting Native Americans may be another explanation for the gap, but that is an unsatisfying answer, too. Grijalva is right when he says, "Part of the law teacher's awesome responsibility for transmitting knowledge must carry with it an obligation to expand her or his own knowledge."[24]

For instructors who do have a working understanding of the Constitution vis-a-vis Native Americans, I suspect that the omission stems from two things.

First is a conceptual inconvenience. Indigenous Peoples upset many of the categories that students bring to con law and that are used in the course. Consider race. BIPOC (Black, Indigenous, and People of Color) is the new, inclusive term that shows how routine it to shoehorn Native Americans into racial categories.[25] Yes, they have a racial designation in the census. They've long been racialized—historically as "uncivilized savages," and today through stereotypes and sports mascots. But they are members of tribes, which is a *political status* that outstrips racial classifications and doesn't jibe neatly with some of the race-based Reconstruction Era amendments con law professors must discuss.[26]

Flowing from their unique political status is a nation-nation relationship that 574 federally recognized tribes individually have with the federal government. That political status makes them akin to (but not exactly like) foreign nations. They have their own forms of self-governance (e.g., courts, police, constitutions). Their existence as nations disrupts ideas about a contiguous, unified territory we call the United States. It ain't that united. The Navajo Nation, located mainly within the boundaries of Arizona, is larger than West Virginia. The Choctaw Nation, located within the boundaries of Oklahoma, is larger than Massachusetts. Native Americans' political status makes it hard to talk about constitutional concepts like federalism; it is no longer about state and federal governments, because a third player is added to the mix—tribal governments.[27]

The second problem is an ideological inconvenience. Talking about Native Americans in con law courses reveals uglier sides of American law. In this sense, I agree with Indigenous Studies scholar Sandy Grande: American Indian tribes expose one of the many "great lies of U.S. democracy: that we are a nation of laws and not random power."[28] Indigenous history undermines the idea that governments derive "just powers from the consent of the governed" and shows how American law has been non-consensually imposed on independent nations.

This is *colonialism*. I don't use the term lightly. The Legal Information Institute at Cornell Law School describes colonialism as "the act of power and domination of one nation, by acquiring or maintaining full or partial political control over another sovereign nation."[29] I frankly don't know how else to describe what happened. As the US exercised control of Indigenous Peoples, it engaged in constitutionally odious behavior: the enforced sterilizations of women, interference with the parent-child relationship, compulsory education, prohibitions on traditional marriages, criminalization of spiritual practices, and detention in camps.[30] Many of these topics come up in con law, but not as they relate to Native Americans.

To make matters worse, constitutionally permitted colonialism is in operation as you're reading this. My colleague Maggie Blackhawk puts it best: "The United States holds hundreds of governments in subordination. *Not historically. Today*. It dominates these governments and their peoples, exploits their resources, prohibits political independence, withholds representation, and imposes its own laws, values, and norms upon these governments without consent."[31] To understand her point, we only need to look at the water rights controversies surrounding the Dakota Access Pipeline, or the federal approval these tribes need to engage in certain economic activities. So when the president and his administration entertain seizing the Panama Canal and Greenland, making Canada the fifty-first state, or erecting a waterfront "Gaza Trump Riviera" that boasts "world class resorts," he is not saying anything historically outrageous—he's expressing openly what constitutional law courses discursively obscure.[32]

And More Colonialism!

The cleansing of colonialism from constitutional law applies to other subordinated peoples, too. If you picked up a casebook, you'd have to search low and high for a discussion of the Constitution's Territory Clause, or what is sometimes called the Property Clause. This provision allows Congress to make all "needful" laws regarding any "Territory or other Property belonging to the United States."[33] This clause facilitated American colonialism by providing a constitutional basis for managing new lands acquired through violence, purchase, and global maneuvering. If you think I'm trying to give you ethnic studies disguised as con law, let's take a brief tour through history. Note how many of these examples involve a belated mea culpa from people in different branches of the federal government.

In 1741, the Russian Empire took over Alaska, but it was "interested only in the extraction of resources, not in governing a distant population."[34] By 1867, the country had lost the Crimean War, was broke, and had started a fire sale. The Russians didn't want to sell to the British Empire, which held swaths of land in present-day Canada, and other countries were not interested. The US, through constitutionally vested treaty powers, purchased Alaska for about $7 million. Although it would take almost a century for Alaska to become a state, that period was marked by hallmarks of colonialism that included:

- Economic neglect once Alaska was acquired;
- A gold rush in the 1890s that "brought whites to Alaska in unprecedented numbers" and disregarded the property rights of Alaska's original inhabitants (Alaska Natives);[35]
- The passage of laws, via the Constitution's Territory Clause, that facilitated the growth of a salmon canning industry that displaced Indigenous Peoples, exploited the Asian men and Native women workers who worked in them, and disrupted subsistence systems;[36]
- The importation of *Plessey v. Ferguson*–styled Jim Crow, with "No Natives allowed" signs becoming common;[37]

- A forced assimilation policy that even the federal government is currently recognizing as traumatic for the more than 180,000 members of the 229 federally recognized tribes in the area.[38]

The annexation of the Kingdom of Hawai'i also pulled from a colonial playbook. In 1887, a militia of white settlers held King David Kalākaua at gunpoint and made him sign a new constitution. The "Bayonet Constitution" was drafted by a secret group of sugar industry–connected lawyers and businessmen who wanted to limit the power of Indigenous Hawaiians. When King Kalākaua's sister Queen Lili'uokalani took over in 1891 and tried to restore Native authority, the US Minister to the Kingdom of Hawai'i, aided by Marines, organized a coup and installed the aforementioned cabal as the provisional government. Yes, you read that right. American businessmen literally held a king at gunpoint to steal his authority, and when his sister tried to take it back, America sent in the Marines to shut that down.

Again, the Constitution's Treaty Clause is what gives the president the power to make treaties with the advice and consent of the Senate. President William McKinley wanted to annex the Kingdom of Hawai'i, which now had an American puppet regime, but he couldn't get the required two-thirds vote, so the annexationists went for a "joint resolution," which only required a simple majority of the Senate and the House. Against the protest of Native Hawaiians, it was successful. People back then and today have argued that this backdoor approach to acquisition was unconstitutional.[39]

In 1993, the US issued an apology that acknowledged that "the overthrow of the Kingdom of Hawaii occurred with the active participation of agents and citizens of the United States." It also admitted that "the Native Hawaiian people never directly relinquished to the United States their claims to their inherent sovereignty as a people over their national lands."[40] In the almost six decades it took for Hawaii to become a state, it was exploited for its sugar and pineapple plantations (think of the company Dole), part of its land was converted into a military outpost (think Pearl Harbor), and its children were banned from using the Hawaiian language in schools. All of this occurred while Native Hawaiians—who did not consent to be governed—were displaced and their culture was suppressed.

At the turn of the twentieth century, the US gobbled up more land by seizing Spain's territories. During the Cuban struggle for independence from Spain, American newspapers published sensationalist stories that created sympathy for Cubans and public pressure for American military intervention. In the meantime, American businesses wanted that Cuban sugar money, and the US government was in expansionist mode. The explosion of a US Navy cruiser in Havana provided justification for the start the Spanish-American War in 1898, and that conflict resulted in the acquisition of Guam, Puerto Rico, and the Philippines.

Beginning in 1901, three years after the American victory, the Supreme Court issued a series of rulings often referred to as the *Insular Cases*. As Boston College law professor Aziz Rana notes, the Insular Cases are taught in few American law classes despite raising significant questions about the reach of the American Constitution. My con law professor was unusual in recognizing the importance of these cases; I felt like I was bestowed with missing chapters of American history when I talked with lawyers after my first year and realized most students skip over this period. The Insular Cases are missing from major con law casebooks notwithstanding the breathtaking import of these rulings.

During this time, the court was drunk on racial pseudoscience and concluded that these darker-skinned people from the new territories were unfit for citizenship and statehood. The court devised a two-tiered scheme to determine who could be in the American family. Incorporated territories received full constitutional protections and were presumed to be on track for eventual statehood. Unincorporated territories got constitutional crumbs. Congress could decide, piece by piece, which rights they deserved. This enshrined a second-class constitutional status for these territories that we would expect to be explored in a con law course.

You don't have to accept these critiques from the Black guy with a long African last name. Take it from Donald Trump appointee and conservative Supreme Court Justice Neil Gorsuch. In a 2022 case Gorsuch wrote, "A century ago in the Insular Cases, this Court held that the federal government could rule Puerto Rico and other Territories largely without regard to the Constitution. It is past time to acknowledge the gravity of this error and admit what we know to be true: *The Insular Cases have no foundation in the Constitution and rest instead on racial stereotypes. They deserve no place in our law.*" And that was just the intro to his opinion! He dissected the contorted logic of the decisions and claimed that they rested on a view about the "Nation's right to acquire and exploit an unknown island" for "commercial and strategic reasons."[41]

The Philippines eventually shook loose and gained independence in 1946, but Puerto Rico and Guam—which were brought under US rule without the consent of their peoples—remain in this liminal status. Other territories in constitutional limbo include American Samoa, the US Virgin Islands, and the Northern Mariana Islands. Law students do not learn how a series of legislative moves and Supreme Court decisions justified the differential status, treatment, and rights protections accorded to more than 3.5 million people in these territories, the majority of whom are non-white. These people have no Senate representation and can't vote in general elections for the president and the vice president. Despite being some of the poorest people in the country they are excluded from some public benefit programs because of geography. Democracy, this is not. But it gets glossed over as students have conversations about the structure of the Constitution, the power of the branches, and "rights."

High-Level and Low-Level Constitutional Interpretation

Curricular inattention extends beyond these historical erasures to contemporary constitutional interpretation itself. That is, when the court bothers to explain itself at all. In the shadow-docket era, blockbuster rulings often arrive as emergency orders with no arguments and barely a sentence of justification; it's almost as if constitutional interpretation is a side gig and the justices have more important errands to attend to.[42]

In some ways, con law professors must act as though Supreme Court justices are driven by principle. This means ignoring examples such as that of Justice Abe Fortas, who "reached decisions first and rationalized them later"—a tendency that is exemplified by the story of Fortas throwing a draft opinion of a case to his law clerk and ordering him to "decorate it" with citations that supported his prespecified legal outcome.[43]

I doubt that professors pretend that politics has no seat at the table; that's difficult to do in a con law course. But how much weight they accord to it as an input for legal outcomes is an open question. One of the areas where politics comes up is in discussions about how to read the Constitution. I'll give you the high-level version of this problem and the low-level version.

The View from Thirty Thousand Feet Above

From above, there is some slippage between, on the one hand, understandings of constitutional *interpretation*, the process of discovering the meaning of the document, and, on the other, constitutional *decision-making*, which addresses "the wider question of how judges should decide constitutional cases."[44] For our purposes, there are three relevant approaches to both. Some scholars refer to them as *modalities* (proper forms of reasoning), *non-modalities* (arguments everyone agrees are illegitimate), and *anti-modalities* (reasoning that clearly influences decisions but can't be openly acknowledged).[45] Since this is quite jargony, I'll instead refer to these modalities as legitimate, nonstarters, and relevant, but forbidden.

In 1982, Philip Bobbitt offered a six-part typology of *legitimate* forms of constitutional argument used to interpret the document. Let's turn to the issue of abortion to tease these out.

- *Historical arguments* focus on the intentions and understandings of the Constitution's framers and ratifiers. *What were the Founders' views on abortion?*
- *Textual arguments* prioritize the plain meaning of the Constitution's words. *Does the Fourteenth Amendment's reference to "liberty" encompass a right to abortion?*

- *Structural arguments* focus on the relationships between different parts of the Constitution. *Does the Constitution's federalist framework suggest that abortion should be left to the states?*
- *Doctrinal arguments* look to precedent and case law. *What about Roe v. Wade?*
- *Ethical arguments* highlight the moral and philosophical principles in the Constitution (e.g., liberty and equality). *The protection of life or the right to bodily autonomy?*
- *Prudential arguments* are somewhat face-saving and concerned with avoiding the undesirable consequences of ill-timed or inappropriate interventions. These are instances when the court occasionally punts. *Are there narrow grounds that the court can use to decide on this new abortion issue that would avoid a political backlash and premature precedent?*

Bobbitt argues that there is "no constitutional legal argument" to be made if it doesn't fit in one of these boxes.[46] Some scholars have offered similar formulations, and others have quibbled with these categories, but they have been described as "invaluable teaching tool[s]" and "central pillars of constitutional theory and pedagogy."[47]

Some forms of constitutional argument are *nonstarters* and will only get brief mentions here. It would be considered absurd for judges to determine the constitutionality of abortion based on astrological arguments, dreams, or a roll of the dice.[48] The exclusion of these kinds of approaches is uncontroversial.

Finally, there are forms of reasoning that could be *relevant, but are forbidden* from explicit constitutional consideration. Constitutional law scholars David Pozen and Adam Samaha have created their own six-part framework to demonstrate the point:

- *Policy arguments* focus on the social, political, and economic consequences of constitutional decision-making. These arguments are frowned upon and understood as extraneous. Under this view, banning abortion may harm women's health, but the Constitution is not a policy report. The constitutional issue in

dispute should lead the way because we don't want judges deciding the law, just interpreting it.
- *Partisan arguments* are based on preferences for a particular group. When Chief Justice John Roberts says there are "no Obama judges or Trump judges," he's trying, in vain, to suggest that judges are above tribalism.
- *Fundamentalist arguments* are based on deep philosophical or moral beliefs that are not widely shared. Religion and social theories offer the easiest examples. It would be considered poor form to rule on an abortion case based on one's Catholic beliefs or based on critical race theory, which highlights how abortion restrictions disproportionately impact poor women and racial minorities.
- *Popularity arguments* are based on the public sentiment surrounding a constitutional issue. Should public opinion on abortion impact the interpretive work of judges? Standard constitutional theory says no.
- *Logrolling* is a form of horse-trading and a compromise technique. The pro-life justices got their way last year, so let the pro-choice justices win this time.
- *Emotional arguments* are centered around feelings and vibes.[49] Appeals to the joys of parenthood or the moral outrage of forcing women to carry pregnancies to term have a place on social media but not in legal briefs or oral arguments.

These forms of reasoning are generally excluded from formal constitutional decision-making and, as a result, mainstream constitutional teaching, but they often operate in court decisions.

Let's stick with abortion and policy arguments. Notwithstanding her critique of *Roe v. Wade* as jumping the gun, feminist icon Ruth Bader Ginsburg was a reliable pro-choice vote in abortion cases. Her background as the cofounder of the Women's Rights Project or her "unequivocal" belief in the right to abortion had nothing to do with this?[50] She was just calling balls and strikes, eh?

The partisan arguments on the other end of the ideological

spectrum are similarly apparent. Donald Trump promised to appoint Supreme Court justices who would overturn *Roe v. Wade*, and he did that by nominating three jurists who understood the assignment.

On the fundamentalist front, am I supposed to believe that a court that is overrepresented with Catholics bears no relationship to its abortion jurisprudence or what Americans describe as a "friendliness" toward religion?[51]

Planned Parenthood v. Casey was the 1992 decision that reaffirmed the right to an abortion when people thought Roe was all but finished; it can help us dispense with popularity arguments and logrolling. On the former, the court had the insecurity of a beginner at a gym. It worried, *in print*, that overturning Roe would bring a "loss of confidence in the Judiciary" and "unnecessary damage to the Court's legitimacy." It was trying to stay popular! *Casey* is one of the rare decisions coauthored by *three* justices (SCOTUS opinions usually have one lead author). Judicial give-and-take and politicking were so evident in this decision that it is sometimes referred to as "Casey's compromise."

Fifteen years after *Casey*, the court gestured toward an emotional argument without owning it. In *Gonzales v. Carhart* (2005), the court considered the constitutionality of a specialized form of abortion that occurs in the later stages of pregnancy. Justice Anthony Kennedy's majority opinion went into arguably unnecessary detail about these "partial-birth abortions." He described abortion as a decision that was "fraught with emotional consequence." He focused on the regret women incur after the procedure, despite admitting that the court could "find no reliable data to measure" such regret.[52]

There are various explanations why some of these forbidden but relevant forms of reasoning rarely surface in constitutional law courses—and why they're a sideshow when they do. Practically, they're not tested on the bar exam. Intellectually, these categories could risk oversimplifying the complex causes of behind-the-scenes decision-making by really smart judges. Socialization is a cause, too—namely, the norm of objectivity and the belief that there is a principled coherence to constitutional law. Ideologically, professors may want to avoid politicizing courts during a time of political polarization.[53] Like the Supreme Court, con law profs may be worried about undermining the legitimacy of courts by pointing out all the pedestrian, extra-legal factors that go into legal decision-making.

The problem with sidelining these relevant, but forbidden insights is that it strips away the moral urgency and human stakes that animate some students' beliefs. It teaches them to perform a particular kind of moral-to-legal translation that diminishes some of what they genuinely care about. They learn that their deepest convictions about inequality, justice, and suffering must be channeled through those staid "legitimate categories" or risk being dismissed as "unlawyerly."

The liberal student who thinks affirmative action is crucial for addressing racism can't argue that directly—they must construct convoluted equal protection arguments about diversity in education. A conservative student who believes gun ownership is essential to exercising a moral right to protect family and self can't make that case. They have to parse eighteenth-century texts about "well-regulated militias." In these instances, and countless others, students learn to treat their moral intuitions as illegitimate inputs for constitutional reasoning.

Engaging the law in this way can produce students who understand the different nuances of con law. But it can also foster a detachment from moral consequences that can be found in legal practice. So when you wonder why lawyers can talk about the most urgent constitutional problems facing this country—voting rights, healthcare, police violence—and it can sound like they're debating building permits, you can see why: They've been partially trained to treat their moral instincts as inadmissible.

The View from Below

A proxy war between liberals and conservatives in the interpretive trenches haunts the modern con law course. It is the debate between living constitutionalism and originalism.

Living constitutionalism and its cousins are often, though not exclusively, associated with liberals.[54] This view of interpretation focuses on the evolving meaning of the document and the ability to apply it to new problems that the Constitution's architects did not encounter.

Originalism, at the most general level, focuses on interpreting constitutional provisions in ways that are consistent with how they would have been understood at the time the draftsmen put pen to paper. These adherents also believe that the document can be applied to modern situations, but they think that happens by focusing on things like the intentions of the drafters, the original meaning of constitutional text, the purpose behind provisions, and the background legal principles from that era.[55]

The ideological chasm between adherents of originalism and living constitutionalism is deep.

On the right, there is a growing "originalist industrial complex" replete with fellowships, access to clerkships, scholarly workshops, and money.[56] Because originalism is the lingua franca of many of the justices on the court, several law schools jostle over originalist academics like Western European countries scrambled for African colonies in the nineteenth century. It's pandemonium!

Meanwhile, liberals, who some say have a Gorilla Grip clutch on legal academia,[57] don't know what to do about the originalist invasion. *The New York Times* has reported on professors crying about redoing their syllabus amid a sea of originalist rulings or bailing from teaching the class outright.[58]

Scholars on both sides accuse the other of being knockoffs—mere derivatives of their own approach. Conservative University of Chicago law professor Will Baude argues that all roads of constitutional interpretation lead back to originalism; even when other modes of interpretation, like living constitutionalism, are used, they only prevail if they don't contradict the original meaning.[59] Liberal Yale law professor Reva Siegel has suggested that originalism masquerades as "value-neutral" but is really a form of living constitutionalism that is "not forthright about its values, aims, and commitments."[60]

I won't wade into the debate except to say this: Both forms of interpretation fetishize a cultural artifact. Originalism does so by using historical methods that professional historians scoff at and, for some reason, often leads to outcomes that disadvantage women and minorities.[61] Originalists get red in the face when they are confronted with the reality that the Fourteenth Amendment was a race-conscious attempt to address the plight of Black Americans and, under an originalist reading, would seem to support affirmative action.[62] Originalism swaps today's judicial preferences for vintage elite ones and throws on lapel pins that say "constraint" and "neutrality."

Living constitutionalists are susceptible to attack from two sides. On the right, critics argue that living constitutionalists and their theory are unprincipled: They embrace judicial activism like a warm hug when it is in service of liberal priorities like abortion and LGBTQ rights but object to judicial innovation that benefits corporations and gun owners. On the far left, critics argue that living constitutionalism prioritizes elite interpretation of a deeply imperfect document that sanctioned slavery for a third of its existence, permitted women's exclusion from voting for half its shelf life, and has a checkered history of subordinating the poor and empowering the rich.[63] Maybe there's a reason why leading liberal law professors—some of whom previously championed versions of living constitutionalism—are saying we need to relinquish our addiction to the document, reimagine it, or abandon it altogether.[64]

My own view: Originalism and living constitutionalism both regularize inequality by making political choices look like legal inevitabilities. Originalist necromancers get into a séance with statesmen who led during a time of rich-white-male rule and ask a diverse America to squeeze into a time machine with them to derive legal meaning. Living constitutionalists embrace incremental reform in ways that remain tethered to unjust starting points, imagine that subordinated communities have unlimited time to wait for justice, and assume steady constitutional progress when recent court decisions prove that advances can be snatched overnight. What emerges is a system where contested fights about humanity get packaged as debates about interpretive technique.

PEEP THIS IRONY: Con law courses help produce lawyers who will shape the lives of countless people whose experiences are absent from constitutional training. These students receive incomplete renderings of our legal order, while entire swaths of law-created suffering—past and present—are ignored or lost in a long list of constitutional rules and precedents. Some students learn to approach legal doctrine as if it can transcend deep struggles over power and the messy realities of inequality. That's how you get an originalism that can bracket all of the original intents many now find abhorrent, as well as a living constitutionalism whose evolutionary timeline consistently prioritizes elite comfort over urgent human need.

The historically selective and politically evasive approach to constitutional law provides some explanation for why the field produces outcomes that feel disconnected from some Americans' ideas about fairness and justice. The uncomfortable truth is that we live under a constitutional system that exalts "equal protection" while protecting inequality with vigilance. What makes matters worse? Con law is the foundational course that trains students to be habitually distanced from these contradictions and inconsistencies.

CHAPTER 7

Civil Procedure and the Architecture of Inequality

PICTURE THIS: You have some kind of common legal problem. Your lousy landlord is trying to keep your security deposit because of minor cleaning issues. Your insurance company discovered an exclusion clause that exists solely to deny your valid claim. Or maybe you encountered some kind of workplace discrimination—you were laid off because of your age, paid less because of your race, subject to sexual harassment, or denied reasonable accommodations for your disability.

You've got smoking-gun evidence and, more importantly, the truth on your side. The apartment was left in impeccable shape, and you have pictures and recordings to prove it. The so-called policy is of recent vintage and actually doesn't apply to your accident. You've got damning emails from your supervisor saying all those discriminatory things.

The merits of your claim are only part of the story. Several rules, filing requirements, and deadlines need to be met for a court to hear your very good argument. Welcome to the world of *civil procedure*, the complex system that governs how noncriminal disputes are conducted that can nix a case before a court hears your meritorious argument.

Civil procedure professors tend to do the yeoman's work of teaching students the nuts and bolts of our legal system and how a case moves through court. Some of the material is mind-numbingly technical. I mean, let's be honest, who likes studying rules? Would you rather use the electric scooter or the Bluetooth headphones you just purchased? Or do you prefer slogging through a double-sided, eight-inch font, multilingual instruction guide?

Because civ pro, as it is colloquially called, is so mechanical, instructors often italicize its importance. The professor might tell the future litigators in the room that it is impossible to win court cases without a sufficient understanding of these rules. Procedure also matters for the people who will never step foot in a courtroom and who will work on the transactional side. They sometimes draft contracts that try to keep their clients out of court, and they try to include favorable provisions should their clients have to litigate. Some understanding of procedural rules is necessary to do either. Civil procedure is one of the most important classes in a student's three years in law school, which makes how it's taught critically important for anyone who might need to extract justice from the legal system.

Here's what stands out to me about civ pro: The course risks normalizing legal inequality by training students to master technical rules via teaching tools that often treat their impact on ordinary people as side issues. The curriculum places heavy emphasis on federal courts, often at the expense of exploring the local and state courts where ordinary Americans and poor people encounter the legal system. Indeed, one has to search high and low for substantive discussions of poverty in the typical casebook, and economic inequality does not receive the serious intellectual attention it merits. Meanwhile, the same intellectual effort professors and students devote to parsing procedural rules is not typically applied to examining how corporations use those rules to avoid accountability.

These curricular shortcomings are tragic because, in its ideal form, procedure is a good thing: a framework that provides order, fosters fairness, and protects people from raw, arbitrary power. But students can't fully understand what procedural rules do—or their real-world consequences—without seeing how they operate as weapons in the hands of well-resourced parties and as barriers in underresourced state courts. This is one way law school teaches its acolytes to ignore what matters—not through cruelty but through benign neglect. It's the kind of professional detachment that allows technicians to operate machines without sufficiently questioning what those instruments do or whom they grind up.

Civ Pro Fundamentals and Federal Fever

Civil procedure courses typically spend a good chunk of the semester walking students through the process of litigation in federal courts. The order may vary, and this is an incomplete rendering, but here are some mainstays of the more than eighty rules that comprise the Federal Rules of Civil Procedure.

For a court to hear a case, it needs *jurisdiction*, which is the power to make decisions about the parties and the type of dispute. You can't go to a California federal court to sue a person you had a dispute with in London when the Brit has never stepped foot in this country and has no ties or connections to the Golden State; the California court has no authority over that person. And you can't bring a divorce to a federal court, because those are handled in state tribunals.

With jurisdiction issues settled, the next step is to file a *complaint* with the court and serve the defendant with a *summons* letting them know that they are being sued. The defendant can then file a *motion to dismiss*, which happens when they claim the case should not proceed further due to some kind of legal defect. Perhaps the complaint was filed past the statute of limitations, served incorrectly, or brought in the wrong court.

If the case survives early challenges, it moves to *discovery*, which is where parties exchange information relevant to the dispute. In an age discrimination case, the plaintiff might ask for his personnel file and the files of younger employees who were promoted instead of him. In return, if the plaintiff is claiming emotional distress because of the termination, that could open the door for the employer to request his medical and therapy records. Discovery aims to get the facts, narrow the issues, and hopefully encourage settlement, because litigation isn't cheap.

At this point, parties might settle, go to trial, or—if one side feels confident about the evidence—they might file for *summary judgment*, which is when one of the parties (typically the defendant) says, "We don't need to go to court. Look at the evidence. Even if you looked at it in a manner that was most favorable to my adversary, the facts say I should still win."

If that doesn't work, things move to trial, which includes jury selection, the presentation of evidence by both parties, and the verdict.

Post-trial moves constitute the after-party. At this stage, one of the parties might ask for a do-over (a new trial). The losing party might ask for the damage awards to be shrunk or the prevailing party might ask for the amount to be increased. One of the parties might request that the trial court's boss (an appellate court) review the decision for error.

This is only a slice of the Federal Rules of Civil Procedure; each of these issues could take a day or a week in the semester. Students spend months trying to master these rules with a monastic devotion. States have their own procedural rules, but the attention is on the feds. The justifications for this focus have the persuasive sheen of a used car salesman: not dishonest, but curated to spotlight the most flattering angles as opposed to the full maintenance history.

The pros. Federal procedural rules are uniform. The same set of procedural rules applies in federal courts across the country, whether you're sweating in Miami or bundling up in Anchorage. State procedure rules are specific to the locality and can vary wildly. What flies in Arizona might flop in Missouri. Within that variance is the reality that many states' rules are modeled after the federal rules, so that's another checked box. And while some states such as California, Florida, and Texas test state-specific procedures, the bar exam tends to use the federal rules as the baseline. Federal procedure is often the basis for important, precedent-setting cases. Students also need to know these federal rules for the fancy clerkships that some of them pursue.

At the same time, the emphasis on the federal level is part of a larger pattern of academic elitism. State laws and rules are sometimes considered the Spirit Airlines of the legal system. Some professors wouldn't say it aloud, but if you gave them enough cognac, they might use the word *gutter* to describe state law issues.

There are good arguments for stronger consideration of state procedure in legal education. To start with the most obvious: The vast majority of cases are filed outside of the federal system. In fact, between 2012 and 2022, 98.5 percent of cases were filed in local and state courts, and the remaining 1.5 percent were filed in federal courts.[1] If the average student ends up practicing in courts, it *may* be in these fancy forums, but it will likely be in the frontline courts where most American litigants battle.

Knowledge of state procedural rules could arguably be more immediately relevant. Yes, teaching one set of uniform federal laws is likely easier, but most law school graduates practice in the state where they went to school, and a few travel to select states. Consider these numbers from a few Chicago schools in 2024: 92 percent of students at DePaul and 82 percent of students at Loyola took the Illinois bar exam alone; 91 percent of students at Northwestern and 74 percent of students at the University of Chicago took the Illinois, California, or New York bar exams.[2] There are similar trends in law schools across the country; most students practice in a handful of states. Nevertheless, federal issues predominate, while the state procedural issues that will govern some of their actual practice gets relegated to secondary status. For some students—especially those who don't go to work at large law firms—it's like training to make soufflés and then working at IHOP during the Sunday brunch rush—both require culinary skill, but the pace, expectations, and resources are completely different.

I am not saying that federal rules should not be taught in the course. Nor am I suggesting the course is devoid of state–federal comparisons. Some locally oriented schools, such as the University of Hawai'i at Mānoa, focus explicitly on state and federal procedure. More generally, there are moments where procedural diversity surfaces. But these are often framed as technical exercises rather than socially grounded inquiries. While federal rules may be a solid proxy on paper, they overlook the resource constraints and local political pressures that shape how litigation actually unfolds in state and local courts. A more deliberate comparative lens could complement existing coverage while producing lawyers who are both more versatile in practice and more attuned to how procedures affect ordinary Americans.³ But the prevailing focus on federal procedure is just the tip of the iceberg—it reflects a deeper problem of how civil procedure education ignores poverty and its consequences.

Ignoring Poverty and the Average Person

Poverty is a non-factor in the standard civil procedure course.⁴ Few of the leading casebooks in the area mention the word or issue—even though a hundred-year-old federal statute governs poor people's access to federal courts and a few procedural rules accommodate their indigency.⁵ Procedural issues facing the average American, oftentimes categorized as "access to justice," may get a little more attention. But some of these treatments can give a sense of begrudging pre-2024 DEI handwaving instead of serious, sustained inquiry. The systematic neglect of poverty makes perfect sense once you understand the social geography of civil procedure—a world designed by and for society's elite.

In the courtroom, federal judges are culled from penthouses of power; wealthy interest groups sometimes influence their appointments.⁶ Some of these judges have spent the past few decades elevating complex white-collar litigation. A former Big Law partner turned law-school dean notes how these judges have deprioritized the "routine pedestrian work often involving unrepresented claimants and poor people."⁷

On an institutional level, the Chief Justice of the Supreme Court appoints members to the Advisory Committee on Civil Rules, which evaluates and updates federal procedure. For more than fifty years, many of its members had a "pro-corporate slant."⁸ One critic went as far as to suggest that many of the members are "demographically predisposed to think like elite white males, or experientially predisposed to think like corporate defense lawyers."⁹ Civ pro expert Brooke

Coleman is not exaggerating when she refers to federal civil procedure as a "one percent regime" focused on "elite litigation."[10]

In the professorial world, poverty is part of a "quotidian corner of civil procedure" and hampered by an academic "instinct" that "equates federal courts with the big case and parties with deep pockets."[11] Michigan law professor Maureen Carroll clarifies the situation. She notes how the filing fee for federal cases is $400. This might be peanuts for the aforementioned judges, private sector attorneys, and law professors—many of whom are six-figure income earners and make more than double the average American income. For some, it's just a wine-soaked, reimbursable dinner with old classmates reliving their law school years.[12]

But $400 represents a week's worth of income to a person who makes the federal minimum wage of $7.25. That's survival money: a few months of minimum-liability car insurance, several weeks of groceries, or a medical bill that can't wait its turn. Yet the assumption in civil procedure is that everyone has four Benjamin Franklins just to *start* a lawsuit.[13] If that's the working premise, then it is no surprise why these courts and their procedures are described as "courts of the elite—jurisdictionally, doctrinally, and socially."[14]

The inattention to issues of poverty is damaging because lawyers and the law have recognized the procedural disadvantages faced by poor people for centuries.

Some scholars have traced federal courts' procedural obligations to mitigate economic inequality to the Judiciary Act of 1789. This law emanates from British legal history and can be traced back even further—to the biblical texts of Exodus, Leviticus, and Deuteronomy. The act created America's federal court system and codified an oath that federal judges take to this day where they promise to "do equal right to the poor and to the rich."[15]

More than a century ago, Harvard law professor John MacArthur Maguire lamented how "poverty, often through the application of some rule of law which otherwise seems eminently reasonable, blocks a civil litigant's path at every stage of the proceedings." Walking through the litigation process in 1923, Maguire explained how a "penniless suitor may lose his day in court because he has no ready money to pay the fees for his writ, for serving process, for entering suit, and for other similar official acts." Should this unhappy fellow get past those hurdles, he will "be helpless because he cannot pay for a lawyer; or he may become helpless in the midst of the case because he lacks funds to bring his witnesses, to pay a stenographer, or to pay a printer." Poor people back then, much like today, had to surmount the "miscellaneous expenses incident to litigation."[16] In civ pro classrooms, litigation tools like depositions, expert witnesses, and appeals are sometimes presented like standard fare on a sleek restaurant menu—unpriced, misleadingly accessible, and stripped of the fact that in practice, their costs are anything but standard or predictable.

In 2007, former legal aid lawyer and now NYU law professor Helen Hershkoff pleaded with civil procedure scholars to integrate poverty into their courses by reminding them of its educational relevance. "Asking students to assess the current civil justice system from the perspective of poverty and inequality comports with the basic aims of the first-year curriculum: to learn to think critically about legal arrangements and to assess dispassionately whether existing rules promote the stated goals of fairness and efficiency for all litigants."[17] This is not a new concept, and it shouldn't be a big ask.

There is also an internal inconsistency to ignoring poverty. Our legal system rests on adversarialism, and it is predicated on the idea that contestants duke it out to produce what legal scholar William Rubenstein describes as "the most accurate and acceptable" legal outcomes. "But for such a system to function properly," he notes, "the parties must be somewhat equally capable of producing their cases." If one side is poorly equipped because "it cannot afford access to the system, or has less time and money to pursue evidence, or less skill in developing legal claims—then what emerges as the stronger case might not necessarily be the better."[18] Truth-finding can become impossible when only one side can afford to find it.

This resource gap has a name. For more than fifty years, scholars have written about *equipage*—the practical resources needed to effectively litigate.[19] Poor people can be less equipped to leverage what procedural rules facilitate. Filing cases, serving defendants, taking depositions, and attending pretrial conferences all require time and resources that poor litigants may not have.

Poverty is consequential to procedure and disrupts ideas of how our civil legal system works, but it has failed to rise to the level of even a subheading in most teaching tools. This is regrettable because a range of procedural issues uniquely impact low-income people, even within the rarefied world of federal litigation—often in cases involving employment discrimination, police misconduct, and disability rights claims.[20] Too often, the teaching of their procedural problems is subject to the whims of a professoriate who *may* elevate them in discrete areas but are unlikely to give these issues the urgency that they deserve.

The 98.5 Percent Down Yonder: Local and State Court Chaos

Moving from the fancy federal courts to the local and state courts unsettles the tidier view of our legal system that first-year civ pro furnishes. These courts serve as "emergency rooms" for millions of Americans who enter them in crisis, whether because of a looming eviction, a child custody battle, wage garnishments, or a domestic violence dispute.[21] Down here, students might see how some of the basic civ pro concepts are undermined.

I remember my first few times in these frontline "lower" courts after taking civil procedure. Some of it felt familiar; I've known poverty, and not the academic kind. But these courts didn't resemble civ pro. It was a surreal sensory overload that never fully left me.

After walking through a separate line marked for attorneys, I stepped into a fog of chaos masked as procedure. Interpreters were nowhere to be found. There were waiver forms that required piles of documentation to prove the poverty most people assumed was obvious. Clerks spoke in acronyms, half-audible, and behind plexiglass—some curt, some kind, all constrained by the system. People being told they were in the wrong location was almost routine. By the time they reached the courtroom door—if they got there at all—it felt less like access to justice and more like an obstacle course.

Inside the crammed courtrooms, rushed decisions were made in cases thick with consequences—determining where someone will sleep, whether they will have their wages garnished, or whether they will see their child again. Most of these people were self-represented, trying to decode rules that didn't feel written for them.

The smell was unforgettable. It wasn't the antiseptic classroom air that is often scrubbed clean of the funk of injustice. It was a mix of cheap cologne, stale courtroom air, and the unmistakable trace smell of someone who'd just finished smoking a cigarette or a blunt outside—perhaps to calm a craving or steady their nerves.

The procedural confusion and frustration were audible. Court staff mispronounced last names and barked out case numbers like deli orders. Grown men raised their voices trying to follow instructions that seemed to keep changing. The crying of children outside the courtroom—overtired, hungry, or just desperate to go home—leaked into the space at random moments. Women litigants managed deadlines and evidence like a second, unpaid job. They shuffled papers and exhaled audibly when no one called their name.

You could feel the stress of people waiting to be called and the humiliation of discussing intimate life details in front of a room full of strangers. Then came the panic as they realized something had just happened, they didn't understand it, and it was already too late. Appeal deadlines had passed. Chances to fix their defective complaint had expired. Others learned that they were barred from pursuing a claim forever.

Meanwhile, judges flipped through mountains of files while rarely looking up—and I couldn't tell if it was indifference, exhaustion, or something else. This version of procedure was messy and far removed from the orderly logic found in casebooks.

One area where this procedural chaos becomes particularly

devastating is debt collection, where the clean rules students learn in civ pro break down and meet messy realities.

Debt buyers purchase delinquent debts on the cheap and try to recoup their funds through fraudulent activity that violates procedural rules. Sometimes they deliver a complaint that fails to meet basic pleading requirements (e.g., the original debt amount, how the plaintiff owns the debt).[22] Or they may engage in *sewer service*, which is when a summons or complaint is not delivered, given to the wrong person, or thrown in the trash.[23] In these instances, there may be a default judgment against a person who didn't show up for a hearing they never knew about. State courts sometimes issue these judgments "with alarming automaticity and speed" and without scrutinizing the evidence of the debt amount or whether the company is suing the right person.[24] One judge told Human Rights Watch he issues default judgments from the comfort of his home on Sunday afternoons.[25]

Then there are the thirty-two states that allow people to be judges without a law degree. In some places, judges don't know the procedural rules and get less mandatory training than states require of barbers and masseuses. These judges take "competency exams" that require sixth-grade reading skills, basic math, and the ability to tell time and identify days of the week.[26] In some of these tribunals, poor people's fates are decided in "courtrooms where either no one knows the law or only one party—the attorney for the more powerful party—does."[27] This procedural albatross is unfamiliar to many.

The inattention to quotidian realities of state courts and procedure is an example of legal inequality reflecting social hierarchies. The curriculum communicates the idea that federal litigation and its elite concerns represent the most serious form of law, whereas ordinary people's disputes are mundane and unworthy of serious engagement. This is a shame because some students may become lawyers who exploit procedural rules on behalf of their clients and to the detriment of poor people. Others will become public interest lawyers or work in law firms doing pro bono work. In all contexts, procedure matters.

As Stanford law professor Norm Spaulding argues, the remedies to some procedural failures "can best be forged by lawyers who are trained in classrooms that are themselves consistently inclusive of the experiences of ordinary people in the courts."[28] Failing to offer representative experiences of people risks turning procedure into "armchair idealism." Others have helpfully noted that "teaching civil procedure is not just about teaching lawyers to implement civil procedure; it is also about teaching lawyers to be the architects of these legal structures, whether as future judges, leaders of the bar, or democratic citizens."[29] We do them all a disservice by neglecting how this area of law impacts society's most vulnerable.

The Corporate Classroom

But the standard civil procedure class is not merely neglectful of the poor—it also understates how deeply corporate interests shape the procedural terrain. If procedural inequality were a house, one of its sturdiest support beams would be American business. But if you parachuted into the typical civil procedure class, you might not encounter corporate influence as a unifying theme. In reality, business interests have used procedural rules to mount one of the most successful campaigns in American history—one that has raised formidable barriers to holding them legally accountable.

The most generous explanation for the thin treatment of corporate procedural warfare points to professors who want to be ideologically neutral. They may want to avoid putting their thumb on the scale of sociopolitical issues. In the last fifteen years, Occupy Wall Street and Trumpism have helped spawn a populist, antiestablishment ethos that some may want to avoid like the plague. The least charitable reasons point to the backgrounds of civil procedure professors—they are likely to have clerked in 1-percenter federal courts, to practice at a law firm defending big businesses, and/or to teach at a law school with tough-to-untangle commercial ties (i.e., they send a lot of students to medium-sized and large law firms). Whatever the reason, conventional civil procedure casebooks fail to capture the democracy-compromising breadth of corporate procedural influence.

Before we get our fingernails dirty, it's worth noting that my point in this section is not that professors should assume an anticorporate crouch. Many of us work for corporations or businesses masquerading as nonprofit entities (e.g., private universities, hospitals, and cultural institutions). As my colleague Liz Pollman notes, there is a rich diversity within the category of "corporations" that complicates homogeneous ideas about who "benefits" from the Supreme Court's "pro-business jurisprudence."[30] The interests of small and large corporations sometimes align—both benefit when the court makes it harder for employees to sue employers. But other times their interests diverge: When the court shields large foreign manufacturers from liability, small American companies lose out while the foreign giants pop champagne and throw themselves a procedural party. All businesses aren't created equal. My point is about honest accounting.

Corporate influence on civil procedure is undeniable. In the last two decades, Nestlé was accused of aiding and abetting child slavery in Ivory Coast. Shell was accused of colluding in extrajudicial killings, torture, and forced exile of people in Nigeria.[31] These were grave allegations brought before SCOTUS, and both times the court ruled in favor of the corporations. Not because the facts weren't serious, but because the procedure gave it permission to look away. The technicalities mattered more than the terror. The court ruled in both cases that multinational corporations with offices in the US can escape accountability in American courts for serious abuses, so long as the harm occurred abroad. (And more often than not that harm is not going to be in places like Geneva or Tokyo but in countries stretched thin by poverty, corruption, and financial extraction.) Both cases involved core civ pro doctrines being used as gatekeeping devices, but they are not considered civ pro cases; instead, they are exiled to international law and human rights courses in ways that obscure corporate procedural advantages.[32]

Bell Atlantic (now Verizon) helped start a trend of federal courts hazing plaintiffs and prematurely throwing out cases if their legal complaint wasn't airtight.[33] The Supreme Court ruling in their favor created more burdensome requirements for people who wanted to sue. Referring to this case and its progeny, a *Bloomberg* article said the quiet part out loud: "Wall Street banks benefit from tougher suit standards."[34]

Comcast and Walmart made it harder for individual plaintiffs to band together and share the cost of expensive lawsuits via class actions.[35] AT&T, Epic Systems, Murphy Oil, and Ernst and Young not only choked out the possibility of class actions but persuaded the Supreme Court to force victims of consumer fraud and unfair labor practices into individual arbitration and out of court.[36]

And these are just Supreme Court decisions. Some of these SCOTUS cases are part of the civil procedure canon and some are not. To the extent that they and their analogs are discussed, the presentation is likely disaggregated and rarely thematized for what it is: an indelible corporate imprint on procedural rules. These decisions exemplify legal inequality by design—the construction of procedural advantages that appear neutral but favor corporate defendants.

One of the blandest treatments of corporate power comes in discussions of forum selection—the process of deciding where a lawsuit will take place. Forum choice can turn on many factors: the reputations of the possible judges, prior decisions issued by the court, or the convenience of the court to the parties, witnesses, and lawyers.[37] Strategizing over these variables is permissible and tolerated; ethical rules governing lawyers require zealous advocacy, and an attorney who fails to maximize outcomes for their clients by picking an unfavorable forum might be accused of malpractice.[38]

For plaintiffs, this sometimes takes the form of what is called *forum shopping*. *Horizontal forum shopping* occurs when plaintiffs choose among states. Suppose you were injured by a product. You can choose to sue in the state where the company is headquartered (Delaware) or the place where the injury occurred (Texas).[39] If one of those states has a reputation for high jury awards, then your attorney knows what to do. Sometimes, a party might engage in *vertical forum shopping*, which involves choosing between state and federal court. Plaintiffs might prefer a federal court if they think the judges are more predictable or the jury pool will be more diverse. In practice, it takes money and a good lawyer to make these kinds of moves. Corporations and repeat players have more ability to cherry pick their courtroom and reserve the playing field before the match starts.

Any flexibility plaintiffs enjoy is tempered by defendants' *forum-limiting techniques*—tools that either predetermine where a case will be heard or undo plaintiffs' choices after the fact—especially when wielded by corporate defendants against resource-constrained plaintiffs.[40] One tool is the forum selection clause that can be found in contracts that are drafted by corporations and specify where a lawsuit can by filed. The stipulated place is almost undoubtedly expedient for the defendant-corporation but inconvenient for the average Jane, who may not have the money or motivation to file a lawsuit on the other side of the country. They may not be able to engage in the suite of activities that come with filing a lawsuit, such as finding a lawyer in a distant state, traveling, acquiring hotel accommodations, securing witnesses, and taking time off from work/family responsibilities.[41]

As one court noted, *forum selection provisions* can "serve as a large deterrent to the filing of suits by consumers against large corporations."[42] These clauses might be found in a credit card agreement, an insurance policy, a rental agreement, subscription services, cloud storage services, a ticket purchase agreement, and many other common sites. The poor souls who sign them, you and I, may technically consent because of our written/electronic signature. But we may not meaningfully consent because we don't read the terms, we don't understand them, and perhaps most importantly, they are "take it or leave it" contracts where there is little room for negotiation. This means corporations can use their phenomenal bargaining power to procedurally disadvantage plaintiffs before a dispute has even begun.

Mandatory arbitration clauses are similarly restrictive. These provisions often preclude people from bringing their claims in court at all, forcing them instead into private arbitration. The estimates of the Economic Policy Institute suggest that more than half of nonunion private-sector employees are subject to mandatory arbitration agreements. Such clauses favor employers and shut the courthouse doors on a variety of issues: employment discrimination claims, labor law violations, disability rights, and family and medical leave laws. Almost two-thirds of companies with one thousand or more employees have these agreements.[43] Though often praised as being efficient, arbitration can transform procedure from a path to justice into a velvet rope that blocks it.

Another weapon is a procedural process called *removal*, which, as mentioned previously, allows a party to have a state case moved to federal court. Scholars have shown for decades how this process can be used in bad faith to slow down proceedings, drive up litigation costs, and exhaust the financial resources of the poorer party.[44] This is not a recent concern. Writing about the late nineteenth century, legal historian Edward Purcell Jr. describes a procedural atmosphere that bears an uncanny resemblance to the current one. Purcell notes how federal suits "were more inconvenient and expensive" for "poor individual plaintiffs." As a result, "corporations were often able to use removal to exploit those practical burdens and thereby induce individual plaintiffs to abandon their claims or settle them for minimal amounts."[45]

Today and looking forward, the advancement of artificial intelligence that can predict case outcomes based on case type, judge, and jurisdiction raises the specter of digitized gamesmanship.[46] In this world, which we may be in by the time this book publishes, corporations could have better access to accurate prediction tools that will allow them to browse for advantageous courts, give them even more settlement leverage, and widen existing power imbalances between them and everyday folk.

Despite the dramatic consequences that corporate procedural asymmetry has on everyday Americans, it remains neither a prominent nor a unifying theme in many civil procedure casebooks. Some texts cover these issues with detail and clarity, but mostly as doctrinal exercises. Corporate defendants surface, but more as background wallpaper for judicial reasoning than as repeat players actively shaping the terrain. The burden of connecting the dots—that procedural rules can function as corporate bludgeons that reshape access to justice— falls on the most discerning student, or on the professor who strays from the casebook to make the case. In any event, the larger picture of corporate influence often stays offstage.

Surfacing the role of corporations in procedure does not make one anti–big business. Besides being intellectually honest—which is the task of institutions of higher learning—integrating these corporate procedural influences into the course would arguably benefit even mercenary students by making them more equipped to advocate for big corporate clients. It could also encourage them to think early about their duties to future clients and ethical duties to justice. Understanding corporate influence could also benefit people who go on to litigate against large corporations on behalf of small businesses, governments, nonprofits, and public interest organizations. It may have the possibility of dissuading some from becoming corporate lawyers, but that isn't a bad outcome if it helps students make more-informed choices about their futures.

Setting aside what students do when they finish law school, my concern is that many students finish the semester with some technical comprehension of procedural rules but a naïve understanding of how the rules and their interpretations have been shaped by corporate interests. If that's right, it becomes easier to adopt pro-corporate perspectives while being inattentive to the procedural barriers facing poor people and average Americans with legal issues. This is bad for democracy, which is premised, in theory, on the equal application of laws to all people (and corporate entities) as well as the ability of citizens to reliably use the legal system when there is a meritorious dispute.

THIS ISN'T TO CRITICIZE individual professors. Some, like my own civ pro prof, are excellent teachers and work within narrow teaching expectations and traditions to meaningfully educate their students. The deeper forces, of course, are structural—the Supreme Court's narrow interpretations of procedural protections, Congress's reluctance to offset those rulings, and chronic underinvestment in state systems. But whether these forces are raised at all, and how they are framed when they are, still matters. When those structural failures are papered over or treated superficially in the classroom, students lose sight of the procedural struggles that matter most to ordinary, individual litigants. The legal ordeals everyday people face—the looming loss of a home, the need for a restraining order, or the recovery of life-changing cash that the legal system demeans as "small claims"—are kicked to the curb despite procedural relevance.[47]

Civil procedure might sound like academic insider baseball, but most people have a stake in how these rules work, whether you have a bit of money, a good education, or social connections. None of these can fully shield you from institutional power if you get into a legal fight. Corporations have a host of procedural advantages and teams of lawyers who may not fully appreciate how those tools exclude ordinary people, or use them blithely in the name of zealous advocacy. Even when lawyers grasp the exclusionary impact, the business of law and client demands often matter more than broader justice concerns. The course is ultimately a value statement about whose issues deserve months-long procedural attention and whose do not merit discussion. This idea should trouble radical leftists, antiestablishment conservatives, and the everyday Americans in between.

PART II

GOVERNMENT LAWYERING

Preliminary Hearing

Former Congressman Thomas Phillip "Tip" O'Neill Jr. famously said that "all politics are local." While that overstates the case, it captures a truth: Political realities shift dramatically across any state. Houston's multicultural metropolitan politics differ starkly from the small towns of East Texas. North Carolina's eastern shores and Appalachian foothills might as well be in different states. Federal and state politics dominate headlines, but government power is exercised most intimately at the local level: in courtrooms, city halls, and administrative offices. These are the spaces where lawyers make decisions that determine who can access services or vindicate basic rights.

By the time students finish the first year of law school and two more years of electives, government lawyering is just one of several paths they can follow—chosen by about 10 to 12 percent of graduates, making it one of the most popular options after law-firm jobs. My perspective on local government attorneys has been shaped by a series of experiences, each revealing different aspects of how these lawyers operate.

The first lens: public interest experiences. These occasions brought proximity, but they were adversarial and came in concentrated bursts.

The summer after my first year of law school, I felt a gravitational pull back to the Bronx, like I owed my neighborhood a debt. So I went to intern at the Bronx Defenders and carried this new legal knowledge like a fragile gift. It was 2014, shortly after *The New York Times* exposed the crushing case backlogs in Bronx criminal courthouses.[1] I observed prosecutors up close for the first time and saw how routine their work was amid dysfunction.

After graduation, I did a pro bono fellowship at Whitman-Walker, a clinic serving the LGBTQ community in Washington, DC. I was inspired by Berkeley friends who challenged me to think about identity more expansively than my heteronormative upbringing had allowed. In a short amount of time, I saw how DC government attorneys bureaucratized bias—making discrimination in healthcare and public benefits seem like neutral-sounding administrative decisions.

As an appellate fellow at the Legal Aid Society of DC, I watched the city deploy its legal resources to deny help to those already deemed eligible for it.

These experiences offered me a front-row seat to government lawyering, but my view remained limited by my role as an advocate on the other side.

The second lens: academic. Returning to research afforded me some breathing room to see additional dynamics.

As a civil rights scholar and a former resident of many of the cities where these lawyers operate, I began to see more dimensions of their work. On the civil side, they enforce consumer protection and fair housing laws. On the criminal side, many prosecutors take on hate crimes and people who abuse children and elders. But these government lawyers reproduce inequality through dogged defenses of government actors accused of wrongdoing and aggressive prosecutions of individuals that destroy families.

The third lens: teaching legal ethics. I've taught this subject at Penn and Harvard, and each time, students' confusion further highlighted the legal system's contradictions.

The unit on government legal ethics is always the hardest. Students are shocked when prosecutors escape consequences that would end other lawyers' careers. Most have never heard of the municipal attorneys who aggressively defend governments in civil rights cases. Their confusion forced me to articulate contradictions out loud. What does it mean to say prosecutors represent "the state" or that city lawyers represent "the city," when their choices can wreck the lives of the very people those entities are meant to serve?

Together, these experiences convinced me that we need to examine the lawyers who wield *local* power. This is where state violence gets personal. It's where legal theory collides with human consequence.

Like many of you, I follow the news, and things are hectic on a state level. State attorneys general (AGs) are deeply implicated in the inequality this book confronts.

On the Republican side, Georgia's AG charged more than sixty environmental and racial justice activists with RICO violations for protesting a $90 million police training complex in an Atlanta forest—an action that some have described as criminalizing First Amendment–protected dissent under the guise of organized crime. In Texas, the AG weaponized consumer protection laws to investigate groups supporting immigrants, gender-affirming care, and diversity initiatives. None of these investigations was prompted by actual consumer complaints.[2]

On the Democratic side, Michigan's AG dropped remaining criminal charges from the Flint water disaster, which was caused by the state's grossly negligent handling of the city's water supply. Despite poisoned children and elders' deaths, the state's top lawyer decided that this was a "whoopsie" and that nobody was criminally responsible enough to prosecute to the end. California's AG spent years defending a prison system so overcrowded that the Supreme Court had to intervene and tell the state to stop cramming humans into cages like livestock. In 2025, this same office was arguing against mental healthcare for more than four hundred inmates, some of whom were trying to cut and hang themselves while waiting weeks for basic care. The $112 million contempt fine imposed on the state shows how far some lawyers will fight to preserve systems that cause human suffering.[3]

At the federal level, the Trump administration has been relentless in pursuing its agenda, with attorneys enabling the effort. The president's got lawyers running around like repo men, slapping executive orders on anything that moves too freely. Your law firm took the wrong case? Revoke their clearance, flag them for "illegal DEI," and call it national security. Too many minorities at your company? There must be some employment discrimination going on, and the EEOC needs to get involved.

Few sectors or issues are off-limits for the Trump administration and its legal background dancers. Universities that promote frameworks that are inconsistent with the administration's ideological line—especially on race, sex, religion, or American history—get rewarded with politically motivated scrutiny from federal lawyers. Those attorneys are the ones helping design, enact, and defend deportation policies so broad and indifferent to status—citizen, documented, or undocumented—that they resemble ethnic population control with citations and justified formatting. And let's not forget the policies that are executed by lawyers that end up backing a form of liquidation dressed up as liberty—dismantling the welfare state while telling poor people, disabled individuals, and rural students to bootstrap their way to the American Dream.

It's tempting to stay with these stories that dominate the news cycle—they're dramatic, loud, and urgent. But they're not the whole picture.

This book turns elsewhere, not because federal and state power don't matter—they do. But constant focus on them can distort our understanding of government lawyering. Practice, research, and teaching have shown me that some of the most consequential choices happen locally and with the least attention paid to them. Federal lawyering today often mirrors partisan warfare. And state AGs increasingly operate as political actors, driven by ideology, ambition, or both. Focusing on lawyers at those levels risks drawing our attention to the most theatrical forms of public lawyering. I'm interested in more subtle and consistent forms of government power.

This part of the book is about the everyday decisions made by attorneys who shape how government functions. The decisions of these lawyers rarely make headlines beyond city limits. These attorneys live among the people they serve; their choices help determine whose rights are recognized and whose lives are disrupted.

Chapter 8 focuses on prosecutors who help enforce criminal law and are likely to be more recognizable to the average reader, as they appear in the news, social media, and popular culture. They may be familiar, but I'm going to take you behind closed doors to show how they decide who gets a second chance and who spends years buried in the system.

Chapter 9 turns to municipal lawyers, who are less visible, but deeply influential. They represent cities and counties in a range of civil issues. They defend allegations of misconduct by a host of government officials—law enforcement, fire departments, public schools, public hospitals, and social welfare agencies. They sometimes do this while undermining civil rights claims brought by their own residents.

Together, these chapters examine how lawyers caught between public service and institutional loyalty learn to extract legal reasoning from its human cost, making inequality look like sound professional practice.

CHAPTER 8

The Power to Choose: Prosecutors and the Criminal Justice Machinery

Long after "The Bronx Is Burning" faded from national headlines in the 1970s, fires claimed the lives of people in my borough for decades. For those of us who came up in the 1980s and 1990s, no one had to explain the consequences of fire-damaged neighborhoods. We could see it, smell it, and step around it. What we knew bore the stamp of heat—rats darting through what used to be front yards, murals painted over burned brick, and rusted fences shut around overgrown lots. Other cities beset by fires and urban neglect carried similar burn marks. We just had our own version.

Fires—like police sweeps, ambulances, and child welfare inspections—were part of the rhythm of life. When sirens blared through the neighborhood, kids continued with their games uninterrupted unless a truck stopped on their block. But it would not be foreign for moms and community caregivers to do a headcount of those same kids once they heard a firetruck. For those who have witnessed or experienced fire-related loss, the images are hard to shake: ash-streaked faces, neighbors handing out jackets, and families standing outside charred tenements holding whatever precious things they managed to grab.

At the time, I, like many of my neighbors, didn't think about the legal response to all of this. Nor did I think about the role of prosecutors—figures who are rarely connected to such suffering. In fact, people rarely think of fires as legal stories. Once I became a lawyer,

I began to see how prosecutors were part of the picture. Prosecutors decide which fires become crimes and which fade into the background.

Permit me to provide very local examples of how prosecutors can move swiftly when firefighters die but remain still when poor or minority tenants perish.

A short ride on the 4 train separated my childhood home and the place where eight-year-old Jashawn Parker took his final breath at 3569 DeKalb Avenue. Jashawn, who also went by Shawn, was nine years younger than me. He could have been one of the students from the Bronx I happen to teach every year, but he never had that chance.

In August 2002, a fire swept through his apartment. His older brother P.J. was badly burned but ran through the flames to a neighbor's house. P.J. and the neighbor unsuccessfully tried to return to the apartment, where they could hear Jashawn crying and yelling from inside. Jashawn's father, Paul, who lost his wife to asthma seven years prior, was awakened by firefighters banging on his window. Instead of following their instructions to exit the apartment, the Jamaican native went to try to save his sons. But the force of the fire blew him backward. Firefighters pulled him through the window and onto the street, where he began asking everyone about his sons.

Jashawn, remembering a firefighter's lesson given to his class, filled the bathtub with water, got in, and covered his face with a wet cloth. Smoke seeped under the bathroom door. His actions weren't enough to save him. His father was hospitalized with smoke inhalation, and when he was told that Jashawn had died, he went into cardiac arrest and had to be resuscitated. When he got to see his other son, P.J., he was wrapped in bandages from head to toe and, in the words of the senior Paul, "looked like a mummy."[1]

Of course, tragedies happen every day. But here lies a truth that should demand both sorrow and outrage: Jashawn's building was a documented death trap.

It had THREE HUNDRED AND EIGHTY-SEVEN (387) housing code violations before the fire. Tenants regularly complained about gas leaks. There was exposed wiring. Some apartments had no smoke detectors (including the Parkers'). A fan was placed in the basement "to keep the wires from overheating." A year before this fatal fire, two separate Housing Court judges independently documented these problems and issued legal orders requiring the landlord to make repairs, but they were ignored.

The Bronx District Attorney declined to file criminal charges; the case wasn't even referred to the office for prosecution and was deemed "an accidental electrical fire." Why? Because to hold landlords criminally liable, prosecutors would have to show that the landlord's conduct went beyond ordinary negligence (a civil issue) and demonstrated a kind of recklessness or criminal negligence. As Pace University law professor Ralph Stein explained, "It's just not a winning thing for a district attorney.... Simply because a building is not maintained is not enough."[2]

The building's ownership was hidden behind shell companies, but records tied the property to a Westchester real estate developer. As of the last known report, Paul Parker has been unable to prevail in a civil lawsuit. He struggled to find his son's unmarked grave because there was no headstone for Jashawn, and he could not afford one.[3]

Fast forward to January 2005, a day referred to as "Black Sunday" in New York City. Now we're just a few blocks from my childhood home—right down the street from the park where I still sit with my 75¢ morning coffee when I visit the Bronx. Tenants in one building used drywall to subdivide apartments on the third and fourth floors, creating smaller, windowless rooms that they subleased for approximately $300 a month. These rooms cut off access to the fire escape. When two firefighters came to the building to respond to a blaze, they were trapped in this confusing layout and were forced to leap from a fourth-floor window to escape advancing flames. They tragically died.

This time, the Bronx DA sprang into action, charging the tenants who built the partitions and the building's owner. Manslaughter, criminally negligent homicide, and reckless endangerment were on the table. The very office that couldn't be moved by an eight-year-old's death mobilized in full force when firefighters perished.

I could compile an exhaustive index of prosecutions across the country where prosecutors knew how to find criminal negligence in cases where firefighters are killed but were meek in other instances. To be sure, firefighter deaths demand accountability. But so do the deaths of eight-year-old Black children. Accountability can take different forms, whether it's criminal charges or civil judgments; what matters is whether the system treats some lives as worth that effort. The firefighter deaths triggered both prosecution and a $183 million civil award, while Jashawn Parker's death produced neither. The disparity lies not just in outcomes, but in what prosecutors even decide is worth pursuing.

These fires and the responses to them expose some of the aspects of inequality that this book has been pointing to: selective enforcement that pursues some forms of negligence while ignoring others; structural incentives that reward prosecutors for winning certain types of cases while overlooking others; and the powerful language that classifies some preventable deaths as "accidents" beyond criminal law's reach while others are considered crimes demanding justice.

Here is where the plot thickens: Robert Johnson, the Bronx DA during both incidents, is a Black man who grew up in public housing in Harlem, went to high school in the Bronx, and worked as a public defender before becoming a prosecutor. He was acquainted with disadvantage, and like many prosecutors, presumably entered the role with some commitment to the community he serves. Yet under his leadership, the office's divergent responses to these two Bronx fires underscore how prosecutorial discretion operates within powerful institutional contexts. Prosecutors exercise judgment at every stage, but they do so facing genuine constraints—limited resources, institutional expectations about which cases matter, and entrenched patterns of decision making that can channel their discretion in ways that reproduce inequality without deliberate malice.

This chapter examines these figures who possess the tremendous power to decide whom to charge and whom to spare. I'll begin by providing some background context and move on to some scenarios that illustrate the complexity of the work. From there, we'll take a quick tour through the criminal process. Through their daily practice, prosecutors refine the distinctly legal skill, first cultivated in law school, of separating what's morally appalling from what's legally prosecutable.

With the best of intentions, they may focus on which cases are winnable, are resource-efficient, and satisfy institutional allies (e.g., other public servants like cops and politicians); but they may do so to the detriment of marginalized groups. The inequalities run deeper when bias, careerism, or indifference enter the equation. The prosecutor—this vital organ of state power—shows us how inequality courses through the veins of America's legal system.

Some Background Information About Prosecution

Local prosecutors go by many names. The head honcho is usually called the district attorney (DA), county attorney, prosecuting attorney, state attorney, or commonwealth attorney. We'll refer to this person as the DA for now. In most of the country, this is an elected position. The jurisdiction they cover might be a city, county, or judicial circuit (which can include a few cities/counties). Office supervisors sit below DAs. Underneath them are the line attorneys or line prosecutors (aka assistant district or assistant state's attorney). They do the day-to-day work of prosecuting people accused of crimes.

Prosecutors wield breathtaking authority over human freedom. They determine whether a person *should* be charged with a crime and *what* they should be charged with—decisions that set the adjudicative wheels in motion. From there, the prosecutor can decide whether they want to plea bargain and strike a deal with this defendant. They also recommend the kind of punishment defendants should receive. And if they think the judge could have been stiffer with the penalty, the prosecutor can appeal that decision, too. With police as allied powers and overwhelmed defense attorneys as their adversaries, it's not unreasonable to say prosecutors have the juice.

Some critics reduce prosecutors to little more than agents of mass incarceration. There's some truth in that view, but it leaves out the broader reality. Prosecutors work on behalf of battered women, put away murderers and child predators, lock up gangs that terrorize whole neighborhoods, and undeniably contribute to *some* level of public safety.[4] They volunteer at the high schools some of their critics don't step foot in, they go to church/synagogue/mosque with your auntie, and they participate in a range of diversion programs for veterans, sex workers, drug addicts, juveniles, and people with mental health issues.

But the public value prosecutors create and the civic good some strive to deliver can't negate the fact that they feed human beings into criminal justice machinery that cages an extraordinary number of people by global standards. This system operates on legal fictions as simple as case names: *The People v. Defendant*—as if teary-eyed family members begging for noncarceral solutions are not part of "the people." It is one in which defendants can be held hostage and extorted through plea bargains. The years of defendants' lives and the cooperation of self-interested informants—the latter of which are sometimes necessary for convictions—are traded away like commodities in a bureaucratic marketplace of prosecution. This legal apparatus allows two people involved in similar street fights to leave court with radically different outcomes— one is seen as having made a "youthful indiscretion" with a "good future ahead," the other as a receptacle for a "message that has to be sent."

Of course, the blame could be spread more widely.

Legislators pass criminal statutes that prosecutors enforce. They can repeal laws that are enforced discriminatorily or are out of step with community norms. Legislators can even turn something that was a crime into a business opportunity. Marijuana legalization is a case in point: in some states, it has given prosecutors one less thing to worry about.

Police officers hand defendants to prosecutors on a plate. They are the "first movers" who conduct stings, make traffic stops, and respond to 911 calls; there is little prosecutors can do without their investigative help.[5]

Judges determine whether to greenlight or pump the brakes on prosecutor-driven plea bargains. In many states, a judge can dismiss a case "in furtherance of justice" if they think the prosecutor's case is lousy.[6]

But prosecutors merit attention because they stand at the critical juncture where potential becomes actual, where a person's encounter with police can transform into a life-altering journey through the penal system. The charging decision marks the point where discretion gives way to process and the adjudicative wheels of criminal justice are set in motion.

Institutions often bear the imprint of the people empowered to lead them. In prosecution that imprint is demographically unrepresentative. In 2019, 95 percent of elected prosecutors were white, and approximately 75 percent of them were white men.[7] The proportion of women climbed from 18 percent to 24 percent between 2015 and 2019, and the number of women of color increased from an impressive 1 percent to 2 percent during that time period.[8] Of course, many parts of the country are predominantly white, but when one looks locally at counties where minorities constitute 50–60 percent of the population, approximately 80 percent of DAs are white.[9] Comprehensive data on the full composition of these offices is rare, but one study in California found more diverse results: Nearly 69 percent of prosecutors statewide were white (despite comprising 38 percent of the population), and men were 52 percent of prosecutors (compared to 50 percent of the state population).[10]

Demographic unrepresentativeness alone does not tell us much; many of these lily-white prosecutorial offices might consist of white angels. Conversely, being a minority or a woman in that role doesn't ensure justice; just google the critiques of former women of color DAs Anita Alvarez (Chicago) and Jackie Lacey (Los Angeles) to disabuse yourself of prosecutorial racial solidarity. But the overwhelming whiteness and maleness of some of these offices can shape prosecutorial work; it can shape how they assess credibility, consider redeemability, and imagine justice.[11]

The impact of this institutional composition extends beyond defendants to the very communities prosecutors claim to represent.

Angela Davis spent twelve years battling prosecutors as a public defender in Washington, DC, before becoming a law professor and authoring a groundbreaking book on prosecution and inequality. Davis observed how "race and class issues can shape prosecutorial behavior, resulting in cases with poor victims and/or victims of color being prosecuted less zealously than other cases."[12]

Beyond race and class lie cultural and communication barriers.

Davis notes that a "prosecutor may find it easier to communicate with a victim who is highly educated and articulate than with someone who has difficulty expressing himself and may feel intimidated by the court system and its procedures." Such distance—across race, class, and culture—can undermine trust between prosecutors and marginalized communities. This space can limit the kind of intellectual diversity that could inform more nuanced approaches to this work.[13]

Resource constraints on prosecutors' offices also harm the communities they represent. Increasingly, recent graduates are looking askance at prosecutorial gigs. In some places, the pay is dwarfed by the pay in the private sector. For example, in 2021, the starting salary for line prosecutors in Houston was $66,000, whereas a person going to a major law firm in the city could make almost three times that amount and have better prospects for the kind of remote work that recent graduates crave but is not possible in prosecutorial practice.[14]

I regularly speak with students at Penn and other schools who feel a pull toward prosecution and view it as a calling rather than a job. But some have concerns about these salaries, not out of greed, but because they are doing the simple math of rent + debt + the modest dream of stability. Criminal law scholar Adam Gershowitz has highlighted this "prosecutor vacancy" problem.[15] He finds that big cities like Miami, Chicago, and Los Angeles have more than one hundred unfilled prosecutor positions each, whereas smaller cities like Athens, Georgia, and St. Louis, Missouri, have more than *half* of their prosecutorial positions vacant.

Prosecutorial vacancies invite harmful consequences.

Such vacancies can mean that younger prosecutors, who have been described as being more aggressive and punitive, rise up the ranks more quickly.[16] These constraints can intensify the pressure to compartmentalize and reduce complex human situations into manageable legal buckets. It can lead to prosecutors failing to dismiss weak cases (keeping them in the system much longer than necessary), having trouble recognizing which defendants deserve generous plea offers (because the attorney can't adequately investigate facts), and being unprepared or error prone.[17] Guilty people going free and innocent people being locked up are inevitable consequences.

But another institutional problem casts a shadow over this whole chapter: absolute prosecutorial immunity. This privilege, granted by the Supreme Court, protects prosecutors from civil liability even for deliberate misconduct in their advocacy role. It is a legal shield stronger than Superman's skin; it fundamentally alters the prosecutorial environment. Immunity shelters the ethical prosecutor who makes a good-faith error. That's fine. But it also protects the unscrupulous ones who knowingly hide evidence, present false testimony, or pursue charges they know to be baseless. Immunity says they can't be sued.

Professional responsibility rules do not fill this gap. State bar officials—the people tasked with regulating the legal profession—have been pusillanimous when facing prosecutorial misconduct. They can suspend or take the law licenses of prosecutors who violate ethical rules but rarely do so, even in clear-cut cases where prosecutorial misconduct led to reversed convictions. One study found that out of 381 homicide cases where convictions were overturned because prosecutors either concealed evidence of innocence or presented testimony they knew was false, not a *single* prosecutor faced serious professional sanctions.[18] In this part of my legal ethics class, I feel silly relaying to students that the so-called watchdogs of the profession don't bite, bark, or wake up when prosecutors are involved. They just sit curled up in the corner, snoring.

This limited accountability creates a system where prosecutorial misconduct faces few consequences, and certainly nothing resembling what ordinary employees would encounter for comparable errors. It shields the deliberate wrongdoer while subtly informing well-intentioned prosecutors that missteps carry minimal professional cost. The result is a segment of the profession operating with extraordinary power and few external restraints.

This practical reality of prosecution—demographic homogeneity, resource constraints, and immunity—creates the partial backdrop against which many prosecutorial decisions unfold. Daily choices in this environment can etch society's inequalities deeper into the legal landscape.

Navigating Inequality: Prosecutorial Dilemmas

With this foundation about who prosecutors are, the hierarchy they are situated in, and the constraints they navigate in mind, we can now explore the deeper tension at the heart of their work: how even well-intentioned prosecutors can become vehicles for inequality. It's too easy to focus on the obvious cases—the vindictive prosecutors who hide evidence or display overt bias. The more challenging reality to confront is how ordinary decision-making by reasonable prosecutors, operating within normal parameters, reproduces inequality. This section is about that quieter, more insidious dynamic. If you grant me this premise—that inequality can be reproduced by the reasonable and in the absence of malice—then the rest of the argument becomes easier to see.

Recall the six forms of legal inequality that we discussed in the introduction and that will reappear throughout the practice-focused chapters of this book. We'll examine them through the kind of hypotheticals I pose to my legal ethics students. These scenarios are drawn from situations that play out in prosecutors' offices across the country. Feel free to annotate or just vibe. You're not being graded.

As you read each one, resist the impulse to default to simple answers of leniency or maximum enforcement. Such dilemmas sometimes defy easy solutions, with different options carrying consequences that can ripple through communities. These six scenarios will illuminate patterns that recur throughout the prosecutorial process—from charging decisions to sentencing recommendations—and set the stage for our examination of how criminal cases actually move through the system. Pay attention not just to the prosecutor's dilemma in each scenario, but to how the very structure of their choices can lead to problematic outcomes. If the issues feel hard, let the discomfort do some of the teaching. And if they don't—if the answers feel too obvious—that might be worth sitting with, too.

1. Legal Inequality as a Reflection of Society—How legal systems mirror existing social hierarchies: Two eighteen-year-olds are caught with a few grams of coke. One works at a grocery store. The other is a freshman at an elite university—like the subjects in the book *Dorm Room Dealers*, which explores how rich students peddle drugs on college campuses and face minimal consequences.[19] The prosecutor's diversion program requires participants to attend weekly therapy sessions, complete forty hours of community service, and pay for mandatory drug education classes—requirements that the college student can more easily meet with parental support. If the prosecutor exercises their discretion uniformly, only the wealthy teen gets a break, but if an exception is made for the working teen, then the prosecutor can be accused of being "woke" and "abandoning equal treatment under the law." What should a prosecutor do when the same rules give better outcomes to those with more money and reinforce the advantage of wealth?

2. Legal Inequality as Discursive Power—How legal language transforms and controls narratives: A prosecutor prepares an opening statement in a case where the defendants allegedly assaulted someone, leaving the victim with significant injuries. The evidence points to some kind of planning and the police report uses terms like "known associates" and "street organization." Anthropologist Robin Conley studies legal language in courtrooms and suggests that prosecutors can "dehumanize defendants and often do so through their linguistic choices."[20] In this case, using terms like *gang* or *crew* or *pack* would likely influence the jury's perception and increase the chance of a conviction. Avoiding those terms might make the case look like typical teenage stupidity. This dilemma might look like ordinary courtroom work—and that's precisely the point. If the tongue is, in fact, mighty, how should the prosecutor aim their linguistic weapon?

3. Legal Inequality as Selective Enforcement—How laws are applied differently across groups: Disorderly conduct citations are issued to a group of protesters who gathered at the downtown plaza after an episode of police brutality. They are engaged in some disruptive behavior: loud chanting, street gathering, and blocking traffic for hours. But sports fans who were celebrating a championship win the previous week engaged in similar conduct and faced no threat of punishment. Each group had similar-sized crowds, but the media describes the protestors as "agitated" and the activity as a "potentially dangerous disruption." Notwithstanding some celebrants' public intoxication, overturning trash cans, and climbing parked cars, the sports celebration was "civic pride," with some cops seen high-fiving fans. The prosecutor could process all the protest-related charges (reinforcing a double standard), dismiss them all (risking criticism for excusing public disorder), or develop a policy that addresses when disorderly conduct merits criminal charges (potentially alienating officers who control his investigations). What's a prosecutor to do when identical behaviors are considered acceptable celebration or criminal disorder depending on who's doing them?[21]

4. Legal Inequality by Design—How laws and regulations explicitly encode disparities: A woman is arrested after defending herself in a domestic dispute and is charged with assault. In a different case, a man is charged with the same offense. They are presumed innocent until proven guilty. The prosecutor recommends $5,000 bail for both. The woman can't afford that amount, so she stays in jail and misses work. She risks eviction and being separated from her children. The man can afford bail and is able to leave. The law is not malfunctioning, but it is encoding inequality by linking freedom to wealth (and in this case, compounding deeper gender dynamics). If the law perpetuates such disparities by design, what moral duty, if any, does the prosecutor have to avoid amplifying such inequality?

5. Legal Inequality as a Structural Imperative—How professional roles require perpetuating disparities: A prosecutor has damning bodycam footage of an officer shooting an unarmed teenager in the back. The video is shaky and partially obscured; it looks bad, but the crucial moment is unclear. The only witness has a history of run-ins with the police and gave inconsistent statements. The public is demanding the tape's release, and rumors are spreading. The prosecutor's boss needs police union support for reelection, and no officer has ever been charged locally. Pursuing charges risks career suicide and police cooperation on hundreds of other cases. Declining to prosecute despite available evidence sends the unmistakable message that protecting law enforcement trumps holding them accountable. As Professor Kate Levine explains, the close relationship between prosecutors and police creates a profound structural conflict when police become suspects. What's a prosecutor to do when ambiguous evidence, political pressure, and structural dependence on the police all collide?[22]

6. Legal Inequality as Contested Advocacy—How competing definitions of justice can reinforce disparities: A reform-minded prosecutor implements a policy declining to prosecute low-level drug possession cases, citing evidence of racially disparate enforcement. This decision immediately generates competing claims about justice. Civil rights groups celebrate it as an overdue recognition of discriminatory policing, but the police union and some minority elders condemn her for "abandoning" these communities to dealers and public drug use that compromises quality of life. Recovery advocates argue that without the pressure of criminal charges, many people with substance use disorders will never seek help. But the civil liberties groups counter that coerced treatment is just another system of control. Everyone's shouting about "justice" and "equality," each with their own definition. How does she navigate these competing visions of fairness when there's no version of "equal" that everyone agrees on?

These six scenarios illustrate some of the complex trade-offs inherent in prosecutorial work—moments where discretion intersects with existing social hierarchies and power dynamics. Reasonable people may disagree passionately about the right and wrong approach to these dilemmas. That is fine. What is important is understanding that these are decision points where inequality can become more deeply ingrained in the system without intent to discriminate. Bear this in mind as we move to a different terrain and I give you a brief tour of prosecution. The bias fest that you are about to see could result from intentional prejudice or the routine mechanics of prosecutorial work. Either way, inequality persists.

This is a journey most would rather never experience firsthand, but instead through the safe distance of film, television, and streaming services. It's not lost on me that my ability to narrate has been granted by way of degrees and legal training, and not by the statistical probabilities that haunted me throughout my youth. A Black male body like mine is more likely to be processed by this system than to interrogate it—to be in a defendant's chair as opposed to at a podium. That's a tension that doesn't leave me—it lingers behind the ideas I wrestle with, the words I speak, and the lines I write. It's a truth worth laying down before we proceed into the maze of prosecution.

As your guide, I'll navigate you through some of the scholarship on prosecutors—a body of work that is immense enough to fuel countless podcasts and documentaries. The research terrain we'll traverse is contested, but beneath the academic quibbling and career-making empirical claims lies a stubborn reality: As cases move through the system, prosecutorial choices accumulate into outcomes that mirror society's deep divisions. To be sure, this isn't the full itinerary—just a few stops: the charging desks where futures are fixed in minutes, the jury rooms where Black and Brown people are pushed out with precision, the courtrooms where prosecutors can lean on loaded narratives, and the post-conviction hearings where they resist revisiting old wrongs.

From Being Cuffed to Sentencing

Step inside the American criminal legal system—the most efficient human processing facility in the developed world. Our first stop is the charging desk, where futures are spared or destroyed. After handcuffs have been applied and booking photos taken, a line prosecutor, sometimes called an *intake attorney*, reviews the file and determines whether to file a charge or pass on prosecution (called *declination*). Theoretically this is where prosecutors could serve as a check on law enforcement and defective police work, but sometimes they do not.

In the misdemeanor world, declination rates hover around a measly 5 percent, which means prosecutors are mostly rubber-stamping police decisions that criminalize racial minorities for low-level offenses such as "trespassing, loitering, disorderly conduct, jaywalking, and traffic violations."[23] The Vera Institute studied the New York district attorney's office, which houses more than five hundred prosecutors and is located in what was known as the racialized stop-and-frisk capital of the country.[24] Vera found that the office "prosecutes nearly all cases brought by the police."[25]

How and what prosecutors actually charge people with is a different story. Some research suggests that prosecutors are not the grand wizards they are made out to be. For example, one randomized control experiment asked a group of prosecutors to examine hypothetical cases and make charging decisions. The researchers found that race had no detectable prejudicial effects on their decisions.[26] A recent computational approach to this issue automatically removed race information from case files in one prosecutor's office and came to the same conclusion: no disparate treatment in charging.[27] Another found that North Carolina prosecutors—both white and Black—*reduce* racial disparities by giving less weight to Black defendants' prior convictions when charging cases, challenging assumptions about prosecutorial discretion and inequality.[28]

These findings are juxtaposed against a buffet of scholarship that finds racial differences in charging. In Michigan, defendants of color were charged with crimes carrying a maximum sentence that was 2.15 months longer than white defendants in similar circumstances—a gap rooted partly in which cases police bring forward.[29] In a system that chews people up by the minute, two extra months for being Black or Latino isn't a rounding error.

In Arkansas, Black defendants were more likely to be initially charged with a more severe offense than white defendants. Let me break that down. Two high school students get caught hacking into their school's Wi-Fi to delay a test. Arkansas's computer crime law gives prosecutors options: They can charge the offense as a misdemeanor or escalate it to a class C felony. The white student gets the lower charge. The Black student gets the felony. That bump changes everything—from plea deals to future job applications. Same keystrokes, different consequences.[30]

Massachusetts researchers controlled for all kinds of variables: criminal history, neighborhood, education, income—everything short of zodiac sign and favorite pizza topping. They found that Black and Latino defendants STILL received longer sentences than similarly situated white counterparts. The type and severity of the charge—the dominion of prosecutors—accounted for 70 percent of these disparities. That 70 percent reflects front-loaded disparity: harsher charges, not harsher judges, are doing much of the damage.[31]

Scaling up to meta-analysis, a statistical method used to aggregate and synthesize multiple studies, is instructive. One meta-analytic review of more than twenty-six separate quantitative studies found that minority offenders had an approximately 9 percent higher likelihood of being charged or fully prosecuted than white offenders.[32] The weight of empirical studies suggests, at a minimum, that race-based charging by prosecutors is not a blue-moon rarity.

With the charge behind us, we enter the next stretch: a series of legal checkpoints on the road to what might become a trial (or, more likely, a plea).

The first option is a case being dismissed after the formal charge. Researchers in Denver and New York have found that Black defendants are more likely to have their cases dismissed. This might look like prosecutorial leniency, but this finding could also be a byproduct of shitty cases that should have never made it past the screening phase.[33] This is the guy arrested for trespassing outside his own apartment because he forgot his key—even after neighbors vouched for him. After a night in jail, a few missed days of work, weeks of waiting, and some lost dignity, a prosecutor finally looks at the file and says, "Oops."[34]

Pretrial diversion is another possibility. This is when prosecutors funnel defendants out of the adjudicative process and toward community-based programs (e.g., community service, drug rehabilitation, victim restitution). A study of pretrial diversion found that prosecutors were more likely to grant these blessings to white defendants than Black and Latino defendants with similar legal characteristics.[35]

Next we move to the bargain basement where plea deals are made. Plea bargaining is the main event of adjudication. In one notable study of Wisconsin, white defendants were 25 percent more likely than Black defendants to have their principal initial charge dropped or reduced to a lesser crime during this phase. When charged with a felony, they were also 15 percent more likely to be convicted of a misdemeanor (punishable only up to a year).[36] Similar results have been found in Florida and New York.[37] In these moments, some get a slap on the wrist—others get the full fist of the state.

There's another backdoor, if you know the password. Deferred judgments are tied to pleas and dismissals; these allow defendants to have cases discarded or have serious charges dropped if they comply with agreed-upon conditions. This is a prosecutor saying, "We'll pretend this never happened—just stay clean for a year." In Denver, white defendants were more than twice as likely to get that deal than Black or Latino defendants.[38]

Down one hallway—if there's no plea and the person opts for a jury over a judge—we arrive at the room where jurors are picked. Here is where the American tradition of discrimination in jury selection rears its ugly face. Racial discrimination in juries has been a problem since powdered wigs were in legal fashion. The Supreme Court tried to prohibit race-based jury exclusion in 1880, but almost 150 years later it is still a problem.[39] In modern jury selection, *preemptory strikes* allow the prosecution and the defense to reject potential jurors without stating a reason. State and federal law prohibit the use of race as a factor, but it happens anyway. If you were a mind-reading fly in a room where jury selection took place, the levels of bias you witness might border *Saturday Night Live* satire territory.

Empirical analyses of jury selection in California provide evidence of racial inequality. Researchers analyzed almost three decades of DA training manuals and found that prosecutors were encouraged to strike jurors based on their clothing, hairstyles, and body language. These materials nudged prosecutors into selecting the ideal juror—people who were "stable" and "professional" while avoiding "less educated people and blue-collar workers."[40]

What was the byproduct of such norms? In seven hundred cases spanning twelve years, researchers found that prosecutors removed

Black jurors 72 percent of the time and Latino jurors 28 percent of the time. At the same time, Asian American jurors were struck less than 3.5 percent of the time, and white jurors got the boot only 0.5 percent of the time. Jury discrimination does damage on two fronts: Minority defendants are more easily denied their right to a jury of their peers, and communities are shut out of a core civic duty.

Some of the reasons racial minorities were struck from juries were seemingly neutral. Many prosecutors excluded potential jurors because of their distrust of the legal system or because they had family who had prior contact with law enforcement. That makes sense, especially if a cop is your star witness. If I were a prosecutor, I wouldn't want myself on a jury; juror Shaun would ruin the entire process. But given what we know about racial distrust of the legal system and the disproportionate contact minorities have with cops, screening out on those bases will inevitably be discriminatory.[41] Indeed, in many jurisdictions, expressing the belief that the criminal justice system treats minority defendants unfairly can get a person struck *for cause*, with judicial approval. As a result, juries are purged of people whose skepticism is rooted in racialized experience and might otherwise check official narratives.

Another set of reasons had clear racial context. Prosecutors excluded people because they had dreadlocks, were from the minority neighborhoods of East Oakland or Compton, or because they wore short skirts and "blinged out sandals."[42] This is just California. Research across the Deep South and Mid-Atlantic has found similar disparities. There are reported cases across the country involving Black jurors being removed because they lived in a "bad zip code" (Maryland), were "heavily tattooed" (North Carolina), had gold teeth (Alabama), or "looked like a drug dealer" (Louisiana).[43]

Language poses a unique, additional challenge for prospective jurors. A 1991 Supreme Court decision permits prosecutors to strike bilingual, Spanish-English speaking jurors (out of a concern that they would not defer to a court interpreter's translation).[44] This means some Latino individuals can be excluded because of pretextual reasons *and* because they are bilingual. The result? Jurors can be excluded for linguistic abilities that might enhance their understanding of a case.

After a jury is empaneled, the next step is trial. The opening statement is a vital moment in which lawyers set the stage and frame the narrative. The thirst to prevail and seek justice can cause government attorneys to lean into explicit racial language that inflames a jury, like the time a prosecutor unnecessarily noted a sexual assault victim's "pasty white" skin tone and the defendant's "dark penis going into a white body."[45] Subtle, though no less gratuitous, language is more common, which brings to mind the case where the "very first words uttered by [the] prosecutor" were references to Latino defendants as "cockroaches."[46] The use of racist rhetoric was so problematic that California passed a law in 2020 prohibiting the state from convicting anyone subject to "racially discriminatory language" by a prosecutor, but the law is *still* violated.

On the other end of the trial, the closing argument is where the government's attorneys can leave a lasting impression before jury deliberation begins. Again, prosecutors have played on racial prejudice in scores of cases: by singing the Confederate anthem at the close of an African American defendant's trial,[47] by using the term "Mexican ounce" to describe 25 ounces of heroin,[48] and by letting jurors know that it is "every mother's nightmare" to "leave your daughter for an hour and a half, and you walk back in, and here's some black, military guy on top of your daughter."[49] One court dealt with a prosecutor's mocking of Black speech and repeated references to law enforcement as the "po-leese." It explained the problem of provocative prosecutorial rhetoric nicely: "arguments based upon racial, ethnic and most other stereotypes are antithetical to and impermissible in a fair and impartial trial."[50]

Even when a case is finished and a person has been convicted, the specter of biased prosecutors remains. Some have highlighted how senior attorneys, despite being in a position to correct past errors, resist reconsidering evidence of innocence after conviction.[51] Professor Laurie Levenson is a former prosecutor who runs Loyola's Project for the Innocent, a twenty-five-year-old clinic that serves Los Angeles and has freed almost seven hundred people. In her dealings with the Los Angeles DA, Levenson finds that confirmation bias, conflicts of interest (e.g., being buddy-buddy with the trial prosecutor responsible for a potentially wrong conviction), and gut instincts about guilt often make senior attorneys unwilling to reassess cases involving defendants claiming innocence.[52] Such stubbornness potentially calcifies bias that may have occurred earlier in the process.

And to put a cherry on top, when inmates seek parole in California, racial disparities in outcomes have been attributed to prosecutorial opposition.[53] Post-conviction resistance reflects a structural imperative within prosecution—the system often encourages standing by prior decisions even when evidence suggests otherwise. This can produce an environment in which preserving the office's image matters more than correcting mistakes. Ultimately, what looks like resolve is sometimes a toxic combination of institutional self-preservation, assembly-line case management, bias, and tunnel vision regarding what constitutes "public safety." The system discourages looking backward, often leaving the original errors intact—errors that disproportionately affect the least powerful communities.

As our journey through some of the stations of the prosecutorial process reveals, this isn't merely about isolated mistakes but a repeated pattern of disadvantage at different points—where case-by-case judgments create population-level disparities. What emerges from our examination of prosecutors is a window into their considerable decision-making power. Their choices about which injustices to pursue and which to ignore—much like those contrasting responses to the Bronx fires—shape not just case outcomes but our collective understanding of justice itself and whose lives truly matter under law.

OUR TOUR ENDS HERE, but the story doesn't. A number of prosecutors recognize some of these problems but are attacked on multiple fronts: by conservative governors and attorneys general who believe these progressives are engaged in public safety–compromising nonperformance of their jobs; by minority communities who believe that they are too permissive when it comes to crime; and by line prosecutors who are resistant to progressive change and try to undermine their bosses.[54]

Ultimately, reform prosecutors face resistance because they are trying to rework a machine that haphazardly dispenses justice. These disparities emerge not just from deliberate cruelty, though that exists too. They emerge through sedimented habits, institutional defaults, and gut decisions that seem normal because they match the social hierarchies we've been taught to accept.

In law school and on the job, prosecutors learn to slice life into legal pieces and human pieces. One prosecutor I talked to called it "emotional triage"—you focus on the facts, evidence, and the law, not the biography. This approach is understandable as a coping mechanism. The volume of human suffering would overwhelm anyone who fully absorbed each case, especially when you've got one hundred cases and only so much heart to go around. But this necessary distance exacts a heavy price: It enables some of the disparities we've observed at every stage of prosecution. The point is not that prosecutors should personally carry every biography into court, but that a system built on bracketing out human context allows inequality to persist unchecked.

What makes prosecutorial inequality so difficult to dislodge is it operates on autopilot; it requires no special effort to maintain. It only requires the absence of active resistance. Meanwhile, challenging disparities demands more than good intentions. It requires sustained work against what might feel normal and efficient; it can involve resistance that brings side-eyes from colleagues. Let's be honest: How many of us can say we'd choose the harder path in our professional lives when conformity offers a safer harbor and sometimes rewards? The difference, of course, is that prosecutors *voluntarily* stepped into roles that determine freedom and confinement. Absent conscious resistance, the machinery of prosecution can transform even the most noble intentions into instruments of the status quo.

CHAPTER 9

Municipal Matters: The Hidden Civil Power of County Counsel and City Hall Attorneys

A CONFESSION: I've lived in the biggest cities in the country—New York, LA, Chicago, Philadelphia, Washington, DC—and for decades, I moved through them with a privileged oblivion.

I thought I understood exclusion by way of my own race, class, and gender. But I walked those streets like someone the city had made room for. The drop from the curb to the street didn't slow me down. The gap between the train and the platform didn't stop me. The bus pulled up close enough for me to board.

It wasn't until I hit my late twenties that I understood the Americans with Disabilities Act (ADA) wasn't some abstract promise but the product of struggle—born from court battles over being shut out of restrooms and blocked at entrances that had no intention of welcoming. It exists because people bled, sued, organized, and refused to disappear.

It took me longer to understand that while many lawyers work to advance civil rights issues like access, some municipal attorneys—working for the very cities we move through—have played a steady role in narrowing those guarantees of equality.

I now understand that some of this unawareness was not just personal but collective. Not just legal, since most people don't know what municipal lawyers do, but something more ordinary and cultural—a quiet consensus that allows many to navigate spaces without registering the violence they can inflict on others.

What makes my ignorance particularly shameful? Evidence surrounded me since I was coming up, but I was unable to connect the dots.

My mother told me how she and other women in her age cohort gave birth under something called "disability leave." Not maternity leave—disability. Even in a unionized job, that was one of the primary mechanisms for leave before the passage of various state and federal family and medical leave laws (and, as a general matter, it continues to be in many workplaces). The leave was short and shaped by policies that treated pregnancy as a brief medical condition rather than a sustained need for care. I filed this example away as one of many early feminist legal lessons—this one shelved under how the law draws hard lines around which bodies it's willing to accommodate.

Meanwhile, my father drove a taxi every day until his body said no. He was physically capable of movement but unable to work those shifts, forcing him onto Social Security disability benefits. I saw my father's struggle as personal hardship, not recognizing how municipal lawyers nationwide were crafting arguments that would make his world smaller if he ever needed to navigate it in a wheelchair.

There were people in the neighborhood—the ones some joked about, pitied, or avoided. The ones everyone called crazy. The man lying down in front of buses, blocking traffic for hours. The woman telling elaborate conspiracy theories to anyone who'd listen. The guy having full conversations with adversaries that only he could see. Back then, I saw spectacle. I didn't understand that these people might have untreated mental illness and nowhere to go. Or maybe these were their survival strategies—perhaps they believed, maybe rightly, that being visibly unwell was the only way to get shelter or qualify for benefits. I definitely didn't think about the city attorneys working behind the scenes—drafting and defending the ordinances that made those people's public presence a crime.

I spent eight years getting a JD and PhD at Berkeley, the literal birthplace of the modern disability rights movement. I watched the paratransit vans pull up to campus. Saw folks using text-to-speech software. Heard the word *neurodivergent* and nodded like I understood. But I didn't. Not fully. Even there, surrounded by innovation, I missed the urgency and the history. The ramp had a backstory. The curb cut wasn't generous—it was fought for.

There wasn't one big moment when it all clicked. No lightbulb. Just a slow stacking of stories and experiences.

Doing intake at the Legal Aid Society of the District of Columbia and representing clients with disabilities forced me to confront what I'd been able to ignore: how the built environment, often reinforced by the state, shuts some people out. Seeing longtime neighbors back home navigate broken infrastructure made those structural failures harder to overlook and more concrete.

Then came friendships with disability scholars and women of color on my faculty—Jasmine Harris, from the Bronx like me, who helped me understand how and why so many people back home were living with chronic illness without ever naming it. Karen Tani, who cotaught a law and inequality class with me, helped me see dimensions of ableism I'd never considered. They didn't force it. They just kept pointing. And eventually, I followed.

Teaching my own courses on antidiscrimination law and social welfare law pushed me beyond the comfortable race-class-gender trinity I'd relied on to explain everything and into something messier but truer—a fuller sense of how law maps itself onto flesh in all its variations. It also helped me see cities and municipal lawyers—the subject of this chapter—much differently.

I can't experience cities the same way anymore.

Walking through the poor, Black, and Puerto Rican parts of Philadelphia feels different. East of 52nd Street, where "Penntrification" takes hold, the streets are smooth, the sidewalks are scrubbed, and the infrastructure is cared for by university, city, and private dollars. Cross over to the side where I get my hair braided, and the investment fades. The concrete buckles. There are fewer ramps. On that side, the message is unmistakable: This part of the city can wait.

When I go back to Washington, DC, I remember the broken

elevators at Dupont Circle station. The alternative to the nonfunctional lift was navigating the longest escalator I've ever seen in my life while officials posted signs directing wheelchair users to stations miles away, as though their time held no value.

The truth is that American cities weren't built to include. That exclusion isn't just architectural; it's legal. It shows up in the arguments municipal lawyers make, the technicalities they lean on, and the hidden calculations that treat some lives as negotiable. This chapter is about those lawyers—the largely invisible actors inside local government whose everyday work shapes civil rights on the ground, often by defending systems that keep certain people out.

A few legal disputes across the country offer a window into how that plays out.

As I WRITE, a federal lawsuit is unfolding where I grew up in the Bronx. The complaint describes how pedestrian pathways are "frequently inaccessible due to parked vehicles that block curb cuts and intersections." The lawsuit catalogues the obstacles faced by bodies that move with care or pain: "trash cans, debris, cracks in the pavement, level changes greater than a quarter of an inch, potholes, and narrow pathways."[1]

Los Angeles had its own accessibility nightmares, especially down in South Los Angeles, where I lived as a carless adult who watched the pavement betray people every day. In that driver-first culture, sidewalks were an afterthought—narrower, more broken, and less maintained than New York's janky paths. Between 2010 and 2020, the city recorded 1,133 pedestrian deaths—second highest in the nation. That isn't a coincidence. When you force vulnerable people into traffic, you've built a killing floor.

In Arlington, Texas, where pickup trucks barrel past pedestrians, wheelchair users described the terrible choice between impossible sidewalks and deadlier streets. As the complaint states, even common sidewalk issues, such as a crack or a slope, can "impede the progress of a wheelchair, damage a wheelchair, or increase the possibility of overturning a wheelchair and seriously injuring its passenger."[2] Feel that fear in those words—the daily terror of navigating spaces built as if you don't exist.

This is not randomized urban decay or urban planning. It is legal inequality as a reflection of society—the physical manifestation of which bodies are deemed worthy of free movement through public space. When people with disabilities took these issues to court looking for justice, not charity, what did they get? A legal stone wall. Municipal lawyers showed up to protect this broken system.

Let's start with the basics: Title II of the ADA says local governments can't discriminate against people with disabilities in any of their "services, programs, or activities." Those services include various things that the government helps provide: public buildings, buses, schools, parks, and sidewalks that help people access public life.

At one point, seventy-six California cities argued that sidewalks weren't covered by the ADA.[3] Not because this was the correct legal argument, but because it would relieve them of liability. The Los Angeles city attorney's office and its privately retained counsel tried to make that hackneyed argument. They could have resolved the problem much earlier, but they fought the plaintiffs for years. It took an L in federal court for them to ultimately agree to $1 billion in sidewalk improvements.

Arlington gave us the remix: years of procedural roadblocks while wheelchair users risked their lives crossing streets with no ramps. When the city finally settled, the city attorney had the gall to say, "This is good for the residents." As if they hadn't spent seven years insisting those same residents didn't matter.

And New York? The lawyers tried something colder. They argued that a previous settlement—one they'd failed to fully implement—blocked new lawsuits. Let that sink in: Their own failure, in some ways, became their defense.

This isn't loud cruelty. It's slow harm. It wears a suit and whispers in legal code. These municipal lawyers weren't spitting ableist slurs. This is legal inequality as a structural imperative. These attorneys were fulfilling their professional obligation to zealously represent their client (the city), even when that representation required fighting against the basic rights of disabled people. That's what makes some of their work so dangerous and worthy of exposure.

And yet—many of these same lawyers are also the reason cities function at all. The park where your kid plays? A municipal lawyer negotiated the land use. Does your toilet flush clean? A county attorney drafted the regulations. The water we drink, the public transportation we use, and the electricity/gas that make our coffee are all partly results of their handiwork. Some of these lawyers work to expand access.

They sometimes draft and enforce local ordinances that go beyond federal civil rights protections and design programs that include rather than exclude. Without the work of municipal lawyers, urban life would fray. There would be bars with no licenses. Construction with no oversight. Public events with no safety rules. They hold the seams of the city together. Honestly, they deserve their own Netflix special—because most people, including lawyers, have no idea how much of city life rests on their steady, often invisible labor.

But this isn't a love letter or a promotional brochure. It is a book about inequality. And we have to confront how the same lawyers who make cities function also help make them hostile, especially to those who need protection most.

These sidewalk battles are just one corner of a much bigger map. In the pages ahead, we take a tour, city by city, following the work of municipal attorneys. We'll see them defending police brutality in one city, fighting housing justice in another, and blocking other civil rights demands across the urban map of America. This chapter is a tour through that legal landscape, where the role of the lawyer is not always to repair, but to protect what already is. It's a kind of work that often requires—and rewards—professional distance, even when real people bear the cost.

Police Misconduct

Social contract theory tells us that we consent to be governed in exchange for certain benefits. Some scholars would go further than that and say the government works for the people. But when I teach the required professional responsibility course that students take in their second or third year, I have to remind my students that legal ethics rules say that the governmental entity or official is the client of these lawyers, not us. The New York City Law Department might say that it "prosecutes and defends lawsuits in the name of the City of New York, its agencies and citizens," but its legal obligations are to the City of New York as a legal entity and officers who act on its behalf.[4] In this regard, municipal lawyers perform functions that are essential to governance. They provide counsel to municipalities, but they are caught in an insurmountable contradiction because their work can destroy lives while keeping the city lights on.

Although the chapter opened with a discussion about access issues, we'll begin our tour of municipal lawyering by focusing on their defense of police misconduct, before circling back to disability rights and concluding with housing justice.

Cases involving police brutality receive the most media attention, making them particularly visible examples of municipal legal work. By examining their approach to these high-profile matters, we can identify an abbreviated playbook of three strategies that municipal lawyers sometimes employ: first, their unapologetic defense of practices later ruled unlawful; second, their negotiation of settlements that avoid admissions of wrongdoing while limiting financial exposure; and third, their weaponization of procedural technicalities to defeat otherwise valid claims. This three-part playbook appears not just in police cases but across various civil rights challenges, from sidewalk accessibility disputes to housing justice litigation.

Government lawyers exacerbate social inequalities when they defend certain types of police brutality claims. Of course, the singular act of representing the government in these cases is not inherently problematic. Public agencies and officials are big targets, and any judicial clerk can tell you about the frivolous lawsuits filed by conspiracy theorists, serial litigants, and opportunistic plaintiffs' attorneys. I'm not talking about these kinds of cases. I'm focused on instances in which there is no question about whether a social harm occurred.

I'm about to fly you through a tour of cases from New York to Chicago to Phoenix—cities with hundred-plus-lawyer municipal departments. Some might dismiss this as cherry-picking the worst examples. But that objection ignores a crucial organizational reality. Some big cities have ENTIRE DIVISIONS dedicated to fighting civil rights claims that hide behind benign-sounding names like "Federal Civil Rights Litigation" or "Government Advice Practice Group." In 2024, municipal lawyers in Chicago handled 122 cases involving payouts for false arrest, excessive force, extended detention, malicious prosecution, and illegal searches.[5] That's two cases per week. For THOSE lawyers, what I am about to describe isn't an exception; it's a Tuesday morning staff meeting. Defense of government officials who engage in constitutionally offensive behavior is part of the job description.

I'm not letting smaller cities slide either. We're going to take the Greyhound to East Cleveland and Camden, places where attorneys don't have the privilege (if you want to call it that) of just focusing on police brutality cases. They are juggling everything from trash collection contracts to sidewalk permits to excessive force lawsuits all at once. The caseloads may vary, but the same playbook strategies can be deployed, whether lawyers work from gleaming downtown offices or county buildings where the AC breaks every summer.

Defending Illegal Stuff: Government attorneys exacerbate social inequalities when they defend certain kinds of police brutality claims involving Section 1983—a federal law that allows citizen to sue public officials. I'm focused specifically on the defense of practices that courts later determined were flatly illegal. These are instances in which attorneys had to know, or should have known that they were defending unsupportable positions.

The New York City Law Department has a Special Federal Litigation division that focuses on police, prosecutor, and correctional officer misconduct. The team has approximately one hundred lawyers, enough to be its own boutique law firm.[6] This city spent years fighting tooth and nail to preserve and defend racially discriminatory policing.

Operation Clean Halls ran from 1991 to 2015 and it involved dirty tactics. The program allowed the NYPD to patrol certain apartment buildings and arrest people for trespassing. When I was coming up in the Bronx, these were the buildings where a lobby could easily transform into an interrogation room, and stairwells became checkpoints. An expert found that in one year alone, 60 percent of the close to two thousand stops were unjustified.[7] A full 100 percent of the stops involved Black and Brown people. Some were getting arrested for trespassing in buildings that they lived in!

By 2011, something extraordinary happened in the Bronx. Assistant District Attorney Jeannette Rucker investigated the NYPD's trespass arrests in Clean Halls buildings. She found that they were routinely violating people's constitutional rights and judges were throwing these cases out. The DA sent official memos that basically told the NYPD, "you can't do this anymore" and "stop bringing us these illegal arrests."

As the last chapter explained, prosecutors depend on cops. Prosecutors can't do their jobs without police cooperation. As the presiding judge put it, "It is no small matter when an ADA publicly suggests that the NYPD has been engaged in a recurring pattern of unlawful stops."[8] No kidding. This is like the CFO publicly announcing the company's books are cooked.

How did the New York City Law Department respond? Its lawyers suggested that the ADA "invented the problem of unlawful Clean Halls trespass stops" under pressure from public defenders and to "lessen the Bronx DA's caseload."[9] Think about what that means.

Municipal attorneys were so committed to defending unconstitutional police practices that they were willing to publicly accuse their prosecutor colleagues of fabricating misconduct. That's how far these attorneys would go to shield cops and the city from accountability. Ultimately a federal court ruled that the implementation of Clean Halls was unconstitutional. The same judge reached the same conclusion about the law department's defense of a stop-and-frisk policy that had terrorized minorities since the 1990s.[10]

Down in Phoenix, the Maricopa County Attorney's Office

defended Sheriff Joe Arpaio's notorious racial profiling regime. This wasn't just any sheriff. This was America's most flamboyant octogenarian—a man who has been described as Bull Connor reincarnated.[11] Arpaio is known as the architect of "Tent City," an outdoor jail where temperatures easily topped 120 degrees and inmates were cruelly served two meatless meals a day while watching the Food Network. The tents were hand-me-downs from the Korean War. (Yes, the one from the 1950s.) Even Arpaio called it a "concentration camp" when answering a question about "illegals" entering the country.[12]

Yet during litigation, municipal attorneys walked into courtrooms and insisted that Arpaio and his colleagues did not "have a policy, pattern, or practice of using race" during traffic stops.[13] The Feds begged to differ. The Justice Department found that 20 percent of immigration-sweep traffic stops were unconstitutional, and Latino drivers were four to nine times more likely to be stopped than similarly situated non-Latino drivers.[14] One DOJ expert claimed that Arpaio oversaw "the worst pattern of racial profiling by a law enforcement agency in U.S. history."[15]

How do we reconcile these two realities? Municipal attorneys said no discrimination was happening whereas federal investigators called it the worst racial profiling they'd ever seen. Either the county attorney's office was staggeringly incompetent, or they knowingly defended systematic racial discrimination. Neither option reflects well on the office. The court concluded that the sheriff's office intentionally discriminated against Latinos.[16] Years after the decision, the county tried to distance itself from Arpaio's practices to avoid legal liability, but it failed.[17] The taxpayer costs for this unconstitutional racial profiling regime that municipal lawyers defended are estimated to reach $352 million by mid-summer of 2026.[18]

This is what legal inequality looks like when it operates through professional obligation and the power of language. Yes, these attorneys had professional obligations to defend their county clients—that's the structural imperative part. But they also deployed their legal skills in an attempt to transform systematic targeting into neutral law enforcement. This is discursive power at work: using legal language to sanitize discriminatory policing. When municipal lawyers can make racial profiling sound like responsible policing, they're not just doing their jobs—they're actively reshaping how we understand justice itself.

Questionable Settlements: A slightly more complicated form of municipal lawyering concerns settling cases. Counties may choose to settle for a range of reasons: to limit financial exposure, avoid prolonged litigation, manage public perception, or prevent damaging details from surfacing in court. It can be hard to determine the true reasons from the outside.

Cost concerns ostensibly drove a settlement in Camden, New Jersey. Cops from the Garden State claimed Xavier Ingram became quadriplegic because he ran and slipped in the rain. According to them, he just... fell.

Ingram's version? Officers stomped on his neck and back while he was face down and handcuffed. The case settled for $10 million. Camden County attorneys, who maintained the innocence of police officers, claimed that the concession "was a business decision spearheaded by the insurance carrier."[19] Ten million dollars for a slip and fall.

Chicago has handled so much police misconduct litigation that its law department also has a separate division that is staffed with forty people who focus on government misconduct. The city's bungling of the Laquan McDonald case shows how settlements can be a byproduct of actual guilt. Chicago officials claimed McDonald, a Black teenager, lunged at cops with a knife despite video evidence showing him walking away from them. The city settled before the McDonald family filed a lawsuit.[20]

What would have emerged had the case gone to trial? We'll never know because that's what settlements are sometimes designed to prevent. Settlements can be a byproduct of fear—fear of a trial that reveals cover-ups, patterns of misconduct, and training deficiencies that could expose a city to *more* legal liability from other plaintiffs. As Michigan law professor Margo Schlanger has explained in the context of inmate litigation, "media coverage of abuses or administrative failures can trigger embarrassing political inquiry and even firings, resignations, or election losses."[21] Settlements "without admission of wrongdoing" can do the work of burying evidence that could trigger systemic change.

Settlements could also be a begrudging concession. In San Diego, deputies are more likely to use canines, chokeholds, tasers, and weapons against Asian/Pacific Islanders than white people.[22] Such was the unfortunate fate for Lucky Phounsy, who experienced a mental health crisis during his son's second birthday. A family member called the police and told the dispatcher that he was unarmed and that no one was in danger. What happened next defies belief. A dozen deputies arrived on the scene, and Phounsy was tased multiple times, punched, handcuffed, and hogtied. He also had two mesh hoods put over his head, was strapped to a gurney, and had prolonged, extreme pressure applied to his head and torso by a 225-pound officer.[23] He ultimately died.

Do you find those actions shocking to the conscience? Most reasonable people would.

Yet the San Diego County Counsel argued that there was no "conscience-shocking conduct" to support a constitutional claim and no "wrongful act" to support a wrongful death claim.[24] Consider the audacity of that position. A man was hogtied, hooded, tased, and crushed to death at his child's birthday party—and government lawyers argued with straight faces that this conduct wasn't even wrong, let alone unconstitutional. A jury saw through this absurdity and awarded Phounsy's wife and small children $85 million. A judge later reduced this amount, and the county ultimately settled for $12 million rather than face a third trial. All of this is against a backdrop of a growing $60 million overall tab for settlements involving county law enforcement. This is what municipal lawyers defend.

These settlements—and the many others negotiated weekly in municipal offices—reveal a tragic subspecialty within government lawyering: constitutional violation cleanup services. The system's design ensures this work will be needed. Cities will inevitably face claims of constitutional violations, and someone must manage the fallout. All too often, this reinforces patterns where legal skill is used to protect institutions rather than pursue justice. When constitutional violations do occur—and they will—these lawyers sometimes take moments ripe for reckoning and reduce them to financial packages tied up with neat settlement bows. Settlements often serve as a substitute for reform, leaving systemic issues intact.

Ultimately, settlements with "no admission of wrongdoing" clauses do even more profound work. They embody discursive power in its rawest form—allowing cities to shape the narrative by framing massive financial payouts as prudent risk management or routine litigation avoidance, rather than acknowledgments of harm. It's moral erasure, plain and simple. What emerges is a system that treats civil rights violations not as the moral or institutional failures they are, but as operational costs to be managed through legal maneuvering and monetized absolution.

Narrow Legalisms: Even in police brutality cases where the facts show misconduct, municipal lawyers often secure victories through procedural technicalities. Recall from our discussion of civil procedure that a buffet of technicalities can wipe out a case that is substantive on the merits. The statute of limitations is the easiest example. Let's say the police falsely arrest you, but you fail to file a lawsuit within the statute of limitations period, which is two or three years in some states. Does that mean no social wrong occurred?

A controversy in East Cleveland, Ohio, illustrates how statute of limitations defenses, though procedurally proper, can feel like a denial of justice. In this poor, predominantly Black city, a group of Black cops engaged in a range of criminal behavior that impacted Black defendants. Calling it mere police misconduct would be like calling an earthquake a gentle rumble. They conjured entire fictional informants out of the air, complete with backstories and motivations, all to justify illegal searches. In addition to stealing people's freedom, they stole the cash of people they arrested. And they lied to grand juries. The scale of their criminal enterprise becomes clear when you look at the aftermath: Prosecutors had to drop charges against forty defendants whose cases were built on lies. Forty human beings whose lives were interrupted by fraud masquerading as justice.

When one of the victims managed to bring a lawsuit, the city's law department argued that the statute of limitations had expired on many claims. The department, like many across the country, was headed by a Black woman. Besides generally showing how women of color are tasked with cleaning up institutional messes they didn't create, this stark example shows how racial minorities can be complicit in legal inequality. Here was a Black woman arguing procedural technicalities to shield a municipal entity that failed to stop Black officers from terrorizing Black defendants. The institutional imperative of defending local government doesn't care about who holds the job or makes the argument. The statute of limitations argument had some success, and the city partially prevailed. The same city that employed these cops, trained them, and failed to stop them got to hide behind calendar dates to sidestep accountability.[25]

Municipal lawyers don't just use technical rules to get cases tossed; they also rely on deeper legal standards to undermine cases brought by people who have been harmed by government officials. Take the case of Anna Barnes. She was driving with her five children when she had a minor accident—no one was hurt. El Paso police showed up and arrested her for driving while intoxicated, even though they never gave her a sobriety test. Barnes says the officers handcuffed her and beat her during the arrest. A later blood test confirmed she was completely sober. The charges were dropped.

Barnes brought a 1983 lawsuit for "failure to train" and the El Paso City Attorney's Office made light work of the case. The city's lawyers didn't deny that Barnes was hurt. They didn't have to. Under Section 1983, they had a better move: Put the plaintiff on defense. These lawsuits require proof that a city's training was so deficient that officials should've known it would lead to constitutional violations.

But Barnes wasn't a police chief or a cadet who sat through officer training. She was a civilian alleging abuse by law enforcement. It's hard to identify structural flaws when you have little access to how the system works. The city's attorneys pointed to general use-of-force policies and said, "We did the training." Barnes's inability to pinpoint an administrative failure that could be linked to the assault led the court to dismiss this claim.[26] Was this a correct interpretation of the law? Unfortunately, yes. But the photos of Barnes after the arrest—which are easy to find online—tell a different story. The bloodied face and swollen eyes show how city lawyers can turn public pain into legal nonliability.

Some might say this is really a critique of procedural or substantive rules, not of municipal attorneys themselves. Or, as one esteemed scholar put it to me, "Don't hate the player, hate the game." But that overlooks something more immediate. In both cases, the rules didn't act on their own. Lawyers did the legal research to support their position. They drafted the arguments, primped them for court, and kept polishing—saving version after version until the one labeled FINAL_v3.docx was ready to go. They presented it to a judge and argued that the city shouldn't be held responsible. These were tactical moves that were tied to a professional obligation to protect the city from liability—even when its employees harmed the public.

Remember that in these cases, municipal lawyers aren't the scrappy underdogs defending powerless individuals against the state. They are the state. Their reliance on procedural rules is expected. It's what the role requires. But when a police beating becomes a question of paperwork, or an invented informant becomes a matter of timing, the injury doesn't disappear. The false arrest still has to be explained to hesitant employers and landlords as well as children trying to understand why their mother's face was bruised and bloodied. And it moves outward—into news stories, into collective memory, and into the shared sense of what justice will and won't allow. That's why we can't stop at the law's conclusions to understand inequality. We have to look at how narrow legal arguments—carefully deployed by lawyers—become institutional shields, even in the face of obvious harm.

Enabling an Ableist World

Having examined how municipal lawyers approach police misconduct cases, we can now return to disability rights with a clearer understanding of their tactics. The same strategies we've just witnessed—defending practices later ruled unlawful, avoiding accountability through settlements, and exploiting legal technicalities—appear in the disability context. The chapter opened with the visible barriers such as broken sidewalks and missing curb cuts, but municipal lawyers wield these same tactics against disabilities that don't announce themselves, such as hearing impairments.

Litigating Poor Policing and Hearing Impairments: Recall that Title II of the ADA prohibits local and state governments from discriminating against people with disabilities in their programs, services, and activities. Policing is the quintessential public service provided by local governments. In many cities across the country, people with disabilities are overrepresented in police use-of-force incidents.[27] People who are hearing impaired are at particular risk.

Let me tell you about Pearl Pearson, a sixty-four-year-old Black diabetic with a hearing impairment. In January 2014, Oklahoma officers stopped Pearson for allegedly leaving an accident scene. His driver's license indicated that he was deaf, and he carried a placard that read, in big font, "Driver Is Deaf." The card also noted, "Failure to follow verbal commands means I am NOT hearing you. Please read the back of the card for communication assistance."

Pearson was not able to show either the front or back of the card because the police officers acted so quickly and assaulted him for disobeying commands he could not hear.[28] Pearson's eyes were swollen shut. He suffered facial injuries and a separated shoulder. After the beating, officers' cameras captured them cursing when they checked his license and discovered he was deaf.[29] Oklahoma County attorneys then spent three years fighting against Pearson's claims, defending officers who beat a man for not hearing their commands. He ultimately received a settlement of approximately $200,000.

Pierson's violent encounter was not a one-off occurrence. There are an estimated twelve million people with hearing disabilities, some of whom inevitably interact with police.[30] Disability rights lawyers have documented instances where deaf people's inability to effectively communicate with untrained cops can lead these officers to mistake their actions or use of sign language as aggression, uncooperativeness, or gang signs.[31]

I do not know what's happening behind closed doors, but I question how well municipal lawyers are advising their law enforcement clients about their ADA obligations (or how much officers are listening to them). How else could you explain "the extraordinary position" taken by the New York City Law Department that it had "no obligation to provide *any* accommodation to the hearing-impaired at the time of an arrest, even if doing so could easily be accomplished without endangering officers or public safety"?[32] The absurdity does not end there.

Battling the Visually Impaired: Two cases brought by the American Council for the Blind, in New York and Chicago, illustrate the defensive and borderline-petty posture municipal lawyers can take in their work.

In the Big Apple, an estimated 205,000 people are blind or have vision difficulties.[33] The Windy City has 65,000 people with vision impairments.[34] These numbers do not account for suburbanites, commuters, or tourists. Between these two cities, we're talking about nearly 270,000 visually impaired people trying to navigate streets and sidewalks every single day.

The intricate work of crossing streets safely often goes unnoticed by sighted pedestrians. As mobility specialist Linda Myers testified, this involves life-or-death calculations. The person uses a white cane to detect a curb, curb ramp, or a detectable warning surface with raised bumps. They assume that is where the crosswalk begins. They try to confirm this assumption by listening for traffic, but that's increasingly difficult with environmental noise on a major city block. For example, construction noise from across the street can drown out signals, the quiet engines of electric cars can make them difficult to detect, overhead trains in cities like Chicago can rattle incessantly, and complex noisy intersections like Columbus Circle in New York can be almost impossible to navigate.[35]

Municipal lawyers in Chicago were so committed to the structural imperative of defending the city that they contested basic realities of navigating the world without sight. An Illinois court had to reprimand Chicago's lawyers for raising "niggling objections" to these tasks. "Common sense and experience suffice to appreciate that these are indeed the essential elements of a safe crossing."[36]

A key tool can help these individuals: accessible pedestrian signals (APS). You might hear these devices at the crosswalk communicating "walk" and "don't walk" to pedestrians; these devices increase blind pedestrians' ability to cross intersections safely.[37] New York had installed these at only 3.4 percent of 13,200 intersections with visual crossing information. Chicago was even worse, with APS at barely 1 percent of intersections. The outcry would be enormous if 97 percent of visual signals didn't work for sighted people.

Disability advocates sued the cities under the ADA for failing to install accessible pedestrian signals for blind and low-vision individuals. New York's and Chicago's law departments made arguments that mischaracterized their demands. The New Yorkers argued that meaningful access under disability law did not require the installation of APS at every intersection in the city with a signal and the Chicagoans maintained that "meaningful access does not require perfection."[38] Classic strawman arguments that the plaintiffs didn't make.

The judge in the Chicago case went to town on the municipal lawyers and wrote exasperatingly, "the City sensibly omits any argument that its provision of APS at around _one percent_ of its pedestrian signals affords plaintiffs and the class members meaningful access to its network of traffic signals."[39] In the New York case, the judge instructed the city to install ten thousand APSs. The plaintiffs in the Chicago case are currently haggling with the city about how many APSs need to be installed and within what timeframe. These are just a small sample of decisions that show big city lawyers sometimes fight tooth and nail to undermine antidiscrimination laws designed to benefit people with disabilities.

Defending Housing Insecurity

Police brutality and inaccessible urban environments often affect poor people, but I'd be remiss if I didn't say anything specifically about government attorneys and poverty.[40] Let's make a few more stops on our municipal tour—this time following the legal arguments these lawyers make that determine who gets to sleep outdoors, and whether those who do have shelter can keep it safe and habitable.

Criminalizing Homelessness: When it comes to homelessness, municipal lawyers have crafted legal arguments and laws that criminalize poverty. More than six decades ago, the Supreme Court ruled that it is unconstitutionally "cruel and unusual" to punish people for things they cannot control. That case focused specifically on the criminalization of being an "addict."[41] To the chagrin of government lawyers, some courts have taken this "involuntariness" principle and applied it to homelessness and ordinances that penalize poverty.[42] In the view of these courts, fining and arresting homeless people—some of whom are involuntarily in that circumstance—was deemed inhumane. One Nevada judge reminded the Las Vegas city attorney in 1967 that "it simply is not a crime to be unemployed, without funds, and in a public place. To punish the unfortunate for this circumstance debases society."[43]

By the end of the twentieth century, advocates brought cases to courts involving the punishment of unhoused people when cities had no housing supply for them. In the late 1980s and early 1990s, Miami police had a practice of recklessly disposing of unhoused people's property—throwing out things like identification cards and medicines that were "reasonably distinguishable from truly abandoned property." What was critical, in this instance, was that low-income housing and shelters were unavailable. In 1988, a class of six thousand unhoused people sued the city. By the time they went to trial, a Category 5 Hurricane (Andrew) had decimated the city and left an estimated two hundred thousand people homeless. Nevertheless, the Miami city attorney had the chutzpah to argue that homelessness was not involuntary or a situation over which "the individual has absolutely no control."[44]

Fifteen years later, the Los Angeles city attorney was pulling similar stunts. At the time, approximately eleven to twelve thousand unhoused people lived in the city, but only nine thousand to ten thousand beds were available, leaving at least one thousand without shelter.[45] Despite a housing shortage, the city wanted to enforce a law that punished any person "who merely sits, lies, or sleeps in a public way at any time of day."[46] When a bunch of unhoused people sued, the city attorney raised several arguments, the most offensive of which was the idea that they faced "no immediate threat of punishment."[47] This is like a boss putting someone on a performance improvement plan but claiming that their job was not in jeopardy. In the Miami and Los Angeles cases, federal courts rebuffed these cities' efforts,[48] and by 2019, a federal court covering eight western states ruled that it was unconstitutional to criminalize camping in public spaces when there was no shelter available.[49]

But in 2024, the Supreme Court intervened and validated the enforcement of anticamping ordinances even when there was no shelter.[50] Here is an abbreviated list of city attorneys who wrote briefs encouraging the court to reach this conclusion: Anaheim, Albuquerque, Anchorage, Honolulu, Las Vegas, Louisville, Phoenix, Portland, Sacramento, Seattle, and Topeka. Even Bismarck, North Dakota, got in on the action. This wasn't a partisan issue or a regional quirk—it was a nationwide coalition of municipal lawyers uniting around the principle that cities should be able to criminalize unhoused people.

A frustrating point made by some city attorneys is that the homeless often refuse offers for shelter; this makes these unhoused people look like brats. But legal scholar Ben McJunkin has offered an extensive list of reasons why such refusals happen. This includes physical safety concerns (some studies suggest that half of shelter residents experience abuse); the lack of accommodations for people with physical disabilities and mental health issues; the prospect of sexual violence in mixed-gender shelters; the separation of couples in same-sex shelters; the ease by which colds, flus, and the like are transmitted in these crowded spaces; and the heightened scrutiny from child welfare services that shelter use can bring for unhoused parents.[51] The indifference to these realities gives off the impression that some of these attorneys care more about business interests and aesthetic complaints than the human beings whose very existence they're criminalizing.

As someone who went to school in Berkeley and walked past encampments, I know that concentrated populations of unhoused people do not come without problems. As the court noted, "adults and children in these communities are sometimes forced to navigate around used needles, human waste, and other hazards to make their way to school, the grocery store, or work."[52] And that's just for outsiders. These spaces also invite forms of violence and public health problems. They are not to be held up as workable long-term solutions.

Nevertheless, the Supreme Court, with the helping hands of municipal lawyers, has given cities the green light to arrest their way out of a housing crisis. After the court's ruling, attorneys for San Francisco "formulated the legal basis for swiftly and efficiently clearing encampments."[53] When lawyers in one of the country's most liberal bastions rush to outlaw homelessness, it's clear this isn't partisan—it's about legal professionals transforming human desperation into a prosecutable offense.

Defending Housing Squalor: When it comes to low- and moderate-income renters, government lawyers play more of a support role—occasionally providing cover for foot-dragging, finger-pointing, and nonresponsive city bureaucrats. Consider the case of Stacey Marable, a mother of five trying to raise her kids in Minneapolis public housing. Over a year-and-a-half period, she went through a gauntlet of housing code violations that were unattended to by local officials.

In her first home, she had to deal with roof deterioration and mold that colonized her walls. She sent multiple notices about the mold to the Minneapolis Public Housing Authority (MPHA), an independent agency that is not attached to the city despite its official-sounding name. Marable asked to be moved, but they denied her request. They insisted that "the property was safe and habitable," even though her children's nosebleeds testified otherwise.[54] She contacted a separate set of bureaucrats from the city of Minneapolis to complain about housing code violations and they played hot potato with her family members' lives. They told her that the city did not have the authority to enforce the housing code on the MPHA properties and pointed the finger back at the agency while her kids got sicker.

Marable made more calls, wrote letters, and had to spend her hard-earned money to hire a private inspector who discovered mold that exceeded safety thresholds.[55] Eventually, MPHA came but didn't do a good job of remediating the problem; Marable hired the same inspector who discovered more mold. This time, MPHA transferred her to another home, and that's where she encountered leaking pipes, drainage problems in the basement, and rodents.[56]

More finger-pointing followed, so Marable had to lawyer up and sue. Throughout the litigation, city attorneys tried to pass the buck to MPHA until an appellate court ruled that the city of Minneapolis was responsible for housing code enforcement. After a $150,000 settlement to Marable, a Minneapolis spokesperson emphasized that "the City embraces its new authority to inspect MPHA dwellings to help facilitate safe, sanitary housing for low-income tenants."[57] It's as if the city's lawyers hadn't just finished arguing in court that Minneapolis had no obligation to protect poor children from toxic mold.

Lead is another issue that government lawyers sometimes try to paper over. Here is the skinny for readers fortunate to have never lived in an older dwelling: The federal government banned the use of lead paint in residential buildings in 1978. When lead paint disintegrates through chipping or peeling, it can turn into particles and dust that can be dangerous if inhaled or ingested and can cause irreversible damage. In infants, it has been linked to premature birth and low birth weight; in children, it can cause developmental delays and learning disabilities; and in adults, it can lead to reduced sperm count, miscarriages, and high blood pressure.[58]

The New York City Housing Authority (NYCHA) is the largest

public housing agency in the country and serves 528,000 residents—a population bigger than the city of Atlanta. For years, NYCHA systematically lied to the federal government about its compliance with lead paint safety regulations. The agency failed to perform many of the legally required lead paint assessments in units where children under the age of six resided. When they did inspect, they found lead in more than HALF of the developments—a pattern that should have triggered urgent action.[59] More than 1,100 poor and working-class children, the majority of whom are Black and Brown, tested positive for elevated lead levels. And that is a less-than-trustworthy estimate that was given by the city and extracted by litigation.[60]

To be sure, New York's municipal lawyers weren't the ones failing to do the inspections. And when inspections occurred, they weren't the ones doing lousy remediation jobs. We must distinguish the attorney from the clients. But the litigation that followed showed how these lawyers fought aggressively for government actors who clearly harmed children.

By April 2018, the lead scandal was public. NYCHA residents and tenant-rights advocates tried to force the agency to get its act together. They wanted a judge to force NYCHA to make a list of all apartments where children under the age of eight lived. This list was to include units that were supposed to get yearly inspections, places where families had complained about lead, and apartments where NYCHA claimed they'd already fixed the problem. Once they had that list, they wanted every single unit inspected within ninety days.

NYCHA's lawyers told the advocates to scram. They questioned the plaintiffs' legal ability even to bring a lawsuit—a common procedural tactic. They suggested that the plaintiffs could not show irreparable harm despite a judge telling them a month earlier that "there is no doubt that lead poisoning constitutes irreparable harm."[61] Finally, NYCHA's lawyers essentially told the court: "Why are we talking about the past? We're in compliance now," to which the court replied, "In a startling display of sophistry, NYCHA posits that it can be trusted to expeditiously complete the requisite inspections and remediations. This rings hollow in light of NYCHA's record of making false statements about its compliance with its lead paint inspection requirements."[62]

NYCHA struck a more conciliatory tone when it was sued by the Department of Justice. It didn't rely on its lawyers or attorneys from the New York City Law Department. It retained one of the best lawyers in the country—civil rights attorney and Big Law firm lawyer Debo Adegbile. Once the feds got involved, the agency settled and fessed up to the lead-based lies and malfeasance. It also admitted to several other failures that impacted NYCHA's residents: a winter in which 80 percent of residents lost heat; a year with thirteen outages per elevator; and a pattern of neglect that included a three-year span with 260,000 work orders for roaches, 90,000 mouse work orders, and nearly 36,000 rat work orders. It's amazing what some pressure from the federal government can do.

IF YOU FOLLOW THE PAPER TRAIL of local civil rights conflicts, you will find the fingerprints of municipal lawyers. Whether a case concerns police misconduct, disability law claims, failure to enforce the housing code, or a range of issues that I didn't have the space to discuss, these lawyers will be in the background. They are trying to keep civil rights plaintiffs out of court by throwing procedural quicksand in their way and endeavoring to limit municipal liability should things move to trial.

Of course, cities deserve vigorous legal defense. Municipal lawyers serve an essential function—protecting local governments from frivolous lawsuits, defending legitimate policy decisions, and ensuring that cities can govern effectively without being overwhelmed by litigation. The issue isn't whether cities should receive good legal representation—it's whether those lawyers should be in the business of making constitutional violations appear like sound policy. It's also about whether the public should accept legal arguments that repackage discrimination as legitimate governance. Problems emerge when municipal lawyers cross the line from zealous advocacy into defending obvious legal violations.

When a prosecutor—someone who depends on police cooperation to do their job—publicly tells the NYPD to stop making illegal arrests, and city lawyers respond by accusing that prosecutor of inventing the problem, we're veering from defense to institutional coverup. When federal investigators document what they call "the worst pattern of racial profiling in U.S. history" and municipal lawyers still argue in court that no discrimination occurred, that's not zealous advocacy—it's institutional denial of reality. When cities spend years fighting accessibility improvements that courts ultimately rule are required by law, they're not protecting taxpayers from unreasonable demands—they're forcing disabled residents to fight for basic civil rights.

Legally thrashing people who bring claims against the local government is an undeniable feature of the municipal lawyer's job. It's not the only part of their work. These attorneys bring actions against predatory businesses that harm consumers, enforce housing code violations against negligent landlords, and do the transactional work of designing different types of socially beneficial public-private partnerships. When read in the most favorable light, one could say that these lawyers are hampered by an institutional role that is designed to protect government entities at the expense of socially marginalized individuals who have experienced legal harm. Even with all of their complications, these lawyers must be brought from their sequestered offices in city hall and the county administration building and into the public square if we hope to understand some of the pressing problems of the day.

PART III

BIG LAW

A Sober View of Big Law

Donald Trump kicked off his second presidency by cracking the back of the American legal market like a butcher snapping a bone. His focus was on *Big Law*, the shorthand term for large law firms that typically have at least five hundred attorneys and often exceed one thousand. These firms often have outposts in New York, Chicago, LA, and DC and international offices in London, Paris, and Tokyo. They also represent major multinational corporations. Bob Nelson has studied Big Law for four decades and faithfully captures its significance when he states, "The large law firm participates in transactions and disputes that have enormous economic consequences for society."[1]

Because of their role in the global economy, Big Law has occupied a VIP section of American politics. That is why observers were stunned when Trump tore down the velvet rope, yanked away the privileges of some firms, and fleeced them like a whiskey-soaked sheriff shaking down a rival saloon. To understand the significance of this rupture, we must first grasp some of the underlying architecture of Big Law, the subject of the next three chapters.

I knew very little about big law firms until I worked at one in DC. During my time, I saw how Big Law has developed an impressive forcefield for itself through money and connections. They host cocktail fundraisers for Democrats and Republicans, employ former SCOTUS clerks with access to the justices' thinking, and provide crisis management for the wealthy. They hedge like centrists, hustle like tech moguls, and do enough pro bono to credibly say they have a commitment to public service.

In the basic structure, *partners* are at the top. They typically have at least eight years of practice experience and an ownership stake in the firm.[2] *Associates* serve them and clients, sometimes with the goal of making partner themselves. The job is lucrative but comes with burdens that are well-known in the legal profession.

The hours are long. Sleepless nights or going home just to shower and change clothes is not uncommon. One of these firms invested $13,000 in "energy pods" that allow attorneys to take twenty-minute naps at work. "It's like, 'Wow, I'm refreshed,'" an attorney remarked after using one.[3] Most people, I suspect, would prefer regular working hours and sleeping in their homes.

The day-to-day work is tedious. It's not a situation like *A Few Good Men* where young attorneys are in court hemming someone up and insisting that they "can't handle the truth!" They're doing hundreds of pages of data entry, proofreading, checking citations, redacting sensitive material, and cross-referencing contractual provisions (though many of these tasks are now being reshaped by AI).

Work-life balance is elusive or nonexistent. You may think that the four-day honeymoon that you planned a year in advance and told all your colleagues about is insulated from work requests. But if there's some kind of client emergency, be prepared to put down the glass of rosé and get to work. I've seen people forgo Beyoncé tickets and front-row seats at basketball games because of an "urgent" matter. The law firm is farming your services out to a client for $900 an hour, so immediate responsiveness and availability is expected.

To many of these complaints, I say: phooey. My perspective is based on a unique experience. I went to a law firm, Sidley Austin, that has a reputation for being relatively family-friendly and low on interpersonal drama. My parents worked blue-collar jobs in the New York City hotel and taxi industries and performed harder, physically debilitating work for an iota of the pay. The same goes for today's blue- and pink-collar workers—in custodial, warehouse, and care jobs. They don't have the luxury of remote work, ergonomic chairs, or standing desks.

Yes, the work in law firms can be monotonous, but at many firms, associates earn anywhere from $175,000 to $225,000 a year! Before starting practice, a lawyer friend—one of the smartest people I know—told me over drinks that 80 percent of her job was copying and pasting terms. She hated it. Meanwhile, I was rubbing my hands in eager anticipation. Where can I sign up?

My background, concern about inequality, and experience in Big Law have helped me develop a sober view of this corner of the profession and Trump v. Law Firms. Such sobriety helps me cut through two dominant views of Big Law, which, for now, I'll call the *cynical view* and the *romantic view*.

The Cynical View

Presidents regularly challenge the media, courts, and federal agencies, but Big Law has traditionally remained off limits. Trump broke that norm. He issued executive orders that targeted law firms that represented his political opponents or employed lawyers who investigated him.

Lawyers in these firms were prohibited from physically entering federal buildings and communicating with government officials. In practice, that could bar them from appearing in court or negotiating plea deals for their corporate defendants. It could also mean that if you represented Bayer or Pfizer, you couldn't communicate with the Food and Drug Administration about your client's new drug.

Government contractors were prohibited from working with these firms. That was painful. The federal government spends approximately $600 billion annually on goods and services. Contracts with federal agencies enable companies to sell a wide range of products, from fighter jets to vehicles to medical supplies. To keep those federal dollars flowing, clients would have to sever ties with these firms; potential clients would likely run the other way.

Finally, Trump revoked security clearances—another body blow. Many of these firms handled sensitive matters requiring access to classified information. Without it, they would be shut out of high-value national security work. No more advising the Lockheed Martins and Boeings of the world.

Some firms tried conciliation and money. Paul, Weiss led the parade by handing over $40 million worth of pro bono services and renouncing DEI in order to have the orders lifted. Other firms followed. Some of this "pro bono" work has even gone to the Commerce Department, where lawyers assisted on international trade deals—a warped use of services meant for clients who cannot afford to pay. The cynical view of Big Law kicked in here as these firms were critiqued for "capitulating" and "bending the knee."

The cynical view is common in the media and portrays Big Law as a villain. Orson Welles's *The Lady from Shanghai* painted the archetype in 1947; shows like *Suits* updated it for streaming. John Grisham is worth nine figures and he has sold millions of gripping books featuring firms as subsidiaries of the Mafia, enablers of poor people's eviction, and defrauders of the government.[4] Then there's the news media and many of the scandals of the past few decades involving these lawyers: the savings and loan crisis of the late twentieth century; Enron; the 2008 financial crash; and the Stop the Steal campaign of 2020. All feed a longstanding distrust of lawyers and a newer anti-elite, anti-corporate mood.

I heard the cynical view in law school at Berkeley, and I know students hear it every year.[5] Sometimes it came from public interest–minded students who saw Big Law as morally bankrupt. Some did not know that their work was being subsidized by law firm dollars. For minority students, the choice to work at a firm is often judged more harshly. As Randall Kennedy explains in *Sellout*, talented minorities are sometimes expected to forego wealth and engage in "martyrdom" via social justice work. In this view, working at a firm aligns with the wrong side of the fight.[6]

This critique paints too broadly. Much of Big Law work is mundane and involves tasks like contract review, regulatory research, and standard corporate transactions. These are not moral crimes. People shouldn't be defamed because clients want to pay them to do inoffensive things misrecognized as evil. I tell my students this often.

As for the law firms that cut deals with the president, the outrage is understandable, but it's also worth remembering that these are businesses, not churches or civil rights organizations. It was a fantasy to expect them to barricade themselves in their Wall Street offices to defend DEI and challenge what some are calling creeping authoritarianism. You might be better off looking for moral clarity elsewhere. Of course, some firms resisted. But that, too, brings complications.

The Romantic View

Firms such as WilmerHale and Jenner and Block challenged these orders and secured early victories. The legal commentariat celebrated this white-shoe resistance and hailed these firms as defenders of democracy. However, we should not confuse corporate survival with a moral stand or ignore that they can coexist. This may have been about principles, but it was also about protecting revenue.

This celebration reflects the romantic view of Big Law: that elite lawyers are stewards of democracy. Some public figures suggested that these resistant firms should be top destinations for students who value the rule of law. Taken one step further, the romantic view suggests that lawyers transcend moral accountability in their legal work. In this framing, law firms should not be punished for hiring or representing people that the president dislikes. Doing so would deter representation of politically unpopular clients.

But there's some dangerous misdirection at work here. Calling these firms guardians of the rule of law does not make it gospel. Yes, they occasionally defend the powerless, but as the following chapters will show, they also help build and maintain systems that harm vulnerable populations and the general public. Moreover, representing a tech company, the Democratic Party, or an elite prosecutor—the reasons why some firms found themselves subject to executive orders—isn't quite riding for the dispossessed.

Defenders of the romantic view sometimes invoke legal ethics concepts like *role differentiation*, which encourage lawyers to set aside personal scruples. Once hired, attorneys become "amoral technicians."[7] If their talents are deployed in service of an outcome that is socially disastrous but legally permissible, shoulder shrug emoji. That posture may be professionally sanctioned, but like the lionization of law firm resistance to Trump, it can mask deeper forms of complicity.

Big Law is capable of both principled and problematic work—its legacy is a mix of both. Any honest assessment must reckon with its power, compromises, and contradictions. The next three chapters examine the work these firms do in healthcare, environmental regulation, and workplace matters—three areas that profoundly affect people's lives and well-being. We'll explore three core modes of lawyering too—transactional, regulatory, and litigation. They provide a more comprehensive view of Big Law's footprint. These chapters complicate the few scripts we have about elite lawyers while showing how, across their many functions, Big Law continues to shape and sharpen the contours of inequality.

CHAPTER 10

Transactional Violence: Healthcare and the Afterlives of Mergers and Acquisitions

Come with me to the forty-fifth floor of a Big Law firm in downtown Chicago. We're talking about the kind of building where you need a keycard to ride the elevator past the twentieth floor. You can see Millennium Park, Soldier Field, and Lake Michigan with ease. The conference room has floor-to-ceiling windows, pristine conference tables, comfy leather chairs, and technology that you didn't know existed.

A partner from the mergers and acquisitions (M&A) group is walking colleagues and his client through a PowerPoint presentation about a hospital acquisition that will affect how three million people access healthcare. He sounds like a corporate poet. He tells a story of "improved efficiency" and "cost savings" but conveniently underplays what might be lost in pursuing those gains.

This wasn't my world when I practiced. I was in litigation—M&A's louder, messier, courtroom cousin. But this room isn't foreign. I know this world as a distant observer, a practitioner, and as someone who teaches courses on the legal profession and law firms. Most of my get-money lawyer friends practiced in the transactional trenches, so I'm conversant in the language. I know that "strategic rightsizing" likely means mass layoffs. That "portfolio optimization" is code for shuttering services that don't generate enough profit. How "stakeholder value maximization" can translate to shedding staff and squeezing every dollar possible out of what is supposed to be a place of healing.

Legal education and the legal profession reward this kind of fragmentation. Law schools teach you to break down complex social problems, and practice rewards lawyers who can move fast and bill hours without getting distracted by "externalities" like community harm. Professional ethics say your job is to primarily serve clients, which creates an inevitable distance between what lawyers do and who pays the price. The result is a system that trains smart people to engineer brilliant solutions while staying disconnected from the human wreckage they might leave behind.

IN AN ICONIC SCENE in the American sitcom, *The Brady Bunch*, Jan Brady, the middle child, complains about all the attention given to her older and more popular sister, Marcia. (You might ask why an eighties baby from the Bronx is referencing this 1970s show; the answer: We didn't have good cable until the mid-1990s.) Jan complains to her parents, "All I hear all day long at school is how great Marcia is at this or how wonderful Marcia did that, Marcia, Marcia, Marcia!" After uttering this famous statement, she says, "I'm tired of being in Marcia's shadow all the time."

This is how I imagine some transactional lawyers think about litigators. Transactional attorneys work in offices drafting legal documents and negotiating contractual terms. They receive less cultural appreciation than their courtroom counterparts. However, in big law firms, transactional attorneys play an irreplaceable role in revenue generation. When President Trump blacklisted the law firm Paul, Weiss and it subsequently gave in, much of the reported concerns were tied to the firm satisfying its rainmaking transactional partners (especially Scott Barshay, the head of the corporate practice who has represented Chevron, GE, Anheuser-Busch, Intel, and United Airlines in eight- and nine-figure deals).[1] The transactional lawyers bring in the moolah. They structure business deals that impact all of us.

When a private company like WWE or Reddit goes through the initial public offering (IPO), transactional attorneys advise on the deal. Sometimes, the financial picture is less rosy for organizations needing transactional lawyers. A company may want to restructure its operations because it is going through Chapter 11 bankruptcy. Maybe it's selling parts of the business to pay creditors or trying to cut costs generally. Transactional attorneys are key to these activities. The breadth of their work spills into the world of multimillion-dollar trusts, sports deals, massive real estate projects, and contracts with the boss of all bosses—the federal government. Some of the work is less exciting and it can be hard to decipher because of the technical jargon.

Private equity has been blamed for the downfalls of Payless Shoes, Deadspin, Toys"R"Us, and RadioShack. Even Taylor Swift, in her battle over her music, placed blame on the "unregulated world of private equity."[2] The transactional lawyers who design these legal structures create agreements that load companies with unsustainable debt to fund acquisitions. Returns to investors are prioritized, sometimes leaving businesses unable to survive.

Real estate development may sound neutral, but the transactional work can involve "investment opportunities" that affect people across the country. Maybe the lawyers structure deals that flood urban neighborhoods with capital and price out minority residents, or they facilitate the purchase of agricultural land by foreign investors that displace rural whites.[3]

International finance involves attorneys helping businesses craft cross-border deals. Anti-imperialists critique this work for keeping poor, postcolonial countries trapped in debt while giving multinational corporations free rein to extract resources. At the same time, isolationists have reasonable grounds to say these lawyers are not "America First" for working on deals at the expense of American jobs and industries.

The well runs deep, and I've only covered a fraction of what's possible through transactional lawyers. This chapter spotlights mergers and acquisitions—one of the most consequential but least understood areas of legal practice. M&A lawyers facilitate critical business deals that can rescue struggling companies, drive innovation, and create efficiencies that benefit consumers and markets. But they also reshape markets in ways that impact all of us. Their dealmaking can reduce consumer choices, increase prices, and limit access to essential goods and services.

Hospital mergers get specific attention because healthcare isn't optional. It involves the most fundamental human need—survival itself—making the human cost of these transactions impossible for anyone paying close attention to ignore. In the healthcare world, M&A-prompted consolidation can disproportionately affect vulnerable groups. Rural communities can lose their only hospital, low-income populations can experience declines in the quality of care, and the social welfare good of healthcare becomes a corporate extraction zone. The complexity and technical nature of this work keep it largely invisible to the public. Meanwhile, the structural imperatives of M&A practice nudge practitioners toward prioritizing technical perfection and client service over community consequences.

To explain how this machinery operates, I'll note a few basics of an M&A deal. I'll then briefly trace the effects of such deals across the banking, grocery, airline, tech, and pharmaceutical industries because this pattern extends far beyond healthcare and into nearly every sector of the economy. Then we'll dive deep into hospital mergers that have life and death consequences for real communities.

What emerges is a portrait of transactional violence—harm that gets inflicted through paperwork instead of physical force; suffering that gets distributed through legal instruments rather than weapons. This kind of sophisticated legal work can become detached from human consequence. It can prioritize profit and efficiency over the realities of ordinary Americans whose lives literally hang in the balance and depend on decisions made in distant conference rooms.

The Corporate Union: M&A Tidbits and the Mechanics of Moral Distance

M&A refers to the process of combining of two organizations. Notable examples include the 1999 merger of Exxon and Mobil as well as CVS's 2018 absorption of Aetna. M&A is a lucrative enterprise. To give you a sense of the scale, the law firm Kirkland and Ellis led the league in 2023 when it advised on $406 billion in M&A transactions, approximately 13 percent of the market share.[4] Kirkland and Ellis's chairman Jon Ballis made at least an estimated $25 million in 2023, putting him in striking distance of Goldman Sachs CEO and banker David Solomon, who made $31 million. The real significance goes beyond these lucrative deals. M&A attorneys have played a significant role in industry consolidation—the process by which businesses are increasingly being acquired by fewer corporations.

Large corporations are more likely to engage in lobbying and increase their lobbying after mergers, which can give them disproportionate influence in politics.[5] Put simply: A merger can help a corporation achieve new scale and get what it wants politically, sometimes to the detriment of the general public. Critiques of large corporations are bipartisan. When two fancy law firms worked on AT&T's $85 billion acquisition of Time Warner, the first Trump administration unsuccessfully tried to block the deal in 2017.[6] In 2022, half of Republicans (53 percent) believed that large corporations should have less power than they do now, whereas 63 percent of Independents and 68 percent of Democrats came to the same conclusion.[7] M&A attorneys play a role in corporate consolidation.

How does M&A actually work? Large corporations typically have a *general counsel (GC)*, who is the chief legal officer, and a team of lawyers, often called *in-house counsel*, who are often former Big Law attorneys. The GC and in-house counsel can do much of the legal work internally, but sometimes they'll retain law firms, also known as *outside counsel*. Sometimes the company retains outside counsel at the tail end of the deal, but the outside firm can also be hired to work from start to finish.[8] These firms specialize in these kinds of transactions and have a deep understanding of the legal requirements necessary to get the deal done favorably.[9]

Lawyers take on various roles when these economy-changing deals go down, most of which are unobjectionable in isolation. The GC is the consigliere. They act as the legal advisor to the CEO and the board of directors. The GC lets the execs know whether the deal is worth doing, hires outside counsel, and ensures that all legal activity serves the corporate strategy. The GC's underlings are part of the larger group referred to as in-house counsel. They sometimes liaise with and monitor outside counsel to ensure they follow through on company priorities.

Within the law firm, some partners easily charge more than $1,000 an hour and are responsible for the high-level strategy. They rely on senior associates, who typically have five to eight years of experience. These field generals quarterback the deal. Sometimes a transaction requires a specialist from another part of the firm to "airdrop" in and mark up a slice of a contract to ensure no major issues (e.g., the tax folks, the employee benefits gurus, or the antitrust specialists).[10] The senior associates are the internal liaisons who help manage the larger team. They may also handle Hart–Scott–Rodino (HSR) filings, which can sometimes involve strategically presenting data in ways that downplay concerns a deal will increase market concentration.

If it were a newsroom, the GC would be the publisher, the partner would be the managing editor, the senior associates would write the story, and the junior associates would be the fact gatherers.

The junior associates do the grunt work. They review the company's existing contracts for *change of control provisions* that could frustrate the deal when ownership changes. Will they get the same deals on oxygen tanks and surgical equipment, or will they get hit with higher costs? The provisions could also involve loans—money the hospital borrowed that might have an earlier due date if ownership changes hands.

These are clean technical questions that can be answered by close reading and legal research. They do not involve thinking deeply about how all those contracts represent lives and lifelines. Those contracts can decide whether the dialysis center that is within walking distance of public transportation stays open; if it were closed, elders who depend on it would be dealt a heavy blow. Such provisions could determine whether the labor and delivery unit stays open in rural Maine, where the next closest hospital is an hour away—ninety minutes if it's snowing. And those terms can dictate whether an after-hours phone line is staffed so that parents who call when their toddler won't stop vomiting can be told to bring the child in for urgent treatment.

Such fragmentation is both the utility and the cost of legal training. It teaches lawyers to break down complex problems into manageable pieces—financial structures, contract terms, legal checklists, and regulatory compliance. Each part gets careful analysis. But that fragmentation keeps the focus on technical pieces rather than human consequences. It's not that lawyers don't care about people—it's that the system trains them to solve the legal puzzle while keeping everything else that puzzle connects to safely in the background.

M&A Gone Wrong?

M&A have an appealing efficiency to them. They can help a company diversify its portfolio, remain solvent, and make more money. Those are presumably good things. But M&A can also be borderline predatory and can eliminate competitors, like the time Google bought Waze in 2013 or when Facebook bought Instagram and WhatsApp in 2012 and 2014, respectively.[11] Good evidence suggests that M&A have played a role in increasing market concentration, decreasing competition, and raising prices.[12] The results harm consumers more generally and historically marginalized groups, especially.

Before analyzing healthcare specifically, let me show how this plays out across other stages of American commerce because this isn't merely a medical melodrama. It's the story of how entire markets get restructured through legal paperwork.

Banking is a good starting point. Bank mergers have been facilitated by law firms and have led to more than one thousand bank deserts—towns or communities that lack independent banks or branch offices.[13] These deserts impact approximately seventy million Americans who cannot access traditional financial services. Bank consolidation makes it more expensive for low-income households to open accounts due to the higher fees and minimum balance requirements of larger banks.[14] This creates a vacuum often filled by fringe banking institutions such as check cashing facilities, payday loan companies, and pawnshops—all of which disproportionately hurt rural, minority, and poor people.[15]

The food industry is another site where big companies are gobbling up smaller ones. By 2020, concentration had reached the point where four firms dominated each major sector: controlling 83 percent of cereal, 73 percent of beef processing, 67 percent of pork processing, 63 percent of salty snacks, 58 percent of bread, and 54 percent of chicken processing.[16] As for milk sales, three companies controlled 83 percent of the market.[17] Again, some of this is due to M&A facilitated by Big Law firms and it has posed a host of issues. Some of these challenges include the recurring theme of increased costs for consumers; employment problems for producers who have fewer entities to sell to; and abusive labor practices for the low-wage (and often minority) workers who have reduced employment options and bargaining power.[18]

On the retail side, the National Grocers Association claims that the big four food retailers—Walmart, Costco, Kroger, and Albertson—"leverage market share to box out suppliers," which leads to price distortions.[19] Some of these names may be less familiar depending on where you live, so let me make this regional to give you a sense of these retailers' breadth: Kroger owns Ralphs in California, Smith's in the Mountain West and Southwest, Mariano's in Illinois, and Harris Teeter in the mid-Atlantic. Albertson owns Vons in California, Safeway in the West, Jewel-Osco in the Midwest, Acme in the Northeast, and Shaw's in New England. The situation would have gotten worse if a Big

Law–orchestrated merger between Kroger and Albertson had not been blocked in 2024. President Joe Biden explained that the high cost of groceries, which rose five times faster than inflation from 2020 to 2022, was a byproduct of sheer market power: "Grocers in consolidated markets charge you more because you have nowhere else to shop."[20]

The airline industry tells a more complicated consolidation story. Since 1960, today's five biggest airlines have absorbed dozens of smaller carriers. However, airfares have fallen by over 30 percent since 1999 when adjusted for inflation; that's the good part.

The downside is that airlines are squeezing customers in other ways via unbundled pricing. The nickel-and-dime tactics include increased checked baggage fees; bans on carry-on items for economy seats (which nudge travelers to upgrade); and seat selection fees that force families to choose between paying more to sit together or having their kid sit between strangers, to name a few. Then there are the hub monopolies—cities where airlines control airports like mob bosses and can extract monopoly rents. Think Delta in Atlanta, American in Charlotte, or United in Chicago. The proposed JetBlue-Spirit merger collapsed in 2024, even with an army of Big Law firms behind it. The Feds thought that eliminating a low-fare airline that forces the Deltas and Uniteds of the world to compete might remove the last check on their pricing power.[21]

Now I know I hit you with a lot of industries, but I needed you to see the pattern before we get to healthcare. These mergers across different industries have led to the same outcome—market power concentrated in fewer hands, reduced choices for consumers, and the power to set prices at will in markets where consumers lack meaningful choice. When this same legal machinery gets turned on hospitals, the consequences become existential.

Vital Signs: Medical Mergers, Money, and Misery

The negative effects of mergers and acquisitions are particularly pronounced in the healthcare system. These kinds of consolidations can lead to the shuttering of facilities, service reductions (e.g., emergency rooms), and the nixing of community health programs. Consolidation can pose problems for elderly individuals who must take multiple buses or trains to reach their closest provider. In rural areas, mergers can have a more dire effect. There's no comparison shopping when you're sick and the one hospital is seventy-five miles away. The closing of one rural facility could spell disaster for patients with time-sensitive emergencies (e.g., strokes, heart attacks). And all of this can happen while hospital execs and M&A teams pad their pockets on these deals.

Between 2000 and 2020, more than 1,500 hospital mergers occurred among the nation's approximately five thousand hospitals. During that same period, the cost of hospital services swelled faster than prices in any other American industry. That increase has been specifically tied to hospital consolidation.[22] Estimates of price increases due to hospital mergers range from 3 to 65 percent.[23]

If you're a middle-class person with good insurance, a 10 to 20 percent price increase borne by the consumer might be annoying and even belt-tightening, but manageable. But for working-class folks who are underinsured or uninsured, such an increase is not abstract. This could mean the difference between a retired person on a fixed income seeking care for heart symptoms or not. It might mean that a patient who was facing a $5,000 surgery now finds the same procedure costs $6,000. It could mean a person has to choose between paying the rent and seeking care, and it could lead to emergency rooms being the first point of medical contact because people can't afford preventative care.

Higher hospital expenses can impact insurers who pass the cost on to employers, which can impact workers' take-home pay since employer-sponsored healthcare is the primary form of coverage for American adults. Higher hospital expenses also exacerbate health disparities between rich people who can foot the bill and poor people who cannot. When a hospital does not accept Medicaid because of the program's low reimbursement rate, these recipients face the same dilemma as the uninsured: the impossible choice between paying out of pocket or forgoing care altogether.[24] The nearly $1 trillion in cuts to Medicaid via the One Big Beautiful Bill Act will certainly not help matters. Most generally, high medical costs play a role in the scourge of medical bankruptcies that impact people across class groups.[25]

Rural hospitals that struggle to staff their facilities are especially at risk of consolidation, and it's worth being clear about who we're talking about in this context. Rural areas have long been home to racial minorities, and that population has grown to 24 percent according to the 2020 Census. However, these areas remain predominantly white, with 35 million white residents accounting for 76 percent of the population. Across racial lines, these communities are disproportionately poorer. The non-metro poverty rate was 15.5 percent in 2022, compared to 12.1 percent for metro areas.[26] The pressures on these rural residents and hospitals are expected to deepen. The American Hospital Association predicts that 1.8 million rural residents will lose health insurance by 2034 due to Medicaid cuts.[27] During an eight-year period, 17 percent of unprofitable rural hospitals became targets of completed mergers, a reflection of how financial vulnerability intensifies as these institutions struggle to serve uninsured populations—particularly poor white communities already living on the edge.[28]

Consolidation can be necessary for hospitals that struggle financially.[29] Whether a hospital is rural or urban, when it is facing consolidation, it has three major alternatives: 1) It can remain open and thug it out. Some do, and about half return to profitability.[30] 2) It can discontinue critical services, like the hospitals in Iowa, which have shuttered a third of their labor and delivery units since 2000. 3) Or it can close altogether, which was the fate of more than 130 rural hospitals since 2010—a timeframe that also included higher rates of mortality from heart disease, cancer, unintentional injury, and stroke for rural adults relative to urban adults.[31]

I and many others might pick a merged hospital over no hospital, especially if it leads to better health outcomes for rural adults. I'll also pick that hospital if it means pregnant women who lack reliable transportation and flexible work schedules can get critical prenatal and birthing services.[32]

However, the evidence showing the actual benefits of consolidation for hospitals themselves is underwhelming. One study has found improved outcomes for consolidated rural hospitals in areas such as heart failure, stroke, and pneumonia.[33] Yet others have found modestly *worse* patient experiences and concluded that mergers *still* lead to reduced access to obstetric services, primary care, and emergency departments. Merged urban hospitals experience reduced pediatric services for children.[34] That is on top of lost jobs and reduced staffing.[35] The basic promise that consolidation improves healthcare delivery is questionable at best.

Corporations benefit from hospital mergers. This is particularly true in metropolitan areas—many of which are highly concentrated; in such locations one or a few organizations can control most of the market.[36] Barak Richman, a health economist and law professor at George Washington University, explains the dynamic nicely. "Reducing competition increases price. We know that, and we've known that for generations, as a matter of rudimentary economics, across markets of all kinds. What's remarkable, and unfortunate, is that we have been less demanding of competition in hospital markets. There seems to be a lingering belief that healthcare providers won't exploit pricing power the same way everyone else does."[37]

Notwithstanding the anticompetitive, high pricing that comes with hospital consolidation, one physician-executive notes that healthcare institutions have primarily relied on M&A activity as a growth strategy and will continue to do so.[38] Transactional attorneys will be right there, ready to supply them with services. A 2024 survey of sixty-two law firms highlighted M&A as one of the most in-demand services among healthcare clients.[39]

The lawyers who work on these deals are part of a larger orchestra of agents who take orders from a principal (e.g., consultants, financial advisors, and hospital administrators). Their work has downstream consequences—some of which are very attenuated and some of which are pretty predictable. Longstanding debacles in the majority Black and poor city of Detroit and the majority white region of Western North Carolina are instructive.

Case Study #1: *Detroit, or How to Legally Destroy a Safety Net.* In 2013, the M&A team at Gibson Dunn represented Tenet Healthcare Corporation in its $4.3 billion acquisition of Vanguard Health Systems. The American Lawyer described the deal as providing a "shot in the arm" to the four law firms involved in the deal: Gibson Dunn, Skadden, Simpson Thacher, and Davis Polk.[40] The Detroit Medical Center (DMC)—which is comprised of dozens of hospitals and health centers in the Detroit metropolitan area—was part of the acquisition. DMC hosts more than two thousand beds and is the biggest employer in a city that is 77 percent Black.

After the acquisition, Tenet went on a slashing spree. It reduced the number of sterile technician staffers who clean instruments by a quarter. It also cut DMC's budget for administering care to poor, uninsured patients from approximately $23 million to $470,000.[41] That's a 98 percent cut in charity care. This is violence by budget line.

The consequence of such cost cutting? Poorly sterilized tools led to complications during people's brain surgeries and spinal fusions. In other cases, operations were canceled altogether—some *after* anesthesia was administered.[42] Imagine entrusting a hospital with your life in this way. You arranged for someone to pick up your kids from school and you spend the night before fasting because they told you not to eat or drink anything. You're lying on a cold operating table with a hospital gown on your body. You're anxious but believe that when you wake up, your body will be healed. You wake up groggy and confused to a nurse telling you that the surgery had to be called off because they couldn't ensure that the instruments were clean.

The situation was so bad at DMC that the Feds threatened to pull Medicare and Medicaid funding, which is usually an enforcement tool of last resort. Much of the blame was placed on Tenet. A group of staff and physicians claimed there was "a fundamental abandonment of a previously developed culture of quality and safety."[43]

Case Study #2: *The Appalachian Extraction.* HCA Healthcare is one of the largest for-profit corporations in the United States. When it purchased the North Carolina–based Mission Health system for $1.5 billion in 2019, eighty-five lawyers from one prominent law firm worked on the deal, the majority of whom came from its Health Care Transactions group.[44] Mission's flagship facility was in Asheville, a city that is 80 percent white and has an above-average poverty rate. The purchased hospital had operated as a nonprofit charitable organization since 1885, and the deal made it the fifth largest for-profit hospital in the country.[45] Mission's profits immediately dipped after the purchase but subsequently skyrocketed and exceeded pre-acquisition numbers.

A study from Wake Forest health law guru Mark Hall has shown that Mission's money-making resulted from cuts in patient-care staffing. Average staffing in North Carolina hospitals was 5:1 full-time staff members per bed in 2019 and remained at that level until 2021. During the same period, Mission's ratio dropped from 6 per bed in 2019 to 3.7.[46] A separate study involving researchers at Johns Hopkins and Rice notes that "after the merger, HCA Mission Health raised its prices by an average 10% almost immediately, while triggering an exodus of physicians."[47] Patients complained about surprise fees that were triple the cost of their copay and that were sometimes incurred without them stepping foot in a Mission office or seeing a specialist.[48]

After the acquisition, Mission was *supposed* to operate more efficiently. It signed an asset purchase agreement that included commitments to retaining certain services, investments in community health, and the hiring of an independent consulting group to ensure compliance. These weren't handshake agreements; they were legal obligations written into the purchase contract.

Folks on the ground suggested that HCA wasn't living up to the deal. One physician told the consultants that "patients are screaming into the hallways: 'Please help! Help!'" They also complained that janitorial services were so short-staffed that "patients are having to clean their own rooms, or their family members [are]." A tearful nurse said more bluntly, "Every single department in that hospital that is designed to help the patient . . . is critically and unethically and inhumanely understaffed."[49]

A letter from the mayor of Asheville, county officials, and state congressional members accused HCA of lying about its intentions before making the acquisition and told a story similar to what occurred in Detroit. "HCA has chosen to make its money by reducing charity care, eliminating medical and unit administrative staff to the detriment of patient care and safety, and sacrificing entire physician practice groups with long-standing contractual relationships by demanding significant reductions in pay."[50]

One Mission executive's faux pas didn't help matters. During an American Hospital Association conference, she claimed that there were "lots of hillbillies" in Western North Carolina before blurting out, "There was a lot of talk about the fact that we are a monopoly, and we are.... We're kind of the 500-pound gorilla in Western North Carolina."[51] She resigned after her comments went public, but her remarks about the hospital said what is usually left unspoken. When you're the primary hospital system in town, you can do whatever you want; raise prices, cut services with abandon, and treat patients how you'd like to—because the people in Western North Carolina have limited alternatives. This is the kind of market power that emerges from deals like this—whether the lawyers structuring them think about it or not.

The Structural Inevitability of Inequality

The lawyers who structured the Detroit and North Carolina deals didn't personally fire the nurses or close the emergency departments. Indeed, transactional attorneys' implication in the consequences of hospital consolidation are arguably more remote. That distance doesn't quite excuse them. These lawyers created the legal frameworks that made these outcomes economically rational for their clients. They helped transform these community institutions into unabashed financial assets, and the result was predictable. This is what I mean when I talk about legal inequality as a structural imperative. No one had to be evil for these tragedies to unfold. The lawyers just had to do their jobs—represent their clients' interests, maximize shareholder value, and ensure regulatory compliance.

But this raises uncomfortable questions about foreseeability and responsibility. Can transactional lawyers working on these hospital mergers reasonably claim ignorance about the well-documented consequences of healthcare consolidation? The cutting-edge research isn't hidden in obscure academic journals—it's reported in major newspapers and discussed in policy circles.

Nevertheless, some lawyers truly may not know—particularly junior attorneys. For them, ignorance is less a personal failing than a built-in feature of law firm work. They are siloed into narrow tasks, kept at a distance from clients, and rarely given insight into the broader context of the deal. That compartmentalization can limit their ability to grasp the larger stakes of these transactions. It also exposes something troubling about legal education and the profession itself: We train people to be technically sophisticated while keeping them socially disconnected.

A second possibility points to the profession's deep faith in optimization. Some lawyers have so thoroughly internalized this mindset that they no longer see cost-cutting, closures, and layoffs as harms.[52] Instead, they regard them as the inevitable price of a "better," more streamlined system—a supposed mark of progress rather than decline.

And then there's the hired-gun approach. Some lawyers know exactly what's at stake and move forward anyway, convinced their duty to the client outweighs everything else. These deals are client-driven, and lawyers often insist their role is to provide counsel rather than determine social policy. If regulators fail to act or drop the ball, the fault lies with government, not with the lawyers or the corporations they represent.

I suspect the truth lies somewhere in the middle. These lawyers exist in professional ecosystems that reward technical competence while actively discouraging moral reflection. That's why the damage doesn't end when the ink dries on the deal. Once charitable hospitals get restructured as profit-maximizing entities, the capitalist version of efficiency becomes self-reinforcing. Many of the subsequent decisions center on shareholder value over community health. Emergency departments, charity care, and rural facilities get eliminated not because they are medically unnecessary, but because they don't generate enough money.

These mergers aren't just one-time transactions. They create ongoing systems of resource extraction that survive long after the lawyers have moved on to their next deals. This is what I mean by the "afterlives" of mergers and acquisitions. The deals themselves might last a few months or even years, but their consequences reshape communities for generations. The lawyers go on and get bonuses and promotions, but the people who rely on these hospitals pay with their health and their lives.

Some lawyers may try to build in protective guardrails. Before one of these transactions, junior lawyers conduct due diligence and investigate risks involved in the purchase. They might note consolidation's economic and social impact on surrounding communities. These concerns can appear in purchase agreements through contractual commitments to charity care, investments in new technologies, and the continuation of certain critical services—kind of like the one we witnessed in Asheville. But these agreements are often time-limited and have an expiration date.

Even when lawyers are aware of potential post-consolidation problems, they may not be positioned to exercise control over what their clients do. The attorney-client relationship often dissolves after the deal closes, and even if it didn't, clients have the prerogative to do as they please. Other times, lawyers adhere to ideas about legal ethics that prioritize their clients' lawful objectives above broader social concerns. In all of these cases, their merger documents might be legally perfect, but the human cost is undeniable.

THIS IS NOT TO tut-tut M&A lawyers. The challenge is structural, as I see it. And I, too, am implicated. I never worked on M&A deals, but I drew a paycheck from a law firm that made millions doing this work. I can teach all the classes on antidiscrimination law and poverty law I want, but the reality is I'm helping furnish big law firms with the talent to do this work. The implications run wide and deep, and they include me too.

Now, an attractive response to the critique in these pages applies to other chapters in this part. Law firms, legal ethicists, and American legal tradition itself insists that these larger corporate clients are entitled to representation. It's a challenging counterpunch, partly because it's professionally convenient for lawyers and corporations and because, in my view, it is correct. But that often stops us from interrogating more deeply.

We must be honest about what's happening. This is a system in which healthcare corporations can hire armies of lawyers for multibillion-dollar deals while patients harmed by dirty surgical instruments can't afford to challenge corporate negligence. This isn't just representation. It's corporate supremacy with a legal cover. When we move beyond the rhetoric and ideal of representation, we can more pointedly ask: Do we want lawyers helping corporations structure deals that create monopolies? Do we want lawyers facilitating mergers that eliminate competition and drive up prices for working families?

Some might dismiss this as just capitalism at work, but the legal profession isn't a passive bystander. The profession is helping architect these arrangements and society pays the price. I'm not saying we should strip corporations of their quality representation. I'm arguing that the current system is so skewed toward corporate interests that it harms patient populations and consumers—especially those from marginalized communities.

When hospital mergers result in emergency room closures, bank consolidations create financial deserts, and tech acquisitions eliminate competition—those aren't just market outcomes. They're the direct result of legal work performed by some of the smartest people in the country.

The issue is whether transactional attorneys and the general public can acknowledge the considerable power that these behind-the-scenes technicians hold and the social responsibility that comes with it. Some may reject any such possibility—in which case, we're back where we started. But for those who accept it, the question becomes whether that power can be redirected toward something more just.

CHAPTER 11

Environmental Degradation in the Regulatory Wild West

Look, I know what you may have been thinking when you saw the chapter title. Maybe after reading the word *environmental*, you worried about science overload and that I was going to hit you with all kinds of words ending in -cide. Or perhaps you saw *regulatory* and thought, "Oh, hell no. This is going to be a PowerPoint in book form."

Bear with me; I'm not about to give you a PhD in pollution.

I'm here to talk about the law. It's not the deal-making, contract-wrangling type we talked about in the previous chapter (though there are overlaps). And it's not the sexy courtroom type involving last-minute verdicts and headlines. This chapter is about regulatory lawyers—professionals who help clients navigate the dense, often confusing world of environmental rules and agency processes. It's the kind of work that happens in the shadow of bureaucracy, far from the public eye, but with real consequences for what industries can do and what communities have to tolerate. To better understand how they do their magic—I need to say a little about the federal bureaucracy, which mostly lived off the grid of public attention until DOGE briefly made it trendy in 2025.

Almost a century ago, the American economy faceplanted and the Great Depression almost broke the country. Congress responded by creating agencies that could impose order and prevent capitalism from cannibalizing the economy again. The Securities and Exchange

Commission (SEC) would keep tabs on Wall Street's next "big idea." The Federal Deposit Insurance Corporation (FDIC) insured deposits to avoid instances where a rumor could spark a stampede of people rushing to pull their money out. The Social Security Administration (SSA) created a safety net for the aged, injured, and unemployed.

By the 1960s and 1970s, it became clear that decades of unchecked industrial growth were harming the environment and people. Smog famously enveloped New York City on Thanksgiving 1966, making the air homicidal. More than 160 people died. The Cuyahoga River next to Cleveland was so slick with oil and industrial waste that it literally caught fire in 1969, and it wasn't the first time. Both events contributed to the creation of the Environmental Protection Agency (EPA) in 1970. In the meantime, an estimated fourteen thousand workers were dying on the job annually, so the Occupational Safety and Health Administration (OSHA) was created the same year.

These days, an alphabet soup of agencies are tasked with regulating various aspects of American life. They all exist in a mini-legal universe. When Congress passes a law like the Clean Water Act, which regulates pollution discharged into rivers and lakes, or the Safe Drinking Water Act, which governs the quality of drinking water delivered to our taps, the EPA passes hundreds of fine-grained regulations defining pollution, how much of it is acceptable, and what happens if you break the rules. If you drink tap water, this is great. But compliance gets costly for industries that produce a lot of wastewater, like refineries. And this is just one aspect of the industrial oversight story.

Regulation gets more contentious when you talk about agency interpretations that impact the culture wars. Title IX, for example, prohibits sex discrimination in educational programs that take federal money. It was passed in 1972, long before the American public developed a more robust vocabulary for sex and gender, so it's up to the Department of Education to determine regulations on whether sex discrimination includes gender identity. (Both Trump administrations have said no, and the Biden administration said yes).

Business opposition to regulation and the culture wars have helped terms like *deep state, administrative state,* and the *DC swamp* slither into our political vocabulary in recent years. The idea is that an army of government bureaucrats or lobbyists is controlling the country, to nefarious ends. In fact, the many thousands of bureaucrats in government have a less threatening task: They are responsible for ensuring compliance with rules across different areas of life. Regulatory lawyers at law firms spend much of their time in direct contact with these bureaucrats, negotiating interpretations, seeking approvals, or trying to avoid enforcement.

Regulatory lawyers wield technical expertise that most Americans cannot access or understand. Unlike litigators who fight in open court or transactional lawyers whose deals eventually become public, regulatory attorneys work in the shadows of administrative agencies that handle things like food, banking, energy, finance, and healthcare. They craft strategies that help corporations navigate complex rules while avoiding public scrutiny. Their specialized knowledge can be a form of power that advantages corporate clients when their interests clash with the welfare of ordinary people—especially since affected communities often have no lawyer representing their interests.

Environmental regulatory lawyers exemplify how technical expertise can perpetuate inequality. The harms their clients are responsible for are tangible, documented, and sometimes fall hardest on communities with the least power—people in poor American communities and poor countries around the world. They help their clients maneuver through environmental rules that are underdeveloped because of the fast pace of industrial change as well as shifting political priorities. Communities, in turn, pay the price with their health. These lawyers' work demonstrates how legal expertise that is abstracted from or indifferent to human impact can enable inequality. In this line of work, questions about community health and planetary survival can easily morph into technical regulatory compliance problems.

To illustrate how this works, I'll begin by describing the general regulatory landscape in relation to large law firms. Then I'll dive into a specific area of regulatory lawyering in the environmental space: *carbon offsetting*. This is how some corporations pay to pollute: They shell out money for environmental projects elsewhere instead of reducing their own pollution. After that, we'll examine how this market that lawyers help prop up creates real consequences for communities here at home and around the world. We'll end with the questionable science behind these projects. Despite mounting evidence of these problems, lawyers continue to structure deals that promise environmental benefits, raising questions about their responsibility to the planet that we call home.

Regulatory Attorneys at Law Firms

In some firms, regulatory attorneys are not separately categorized but are grouped with transactional attorneys or litigators. A transactional lawyer might do the regulatory work of making sure that a client's employment benefits are in accordance with Department of Labor rules, and a litigator might provide compliance advice before putting the gloves on and going to court.

Some firms distinguish regulatory work because the specialization is particularly intense. The Code of Federal Regulations, which contains all the regulations of federal agencies, is 185,000 pages, which is almost four times larger than the United States Code of laws that holds statutes passed by Congress.[1] And that is to say nothing of various regulations passed by states as well as other countries where Big Law clients have a foothold. There's a reason why President Trump complains about overregulation and why Elon Musk brought a literal and figurative sledgehammer to federal agencies. Helping clients comply with a web of state, federal, and international laws is a special talent and costly.

Regulatory lawyers often provide advisory services, like helping a pharmaceutical company prepare for an audit by the Food and Drug Administration (FDA). Other times their work is more dramatic—for instance representing an employer in front of the National Labor Relations Board (NLRB) against charges of interfering with workers' right to organize a union. Regulatory attorneys are, in some ways, Swiss Army knives.

Unfortunately, regulatory attorneys camouflage the inevitable tensions that arise between profit-seeking, liability-avoiding corporate clients and the general welfare of society. The magic word *compliance* does much of the concealing. It depoliticizes very technical but grave regulatory issues and reduces them to mechanical rule-following. Corporate and public interests do not always clash, but when they do, the legal ethic of attorney loyalty and the business-to-business nature of Big Law representation make it easy for corporate interests to prevail. In those instances, consumers, workers, poor people, and the environment can be some of the casualties.

Many Americans carry what corporate law scholar Victor Fleischer calls "a vague intuition that the rich, sophisticated, well-advised, and politically connected somehow game the system to avoid regulatory burdens the rest of us comply with."[2] He's on to something. Here's a quick potpourri of regulatory shenanigans compliance attorneys are implicated in but that are not part of our national conversations about inequality.

First up: *regulatory arbitrage*. This sounds fancy, but it's when business activities are structured in a way that takes advantage of regulatory gaps, kind of like Black Friday shopping for weak rules. The simplest example is incorporating a company in a country that provides favorable tax treatment. This is legal and defensible in a globalized world that permits the movement of money. But it also benefits the wealthy, reduces tax revenue that could be used for public welfare, and shifts tax burdens onto others.

A newer flavor of regulatory arbitrage is Uber's classification of its workers as independent contractors as opposed to employees. This designation allows it to avoid providing certain legal protections to its workers. That is great for Uber. It is not good for the drivers who are in states where independent contractor status means unemployment insurance and minimum wage standards don't apply.

Second, there is the *regulatory lag* (RegLag). This refers to instances where new activities or technologies *should be* regulated but are not due to some kind of delay. The lag could be a byproduct of uncertainty about which agency would be the optimal regulator, political resistance to creating yet *another* agency, or good old-fashioned congressional dysfunction, among other reasons.[3]

RegLag is well-illustrated by the nine-year gap between the arrival of e-cigarettes in 2007 and the FDA's 2016 move to bring them under its authority.[4] This "lost decade of inaction" was a byproduct of "an intense lobbying effort by the e-cigarette and tobacco industries." There were also "fears of a political backlash in tobacco-friendly states," bureaucratic delays, and a foot-dragging FDA commissioner who "previously served on the board of a chain of vaping lounges."[5]

During this period of lethargy toward e-cigs, regulatory attorneys in law firms of all sizes advised these companies like they were handling any other consumer product. Highly addictive vape juice hit the market. Youth-enticing flavors like crème brûlée, lychee, cotton candy, and churro contributed to a teenage public health emergency, with national surveys indicating that approximately 25 percent of high school students reported e-cig usage.[6] Exploiting and slowing down regulatory development is all "fair" in our system, and it is not limited to the vaping industry. Over the past decade, law firms have established regulatory practices in social media, artificial intelligence, and financial technology (fintech)—all of which significantly impact the public but often outpace government regulation.

A third issue is the *revolving door* between the government and Big Law. One can go from making $175,000–$200,000 at a federal agency to making $700,000 as a law firm partner and well into the millions if one has a large client base.[7] Some of these people have families to feed, so I can't knock the individual hustle, but the systemic implications are profoundly alarming. This lawyer carousel means that former public servants are selling their insider expertise to the highest bidders. Again, when corporate interests clash with public welfare imperatives—such as food, workplace, health, and consumer protections—you can make an educated guess about who the duty-bound regulatory attorney is going to prioritize.[8]

The revolving door is a bipartisan phenomenon. Eric Holder was a $2-million-a-year earning partner at Covington and Burling before becoming Barack Obama's Attorney General. Holder caught flak for not prosecuting the banks that were responsible for the 2007–2008 financial crisis (some of whom were Covington clients). A successful prosecution at the time would have been difficult considering the state of the law and the complexity of financial crimes. Still, Holder's Covington ties and return to the firm underscored public perceptions that the revolving door causes lawyers to tread lightly while in office and underregulate powerful corporations.

The firm reportedly kept a high-rise corner office empty during his six-year absence, like a friend saves a barstool at a tavern. During his homecoming, an excited Holder remarked, "I'm going to have the ability to use all the things I've learned over the years, not only domestically but internationally in a way that's going to be fun." Using insider, expert knowledge was going to be fun. "Big Fun," I suspect. Holder would go on to charge as much as $2,295 an hour.[9]

On the other end of the aisle, Eugene Scalia, the son of Antonin Scalia, has been described as "a skilled lawyer with a broadly conservative, pro-business and anti-regulatory agenda."[10] He has circulated between being the Secretary of Labor and the law firm Gibson Dunn, where he helps lead its regulatory group. He is one of the "go-to guys for challenging financial regulations."[11]

Government officials are scared to issue new regulations for fear of being sued by Scalia. When the Federal Trade Commission (FTC) banned non-compete clauses in 2024, Scalia filed a lawsuit *the same day*. Overall, much ink has been spilled on the revolving door's complex effects, but the core issue is straightforward: Former officials monetize their government experience for corporate benefit.[12]

With an understanding of how regulatory attorneys can finesse the system via arbitrage, lag, and revolving doors, we can now consider an area they help shape: our physical environment.

A critical caveat: The rest of this discussion proceeds with the presumption that climate change is human-caused and serious. The fact that I've worn open-toe sandals on Christmas in Philadelphia is a problem. But one does not have to accept that premise to get something from what follows. Whether you are a populist who thinks climate change is an elitist project; an industrialist who believes, in earnest, that economic development trumps environmental concerns; a fossil fuel lover (from executives down to workers) who thinks green initiatives threaten your livelihood; a conservative who looks askance at woke "green" agendas; or a libertarian who sees climate action as another form of government creep—by the end of this chapter, you may be even *more* likely to see what I'm describing as a big multibillion-dollar scam.

Carbon Offsets and the Pollution Trading Floor

Climate change can feel abstract or complicated, but at its core, it refers to the long-term changes in global weather patterns, specifically the warming of the planet. It has been tied to human activities such as cement production and different types of fossil fuel use. These pursuits increase the presence of carbon dioxide, the primary greenhouse gas in the atmosphere. Carbon dioxide accounts for about 80 percent of greenhouse gas emissions, so that's where we'll spend most of our attention.[13] An added point: When people cut down forests (deforestation), they remove critical vacuum cleaners—trees—which suck carbon out of the air. This also impacts climate change.

Climate change has touched every part of the country. Wildfires in the Pacific Northwest, megadroughts on the West Coast, floods in the Midwest, rising sea levels in the Gulf South, hurricanes on the East Coast, 90-degree weather in Alaska, and national heatwaves across the country have all been linked to global warming. Failure to address climate change means more of these extreme weather events, the extinction of entire species of plants and animals, disruptions to our food supply, and water shortages. Here are the key numbers: The Earth's average temperature has already increased by 1.9 degrees Fahrenheit since 1880. The international goal is to keep that increase under 2.7

degrees—a target that would require global net-zero emissions within the next few decades.

Regulatory attorneys play a role in climate progress by advising clients on how to meet emissions rules, reduce their footprint, and take part in carbon offset programs. The specifics are complex, but carbon offsetting allows entities to pay to pollute while saying they are working toward ending climate change. Think of it like this: Some companies inherently produce massive carbon emissions—oil companies engaged in refining, airlines flying planes across continents, and manufacturing plants running energy-intensive operations. But even seemingly benign institutions participate in this market. Universities, for example, burn enormous amounts of natural gas heating and cooling their campuses.

These entities can "offset" their carbon footprint by paying for projects that reduce carbon emissions elsewhere. That other place might be in Uganda, where forestation projects aim to plant trees that absorb carbon from the air; India, where the creation of wind farms has helped generate electricity without burning carbon-emitting fossil fuels; or Honduras, where energy-efficient, air-quality-improving stoves have proliferated.

There are two kinds of "markets" for carbon offsetting.

Voluntary markets are optional and the bigger of the two. In this instance, a tech company might estimate that its carbon footprint is one hundred thousand tons a year. It may go all in and decide to purchase one hundred thousand offset credits from the developer of a forest conservation project, even though they are not legally required to do so. Why? The reasons vary. Leadership might believe that decarbonization should be a corporate priority. The company might want to distinguish itself from its competitors as being *more* ecofriendly. However, a company might participate in offsetting to window-dress, distract the public from its environmentally harmful practices, and/or delay the inevitable need to change its operations. Irrespective of intentions, loose rules in the voluntary markets help companies conjure whatever climate story they want to tell.

Compliance markets, by contrast, are grounded in law. California has one of these systems and seeks to limit greenhouse gas emissions. To illustrate how it works, imagine the state sets a cap of one million tons of carbon annually and the California Air Resources Board issues one million allowances that allow entities to emit a ton of carbon per allowance.

Suppose Chevron is issued 380,000 allowances, but it expects to emit 400,000 tons of carbon, leaving a 20,000-ton shortfall. Chevron has a few options. It could invest in a reforestation project that offsets the 20,000 tons of carbon, or it could buy allowances from another company. Assume here that Amazon has an allowance of 210,000 tons but only used 190,000. It could sell the remainder to Chevron. If one allowance costs $30, then Chevron would have paid $600,000. Either way, Chevron can continue to pollute as usual without reconfiguring its operations.

Carbon offsetting is not a bad idea. Some say the point is to make pollution expensive. Offsetting can be an important stopgap measure that reduces emissions in the short term while long-term solutions are being developed. The trouble is when good intentions enable bad habits. Think of it this way: Some days I run five miles, or lift weights, and then turn around and eat a carnitas sandwich slathered in butter (a torta). I'll also delude myself into thinking "I earned it" and that this is a good source of protein. To put it crudely, carbon offsets are akin to trying to out-exercise a bad diet. It's hard to argue that exercise or offsetting itself is unwise. But if Chevron is still emitting the same levels of carbon and I'm not actually reducing my overall calorie intake, both exercises offer marginal gains while avoiding the hard work of cutting out the vice.

The Slow Violence of Carbon Offset Lawyering

Where do lawyers fit in the picture? Regulatory attorneys who work on carbon offsetting are helping transform the climate crisis into a financial product. They lend their expertise to an enterprise that has a jagged set of regulations, is globally stratifying, and is domestically uneven. This is the kind of "slow violence" described by environmentalist Rob Nixon that "occurs gradually and out of sight" and is "dispersed across time and space."[14]

On the global level, a post–Paris Accord framework aims to facilitate cooperation between countries seeking to engage in carbon trading. But when you look at the countries that host offset projects, the picture is murkier. One study focused on the stewards of these lands—Indigenous Peoples, local communities, and Afro-descended People.[15] It found that only half of the total land held by these groups is recognized by local governments. This means they have limited property rights or ability to stop corporations from taking their ancestral land for offset projects. Very few countries have regulations that specify a definition of carbon credits, who owns them, or how they are traded. Only a handful of these communities have established feedback or grievance mechanisms. This lack of legal recognition and regulation is a recipe for massive land grabs in the Global South facilitated by corporations and local foreign governments, with lawyers playing a quiet background role.

In the context of American regulation, about a quarter of American states have cap-and-trade programs like California's. There is no national regulatory framework for carbon offsets as the impacted industries are too powerful and climate change legislation is too controversial. A few agencies that deal with financial instruments dabble (e.g., the Commodity Futures Trading Commission [CFTC] and the SEC). The FTC tries to regulate the marketing side of carbon offsets to avoid deceptive advertising, but there is no central regulatory figure. Under the Biden administration, federal oversight remained minimal; during Trump's second administration, what appears to be RegLag may simply become regulatory abandonment.

For offset lawyers, this regulatory uncertainty creates expansive opportunities to navigate gray areas and exploit oversight gaps on their clients' behalf. In the local and international contexts where regulations exist, attorneys get approvals from governmental bodies and stretch the rules as far as possible to keep compliance costs down for their clients. They work on the side of carbon offset buyers and sellers, helping clients navigate the various standards that are supposed to determine project quality.

The corporate descriptions of carbon offset work reveal Big Law's discursive power. Community displacement and pollution get transformed into financial products, while questions about real-world impact fade into the background. One major law firm in the field describes having a "deep bench" of lawyers who work on "all aspects of carbon finance including derivative products and securitization, and carbon funds."[16] This is a fairly technical description of their work that masks the reality that they participate in the creation of a legal infrastructure that uses financial instruments to permit the trading of pollution rights.

Another firm notes how a senior partner helped clients "monetize the environmental attributes of clients' innovative practices and materials to earn recognition as carbon offset credits."[17] This is code for: "We will help you simultaneously profit from your innovations while presenting them as atonement for the world's climate sins."

A competitor touts helping carbon offset clients with the "monetization of new and emerging pathways for traditional oil and gas producers."[18] Dissect this sentence for a moment and its true meaning becomes clear: Lawyers helping fossil fuel companies—the primary drivers of climate change—find new ways to profit from the environmental crisis they helped create.

Many firms are often coy about *who* they represent. This may be because the client prefers confidentiality. There is also the phenomenon of *green hushing*, which is when businesses don't talk about their climate goals to avoid regulatory scrutiny and reputational harm.[19] Firms may also want to maintain a competitive advantage over other firms, avoid the watching eyes of climate change activists who might want to sue, or preserve space for plausible deniability should an offset project go awry. A representative description of prior work is more likely to look like this:

> "Advised a sovereign wealth fund and Macquarie on their potential investment in a forestry project in the DRC, including the due diligence of the project."[20]

What does this even mean? A sovereign wealth fund is a state-owned entity that invests money on behalf of a country, like the Norway Government Pension Fund Global, the China Investment Corporation, or the Abu Dhabi Investment Authority—all of which are individually worth a trillion dollars, give or take. The Australian investment bank Macquarie is the world's largest infrastructure manager and is nicknamed the "Millionaire's Club" because of its history of profit generation.

So we have a bank and an anonymous country with dollars to spend interested in the Democratic Republic of Congo (DRC). The Congo Basin has been referred to by the World Bank as the "lungs of Africa" because it's the world's largest carbon sink, meaning it absorbs massive amounts of carbon for the atmosphere. This makes it an ideal candidate for offsetting projects.[21] What could possibly go wrong when a richer country and a multinational bank team up to develop a carbon offsetting project in the DRC? This is the same Congo where Belgium's King Leopold once turned rubber extraction into an enterprise that killed *millions*. For over 150 years, this region has been a source of exploitation for Europe and America.[22]

The devastating consequences of carbon offsetting are found throughout the Global South. Indigenous People manage or hold tenure on 25 percent of the world's land surface, and their territories are home to 80 percent of the world's plant and animal species.[23] Their native lands are often targeted for carbon offsetting projects despite their lower culpability for climate change. One study found that in 2019, the richest 10 percent of the global population emitted approximately 48 percent of global emissions, whereas the poorest half of the global population was responsible for only 12 percent.[24] This means the communities that contributed the least to this climate crisis are now watching their ancestral lands get signed away by governments, developers, corporations, and the lawyers who make these deals possible—all to fund projects that let the biggest polluters claim environmental virtue.

Tom Goldtooth (Diné and Dakota) is an award-winning executive director of the Indigenous Environmental Network in the United

States. He has described carbon offsetting as "part of a system that privatizes the air that we breathe" since it "allows polluters to buy and sell permits to pollute instead of cutting emissions at the source."[25]

Fany Kuiru Castro, an Indigenous Uitoto leader from the Colombian Amazon, has described how carbon pirates "arrive in communities with long legal documents in English and don't explain what's in them" even though "many Indigenous communities don't read or have low literacy, so they don't understand what they're agreeing to."[26] The work of regulatory attorneys in global law firms legitimates and institutionalizes the expansion of offset mechanisms that have been described as "carbon colonialism."[27]

One law firm remarks on how its leading partner helped "open the gates" for carbon offsetting in Cambodia.[28] But Human Rights Watch has found that Indigenous Chong people in that country have been subject to forcible evictions and arrests while not getting access to contractual sharing agreements that would allow them to benefit from carbon projects.[29] The question is not whether this particular lawyer directly caused these specific harms—that would be difficult to establish considering the aforementioned evasiveness law firms maintain about some offset projects. What is more important is how law firms contribute to building legal frameworks that reflect and institutionalize global power imbalances. They are helping create structures that make such dispossession possible, even when individual lawyers never intended these outcomes for particular communities.

A still-unfolding example from Brazil puts a finer point on the problems of carbon offsetting. The Lowering Emissions by Accelerating Forest Finance (LEAF) Coalition is a public-private partnership that protects tropical forests. The United States, United Kingdom, and Norway are some of the "donor governments" involved. "Corporate participants" include Airbnb, Delta, and Walmart. Emergent is the "plug"—a nonprofit that connects corporate buyers of carbon credits to countries. The law firm Latham and Watkins has provided ongoing support to Emergent since 2019, helping the company navigate multimillion-dollar deals "involving more than 25 lawyers across offices in the US, UK, EU, and Asia."[30]

In 2024, Latham advised Emergent on a $180 million forest protection deal. When Brazilian Governor Helder Barbalho announced the agreement, he claimed Indigenous Peoples had input. Weeks later, thirty-eight Indigenous and community organizations called his bluff and said they were not consulted.[31] They accused the Brazilian government of violating the internationally recognized right of "Free, Prior and Informed Consent." This is the right of local communities to be involved in development projects that impact them without coercion (free), before a project commences (prior), with complete information about its impact (informed), and in good faith dialogue (consent).[32]

After the bad publicity, the Brazilian government walked back their comment and clarified that though an agreement was in place, things would not be finalized until 2025, after a "collective construction process" and "a new phase of dialogue" with local communities.[33] The whole process was giving "secure this Amazon and Bayer money first, and sort out nagging details about Indigenous rights later" vibes. Indigenous Peoples in Brazil should be worried about what looks like a slow-motion tragedy.

Activists have complained that Latham's client, Emergent, has failed to conduct meaningful consultations with Indigenous Peoples affected by carbon offsetting. The response signifies some of the problem. Emergent executive vice president Philip Brady replied, "We have to be really clear that Emergent and the LEAF coalition's role in terms of engaging with Indigenous peoples and local communities" is to "make them aware and assist their understanding of the process and, yes, to gain their support because that is crucial. But it is not the responsibility of Emergent and LEAF to consult with an [Indigenous] group on their involvement in a particular host jurisdiction."[34]

Brady is saying that they will *talk* with these impacted groups and educate them, but they will not *consult* with them about a specific project in their country. Look to the local government if you want that kind of engagement. Under "Free, Prior and Informed Consent" principles, Emergent is probably right, as such consultation is likely a governmental obligation. But when local governments want foreign investment, and carbon brokers disclaim responsibility for community engagement, what protection do affected communities actually receive? What's the role of the Big Law attorney a thousand miles away?

Whether lawyers have broader obligations to these communities is debatable. However, providing technical expertise to a client that takes a hands-off approach to Indigenous rights isn't neutral. Carbon offset lawyers structure the transactions that keep this market afloat and help dictate winners and losers. Given the financial incentives involved, Brazil's history with carbon offset scams, and law firms' historical role in facilitating dispossession, this looks like another chapter in the annals of legal exploitation.[35]

Back in the US, regulatory attorneys work in states with carbon offsetting programs that are beset by criticisms over racial and socioeconomic disparities.

Scholars at the University of Southern California have found that large industrial facilities that emit the highest levels of greenhouse gases in the Golden State are more likely to be located in poorer, minority communities.[36] These researchers, along with a separate team at UCLA, found that many facilities *increased* their emissions in these disadvantaged neighborhoods while meeting their compliance obligations by using offset projects located *outside* of the state.[37] Similar results have been found in the eleven eastern states that have their own offset program. This has led critics to describe the carbon offsetting enterprise as a free pass that allows the fossil fuel industry to externalize the cost of pollution onto poor minority communities and transform those places into "sacrifice zones."[38]

Carbon offsetting is a form of environmental capitalism premised on the questionable idea that free markets can moderate climate change. There is also an inherent tension between the short-term focus on quarterly earnings that corporations have been criticized for and the long-term costs of mitigating climate change.[39] Put differently, carbon offsetting is a profitable form of climate delay. Institutional polluters, counseled by regulatory attorneys, can comply with regulations and voluntary commitments more cheaply than by promptly reducing their emissions. As a result, both buyers and sellers can transform pollution rights into what Columbia professor Katharina Pistor calls "coded capital"—assets that preserve or generate wealth.[40]

Scrutinizing Junk Carbon Credits

If the perverse incentives and sketchy nature of carbon offsets haven't convinced you, then investigative journalism, scientific studies, and new litigation may do the job. These revelations raise uncomfortable questions about the regulatory attorneys who spent years working within the legal architecture that legitimized what increasingly appears to be a global environmental shell game.

Verra is one of the world's leading certifiers of carbon offsets. In theory, its standards do the work of assuring the quality of carbon offset programs and are referred to by some lawyers in their description of their practice. The current board of Verra is led by a partner at Akin Gump, a law firm renowned for its work with the gas and oil industry. In 2023, *The Guardian* led a nine-month investigation that found that more than 90 percent of Verra's rainforest offset credits are likely "phantom credits" that do not represent real carbon reductions.[41] Verra fought back and argued that the investigation was methodologically flawed. But the subsequent resignation of its CEO, who confessed to some of the organizational shortcomings, and Verra's promise to phase out its methodologies in 2025, are telling.[42]

Other journalistic investigations that have looked beyond Verra have not been subject to the same falsification. Investigators at *Bloomberg* examined fifty thousand transactions from major offset databases that took place in 2021. They found that 40 percent of carbon offsets came from renewable energy projects that were ineffective and added no additional climate benefits.[43]

The New Yorker put the magnifying glass on South Pole, one of the world's largest carbon-offsetting firms. One of South Pole's projects covered a region of Zimbabwe that was ten times larger than New York City and involved the sale of approximately $100 million of credits to

Volkswagen, Delta, and Gucci. The firm discovered that only fifteen million of the forty-two million carbon credits were backed by real emissions reductions. Notwithstanding this evidence, the company continued to sell more than three million "environmentally worthless credits" to Porsche, Nestlé, and Nando's.[44]

A group of scholars from Stanford, Berkeley, Columbia, and other research entities examined California's carbon market and found that 29 percent of the credits they analyzed were not offsetting. Put simply, for every one hundred million tons of carbon companies claimed were being offset, twenty-nine million tons were not being balanced out. This 29 percent failure rate represents $410 million in credits purchased without real climate benefit—and, more gravely, pollution released into the atmosphere under the illusory guise of emissions reduction.[45] This is on top of research showing that many offset projects provide no additional environmental benefits.[46]

In late 2024, the Biden administration took on a set of federal prosecutions targeting the carbon offsetting industry. The cases center around Kenneth Newcombe, a founder and CEO of C-Quest Capital. C-Quest makes its money by developing carbon credit projects and selling them to companies that want to offset their emissions. One of their signature projects focused on bringing cookstoves to rural parts of Africa and Southeast Asia. The goal was to replace emissions-intensive forms of cooking, such as outdoor wood burning and traditional charcoal stoves.

Unfortunately, C-Quest provided misleading information about the effectiveness of these projects. Regulators from the SEC, CFTC, and DOJ came after them in what one firm described as "the first federal enforcement action related to fraudulent practices in the voluntary carbon market."[47] According to the DOJ, C-Quest lied about stoves that were never installed and claimed credits for stoves that were missing, broken, or installed at the wrong location.

In one inspection of a home where a stove was supposed to be installed, a C-Quest employee discovered that the house was no longer there—the beneficiary was living in a makeshift structure. COO Jason Steele replied, "Hmm, instead of losing all the carbon as a result of getting 19 out of 20 samples, can we ... build a stove in a nearby house, and say the person moved but gave the stove parts ... to another household."[48] In other words, when confronted with a missing house, the executives' solution was to invent a fictional stove relocation story to keep the carbon credits flowing.

CEO Steele pled guilty to wire fraud conspiracy, commodities fraud conspiracy, and securities fraud conspiracy and is cooperating with the Feds, while COO Newcombe is currently fighting the case. Due to this debacle, Verra—the registry that had certified C-Quest's projects—canceled five million overissued carbon credits in Angola, Kenya, Laos, Malawi, Mozambique, Tanzania, Thailand, Vietnam, Zambia, and Zimbabwe.[49]

The federal prosecution of C-Quest reveals the fraudulent foundations of a major carbon offset operation. Firms like Dentons, Latham and Watkins, Akin Gump, and Norton Rose Fulbright have all worked on cookstove projects similar to those at the center of the case.[50] While it's unclear whether any of these firms worked on C-Quest's specific fraudulent schemes, the prosecution raises broader questions about the legal profession's role in the carbon market. For years, C-Quest issued hundreds of millions of dollars in credits across multiple countries and carbon registries using standard methodologies— which suggests that the governing legal frameworks were insufficient to prevent or detect fraud. That design failure, and continued dealmaking, forces us to ask: How do we think about regulatory attorneys who hold themselves out as market leaders and experts in an area that has proven itself to be ripe for abuse and that rests on questionable scientific foundations? The 2008 financial crisis from just under two decades ago provides a troubling answer.

THE 2008 FINANCIAL CRISIS involved a different regulatory environment and distinct economic harms as compared to the offset industry issues just described. Yet there are still some striking similarities.

Both involve the creation of new financial instruments. In the leadup to the financial crisis, banks, with the help of lawyers, took risky subprime loans and bundled them with other mortgages into a complicated financial product called *collateralized debt obligations*. The riskiness of these financial instruments was masked from the world. Similarly, with carbon offsetting, lawyers take these permission slips for polluting and bundle them into derivatives in a context where their efficacy is questioned.

Both involve creating new markets. Before the 2008 crisis, banks and their lawyers designed the legal frameworks for the purchase, sale, and trading of these risky assets. Carbon-offset lawyers today perform similar work in a market already worth billions—and projected to reach a trillion within a generation.

Both the financial industry prior to 2008 and the current carbon offset industry involve lawyers who assist clients in navigating gray regulatory areas. Before the financial crisis, attorneys provided legal opinions to bank regulators regarding the permissibility of these instruments while they advised clients on how to navigate regulatory gaps. Today, carbon credit lawyers assure the few regulators that exist about the soundness of offsets while counseling clients about how to operate in a jagged regulatory environment.

Both instances presented verification challenges. In 2008 there were loud critiques about the failure of lawyers and others to conduct due diligence on the quality of the underlying mortgages, and today a steady stream of reporting and research questions the value of offsets.

In addition, both these industries involve profound systemic risk not just to historically marginalized communities, but to society writ large. In the 2008 crisis, Americans lost $9.8 trillion in wealth and the world lost an estimated $50 trillion.[51]

If one is skeptical of climate change, then the price of offsetting is the cost of an artificial market that defrauds consumers and third parties. Climate believers face their own problem. Even assuming the offset industry improves, the solution's modesty remains troubling. As one booster admits, "We can't offset our way to a solution.... Let's be honest. The voluntary carbon market only exists because there isn't the political will to introduce a carbon tax economy-wide."[52]

If one believes in climate change and the offset industry retains its current form, then the stakes will far exceed those of the financial crisis. As long as these markets continue feeding us the fiction of climate responsibility while delaying genuine environmental progress, we won't be talking about foreclosed houses and depleted bank accounts—we'll be talking about the inhabitability of our planet itself.

CHAPTER 12

Litigating Labor: Class Action Killers, Wage Theft Accomplices, and Union Busters

Before I worked at a law firm, I was confused about a lot of things. I mistakenly believed *litigation*—the resolution of legal disputes through courts—made the world go around. I narrowly understood transactional work as haggling and doing deals; it seemed like a sideshow. Regulatory work was too mysterious and gray. But litigation? That felt like the main event. I thought I understood legal practice, but in hindsight, my views were laughable—in the same way a toddler thinks they're helping you cook because they stirred stuff in the bowl a few times.

But I was crystal clear about one thing: I wasn't doing employment discrimination defense. Not ever. Not for nobody.

Two of my mentors from my days as a researcher at the American Bar Foundation were sociologists Laura Beth Nielsen and Robert Nelson. They were working on a book with Ellen Berrey about workplace discrimination, and their research painted a stark picture of how these cases actually played out.[1]

At Berkeley, I took courses with employment specialists and understood the basic framework—that employment discrimination consists of workplace violations grounded in differential treatment based on race, gender, age, disability, religion, and other categories of difference. And I knew who Big Law worked for in these cases: the companies. Almost always companies.

As a late bloomer—graduating from law school nine years after college—I had friends knee-deep in the workforce and they told me tales of workplace discrimination. The stories were consistent and spooky.

Don't get me wrong—I wasn't judging the lawyers who did that work. Most of my scholarship at the time focused on public defenders—lawyers who represent the marginalized, yes, but also people who've done reprehensible things. I may have been confused about the contours of corporate practice, but I wasn't naive about the moral complexities of legal representation. Having grown up around hustlers and opportunists, I knew that employers sometimes faced frivolous lawsuits from individuals trying to exploit the system.

But I knew myself well enough to recognize that this particular compromise—defending systematic workplace discrimination against people who looked like me, my family, and friends—would have corroded something in me that I wasn't willing to sacrifice. This wasn't misguided idealism, but self-knowledge.

When I got to Sidley Austin, I did mostly general litigation. Think of it as being a substitute teacher, but for lawsuits. People in general lit don't have their own specialty; instead, they get pulled into whatever legal fight needs extra bodies with law degrees. The firm had a staffing system that tracked everyone's workload and assignments were handled through a mix of coordination and consultation. Sometimes you'd get assigned to a case because the system showed you weren't swamped with other projects; other times, coordinators would reach out asking if you had a few hours to work on a particular matter.

I always worried about the request for help with an "employment discrimination" matter but fortunately dodged it because of geography; most of the partners doing that work were in Chicago, and I was in DC. Besides general litigation, much of my other work was in the healthcare space. However, as a generalist, I learned a few things about litigation that apply across many fields but have unique expressions in workplace disputes.

In much litigation involving a company versus an individual, a company can outspend the other into submission. In this context, unlike transactional or regulatory work that tends to unfold at a greater remove, real people are describing real harms—and depending on the stage of the proceedings, they are doing so right in front of your face. Similarly, corporate defendants have to defend morally questionable positions in public documents and even in open court with a straight face.

Workplace litigation reveals American inequality in its full regalia. You see the power imbalances in ultra-high resolution. On one side, you see the team lawyers: a cavalry of sorts. On the other, you see the housekeeper with arthritis. She faces a blitzkrieg of motions and requests for information while being represented by a public interest attorney who is juggling dozens of cases. During depositions, you might see these corporate attorneys stare down an immigrant cafeteria worker as she describes being threatened with deportation for even thinking about unionizing. In federal court downtown, you see the law firm partner stand before a judge and argue that a bathroom break for a pregnant woman or a person with a disability would unduly burden an employer.

Some of these things are even clearer to me as someone who now teaches courses that cover workplace disputes. When I lecture on antidiscrimination law, I must cover the many laws that prohibit differential treatment of workers on the basis of race, sex, religion, disability, age, and national origin. When I teach in my social welfare law class—a course about how our safety net is supposed to work—I'm covering the laws about minimum wage, overtime pay, workers' right to form unions, and the unemployment benefits that keep people from going hungry between jobs.

In this chapter, I'm going to show how workplace litigation serves as a perfect microcosm of how lawyers perpetuate inequality. Workplace litigators operate within massive resource disparities that mirror broader class inequalities—corporate defendants can assemble teams worth millions while workers face barriers to getting a lawyer. These resource advantages don't just win individual cases; they reshape the entire legal landscape to favor corporate clients. To top things off, the professional demand and client expectation for zealous advocacy means participating in this kind of inequality looks like competent legal practice.

To illustrate how this system works, I'll start by describing the

David vs. Goliath–like dynamic that characterizes some workplace disputes. From there, we'll see how large law firms use procedural warfare to make workplace discrimination difficult to challenge. Then we'll drill down into wage theft cases—a capacious category that includes much more mistreatment than people might recognize. I'll conclude by turning to unions. In this world, litigators play defense and offense; they defend past workplace violations and help employers aggressively prevent worker organizing.

This isn't abstract legal theory—this stuff might impact your own life. Some of these tactics might be used by a current or future boss. (My own employer shows up in these pages.) And it might be uncomfortable. Some of the places you shop and services you use every day—Walmart, Whole Foods, Trader Joe's, Amazon, Uber, Lyft, DoorDash—are all part of this story. They've all hired large law firms to reshape the rules around how they treat their workers. The convenience economy we all enjoy operates on legal foundations that rarely get public attention.

The Artillery Gap:
Resource Disparities Between
Labor and Management

It's hard to understand employment litigation without understanding the artillery that workers and management bring (or do not bring) to these legal showdowns.

Many law firms have some kind of "employment and labor group" that is staffed with badass attorneys who represent employers. These groups actually cover a wide range of practice areas, but for our purposes, we're focusing on two. The first is employment law, which involves workplace bias, wage theft, and other violations of workers' individual rights, and is the subject of the first half of the chapter. The second is labor law, which concerns workers' right to organize, form unions, and engage in collective bargaining—the substance of the second half of the chapter.

Companies facing employment issues can receive a range of services from law firms. They might have a team of lawyers that handle everything from the employee's complaint to the judge's final decision. But there's more they can offer: economists who can make pay gaps look like the invisible hand of the market giving you a thumbs-up; jury consultants who know how to get regular people to side with corporations; private investigators who dig through employees' social media; and expert witnesses who reassure that disputed conduct is standard industry practice. Money can buy nice things.

Plaintiffs often lack access to this level of human capital or the funds to pay for it. If a person without wealth brings a lawsuit for being wrongfully terminated, they face barriers just getting a lawyer. Voluntary pro bono help is a longshot.

Contingency lawyers get paid only if they prevail, but this option raises problems since wages often determine the amount of recovery. Assume the plaintiff makes minimum wage, and the recovery is $3,000. If the contingency fee is 33 percent, the lawyer may not want to spend weeks working for a thousand bucks.

Some lawyers want an upfront retainer fee, which is going to be hard for plaintiffs to come up with without savings. In a study of employment discrimination attorneys, one plaintiff's lawyer said that he uses the retainer fee as a screener to force clients to "decide whether it's worth it to proceed with a case and to give them an awakening regarding the risk of losing."[2]

If the plaintiff-worker navigates these barriers and many others, they will likely be working with a smaller plaintiff-side law firm or a public interest organization that may be equally talented, but will not have a legion of lawyers to work on the matter.

The feds can get outgunned by corporations too. The Department of Labor (DOL) administers laws on workplace safety, minimum wage, and workers' compensation. Its legal office has received the same amount of funding in 2024 as it did in 2013, with zero adjustment for inflation. Meanwhile, personnel shrank by 17 percent and, in the words of the department itself, it has "restricted the provision of legal services, particularly in enforcement." A former DOL official in the George W. Bush administration noted that these resource constraints "have been a fact of life for a long time."[3]

These resource disparities sustain inequality in several ways. First, they deter plaintiffs from filing legitimate claims, keeping the status quo in place. Second, they allow law firms to use money to pummel opponents into submission through "litigation by exhaustion," leading to suboptimal settlements. Finally, these disparities enable firms to shape legal precedents favoring corporate clients, sometimes to the detriment of American workers.

Corporations face costs too. A $400 million class action could bankrupt a company. In these cases, and litigation involving smaller amounts, the employer might assess the case, and find that it's meritless. But the "nuisance value" of the suit might lead a business to resolve the case out of court. That settlement cost accounts for lawyer fees, reputational harm, and the hit to stock price that comes with being in a public legal fight, even when the company, in fact, did nothing wrong.[4]

Besides groundless litigation, perfectly legal behavior is misrecognized as a legal wrong in some instances. Labor law specialist Cynthia Eastlund explains how employer conduct is informed by legitimate economic motives—namely minimizing labor costs—that are not indicative of any kind of discrimination.[5] Nevertheless, the weight of documented evidence of employment discrimination and the billions stolen in wages annually suggests that worker exploitation is a bigger social problem than frivolous lawsuits.

The Employment Discrimination Defense Industry

Employment discrimination is a broad legal category that covers different kinds of "adverse actions" taken against someone because of their identity. These include actions involved in the areas of hiring, compensation, and termination, as well as more subtle actions like demotions and unreasonable schedule changes.

Let's get more concrete. Say a hijab-wearing Muslim woman or a yarmulke-wearing Jewish man works for a large corporation that has a dress policy that prohibits "caps." The company refuses to make a religious accommodation. Suing individually is difficult, so the employee decides to pursue a class action, which can address cost constraints. And since class members can be anonymous, class actions can also help mitigate fears of employer retaliation.

Large law firms have a less rosy view of employment discrimination class actions and sometimes brag about crushing them. Paul Hastings has one of the best employment and labor practices in the country and they have been described by *The American Lawyer* as "class action killers"—a title the firm proudly touts on its website.[6] Proskauer Rose defends "many of the world's largest and most well-known employers in class and collective action suits and expedites their resolutions creatively, *aggressively*, and efficiently."[7]

To get a better sense of Big Law's posture toward class actions, let's focus on *Wal-Mart v. Dukes*, a landmark 2011 Supreme Court decision that made it more difficult for women workers to band together and challenge sexist policies.[8] Betty Dukes, a Black woman who worked for Walmart as a greeter, sued her employer on behalf of 1.5 million female workers for sex discrimination. The plaintiffs argued that the company maintained a culture that enabled gender bias through decentralization and informality. Local managers had discretion over pay and advancement, but there were few standards, available jobs were not posted, and promotion was characterized as a "tap on the shoulder process."[9]

The "largely uncontested descriptive statistics" were damning. Women were paid less than men in every region and the salary gap widened over time. They were also "paid less than men across stores, even when controlling for experience, performance, and position."[10] Women also worked 70 percent of the hourly jobs but made up only 33 percent of management. A committee of female Walmart executives admitted that stereotypes limit the opportunities offered to women."[11]

The workplace stories were similarly striking. If a woman was interested in leadership, Walmart required her to relocate for management training, which was a non-starter for many women with families. If she stayed in the regular employee pool, she was funneled into stereotypical roles like cosmetics and baby clothes, while men were placed in more remunerative departments like sporting goods and electronics. To add insult to injury, women were repeatedly passed up for promotions and had to train the less-qualified men who jumped the queue.

The plaintiffs prevailed in lower courts, but Walmart pulled out the big guns on appeal and hired Ted Olson—the lawyer who helped George W. Bush win the 2000 election. Several Big Law firms filed briefs for Costco and the Chamber of Commerce—corporate allies who backed Walmart in this fight against workers.[12] They were reasonably concerned about big companies' exposure to class actions if the plaintiffs won. Optically and in the facts, the case was a proxy fight between labor and big corporations.

Walmart secured the victory not on the issue of whether its policies were discriminatory but on a technical question about class action requirements. The opinion was written by Justice Scalia, who, one study shows, was one of the top ten most business-friendly justices in the late twentieth and early twenty-first century.[13] He ruled that the plaintiffs couldn't meet the procedural requirement of sufficient "commonality." In short, Scalia was asking for a more common thread among the plaintiffs; something like evidence of "discriminatory bias on the part of the *same supervisor*."[14] Since Walmart was so decentralized, the women's experiences were too varied to challenge collectively. Pervasive bias became a procedural escape hatch rather than proof of guilt.

The *Dukes* decision made it more difficult for employees to bring class actions for discrimination.[15] Assuming an aggrieved employee isn't forced into arbitration, they could bring smaller, regional class actions, which have had mixed success.[16] The alternative—individual lawsuits—faces all the resource barriers I described earlier. Such scattered individual cases may not provide enough incentive for national corporations to change their behavior.[17] Walmart might stay in the news with gender discrimination lawsuits because it is the biggest employer in the country.[18] And/or it could be because the retail chain, like many others, has a sex discrimination problem.

What's maddening about *Dukes* is how the legal system rewarded Walmart for being really good at discrimination. Walmart's lawyers did what law school trained them to do: Identify procedural requirements and exercise them with skill. They successfully transformed a massive civil rights violation involving 1.5 million women into a procedural technicality. They didn't need to deny the sexism to prevail, they just had to make it harder to challenge.

The import of *Dukes* applies not just to sex discrimination at Walmart but also to discrimination based on race, color, disability, religion, age, and national origin. In their advertisements to the world, many employment groups at law firms emphasize their ability to thwart class actions. *Dukes* remains one of their most powerful precedential weapons.

The Many Faces of Wage Theft

Obliterating class actions is only part of the story. The employer defense bar represents corporations in cases of wage theft—the withholding of wages and benefits that employees are legally entitled to. There are many variations of this. Employers might pay less than minimum wage, steal tips, refuse to pay overtime, or misclassify people as independent contractors. Despite the sound of the term, *wage theft* can occur for innocuous reasons, such as payroll errors or a manager's misunderstanding of complex employment regulations. Even if wage theft emerges from mistakes, it is unlawful and disproportionately impacts women, immigrants, and racial minorities who are more likely to work in low-wage jobs.[19] But with fifty-three million people working low-wage jobs—more than half of whom are white—Big Law's anti-worker efforts can end up cutting across racial lines.[20] The battles take several forms.

Minimum Wage: Analysts have estimated that minimum wage violations cost 17 percent of low-wage workers approximately $8 billion annually (or $3,300 per person). The Papa John's cases show how this plays out in practice.[21] The pizza chain was accused of paying approximately nineteen thousand delivery drivers in six states less than the federal minimum wage. The IRS recommends a wage of 45¢ to 60¢ per mile, but Papa John's paid drivers $1 to $1.50 per delivery irrespective of distance traveled; deliveries four miles or greater would easily wipe out their earnings. Lawyers at Ogletree Deakins tried to fend off the case using a host of technical arguments but failed. With a class action looming, Papa John's settled for $12 million in 2015.

After shelling out $12 million, you might think the company would adjust its practices. Instead, another class action involving 120,000 drivers in seven states made similar allegations. After seven years of litigation, what could have been a $750 million judgment settled for $20 million. Gerald Maatman has been one of the top class-action defense lawyers for almost two decades. In 2023, the same year the case settled, *Law360.com* designated him as 2023 Employment MVP because he took "mammoth employment law class action cases and successfully whittled down the suits." In his reflection on the case, Maatman sounded like a basketball player fresh off the court, still dripping sweat and adrenaline. "Of all the cases, that one was the most gratifying."[22] As I write, another class action involving *the same issues* is pending.[23]

Tip Theft: When an employer pockets tips for themselves or improperly distributes tips from a tip pool, they are engaged in tip theft. Though it is associated with the restaurant industry, it also applies to Uber, whose drivers have been described as existing barely above the federal poverty line.[24] In 2014, a rider pursued a class action against the company.[25] She alleged that Uber took a little less than half of a 20 percent gratuity fee that was supposed to go directly to drivers. Uber retained lawyers from Quinn Emanuel. They tried to use the *Dukes* ruling to prevent the class from being certified, to no avail. Uber settled for approximately $340,000, but refunded customers instead of giving the money to the drivers it cheated.

Misclassification: This form of wage theft involves stripping workers of most of the basic protections the labor movement fought for over the past century. Misclassifying workers as independent contractors allows employers to avoid paying into Social Security and Medicare. It also allows them to skirt minimum wage and overtime requirements and exempt themselves from discrimination and organizing laws that technically apply to employers.

Some people may want contractor status (for the independence, the ability to work remotely for multiple clients, and/or the tax implications). And in numerous instances the status is appropriate. DJs, freelance journalists, expert witnesses, and many others fit the definition of independent contractor. However, some people want the protections and benefits that come with employee status, and their work demands that they be legally categorized as such.

Women and minorities are overrepresented in seven of the eight occupations at the highest risk for misclassification.[26] David Weil is a former Department of Labor bureaucrat who recalls how "week after week" he witnessed investigations involving "the incorrect classification of all types of workers: janitors, home health aides, drywall workers, cable installers, cooks, port truck drivers, and loading dock workers in distribution centers." He rightfully observed that classification is "about protecting people in what is inevitably an unequal bargaining relationship: employment."[27] A judicial and legislative saga in California provides more context into the problems of misclassification.

In 2004, the delivery company Dynamex converted its California drivers from employees to independent contractors to generate savings.[28] When drivers challenged this reclassification, Dynamex assembled a legal team from three Big Law firms. They lost in court, and California subsequently passed AB5, a law that presumes workers are employees unless the company can prove otherwise. Backed by different Big Law entities, the California Trucking Association, Uber, and Postmates all challenged this unwelcome business threat—and lost.[29] This was a war against having workers classified as employees.

Gig companies—Uber, Lyft, DoorDash, and Instacart—responded by pouring more than $200 million dollars into a tailor-made law, Proposition 22, that exempted them from AB5. A majority of California voters supported it, and the California Supreme Court upheld it, thanks in part to advocacy by lawyers at O'Melveny and Myers, among other firms. Views on the law were complex, but the result was clear: Big Law helped companies systematically deny workers employee benefits while reshaping the legal boundaries of employee classification itself. It was a perfect example of legal inequality by design—the crafting of laws to primarily benefit employers.[30]

What binds these wage theft cases together—from Uber's tip skimming to misclassified gig workers—is how employment lawyers try to systematically redefine the boundaries of what employers owe their low-wage and blue-collar workers. These courtroom victories don't just harm the workers directly involved; they create legal precedents that make similar violations easier to defend in other industries. This pattern of making worker justice harder to achieve reveals the stakes in our next area. Unions represent one of the few remaining institutions capable of challenging worker exploitation and its normalization, which is why Big Law firms devote so much energy to helping their clients fight them.

Union Busting

So far, we've discussed employment law, which focuses on the employer/employee relationship. Labor law adds unions to the mix. Many large corporations either have unionized employees or want to ward off unions. Big Law equips them to handle both.

A *union* is an association that represents workers' interests on issues such as wages, benefits, work conditions, and grievances. The National Labor Relations Act of 1935 (NLRA) protects workers' rights to form unions, engage in collective bargaining with employers, and strike in certain instances. The law also created the NLRB, the federal agency responsible for enforcing American labor laws.

Before describing how management-side attorneys pummel unions and union mobilization, I have a disclaimer/admission: I'm mixed on unions. My mother's unionized hotel job kept a whole family afloat. It even had a college scholarship that my brother and I benefitted from. But I'm a scholar who knows unions have struggled with exclusion, corruption, and accountability.

Personal experience aside, the evidence suggests that unions are generally beneficial to workers. Union members cannot be fired "at will," which gives them higher job security. They also receive higher wages, have better access to health insurance, and accrue more paid sick days than workers who are not in unions.[31] Unions can also reduce wage gaps, as unionized women, minorities, and workers with disabilities earn more than their nonunionized counterparts.[32] Seventy-one percent of Americans approve of labor unions, the highest number in almost fifty years.[33]

But unions can be flawed. They have long histories of exclusion and discrimination. Unions were a driving force in the passage of the Chinese Exclusion Act of 1882, which prohibited swaths of Chinese immigrants from entering the country for more than fifty years.[34] The Teamsters has not been able to shake its association with the mob, or that time the Supreme Court said it funneled Black and Hispanic members into less desirable jobs.[35] Unions have also struggled with reigning in sexual harassment. Wilma Liebman, who chaired the NLRB under President Obama, described sexual harassment as "an ongoing problem for unions, especially those that were initially heavily male."[36] From the perspective of management, their collective nature can shield underachieving workers and hurt bottom lines.

Suffice it to say that I don't romanticize unions. They are imperfect institutions, but they can be critical counterweights to corporate power. Perhaps because of this reason (or in spite of it), management-side law firms try hard to squash unions where they exist and ward them off in workplaces where they do not. We'll cover the preemptive work here.

Big law firms often act as union busters. *Union busting* can be considered a derogatory term as it evokes images of late nineteenth-century gun-toting Pinkerton security guards clashing with organized labor. But the *Oxford Reference* tells us that union busting includes "attempts to pre-empt unionization" and "union organizing," as well as efforts "to break and remove a trade union in order to secure a non-union workforce."³⁷ By those standards, that's right in the wheelhouse of many law firms.

Some law firms are not sheepish about their anti-union work. The law firm Barnes and Thornburg advertises services in a soothing fashion: "A union flyer was posted on one of your facility's employee bulletin board last night. What should you do next? Fortunately, you don't have to know the answer—because we do.... We will get you through this.... *Our passion* is to preserve a client's freedom to manage and to assist our clients in helping them remain union-free." The firm then proceeds to list its adversarial conquests. "Our team has also helped companies avoid hundreds of campaigns across the country, including UAW, Steelworkers, Teamsters, CWA, IBEW, UFCW, UNITE-HERE, IAM, AFTRA, SEIU, the Laborers, GMPP, Sheet Metal Workers, [and] 1199, *just to name a few*."³⁸ Each acronym probably represents hundreds of workers who tried to organize and lost.

Other firms are a little more discreet about union avoidance activity and use the plain language of "labor relations." Much of their work is opaque because of weak disclosure laws.

A 1950s congressional investigation revealed unsavory antiunion conduct, including fake "company unions" that undermined real union efforts, disinformation campaigns, bribery, and extortion. Congress passed the Labor-Management Reporting and Disclosure Act (LMRDA) in 1959 to require public disclosure of money spent persuading employees about unions. But enforcement was sparse from the start.³⁹ By the deregulatory 1980s, the Department of Labor's handling of disclosure became so lax that a congressional committee called it an "abandonment of its enforcement obligation."⁴⁰

LMRDA exempts lawyers from disclosure requirements when they're giving legal advice or doing work that doesn't involve communicating with employees. As a result, much legal work opposing unionization remains confidential. Multiple administrations have tried to narrow this exemption, but business groups have successfully fought these efforts. Today, corporations spend an estimated $340 million annually on union avoidance.⁴¹

The unionization process provides many opportunities for these techniques. Workers can unionize in two ways. First, if a majority of workers sign authorization cards indicating they want union representation, employers may voluntarily recognize the union and begin bargaining. If the employer refuses recognition, workers must undergo a more contentious NLRB election process. They have to gather authorization cards from at least 30 percent of employees, then petition for a secret ballot election. If a majority of workers vote for the union, then it becomes certified as the representative for the workers.

Union avoidance sometimes involved regulatory lawyers and litigators. Overall, these labor lawyers are "writing speeches, training supervisors, [and] making videos and websites to convey the antiunion message," explains labor expert John Logan.[42] Union avoidance involves a smorgasbord of styles.

Sometimes it involves challenging workers' basic right to organize. This happened with graduate students at Duke and the University of Chicago. These billion-dollar institutions tried to prevent students from unionizing for better pay and benefits. They were told by university counsel, Proskauer Rose, that their teaching and research work wasn't really "work" and didn't entitle them to organize as employees.[43] (My employer used the law firm Cozen O'Connor to pull the same stunt.)[44]

Union avoidance could involve the tried-and-true tactic of delay—an allegation that has been lodged at Starbucks and its legal counsel at Littler Mendelson. Between 2021 and 2024, ten thousand workers at four hundred Starbucks locations agreed to unionize. Littler has been known for "using the intricacies of labor law to thwart organizing and, if unions win elections, to delay the bargaining indefinitely."[45] Delays slow down the prospect of improved work conditions that potential unions desire and can bleed union support over time, as workers may grow frustrated or lose faith in the process.[46]

Other hardball tactics include challenging the validity of the authorization cards and suggesting that signatures were collected improperly; accusing union members of unfair labor practices; and challenging as many ballots as possible after elections. Many of these employer challenges are technically legal and rational for an employer wanting to ward off unionization. "You've got to be kidding me if you think an employer should just sit back and take it," one management-side lawyer explained.[47]

Union avoidance work can maintain uneven power relations between employers and management. Stagnant wages play a critical role in economic inequality, and union avoidance can deprive workers of a mechanism that could help them secure higher wages, leaving that prospect to the vagaries of the market or an employer's discretion. This line of work also fosters political inequality by reducing the collective organizational voices of workers while giving business interests a louder say in public policy.

Large for-profit corporations are not the only ones relying on the union avoidance talents of Big Law firms. Lefty organizations also sometimes engage in union busting. The Center for Family Representation (CFR) provides legal assistance to Black and Brown parents in New York City with the goal of reducing youth incarceration and reliance on the foster care system. Workers there tried to organize, so CFR retained Winston and Strawn, a law firm that had a partner on its board of directors. The firm deployed attorneys who fulfilled their pro bono requirement by helping CFR stave off the unionization effort.[48] This meant lawyers literally performed charity work by crushing other workers seeking better conditions.

When employees at the ACLU of Kansas desired unionization because of a "toxic work environment," it hired Ogletree Deakins, leading one critic to say: "in Kansas, 'ACLU' apparently stands for 'Another Corporate Lackey Unmasked.'"[49]

Liberal newsrooms and media outlets have been bleeding jobs for the last decade, and staffers have increasingly looked to unions for job security. Months before employees at *New York Magazine* announced a unionization drive, management at the outlet held a "union-busting meeting" by Proskauer Rose.[50] When *Slate* inched toward unionization, Mark Joseph Stern, the well-respected legal writer, decried the "appalling" hiring of "notorious union-busting law firm" Jones Day.[51]

Politics and Prose is a popular independent DC bookstore that has been described as "liberal Washington's most sacred space."[52] The owners of the store were former union members but did not feel that a union was compatible with the thin profit margins of the book industry, or appropriate for their "three stores with a total of 104 employees." They tapped Jones Day when staff wanted to unionize.[53]

These scenarios and many more suggest that union avoidance is not necessarily a left/right issue but a labor-management concern. Things get uglier when you move from preemptive work to conflicts involving existing unions and for-profit employers.

Undermining Worker Power

Beyond preventing workers from organizing, law firms also help employers attempting to undermine collective worker power through aggressive interpretations of labor law.

The hotel industry, where housekeepers face particularly dangerous working conditions, provides a glimpse into how some of these legal strategies operate in practice. Housekeeping work involves an inordinate amount of standing, lifting heavy objects, repeated squatting, and kneeling that compromises joints and backs.[54] The work exposes the predominantly female workforce to toxic cleaning materials, bodily fluids, and bacteria.[55] Sexual harassment from colleagues and guests is common but can be undernoticed because of the vulnerability of these workers and the fear of repercussions that come with reporting.

Competition within and outside the hotel industry (e.g., vacation platforms like Airbnb and short-term rentals like Sonder) can encourage management to keep labor costs down. This can lead to stagnant wages and skimpy health benefits that don't match the increasing cost of living in some cities. Noteworthy labor protests and strikes have taken place at hotels in Boston, Chicago, Detroit, Las Vegas, Los Angeles, San Francisco, and Honolulu since 2018. Many of these employers secure top-notch Big Law attorneys to handle these disputes.

Such was the case in Alaska. Picture Yocasta Guerrero, Ana

Ynfante, and Sung Hee—three housekeepers at the Hilton Anchorage whose names tell you everything about who does this back-breaking work in America. These housekeepers were required to clean seventeen rooms per eight-hour shift. In 2018, the hotel underwent a renovation. It replaced old bathtubs with walk-in, glass-walled showers. It also added more sofa beds to rooms and replaced all pillows with longer and heavier ones.

These might seem like minor amenity improvements that make life nicer for Hilton Honors reward members, but they made the work harder, and the quotas remained the same.

These housekeepers now had to clean both sides of a sixty-three-square-foot glass enclosure and make sure that it was free of streaks, smudges, and watermarks. "As a direct result of performing those additional new bed-making tasks, combined with changing the numerous, heavier, and longer new pillows, and cleaning the renovated glass showers," housekeepers had to "work harder and spend more time cleaning the renovated rooms."[56]

When the housekeepers complained through their union, management forced them to sign documents acknowledging that failure to accomplish their quotas could lead to termination. The union filed a charge with the NLRB, alleging that the hotel violated various labor laws that prohibit employee coercion and require bargaining over changes in work conditions.[57]

The hotel hired Littler Mendelson. The lawyers did what they were supposed to do by rattling off a series of arguments designed to exonerate their client. They claimed that the renovations were simply business decisions not subject to collective bargaining. The firm also maintained that requiring workers to clean new fixtures didn't constitute a material change in working conditions. And to add a cherry on top, they maintained that the threat to terminate wasn't coercive.

If Hilton won, its arguments could have set dangerous precedents. Employers could more easily bypass bargaining by calling changes "business decisions." They could also pile on new, time-intensive, arduous duties without negotiating. And threats to terminate could be considered noncoercive. To be sure, the lawyers were doing what they were paid to do—following the playbook of zealous advocacy. But this is how unions lose power: through legal arguments that sanitize employer abuse and redefine worker protections out of existence. Fortunately, the DC Circuit Court of Appeals—considered the second most important court in America—ruled against Hilton.[58] But this loss hasn't deterred more ambitious, Big Law–fueled attacks on unions.

More recently, Starbucks, along with Whole Foods, Trader Joe's, and SpaceX have cut to the chase and said, "No more playing defense." Instead, these companies—all subject to unionization efforts—have made the bold argument that the NLRB judges are unconstitutional. This is part of a larger maneuver by big businesses seeking to challenge the practices of federal regulators and the agencies themselves.[59] My guess is that by the time this hits the shelves, the NLRB will have less power.

This may sound drastic, but as of this writing, the NLRB is stalled at the top. In January 2025, President Trump fired Gwynne Wilcox, one of the board's Democratic members, even though the law says she can only be removed "for cause." She sued and initially won in a lower court. But when the case reached the Supreme Court in May, the justices issued a stay—pausing her return without making a final ruling. For now, the firing stands. And the legal argument backing it? It's similar to the one raised by Starbucks, SpaceX, and Whole Foods through their attorneys: that the NLRB's structure is unconstitutional.

The agency isn't shut down completely—its regional offices still function—but at the top, it's inoperable. Whatever comes next—whether the NLRB is restructured, sidelined, or dismantled—one thing's certain: Big Law won't just be in the room. It'll be helping write the rules.

THE EMPLOYMENT AND LABOR DEPARTMENTS in American elite law firms possesses a power that goes far beyond individual client representation. These attorneys are actively shaping the material conditions of American working life—the place where many Americans spend their conscious hours; the site that determines some people's ability to care for aging parents and craft a new future for their children. In many ways, they are shaping the American Dream.

When they argue that 1.5 million women cannot challenge systematic discrimination because their experiences are insufficiently uniform, they are not simply defending Walmart—they are encoding inequality into legal precedent itself—creating uphill battles for people to collectively challenge workplace discrimination. And when they argue that the NLRB itself is unconstitutional, they're not just defending individual companies—they're dismantling legal protections for one of the few counterweights to corporate power. These high-profile attempts, as well as under-the-radar decisions that do not capture mainstream attention, push more and more of the burden of challenging systematic inequality onto isolated individuals who lack the resources to sustain such challenges.

All of this is happening through what appears to be neutral professional practice—people simply doing their jobs. These lawyers inhabit a spectrum of motivations that resists simple categorization. Some are true believers who fervently champion their corporate clients' interests; they're genuinely convinced that what serves business serves society. The consummate professionals deploy their considerable skills with studied indifference to the cause they serve. For them, the law is the law, and a client is a client. Still others focus on preserving what they see as the integrity of the adversarial system, believing that zealous advocacy on all sides ultimately produces just outcomes. Some lawyers—especially junior ones—aren't operating from any grand motivation beyond doing well at the discrete task they've been assigned. They might be asked to draft a memo on state overtime rules with little sense of the dispute itself or how it fits into the bigger picture.

But what emerges from this machinery—regardless of the private reckonings of those who operate it—is the slow erosion of already-compromised democratic ideals: equal treatment, fair pay for work, and the ability to organize.

PART IV

PUBLIC INTEREST LAWYERING

Intake

Public Disservice and the Paradox of Good Intentions

IN SOME WAYS, this part wrote itself. In others, it was the most difficult section of the book. I knew I had to write it, but it was the one that weighed on me the most.

I've either interviewed with or given talks at more than sixty of the approximately two hundred accredited law schools in the United States, and if you ask any law professor who has a faint idea of who I am, I'm the guy who writes about public interest attorneys—public defenders and lawyers in nonprofit and civil rights organizations.

I did a short stint as a lawyer in one of these public interest organizations—at the Legal Aid Society of the District of Columbia, where I worked on cases where upstanding working-class folks were simply trying to get Medicaid benefits that they were entitled to or remain in houses that sleazy landlords were trying to kick them out of illegally. People who work in public interest law are the people I talk to the most. Their labor is arguably closest to my moral commitments.

About a third of aspiring undergraduates consider law school because they "want to advocate for social change."[1] Only a portion of them actually go into public interest lawyering. At my institution and others, a non-negligible number gravitate toward me. For most of my career, I've either taught antidiscrimination law or poverty law every year. This is what I do.

But here's the challenge. Public interest lawyers perform the highly admirable work of advocating on behalf of society's most vulnerable populations. Criticism of them can seem misplaced and akin to dissing firefighters. You *could* criticize them, but they are not the first group that comes to mind when one thinks about the reproduction of inequality.[2] You could more easily point to police officers, prosecutors, and judges as sources of injustice. And with civil rights and civil liberties increasingly under siege, the work of these lawyers is indispensable. Still, that reality cannot exempt them from scrutiny because even the best-intentioned actors can reproduce the very hierarchies they are fighting against.

A maxim in subsects of the Black community applies with real force here: Some things in life are hard but fair, sad but true. Equality-focused lawyers and scholars—a category I'd put myself in—are implicated.[3] If you've gotten this far in the book, you've likely learned that I'm equal opportunity with my commentary. I won't disturb tradition here.

Why is it hard to talk critically about these lawyers?

First, these people have dedicated their lives to helping the marginalized; some may feel beyond reproach, *especially* from people who are not in the trenches with them. Some of them made the sacrifice of taking out six-figure debt to make five-figure salaries. To put things in perspective, a recent college graduate beginning their career as a teacher in Kentucky would start at a minimum salary of $56,421.[4] A recent law graduate beginning as a public defender in the same state would make $42,373, and that figure would jump to $57,000 once they passed the bar exam.[5]

Perhaps these lawyers have attended an Ivy League law school that costs around $75,000 a year. Public interest jobs in urban cities are competitive, so they may be like the smug rich kid I met in law school at a public interest event. Said dude told me he was going to go down South to begin his career and cut his teeth because "that's where you can get some real litigation experience." After gaining this proficiency, he planned to return to his hometown in the Northeast.

Or maybe they are a sweet student who was born and bred in rural Kentucky, is committing their life to serving the underserved, and attended the University of Kentucky for law school, which costs about $26,000 a year for in-state students.

Imagine telling these people, who may have paid anywhere from $75,000 to $250,000 for school, that they are part of the problem. It's hard to tell self-satisfied and well-intentioned people that they are implicated in the structures of subordination they are fighting on a daily basis. In a context where the federal government is increasingly moving toward austerity, which will make the lives of poor people harder, highlighting the faults of their legal allies becomes more challenging.

Reflecting a mirror back on public interest attorneys is also difficult because they are deeply wound up in liberal orthodoxy. Some have sincere ideological commitments to racial equality and the like, but sometimes an unstated assumption for them is that conservatives have a monopoly on the -isms and -phobias of the world. It's as if the last two two-term Democratic presidents didn't each have their hands in policies that progressives now disavow: Clinton helped shepherd mass incarceration and end welfare as we knew it, while Obama initially defended "traditional marriage" and oversaw a massive expansion of deportation.

I'm referring here to the "smooth-talking, self-congratulating white liberals" that *The New York Times* columnist Frank Bruni writes about. "They open their arms to a black visitor. Don't be duped. They're wolves in L. L. Bean clothing. There's danger under the fleece."[6] Setting aside Bruni's hyperbole, the challenge here is ideological certainty. Some people believe that because they have the right politics, they can't be part of a problem. Such certainty transcends identity and applies to racial minorities, women, and those born working-class.

Another reason why it's tricky to talk soberly about public interest lawyering is the murky definitional boundaries. In the mainstream legal world, most people use the same definition of public interest as Equal Justice Works (EJW)—a vital nonprofit organization that provides two-year, $63,000 post-graduate fellowships for people who want to enter this field. According to EJW President Verna Williams, public interest lawyers "focus their practice on helping low-income, marginalized, or vulnerable populations."[7] This is exemplified by organizations like the Women's Law Project in Philadelphia, which focuses on gender discrimination and addresses issues such as domestic violence and reproductive health. Or it could be an org like AppalReD, which directed some of its early efforts in the 1970s to helping coal miners in Appalachia and now has programs like a low-income taxpayer clinic for people in the region. Public interest groups also focus on LGBTQ+ rights, immigration reform, disability rights, and elder law. Championing these issues is something that many people would agree rightfully deserves a round of applause.

But the mainstream definition of public interest law is limiting. When people criticized Michael Jordan's disengagement in electoral politics, he famously said, "Republicans buy sneakers, too." Let's remix this. Conservatives engage in public interest, too, but they are rarely considered in this context. For example, the Alliance Defending Freedom (ADF) created the playbook for the overruling of *Roe v. Wade*, the American Center for Law and Justice (ACLJ) focuses on school prayer as protected speech, and Students for Fair Admissions (SFFA) put affirmative action in peril. Their positions may be anathema to *some* liberals, but they have public constituencies who either understand themselves as marginalized or are defined as such. However, mainstream organizations that underwrite public interest lawyering generally don't support this work (though the conservative donor network funds their own version of legal advocacy).[8]

The Skadden Foundation is another organization that funds more than two dozen law graduates who want to work in public interest. They provide $65,000-a-year salaries for two years. In their thirty-year history and in EJW's forty-year history, you'd be hard-pressed to see them fund lawyers who want to work on conservative issues such as gun rights or school choice vouchers, even though those issues impact marginalized groups, too. That's fine. They are entitled to do what they want with their money. But funding patterns speak to my point about definitional problems (of which there are many more) and the previous point about liberal orthodoxy.

Scholars of the legal profession have a much broader understanding. In their six-hundred-page book on public interest law, Scott Cummings and Alan Chen define the field as the "broad and contested range of activities that includes legal advocacy focused on the representation of individuals shut out of the private market for legal services." Sometimes the small business owner facing a discrimination lawsuit or the farmer fighting environmental regulations that threaten their livelihoods can't afford those services and fit within the definition. But Cummings and Chen don't stop there. Their definition also includes impact litigation handled by lawyers who "advance the collective interests of defined groups of constituencies." Some of these conservative organizations and their causes fit that mold, too. But this broader understanding of public interest is less sexy because it raises harder questions about who constitutes the public."[9]

Can you see some of the difficulties here?

Evaluating a field involving many dedicated public servants—some of whom are ideologically insistent and have a particular view about who is an insider—is no easy task. On balance, they unquestionably do more good than harm. But they too are subject to various kinds of implicit biases irrespective of their backgrounds, which makes this topic more sensitive than a loose tooth. But the gravity of public interest law's underbelly is too important to avoid.

This part takes on the challenge by outlining the inequality-producing features of a field focused on addressing inequality. Chapter 13 provides a brief history of the legal and political developments that shaped the field. Chapter 14 looks to the bottom and focuses on public interest lawyers who provide direct services, whereas Chapter 15 spends time on the high-level, policy-focused impact litigation taken on by liberal and conservative public interest organizations. As the cartoon character Darkwing Duck used to tell me on television in 1990: "Let's get dangerous."

CHAPTER 13

How We Got Here: The Political and Economic Straitjacketing of Public Interest Law

Every day in America, a special group of lawyers shows up to fight for people who have nowhere else to turn. These are the public defenders of the world who represent poor people accused of crimes. They are the legal aid lawyers fighting for people who are being evicted, denied disability benefits, or separated from their children by the state.

This might sound conspiratorial to some, but the legal system was intentionally designed to make these lawyers less effective and their jobs harder. Purposely and with precision. The proof is in the history, statutes, cases, and funding decisions.

In this chapter, I plan to show you how America perfected the art of defanging public interest lawyering. How so? By ensuring it could never fully challenge the systems that create its clients' problems.

Before the early twentieth century, legal representation for the poor operated on a volunteer model with minimal state obligation—if you couldn't afford a lawyer, you relied on pro bono work or went without.

The New Deal and civil rights movement expanded these obligations. The federal government slowly recognized that constitutional ideals might require actual legal representation as opposed to words and procedural promises. This culminated in the 1960s War on Poverty, which briefly promised a form of access to justice for marginalized communities.

But public interest law was systematically designed to fail through a process of political and economic strangulation. The 1970s inaugurated a conservative backlash that included funding restrictions that tied public interest lawyers' hands, Supreme Court decisions that rolled back constitutional protections, and eligibility requirements that turned away most people who needed help.

These moves created a system in which lawyers dedicated to fighting inequality find themselves trapped within constraints that were deliberately constructed to ensure that their work remains individually helpful but systemically compromised. This inequality by design mirrors society's approach to social welfare problems: interventions that inadequately address needs while avoiding fundamental changes.[1] The blueprint for this state of affairs was not drawn overnight.

The Mid-Twentieth Century Opening and Closing of Poverty Law

There is no need to luxuriate in a full history of public interest lawyering—a field that stretches back as far as the Founding Period, when white, antislavery activists created abolitionist organizations to raise legal challenges to slavery as well as to help free and enslaved Black people. I've done that work elsewhere.[2] For our purposes, the relevant starting point is the mid-twentieth century. At that point, tectonic shifts occurred in our civil and criminal justice systems. Both concerned the government's responsibility to provide lawyers to poor people who could not afford them.

Before the 1930s, the Sixth Amendment right to counsel, like many other constitutional provisions, was understood as a negative liberty. Just as the First Amendment prohibits the government from restricting speech, and the Fourth Amendment limits its ability to engage in unreasonable searches and seizures, the Sixth Amendment was understood as a restraint. The government could not *prevent* a criminal defendant from obtaining a lawyer, but it had no affirmative obligation to *provide* one. Some localities provided lawyers to poor people out of the goodness of their hearts, but this was not required as a matter of federal constitutional law.

During the New Deal period, the Supreme Court revisited this arrangement. Lawyers slowly became a constitutional requirement in limited contexts—mainly state death penalty cases and federal felonies. There was no federal legal right to an attorney in civil matters, so these litigants had to proceed on their own, rely on pro bono efforts, or approach the few local legal societies that were in operation.

By the 1960s, the federal government made some important moves on both criminal and civil matters.

On the criminal side, the Supreme Court ruled that lawyers were required in state felony cases. Felonies are serious crimes—things like murder, robbery, and aggravated assault. They can send you to prison for years. The court's ruling meant that if you couldn't afford a lawyer for these cases, the state had to provide one. The court also required police to inform people of this obligation—the Miranda rights often recited in television arrests.

On the civil side, Congress and the president authorized a War on Poverty that opened up the treasury and provided money for lawyers. In the early years of that initiative, the federal government dropped between $22 million and $60 million annually to underwrite the costs of lawyers for poor people facing housing, welfare, and civil rights issues.[3] This is when public interest lawyering took on the left-leaning character attached to it today. The field increasingly became associated with forms of government welfarism and social justice that some conservatives abhor. In any event, the expansion of the right to counsel and the funding of civil legal aid broadened a public interest law world previously occupied by a handful of civil rights and civil liberties groups and a smattering of legal aid organizations.

These public interest lawyers were bold. They walked into housing court challenging eviction notices that violated tenant rights, and they pushed back against welfare caseworkers who cut off welfare benefits because they felt like it. They used shiny federal dollars to sue under-resourced police departments for brutality. They were engaging in forms of legal aid that were radical and unfamiliar in American history—defending the use of Medicaid for abortions and representing Black and Brown militants in court. You can likely see where this was going.

In the 1970s, conservatives cried "malarkey" and launched a countermove. Their complaints had some merit, but they added racism, classism, and sexism as chasers, so they had what lawyers call "mixed motives."

On the criminal side, factually guilty people were getting their sentences reversed on legal technicalities that were exploited by government-funded defense attorneys—hardly good press for a War on Poverty.

On the civil side, federally funded lawyers went beyond working on garden-variety legal aid issues like evictions or family disputes. They were out challenging fees assessed on poor people trying to get a divorce, they were trying to expand welfare benefits, and they defended student protesters during the height of campus upheaval. For some conservatives, this was a revolution to oppose.

Black and Brown men who were beneficiaries of criminal legal aid were viewed with suspicion by conservatives as mass incarceration was taking shape. Their sistren, beneficiaries of civil legal aid, were stereotyped as Cadillac-driving, no-job-having, food stamps–using con artists. This played out during a decade marked by stagflation and recession.[4] It became too easy for a combination of genuine and insincere small government, cultural, and fiscal conservatives (along with some liberal coconspirators) to point a finger at lawyers and say enough is enough. The backlash targeted both civil and criminal legal aid, but the particular methods used in each area show just how surgical this dismantling really was.

The Art of Inadequate Criminal Defense

In the 1970s and 1980s, politicians shoveled money into police and prosecutors' offices while leaving indigent defense gasping for scraps.

Doing otherwise was political suicide. Then in 1984, the Supreme Court decided *Strickland v. Washington*. This case epitomized the judiciary's tolerance of indigent defense systems that were, in many places, starved into chronic dysfunction.[5]

Strickland created a standard that defendants must meet if they want to show that their lawyer sucked (in legal terminology, "provided ineffective assistance of counsel"). The defendant—who, to be clear, is challenging a sentence of guilty and likely doing so with a different lawyer—must show that 1) the performance of their initial lawyer at trial was unreasonably deficient and 2) such performance impacted the outcome. Both are hard to prove.

For example, let's say you're falsely accused of theft. There's a witness who can attest to your innocence, but your lawyer fails to call them to testify because they worry about his trustworthiness and fear that he will alienate the jury. *You* might think that was an unreasonably deficient performance, but a reviewing court might say: "Meh, your lawyer may have dropped the ball, but he was not *unreasonable*." If the first prong is not met, we don't move to the next step. Claim denied.

But let's assume that you can show the that the lawyer's performance was unreasonably deficient. The next task is to prove that said performance prejudiced the outcome. This is difficult for two reasons. First, many defendants are guilty irrespective of their lawyer's performance. Second, even when a defendant is innocent, proving prejudice is Monday morning quarterbacking. On appeal, the reviewing court may be looking at a defendant who has already been convicted, is still in prison, is unshaven, and is wearing some last-minute baggy zebra suit that their new lawyer got them "to look professional." It's going to be hard for a court to look at this person, who has already been determined guilty, and say, "This outcome would have been different." There are all types of motivated reasoning and hindsight bias in the air.

Consider the low bar this *Strickland* standard permits. In one noteworthy case, a federal court ruled that an attorney who slept while his client was being cross-examined *was* unreasonably deficient but said his REM sleep didn't impact the outcome of the case.[6] In another, a court found no deficiency or prejudice where a famously racist attorney known for "the three-martini lunch" referred to Black people as "jungle bunnies" and called his colleague "a big black nigger trying to be a white man." As for his client, the lawyer called him a "nigger" and expended relatively little effort or money on his client's death penalty case.[7]

The low *Strickland* standard further weakened government incentives to fund adequate defense. Why spend more when almost anything passes constitutional muster? Local officials also face real trade-offs—more money for public defenders can mean less money for things people may care *more* about (e.g., education, healthcare). There can also be a general unwillingness to allocate money to defendants—a constituency that in some places will be replete with names like Dewayne and Carlos; this group is certainly not organized or powerful like the American Association of Retired Persons (AARP). Chronic underfunding and judicial complacency have a predictable result: inequality baked into the structure of criminal defense.

Regulatory Extortion and Civil Legal Aid

In the last quarter of the twentieth century, things were not much better on the civil side. Federal dollars for civil legal aid attorneys not only dried up but were almost eliminated altogether. In the late 1960s and early 1970s, California Rural Legal Assistance, a legal aid group renowned for its work with Chicano farmworkers, dealt then-California governor Ronald Reagan some embarrassing legal losses. When he reached 1600 Pennsylvania Avenue in 1980, it was time for payback. President Reagan tried to nix federally funded services entirely. He failed, but the broader assault on legal aid had been building throughout the 1970s.

Throughout the last three decades of the twentieth century, Republicans, joined by some Democrats, continued to impose restrictions on legal aid attorneys who received federal funding. These restraints are somewhat akin to what libertarian professor Philip

Hamburger calls "purchasing submission." The feds essentially said, "Take our money and follow our rules about who you can represent," or get no funding at all.[8]

The prohibitions imposed on civil legal aid focused on lawyers who worked in the tradition of the 1960s' progressivism. The restrictions were knife work in a Michelin kitchen: sharp, controlled, and intentional. Two of the most vulnerable groups that desperately need lawyers—prisoners and undocumented immigrants—were cut off from federally funded legal aid.

Those class-action lawsuits that allow people to pool their grievances? Restrictions were imposed on those, too. Limitations on the collection of attorneys' fees further deprived already underfunded lawyers of another source of financial support. Legislators preferred isolation over solidarity; individual tragedies were less threatening than collective action.

Legal aid lawyers now face an impossible choice—federal dollars that come with strings and shackles, or the freedom to fight without the means to do so. Legal philosopher David Luban argues that these restrictions, and many others, "ensure that entire subgroups of low-income people will never be heard in the legal system."[9] The overall result in this highly constrained, underfunded corner of the profession is a situation where *millions* of people's legal needs are unmet and existing social disparities are reinforced. These constraints ensure that some public interest lawyers become complicit in rationing justice rather than expanding it, regardless of their personal commitment to equality.

In Their Own Words: How Structural Constraints Break Criminal Defense Attorneys

We now have a sense of some of the structural constraints that shape the work of public interest lawyers—some financial, some legal—but how do these restrictions impact the people they serve?

The conundrum of poor funding and compromised representation faced by public interest lawyers is what anthropologist Michael Taussig refers to as a *public secret*: forms of shared knowledge within a community that are not always openly discussed.[10] The reticence is tied to public defenders themselves, who are reluctant to discuss the poor representation component of the equation. Who wants to admit that they are doing a subpar job? Many defenders acknowledge crushing caseloads yet still insist they can be effective; admitting otherwise feels like defeat and can be a step toward leaving the work. That cognitive dissonance, reinforced by the hard-fought victories they sometimes win, helps them endure even as it obscures structural failure. But some attorneys have spoken publicly about the problems in indigent defense. Listen to the confessions of practitioners trapped in this system.

Jenny Egan has worked as a public defender representing juveniles in Baltimore. Egan, a white woman, described herself as "a queer, antiracist, feminist who works to fight injustices rooted in structural racism and economic inequality."[11] She worked with juvenile defendants in a city known for criminalizing Black children, and Black girls specifically.[12] When she told *Slate* that she had "the honor of setting kids free from chains back into their mothers' arms," she won me over.[13]

Egan has acknowledged that there is a dark underside to indigent defense: "I am a cog in that same machine, and my participation might be holding that system up as well." This feeling of complicity is shared by some public defenders and their clients, and it is tied to lack of time, lack of resources, and, as Egan says, high "caseloads that don't allow me to actually represent the way that I would."[14]

In Miami, the former chief defender admitted that his office could not afford to pay new lawyers a competitive salary, so they hired people straight out of law school and threw them into "little league" misdemeanor court.[15] The fallout from misdemeanor convictions is far from minor. A single conviction can trigger probation, eviction, loss of public benefits, separation from children, or even deportation. In other words, new lawyers learned on the job while people's lives were at stake.

New Orleans public defender Tina Peng was more confessional about the problems she faced representing poor criminal defendants in the Big Easy. Writing in the *Washington Post*, Peng explained, "An unconstitutionally high caseload means . . . that I miss filing important motions, that I am unable to properly prepare for every trial, [and] that I have serious conversations about plea bargains with my clients in open court because I did not spend enough time conducting confidential visits with them in jail. I plead some of my clients to felony convictions *on the day I meet them*."[16]

For the more quantitatively inclined, put it this way: Under national workload standards, a full-time lawyer should handle no more than 93 high-level misdemeanors or 150 low-level misdemeanors annually. In reality, each defender in New Orleans was handling the equivalent of *nineteen thousand* misdemeanors a year and spending approximately seven minutes per case.[17] Seven minutes to defend someone's freedom in the land of the free.

Former public defenders-turned-law-professors have offered similarly grim observations. Michigan law professor Eve Primus is one of the leading scholars of indigent defense. She has worked in this space in different capacities. "As a trial-level public defender . . . I have been in the jail lock up at the courthouse and seen appointed attorneys walk into the cell block on their client's trial date and say, 'Hi. I have been appointed to represent you. Here is what is going to happen. The prosecutor has offered you a really good deal, and I think that you should take it.' No introductions, no questions, no attempt to hear the client's story, no respect."[18] This was when she was in the trenches. Recalling her time doing appeals, she notes, "I have called trial attorneys to get a sense of what happened at trial only to hear them say things like, 'the client was obviously lying so I didn't bother to investigate.'"[19]

MacArthur Genius Award winner Jonathan Rapping argues that budget constraints force defenders to "shoot from the hip." Without paralegals or investigators, and with no time for research, these lawyers file "boilerplate motions" and raise only routine legal issues.[20] All of this is happening to the average criminal defendant, who, Harvard law professor Alexandra Natapoff notes, "has numerous personal attributes that make the attorney-client conversation challenging, including substance abuse, mental health problems, and functional illiteracy."[21] It's unfortunately a perfect storm: The most vulnerable defendants getting the most overworked lawyers.

Such anecdotes are borne out by more empirical data. Quantitative researchers have found that approximately three out of four public defender offices did not have enough attorneys to meet national caseload standards guidelines.[22] Qualitative studies have also shown how these constraints can cause defense attorneys to cut corners in ways that harm their clients.[23]

Overall, public defenders' inadequate funding and high caseloads lead to poor outcomes for their clients: languishing in jail before trial (when they shouldn't be), being pressured to take a plea bargain, being wrongful convicted, and being dealt excessive sentences that are not individuated because courts don't have all of the facts.[24] Public defenders work within what's often called an assembly line system of justice. Criminal law scholar Zohra Ahmed argues that at their best, defenders can "slow down the conveyor belt and create off-ramps" for their clients.[25] At worst, these overworked lawyers continue the rapid processing of defendants, which can exacerbate inequality in a flawed criminal justice system.

How Structural Constraints Shape Direct Services and the Civil Legal System

Civil legal aid is sometimes understood as less urgent because it doesn't involve incarceration. That reflects potentially impoverished ideas about state violence. The termination of parental rights based on false accusations of neglect represents its own form of kidnapping. Sending someone back to a war-torn country they barely remember can be crueler than incarceration. The denial of Medicaid coverage for a life-saving medication can be a death sentence.

Like public defenders, civil legal aid lawyers are underfunded and overwhelmed. But there's no constitutional right to a lawyer in a civil case, which means some people get no help at all. The Legal Services Corporation (LSC) is the biggest funder of legal aid and received $560 million from Congress in 2024, which is barely a third of what it requested. LSC and the organizations it funds must ration legal services like soup during the Great Depression. Who they help is determined by the meager federal poverty guidelines. To qualify for assistance, a single person seeking help typically needs to make under $18,825 before taxes (125 percent of the federal poverty level). That might work for people who make the federal minimum wage of $7.25. But if you live in a state like Nebraska or Nevada, where minimum wage is $12, you'd be above the eligibility cutoff and better pray that the provider makes an exception (which they sometimes do).

Eligibility restrictions are reasonable in principle, but in practice, these thresholds have the effect of turning away people in desperate need of help—many of whom would not be categorized as "privileged." These kinds of restrictions can lock out the white working class that the mainstream media discusses every election cycle and whose economic fragility is poorly understood. Eligibility restrictions can also impact a diversifying middle class. These individuals typically do not qualify for legal aid but cannot afford private lawyers. They are just one legal setback away from slipping down the social class ladder. An aggressive debt collector here or a Medicaid denial-of-service issue there could be disastrous.

And this doesn't even take into consideration the approximately one million people who *are* eligible, who come to one of these legal aid organizations, and who are turned away because it has limited resources.[26] One lawyer recounted, "We only represent probably 5 percent of the people who request assistance ... we're just continuously telling people: 'Well, no, I'm sorry you're going to lose your children, but I can't do anything for you.'"[27]

The sad but unstated reality is this: These legal aid orgs are implicated in a legal system where *some* of the poorest and all of the richest get at least some help, but everyone in between, from the working class to the middle class, is screwed. Through no fault of their own, these lawyers work in a system where a person who faces eviction, aggressive creditors, or a spousal batterer may not be able to get the legal services they deserve because they have committed an ungodly sin: working for wages that place them above the poverty line but below the threshold of actual security.

Those fortunate enough to receive help from legal aid offices are sometimes harmed by the economic circumstances of their representation. In an ideal setting, a paying client facing a civil issue has all types of capital to keep their lawyer accountable. They have the human and cultural capital to communicate with their lawyers as equals and the social capital that could influence referrals in ways that could keep a lawyer on top of things. Perhaps most importantly, they have money; they can walk and take their business elsewhere. This is the case for the corporate parties I discussed in Part III, but not so much for the poor client receiving legal services. They have little economic or social leverage, as legal aid is likely their only option. The representation, conditions, and quality of work are all "take it or leave it propositions."[28]

Limited leverage, accountability mechanisms, and resources often mean people receiving legal aid are subject to the kinds of corner-cutting experienced by criminal defendants. Legal aid icon Gary Bellow saw this problem during the heyday of poverty lawyering. Many lawyers try earnestly to help as many people as possible, which can lead to exhaustion and a troubling transformation. As Bellow observed, lawyers quickly develop "the same self-protective formality, the same need for categories, the same dehumanization" found in welfare agencies. The quality of their legal work suffers as they ignore issues "in the name of a quick compromise and in the face of the growing caseload." Cases appear simple only because they're "superficially handled." With proper time to investigate and research, Bellow argued, lawyers could far better protect their clients' interests.[29]

Crushing caseloads can result in some attorneys treating all cases similarly and failing to recognize crucial differences that might prevent clients from being evicted or help them keep their disability benefits. These lawyers may cut off a client interview once they discover an easy solution to one legal problem, while ignoring many others. Or they may narrowly define a legal problem in ways that preserve their scarce time but resolves only a portion of the client's problem (e.g., recognizing that a client's denial of Medicaid assistance was improper but missing the fact that the client may not be getting reasonable accommodations at work for their disability).[30]

In some of the few studies of civil legal services, lawyers have confessed to interviewers that "they spend insufficient time with clients" and do not "devote enough time to each case in order to do everything that needs to be done."[31] To be clear, this reflects structural constraints more than personal failures. But it does mean they sometimes furnish lackluster legal services that hurt the same marginalized groups they care about.

Perhaps most revealing is how legal aid organizations present their work to the public. If you pull up the annual report for any legal aid organization, you're likely to find some remarkable victories notwithstanding the constraints I've already mentioned. You'll also find a long list of donors and client narratives. One legal aid attorney in Washington state, Beth Leonard, and her colleague Jay Doran described the sanitizing and stereotype-fulfilling nature of these client narratives. In their own experience writing these stories and their national review of similar narratives, they found that legal aid organizations must delicately craft accounts of their clients' lives that appeal to the broadest audience so they can raise money.

Appealing to potential donors' ideas about worth can quickly become entangled with ideas about deservingness, a morally fraught concept in American history and social policy.[32] Leonard and Doran describe how "deserving clients are the most commonly marketed" fundraising efforts. They're talking about the "the veteran father wrongly denied housing, the single mother escaping a domestic violence situation, or the senior citizen being taken advantage of by a relative."[33] The fentanyl-addicted mom who's legally owed benefits or the gambling father fighting for his rightful visitation won't be front and center; they may not be present in the report at all. Leonard saw this firsthand with one client. The Muslim Iraqi immigrant who did not speak English and was likely discriminated against because of her religion and nationality was repackaged and transformed into a palatable story: a generic mom of two who lost her job, faced eviction, and was rescued by legal aid.

Strategic choices regarding the presentation of clients to the public make sense. Many people, including myself, might think long and hard before donating their money to less-than-sympathetic causes or persons. But there are two tragedies here. First, these organizations *do* help people who may be deemed undeserving, so they are somewhat in the closet about this aid. Second, this approach to fundraising allows the public "to ignore the realities of systemic poverty" and "reinforces the idea that not everyone deserves access to the justice system—only those that the public deems worthy."[34]

PUBLIC INTEREST LAWYERS demonstrate that the trope "Equal Justice for All" should include the disclaimer "eligibility rules apply." These attorneys have been air-dropped into a storm of inequality—a trifecta of economic, political, and social hurdles. They are held back by shoestring budgets. They are shackled by legal limitations on the work they can perform. They advocate on behalf of disadvantaged people who were either born poor or slipped into poverty. And their clients often face additional discrimination based on race, gender, disability, or immigration status. Public interest lawyers inherit all this weight.

The structural constraints of public interest work shape who gets legal help, the type of help they receive, and how their stories are told—all of which can exacerbate disparities in our legal system. In these instances, inequality is encoded and perpetuated in a system designed to combat it. The unfortunate reality is that the good intentions and good people that populate this world cannot overcome a framework that permits legal wins within very circumscribed limits.

CHAPTER 14

Power, Prejudice, and Paternalism in the Pink Ghetto

Public interest law operates within a complex web of economic, political, and social constraints that produces odd dynamics. In conference rooms across urban America, overwhelmingly white and wealthy boards make strategic decisions about legal help for poor, racially diverse communities. In many offices below, women lawyers perform the day-to-day work of providing direct services and earn a fraction of what their private sector colleagues earn. These scenes reveal some of the demographic complexities that run throughout public interest work. This chapter delves deeper into how racial and gender dynamics influence the provision of direct legal services.

A tiff between a Black prosecutor and some public defenders is illustrative. Rachael Rollins was a Massachusetts-based Black prosecutor who was a guest on Boston Public Radio when a caller going through a criminal case reached out to the show and complained about his inability to reach his attorney at the Committee for Public Counsel Services (CPCS; the state's public defender).

Rollins pulled no punches. She suggested that the caller reach out to a local prosecutor if the communication problems continued. She called the good people at CPCS "overwhelmingly privileged" and criticized the lack of diversity at the office. "Ask some of the criminal defendants who are incarcerated—is this a rainbow coalition of people who are representing these individuals?" She added, "I refuse to pretend like this is Thurgood Marshall and Martin Luther King working for CPCS right now and running this operation."[1]

Rollins brought racial justice credentials to her criticism; she served as president of the Massachusetts Black Lawyers Association and legal redress chair for the NAACP Boston Branch. She was calling out a majority-white public defender office that was in a state with some of the starkest racial disparities in its prison population.[2] All hell broke loose. How dare she question these civil servants?

People were pissed and minority lawyers were some of Rollins's biggest critics. The Black Public Defender Association admitted that Rollins may have raised some points that were worthy of discussion but argued that "progressive" prosecutors like Rollins had "no standing or credibility" to talk about public defenders or minorities who were "disproportionately targeted by the unjust criminal legal system."[3] Jullian Harris-Calvin and Premal Dharia, two highly regarded former public defenders and women of color, called her comments "tone-deaf" and unethical.[4] But Rollins was highlighting the contradiction at the heart of public interest law that makes many of its practitioners uncomfortable: The people making decisions about poor people's freedom, housing, child custody, and access to public benefits are sometimes socially distant from them. That separation can be along the lines of race, class, personal experience, or what legal scholar Alexis Hoag-Fordjour calls "embodied empathy."[5]

I get it. Poverty lawyers are embattled, underfunded, poorly understood, and woefully underappreciated. Like many groups, they don't take criticism kindly and will circle the wagons. Rollins's critics were not entirely off-base, but there's something unsettling about a prosecutor, no matter how enlightened, stepping into the pulpit to preach to defense attorneys about their shortcomings. But the frustration revealed something deeper: how the most well-meaning lawyers can be so invested in narratives of their own goodness that they resist having their contradictions named by outsiders.

Direct services attorneys represent the ultimate test case for the legal profession's capacity to produce justice. These are the lawyers in the trenches, the ones with thick case files bursting out of beat-up briefcases. They sit side by side with domestic violence survivors, have hard conversations with teenagers aging out of foster care, and explain complex immigration law to clients who barely speak English as deportation officers loom outside. In some instances, they are the closest thing to champions that poor communities have. If inequality can be detected here—among some of the most well-intentioned lawyers in the most justice-oriented corner of the profession—it shows us that no corner of the bar is immune. Indeed, in this space, good intentions can coexist with a detachment from the human consequences of legal work—a distance sustained not just by habits of legal reasoning but also by resource constraints and the comforting belief in one's own goodness. This chapter reveals how even lawyers dedicated to fighting inequality can play a role in its reproduction.

We'll proceed in four steps—two about the composition of direct services and two about day-to-day work.

First, I'll show how the field replicates the hierarchies it claims to challenge. Women dominate direct services, reflecting how society feminizes and devalues caring work. Up next is the underrepresentation of minorities in leadership positions. The boards and executive directors of these organizations are approximately 75 percent white despite serving often predominantly Black and Brown clients. Representative politics aside, this mismatch shapes who has decision-making power and sets agendas—no small matter when dealing with marginalized communities. Ultimately, organizations meant to challenge inequality deliver services through structures that mirror the hierarchies their clients face.

The next two areas focus on service delivery. I'll show how the ethical requirement for "zealous advocacy" permits progressive lawyers to intentionally exploit the same prejudices that oppress their clients—even when they do so for their clients' benefit. The chapter lands with a discussion of how direct services attorneys can be unwittingly biased in their representation despite their best intentions.

You may not like what follows, particularly if you are one of these lawyers, know one, or believe in the stories of public interest law's purity. That's okay. It unsettles me too. If we believe in the power of honest reflection, we can't exempt people from it. In my view, the people most affected by legal aid deserve more than good intentions—they deserve the same rigorous reflection applied to the rest of the legal profession.

Race, Gender, and Inequality Inside Public Interest Organizations

Direct services attorneys occupy a paradoxical position in American society. They are entrusted with some of society's most vital justice work, undervalued within their profession, and still far better off than the vulnerable clients who depend on them. Rutgers law professor Sandra Simkins notes how neglected children, deportation, solitary confinement, homelessness, and domestic violence are some of the issues lawyers' clients face. Thinking back on her experience in the late '90s, she admits: "my $33,000/year salary with good health benefits felt like luxury by comparison."[6]

Pink collar is a designation often used to describe various forms of labor typically and historically performed by women (e.g., childcare, nursing, social work). *Ghettos* refer to areas where people are isolated because of sociolegal pressures. Although *pink ghetto* has been applied to a variety of places where women are occupationally segregated, Simkins uses the term to refer to the low-paying, low-status public interest world that has limited opportunities for professional advancement.[7]

Historically, legal aid has long been considered feminized work, even when law was a male-dominated profession.[8] In today's world, women are overrepresented in public interest compared to the rest of the legal profession. Between 2013 and 2023, the percentage of female lawyers in the US went from 34 percent to 39 percent.[9] Meanwhile, in the two most recent years for which there is data, 2016 and 2021, they constituted between 56 percent and 60 percent of public defenders and between 68 percent and 70 percent of civil legal services attorneys taking jobs in these fields.[10]

The numbers reflect a troubling pattern: Women may be gaining ground in law, but that ground is often in public service roles with the least pay and recognition. Of course, many women *opt* into this line of work. But in law firms and prosecutors' offices where women are underrepresented, institutional barriers and gender stereotyping effectively tell women they're unsuited for aggressive, male-dominated workplaces and should choose public interest law instead.[11]

Direct legal services are a form of care work and society often expects women to perform this labor. Clients have often waited weeks to chat with an attorney and they are trying to distill a legal problem amid anger, fear, and desperation. They sometimes communicate to an attorney who is asked to "be a therapist, marriage counselor, social worker, friend and confidante, and innumerable other roles for which they are not trained nor qualified to fill."[12] A problematic societal norm says women should engage in this kind of intellectual and emotional labor and that they should do so on the cheap.

People typically don't become poverty lawyers for the pay. In year one, they may make in the high $50,000s or low $60,000s. At five years, they make between $74,000 and $90,000.[13] This is good money, but a fraction of the $200,000 some first-year associates make or the $265,000 their fifth-year colleagues earn.[14]

Attorneys in the feminized public interest workforce might be paid less because society and government funders do not value the relative work they perform. Their low pay might be a result of a broader socialization of women into caretaking roles. There is also a specific legal culture that encourages them to be "selfless caregivers" who derive little satisfaction from material rewards but are content with the "gift" of helping others.[15] Men get the money, and women get the psychic and moral rewards.

Beneath the rhetoric of service and sacrifice lies an unsettling fact: Some women are only able to enter and remain in these careers because of their spouses' higher salaries. As sociologists Cynthia Epstein and Hella Winston observe, women lawyers are often married to male attorneys. They sometimes have a collective "normative assignment" where "the man works in a high-demand and higher-paying sector, while the woman works in the 'do good' sector." In this set-up, "the husband's high salary subsidizes the wife's public interest work while also relieving him of the moral burden of not doing socially useful labor himself."[16]

This arrangement—which can extend to husbands who work in tech, finance, and consulting—reinforces the gendered assumption that women should prioritize moral fulfillment over financial compensation. In some instances, entry and survival in certain public interest jobs depends on high-earning marriage partners and economic safety nets that aren't available to all women.[17] These conditions help sustain a form of occupational segregation that keeps women concentrated in caring professions.

Occupational segregation in direct services reflects a familiar gendered devaluation: like teachers and social workers, these lawyers are told they are not in it for the money and should be satisfied with "making a difference." In this altruistic world of poverty lawyering, women attorneys may be led to believe that success only comes with forms of selflessness shown to lead to burnout.[18] Such burnout, in turn, manifests through behaviors that can harm clients: irritability, poor job performance, and compassion fatigue.[19]

The field is caught in a bind. The passion that drives lawyers to choose justice over money contributes to society's perception that care work should be compensated less. When these organizations frame sacrifice as necessary for meaningful work, they inadvertently reinforce that this work is worth less than other legal practice. That puts these lawyers in an impossible position—they're fighting inequality while working in a field that segregates women into low-paying jobs and calls it virtue. In doing so, they end up mirroring some of the gendered hierarchies they challenge in their work.

Power at the Top, Service at the Bottom

The racial composition of public interest organizations is another concern. The boards of civil legal aid organizations are 73 percent white, 13 percent Black, 5 percent Asian, 5 percent Latino, and .08 percent Indigenous.[20] But this is somewhat misleading since the law requires that some federally funded groups have a board that includes representatives from at least one-third of its client population.[21] Organizations that don't take federal dollars see minority numbers dip to 21 percent.[22]

Racial tokenism has been a longstanding complaint about these boards.[23] In any event, the majority of public interest boards are populated with corporate lawyers who are there because they can get money to the organization and/or have the financial chops to perform the board's fiscal oversight functions. That's reasonable and arguably desirable. But there can be an economic and racial mismatch between the poor minority recipients of legal aid and the mostly white and wealthy board members who have "limited industry expertise or knowledge of the client population."[24]

These boards are typically responsible for hiring executive directors (EDs) whose ranks look quite similar, which is to say, unrepresentative. Approximately 75 percent of EDs are white, 9 percent are Latino, 8.1 percent are Black, 4 percent are Asian, and .05 percent are Native American.[25] EDs, in turn, often recommend individuals to the board to be future members. Here is where you really see the power of social networks and the shocking finding that 75 percent of white people have no Black friends.[26] In her empirical study of public interest leadership, legal sociologist Tinu Adediran discovered borderline incest between board members and EDs. One member described to her how she got on the board:

> I went to the annual dinner or fundraiser quite frankly with my then brother-in-law . . . because his boss . . . was on the board and he had extra tickets for this event. It was this great event and [the ED] stood up and she was so inspiring about how this is really going to make systemic change . . . and I just remember being just overwhelmed at that point like, yes, that's what we need to do! So, I set up a meeting with [her] and basically, it was, like, "I want to join your board." And so, I did. And then, this is my second year as a board chair.[27]

See how easy that was? The dynamics of insularity and exclusion that shape board composition often carry over into decisions about who becomes executive director. And in case you're thinking about it, there's no pipeline problem here. Racial minorities have high representation as staff attorneys within some of these orgs, making up between 42 and 47 percent; white staff attorneys are promoted to ED positions at disproportionately higher rates than minorities.[28]

Why does unrepresentative leadership matter? First, this composition means racial minorities have limited decision-making authority in organizations that disproportionately serve them. Put differently, there are unequal power dynamics tied to race and money. Relatedly, this whole set-up reeks of a kind of white saviorism that can easily breed top-down approaches to legal services that are unresponsive to communities' needs. Finally, since boards and EDs set organizational direction, they share responsibility for institutional failures and internal disparities.

Strategic Stereotyping and the Costs of Winning

If you come down to gen pop where staff attorneys work, you might hear comments and strategies that are surprising. Lawyers are required to represent clients zealously, and doing so might mean marshaling social distinctions that reify problematic stereotypes.

Consider the case of disability rights lawyers.

Ableism refers to practices that reinforce the subordination of people with disabilities.[29] UCLA law professor Jamelia Morgan shows how lawyers sometimes traffic ableism when "they are forced to represent their clients as physically, mentally, and emotionally damaged."[30] She admits that this form of representation might be reasonable, but she also rightfully observes that this kind of presentation of disability as "a type of weakness, pathology, or deficiency" can reinforce "a set of beliefs which normalize the mistreatment and abuse of people with disabilities."[31]

This creates a devastating contradiction: Attorneys advocating for disability rights find themselves trafficking in narratives that reinforce the very stereotypes that justify discrimination against disabled people.

Every time they win a case by painting their clients as broken and helpless, they're teaching judges, juries, and society to think about disabled people as damaged goods who are in need of saving. The result is that individual legal wins can undermine broader struggles for disability equality, and make it harder for disabled people to be seen as full human beings deserving of accommodation rather than charity.

Gender can influence how a public defender strategically describes a client with mental health problems. Their male defendants may have "anger issues," whereas the female defendants suffer from "co-dependency, trauma, and anxiety."[32] Gender shapes ideas about leniency, with women clients being portrayed as "good caretakers," and male defendants being described as "good providers."[33] Or gender could come up when a woman is an accomplice in a crime, and her attorney insists that she was just passively following along with the male perpetrator's conduct (or coerced into collaboration).[34]

Some have argued that attorneys must go full throttle and exploit every category necessary to secure a W for their client. Abbe Smith is a former public defender, professor at Georgetown, and one of the country's most cited legal ethics scholars. She has been a booster of such usage. If a young Black man is accused of drug possession, her approach would permit his public defender to go Huey P. Newton and emphasize how the "racist, fascist pig power structure" refuses to surveil the white fraternity boys who live across the street and snort big lines of coke. Immigrant accused of petty theft? Accentuate the poverty and violence faced by this young man in Guatemala. The so-called LGBTQ+ panic defense involves a defendant arguing that their homophobic or transphobic violence should excuse liability. As this argument goes, the fact that he, a cisgender male, attacked a transgender woman who made a pass at him is a rational response when one's heterosexual honor is threatened. Such capitalization on identity would be permissible to get the legal victory.

There's principle underneath this. Smith is a lefty, and she makes her politics clear: "I do not enjoy stirring up or manipulating homophobia or race, gender, or ethnic prejudice in the course of representing a client. However, my own ideological values cannot be the determining factor."[35] She's firm in her belief that lawyers shouldn't be in the business if their politics will get in the way of representing clients zealously. She is unpersuaded by the idea that the harms that come to marginalized communities should foreclose the use of identity in criminal defense.

Smith is not completely off base. In her view, public defenders represent disproportionately poor and minority clients who are subject to daily bias. Why should these lawyers and their clients shoulder the *additional* burden of caring about the third-party implications of their tactical behavior when 1) the client's life or liberty is on the line, and 2) the client herself might be fine with exploiting social categories.

There's something simultaneously uncomfortable and attractive about this view, and others have supported it by suggesting that the instrumental use of bias is justifiable under an adversarial system that privileges loyalty to a client and often includes disadvantaged defendants going up against a powerful state.[36] Importantly, blatant appeals to prejudice are not the norm. "Subtle approaches are far more common," are permitted by ethical rules, and have been identified in qualitative work on public defenders.[37]

But this instrumental use of identity—turning disability, gender, sexuality, and race into courtroom tools—reveals how the adversarial system can transform even progressive lawyers into merchants of stereotype. This legal inequality is structural imperative made manifest. Lawyers who deploy identity in this way may see it as part of their professional obligations. The fact that their zealous advocacy might reinforce the very prejudices that landed their clients in the system becomes collateral damage in a public interest world that often prioritizes individual victories—especially when systemic change is elusive.[38]

When Helpers Harbor Harmful Assumptions

Purposeful weaponization of prejudice may be bad for marginalized communities and good for clients, but the separate problem of implicit bias serves no one. These are unconscious stereotypes and attitudes that people make about social groups.

We're all susceptible. I've lived in the South Bronx, the South Side of Chicago, and South Los Angeles. When I go back to any of those places and see a bunch of young Black and Brown men smoking weed and talking shit on the corner—which they are legally entitled to do under local law—I juke to the left and cross the street. And I've done the same when I've walked on college campuses and encountered drunk white bros. When I'm walking around anywhere late at night in street clothes, I accept the fact of my blackness and charge it to the game when white people socially distance themselves like its 2020 and we're still in the midst of COVID.

Implicit bias is especially problematic in legal aid because it's harder to detect. In the criminal context, there is much more commentary on bias by cops, prosecutors, judges, and juries. When such bias occurs in a criminal proceeding, it is the defense counsel who is likely to uncover it and possibly litigate it; however, they may be less likely to examine their own potential biases.[39]

The available research demonstrates that such bias is something we should worry about. One study of defense attorneys found that they had more automatic associations of white faces with "good" and Black faces with "bad."[40] In another experiment, defense attorneys recommended plea bargains for Black clients that entailed longer sentences than the deals they recommended for their white counterparts.[41] Stanford sociologist Matthew Clair's study of Boston courts found that defense attorneys actively participate in institutionalized forms of "covert" discrimination. Brown University sociologist Nicole Van Cleve found that Chicago defense attorneys' representation was shaped by a "racialized understanding" of their clients that derived from assumptions about their worthiness and morality.[42]

To illustrate how a defense attorney's implicit bias can be expressed, let's walk through the juvenile justice system. The insights of former public defender turned Georgetown scholar Kristin Henning guide this analysis. She notes that when public defender offices have units that focus on juveniles, they are often the least funded in the organization. These units sometimes serve as the training ground for wet-behind-the ears lawyers or spaces for attorneys who are burned out from adult work.⁴³ Their young client—likely Black or Brown because that's who we're usually talking about—gets arrested for drug possession. The defender, at first, would have to make a triage decision around how much time she'd want to spend on the case.⁴⁴

Triage calculation might be based on a brief interview that went poorly. Maybe the young person thinks the attorney is paternalistic and the defender thinks he is "recalcitrant" or "uncooperative." Age and power dynamics could be getting in the way. Or maybe the youth is overwhelmed by the court system and the fast pace of things? If so, he might withdraw and withhold important information that might be helpful to the case. Implicit bias could fill in the gaps. Perhaps he *does* provide information, but struggles with language, cognitive, or emotional issues that impact his ability to tell his story. Or, because he is a kid, he is unable to stay on track and ask good follow-up questions. Implicit bias and fatigue could lead the defender to not meaningfully investigate.⁴⁵

Home environment plays a critical role in juvenile proceedings and is a place where implicit biases can thrive. This environment can decide whether the youth is released from detention and the punishment they receive. At this stage, the defender aims to demonstrate a stable home environment, which is easier when is the child lives in a two-parent, middle-class household. "When families do not comport with these norms, defenders may overgeneralize and make assumptions, especially about parents who are hard to reach, miss court proceedings, and frequently change residences."⁴⁶ Being poor, minority, immigrant, or having a criminal record can confirm racialized narratives about home stability.⁴⁷ Assumptions about home life can play a role in whether the child gets probation, is assigned counseling, is placed in a foster home, or is committed to a juvenile facility.

Other factors that can be shaped by implicit bias matter as well. School attendance is relevant; implicit bias might cause a defender to view the absenteeism of a white child as legitimately tied to illness and that of a minority child as related to delinquency. Remorse is also important. When minority children engage in normal adolescent behaviors like "inarticulate apologies, flat facial expressions, or apparent disinterest," such conduct can be misread as evidence of remorselessness and lead to less desirable outcomes.[48]

Before white readers get fragile and minority readers get on their high horse, it's worth emphasizing that defenders of all racial backgrounds are susceptible. Implicit bias research has shown, for example, that 75 percent of white people and 50 percent of Black people demonstrate anti-Black bias.[49] Very few people are immune.

ONE OF THE MOST CRYSTALLIZING MOMENTS I experienced in my scholarly work was when I interviewed a Puerto Rican woman who worked at a legal aid organization helping people with public benefits that were wrongfully denied or terminated. When she was a child, her family had been on food stamps, back when it came in the stigmatizing paper-coupon form. She reflected on interactions she and her mom would have with welfare administrators and observed, "I see my family in some of my clients, and I worry that if I'm not vigilant, I'm going to be like those welfare officials I used to despise. They were so impersonal and [it] felt like they were processing another case file instead of dealing with needy people. But when you have double the recommended caseload and half the resources you need, it's easy to be biased and not see it." Her words reveal the impossible position that even self-aware advocates find themselves in when resource constraints make fighting bias a vigilant battle.

What emerges from this examination is a field caught in a web of contradictions. Public interest law is a space where some of society's most persistent inequalities get reproduced through the very people trying to eliminate them. Women find themselves channeled into work that mirrors their broader relegation to undervalued caring roles while leadership often fails to reflect the demographics these organizations serve. Meanwhile, some lawyers' daily practice of advocacy can involve them relying on problematic stereotypes and assumptions. These contradictions don't negate the justice these committed advocates deliver. They underscore the urgent need to better align the field's ideals with its practice while recognizing the quiet distance that can persist between those who challenge inequality and those who live with it.

CHAPTER 15

High-Level Impact Litigation and Inequality

PUBLIC INTEREST LAW has its headliners and its lifelines—the ones who get the spotlight, and the ones who do the daily work of keeping people from sinking.

If you go to the legal aid office in your city, you'll see crisis unfold in real time. Stressed-out clients sit on wobbly folding chairs holding eviction papers in reused envelopes. Attorneys skip lunch because there's no time to eat, printers seem to go on strike every other day, and a missed deadline can mean deportation or eviction. The attorneys don't talk much about legal precedent but instead the immediate needs of their clients today.

On the other hand, if you go to the big-impact litigation office in the same city, you are apt to find something different. The air conditioning is cooler, quieter, and more reliable. The staff has just finished a catered lunch. No clients are in the waiting room. The work is slower, more abstract and focused on strategy. Their matters are urgent, but they have time. They think in years and their wins make headlines. They are not focused on an immediate eviction but on a reinterpretation of the Fair Housing Act that would impact the lives of thousands. These are the folks this chapter focuses on.

Impact litigation is a form of legal advocacy that focuses on strategically filing cases and appealing decisions that affect specific interest groups. The goal is to remake social policy through courts. Some of these organizations predate federal legal aid funding and operate outside its restrictions. Others emerged as a direct response to those limitations and are free to pursue the broad systemic challenges that federally funded attorneys cannot touch.

In the public interest world, impact litigation is considered elite work for top law school graduates and seasoned lawyers. The classic organization here is the NAACP Legal Defense Fund (NAACP-LDF), but some other organizations engage in impact litigation even if it's not their specific mission, for example, the American Association of Retired Persons (AARP) or the National Federation of Independent Business (NFIB). A few organizations engage in impact litigation and direct services, but they typically lean heavily toward one model, and the work itself is usually separate. Impact lawyers and direct services attorneys often operate in different worlds, even under the same organizational roof.

Across the public interest world, the pursuit of justice increasingly plays out through competing claims of harm, where victimhood is the hottest commodity in American politics.[1] Whether the injury is tied to discrimination, attacks on liberty, or exclusion, this sense of grievance generates legal disputes. Liberal and conservative organizations alike turn to impact litigation to vindicate their version of justice. But here's the kicker: Because these claims rest on competing accounts of harm, both sides can present themselves as fighting inequality even while critics argue they are entrenching it.

This doesn't mean all claims about inequality are equally valid—some forms of harm are more documented, more systematic, and more devastating than others. But impact litigation operates in a space where sincere disagreement about inequality is possible. Unlike clear-cut disparities—whether poor defendants get worse legal representation than wealthy ones or whether workers with disabilities face discrimination—these constitutional battles involve competing claims that have some legitimacy.

To show how this dynamic works, I'll draw examples from some of the most contentious issues in contemporary American politics: free speech and platform regulation, gun rights and public safety, affirmative action and racial preferences, and religious liberty and civil rights. I'm not here to settle these debates or declare winners—that's not the point. Instead, I want to show how lawyers across the ideological spectrum can become so immersed in legal reasoning that they overlook, bracket, or disregard the human consequences of their work. That detachment is what allows critics to reasonably argue that the legal profession, for all its talk of justice, often perpetuates inequality.

Liberal Speech Rights and Expressive (In)equalities

The American Civil Liberties Union (ACLU) has fiercely defended First Amendment rights for over a century, and in this moment—when protest restrictions, book bans, censorship, and other speech crackdowns are spreading—the organization's role remains indispensable. As its legal director noted in 2024, the ACLU takes a certain kind of pride in defending the speech rights of people with whom they disagree. Since 1920, that score includes "the speech rights of neo-Nazis, white supremacists, religious fundamentalists, anti-LGBTQ individuals, and more."[2]

This content-neutral approach could be considered an honorable form of equality—free speech rights for everybody. "That's the guiding principle," explained one prominent ACLU figure. "No matter how obnoxious it is, how racist it is, we don't want the state to decide who has the right to speech. We take this very, very purist position that the price we pay for a free society is putting up with this crap."[3]

In 1934, a year after the German government began passing a series of anti-Jewish laws that would culminate in the Holocaust, the ACLU defended the rights of Nazis in the US. "Our attorneys, both Jews," the ACLU noted, "urged the Mayor of New York [to allow] the use of city property for a meeting of *the persecutors of Jews*, the Nazis."[4] This was, in effect, advocacy for equal application of free speech rights. But it also gave legitimacy to one of the most reviled ideologies in global history. Maybe it was just a tradeoff, but not a small one. One might think of a statement issued by the US Holocaust Museum: "The Holocaust did not begin with killing; it began with words."[5]

Thirty-three years later, when some Chicago-area Nazis wanted to demonstrate in the Jewish suburb of Skokie, the ACLU, led by a Jewish attorney, came to the defense of the Nazis. The prospective intimidation and trauma imposed on this city—*home to Holocaust survivors*—be damned.

Then there's Charlottesville.

The 2017 Unite the Right rally involved a medley of neo-Nazis, white nationalists, neo-confederates, and members of the alt-right. One of them drove his car into a group of counterprotesters, which led to the death of one woman and injuries to dozens. In the lead-up, the city revoked the permit for the march, and the ACLU of Virginia stepped in to provide representation. It wasn't about the views underlying the event (which they abhorred), but rather the principled commitment to free speech coupled with the mistaken belief that the protest would be peaceful. "History can be an unforgiving tutor," the ACLU admitted, and the debacle caused it to revisit its policies and scrutinize the proposed "facts of any white-supremacy protests with a much finer comb."[6]

The ACLU's content-neutral stance doesn't immunize it from criticism. Dennis Parker, the former director of the ACLU's Racial Justice Program, claims that "First Amendment protections are disproportionately enjoyed by people of power and privilege." Former ACLU legal director David Cole replied, "Everything that Black Lives Matter does is possible because of the First Amendment."[7]

The problem, however, is that free speech assumes speech among people equal in power.[8] Some people, like constitutional law professor Mary Anne Franks, believe that "racist and misogynist speech is in no danger of suppression" and that "there has perhaps never been a safer time in America to express virulently misogynist, racist, and xenophobic speech." She would likely point to the last three election cycles (2016, 2020, 2024) as proof.[9] Even if one disagreed with her, they could look at the internal fracturing within the organization.

A newer generation of ACLU employees has focused more specifically on immigration and transgender rights and are not as absolutist as their predecessors.[10] They see the equal application of one principle—free speech—as potentially exacerbating other inequalities. Both perspectives identify real tensions in how free speech operates in an unequal society. This internal divide within the ACLU—between protecting speech as an abstract right and protecting people from harmful speech—reflects broader challenges. And it illustrates how competing visions of equality can coexist within the same organization.

Robust free speech has equality implications in the digital realm—an area in which the ACLU and several left-leaning groups have been similarly resolute. The Electronic Frontier Foundation (EFF) merits some attention here. EFF was founded in 1990 and focuses on digital civil rights. I got my legal education at Berkeley—a school with a strong public interest orientation that is located not too far from the tech capital of Silicon Valley. EFF is where many of the lefty students wanted to work. EFF focuses on technological innovations that benefit us all—issues like illegal surveillance, which many likely detest, and government regulation of online activity, which some disfavor.

EFF vigorously defends Section 230, a 1996 communications law that helped create the modern internet. In simple terms, Section 230 protects online entities (e.g., websites, social media, and video-sharing platforms) from being legally responsible for content posted by users.[11] If a user posts a blog on *Medium* that starts a fight, posts unflattering images of a personal enemy on TikTok, or uploads a false advertisement on YouTube, that platform can't be liable for legal wrongdoing.

EFF believes *people* should be liable for their bad online conduct, not some intermediary like X. According to EFF, Section 230 allows for a more light-touch approach to content moderation since providers can worry less about liability. They worry that if Big Tech entities like Meta and Google faced liability, they would become "free speech gods" who over-police controversial ideas and take down anything remotely controversial. Such action, they believe, would impact "disempowered individuals and communities' voices."[12]

EFF is not a bunch of white tech bros talking about inequality. A group of social justice and tech scholars—all of whom either graduated from or taught at the Black legal mecca, Howard Law, agree. They have italicized EFF's concern about Section 230 and disenfranchisement. They argue that Section 230 democratized the public sphere by allowing platforms to host minority activists who "ruffle the feathers of those perched on top." (Think Black Twitter). These users now have elevated platforms to speak instead of being relegated to "graveyard TV and radio slots."[13]

These scholars also see Section 230 as benefiting the #MeToo movement. In the absence of 230's protections, they believe platforms may have been more cautious about hosting content that could be viewed as defamatory against "powerful and litigious men" accused of sexual misconduct.[14] Section 230 also impacts the LGBTQ community, as it has allowed various online sexual communities to thrive (e.g., dating apps like Grindr, HER, and Scruff). Without 230, some worry that platforms would be subject to aggressive prosecutors who find ways to sue them because they violate majoritarian gender and sexual norms.[15]

EFF and their allies have legitimate concerns about how online regulations of speech will hurt historically marginalized groups. But it's also fair to examine the other side of the inequality coin: How does this deregulatory, liability-shielding law *harm* these groups and others? The easiest answer is online abuse. "Harassing people online is far cheaper and less personally risky than confronting them in real space," privacy law expert Danielle Citron notes.[16]

Cyberharassment is the use of an electronic device to seriously alarm or threaten a person in a manner that causes substantial emotional distress or fear of injury.[17] A third of young women under the age of thirty-five report being sexually harassed online compared to 11 percent of men. And more than half of lesbian, gay, and bisexual adults report severe forms of online abuse compared to 23 percent of heterosexual adults.[18]

Two cases involving cyberharassment highlight the problems with Section 230.

In 2003, one of the most liberal federal courts helped the online dating site Matchmaker escape liability for sexual harassment. It all started when some rando in Berlin created a fake Matchmaker account impersonating actor and singer Christianne Carafano (aka Chase

Masterson) and said "she" wanted a one-night stand. This unknown person also claimed that "she" was looking for a "hard and dominant man" with a "strong sexual appetite" because "she" liked being "controlled by a man in and out of bed."[19] This person included Carafano's address and phone number, which caused Carafano to feel unsafe in her home and led her to shuffle between hotels for months. She sued Matchmaker, but the court said Section 230 barred liability.

In 2016, Matthew Herrick was stalked by his ex-boyfriend on Grindr, a dating app geared toward gay and bisexual men. The ex impersonated him, and noted that he was interested in "serious kink" and "hardcore unprotected group sex." These advertisements led about 1,400 men to come to Herrick's house and job in just ten days. He reported the impersonations to Grindr approximately one hundred times and sued.[20] Again, a federal court said no liability under 230.[21]

Doxing—the nonconsensual publicization of one's private information—uniquely impacts racial and religious minorities.[22] Black Lives Matter activists—who Section 230 supporters believe are empowered by the law—have long been subject to doxing.[23] It has even spilled into the touchy topic of Israel and Palestine, where campus controversies have led to doxing incidents affecting students across the political spectrum.[24] The Anti-Defamation League (ADL), which had been tracking prejudice-based doxing for years before October 7th, has consistently called for Congress to reform Section 230 to address such harassment campaigns. In its view, that kind of legislative fix and the passage of new laws would protect people from being "harassed and terrorized online based on race, religion, [and] sexual orientation" and prevent them from being "forced out of digital spaces, silenced, harmed, and left without recourse."[25]

Doxing campaigns have been launched from across the ideological spectrum. Some have accused the Canary Mission—a group designed to combat far-right and far-left antisemitism on college campuses—of being responsible for the doxing of pro-Palestinian college students after October 7th. If you went to their website, you'd find a long list of students, professors, professionals, and organizations that the Canary Mission accuses of antisemitism. Anti-fascist lefties also engage in "cybershaming" and reveal the identities of neo-Nazis. Indeed, after the Charlottesville Unite the Right rally, some participants reportedly lost their jobs after being unmasked.[26]

The same behavior gets labeled as either dangerous doxing or important transparency work, depending on who's doing it and who's being exposed; sometimes it's characterized as both.[27] But the point here is that Section 230 permits this behavior—which has been deployed across the ideological spectrum.[28]

This illustrates how contested advocacy works across the speech landscape: The ACLU defends Nazi marches as constitutionally protected while critics argue doing so enables violence; EFF champions Section 230 as democratizing speech while reformers document how it facilitates harassment. Each side can marshal evidence of real harms and real benefits. The law sometimes forces choices between these competing visions of equality and those choices inevitably privilege some forms of protection over others.

Bipartisan Trigger-Happy Advocacy

Gun policy is another area where left-leaning public interest organizations have advanced positions that arguably produce socially bothersome results. *NYSRPA v. Bruen* will be our unfortunate muse.[29]

Until the twenty-first century, it was unclear whether the average citizen had a constitutional right to individual firearm ownership under the Second Amendment. In 2008 and 2010, the Supreme Court ruled that the amendment protects individual gun ownership for lawful purposes—namely, self-defense in the home.[30] In 2022, the Supreme Court addressed the scope of this right in *New York State Rifle & Pistol Association, Inc. v. Bruen*.[31]

The specific laws at issue in *Bruen* were arbitrary. For residents of New York City who wanted to exercise their new constitutional right to own a gun at home, they had to convince an official in the NYPD, an agency with a well-documented history of racism, that they were of "good moral character."[32] To possess a gun outside the house for self-defense, the applicant had to show "proper cause"—a demanding standard that involved "a special need for self-protection distinguishable from that of the general community." Living in a high-crime neighborhood wouldn't cut it.[33] Put differently, New York's legal system thought that the constant threat of violence was just part of the urban experience, not grounds for self-defense.

Unlawful firearm possession can earn a person 3.5 to 15 years, and that will be on the higher end if the gun is loaded. But check this out: New York law considers a gun "loaded" if a person possesses ammunition at the same time as a firearm, even if they are separate![34] The result? Even though African Americans were 18 percent of New York's population in 2022, they comprised 78 percent of the state's felony gun possession cases. Justice Clarence Thomas would have none of this and wrote the decision striking down the New York statute and similar laws that inhibited people's ability to lawfully possess a gun outside the home.

Several New York public defender groups stepped into the impact litigation arena and filed an amicus brief in support of the gun rights position. They focused on racial justice. Some of the questions underlying their position were straightforward. Why do people in the Bronx, the poorest congressional district in the country, have to pay $400 in fees to get a license? Why do they have to prove their moral worthiness to a police department with an ongoing racial subordination problem?

Elsewhere, one of the lawyers remarked, "Over a quarter of my felony caseload as a public defender consists of people possessing—not using, just possessing—a firearm without a license."[35] New York's gun law led to unlawful arrests, unnecessary pretrial confinement, and convictions of a swath of Black and Latino New Yorkers who simply wanted to protect themselves. The downstream effects of such criminalization included lost children, jobs, and homes for people engaged in acts of possession that people in other parts of the country exercised freely. These lawyers wanted equal treatment under the Second Amendment for their clients.

I'm sympathetic to these advocates' points, especially as a Black man from the city who has been subject to stop and frisk and as someone who interned at the Bronx Defenders. But they lent intellectual support to a constitutional state of affairs that some critics believe endangers minority communities.

The public defenders' argument, however compelling, runs into a brutal reality: Licenses won't stop police harassment and might give officers new justifications for violence. As the legal pundit Elie Mystal points out, "If a cop shoots a Black person to death and that person is belatedly found to have had a weapon anywhere near their grabbable area, the cop will not be charged with a crime, much less convicted."[36] That's what happened to Philando Castile in Minneapolis. Castile had a license to carry, told the cop about his weapon, and was shot anyway. The same shoot-first-ask-questions-last difficulties apply to cops who shoot unarmed minorities. But in a *Bruen* world, officers may be *more likely* to presume that people are armed, which could justify *more* surveillance and violence.

A gun could be useful for a person facing potential harm, though this assumes they know how to shoot, which is questionable given weekly stories of innocent bystanders being killed. Notwithstanding that utility, there is compelling empirical evidence about the hazards of increased gun ownership. Concealed carry laws are associated with a 9 percent increase in assault and homicide.[37] Stricter permit requirements for concealed firearms are associated with lower homicide rates in both white and Black populations.[38] The data suggest that looser gun laws cost lives. The effects of lax gun restrictions will likely fall disproportionately on minority communities, which already experience higher rates of gun violence; 31 percent of Black Americans and 22 percent of Hispanic Americans have personally witnessed a shooting, compared to 14 percent of white Americans.[39] The communities these advocates sought to protect may bear the heaviest costs of the policies for which they advocated.

There are also worrisome gender implications of loose gun laws. More than 50 percent of homicides committed by partners involved guns, with American Indian, Alaska Native, and Black women experiencing disproportionate rates of gun violence.[40] That's why it was a surprise when another group of public interest lawyers and the

National Association for Criminal Defense Lawyers (NACDL), the leading professional group for defense attorneys, advocated for *stronger* Second Amendment rights after *Bruen*. Their target? People who have been subject to civil domestic violence orders.

United States v. Rahimi involved a man who shoved his child's mother into his car, retrieved his gun, and fired as she escaped. He warned he'd shoot her if she reported it. She successfully got a restraining order, which was violated that night when he contacted her on several social media accounts (back to the cyberharassment). Federal law prohibits people subject to such orders from possessing a gun if they are a credible threat to someone's physical safety, and Rahimi was definitely that. He subsequently threatened another woman with a gun, shot at a drug customer, had road rage shootings, and shot into the air after his friend's credit card was declined at Whataburger.

Various criminal defense organizations supported Rahimi's constitutional argument. The Bronx Defenders Union and the NACDL wrote a brief urging the court to protect Second Amendment rights for people subject to restraining orders. They rightfully highlighted how the issuance of protective orders was often superficial, based on hearsay, and lacked due process. Put differently, they believed these orders were fast-tracked in a way that created a backdoor for stripping constitutional protections from minority defendants who never received a fair hearing. But even a super-conservative, Heckler and Koch–loving Supreme Court rebuffed these defenders and ruled against Rahimi. They likely worried about the optics and implications of a domestic abuser's right to bear arms.

I don't consider these public defenders who fight for gun liberalization to be harmful agents of inequality per se. They have a specific and plausible vision of racial justice tied to their work and the clients they serve—defendants who continue to lose gun rights through summary proceedings that disproportionately impact minorities. My purpose here is to show you dueling and reasonable conceptions of inequality, and how public interest organizations sometimes advocate for one of them. The reality is complex. Much like the speech context, advocates on both sides can be sincere in their equality-focused intentions even as they overlook, minimize, or rationalize the harms their arguments inflict on others—illustrating how legal reasoning can sever law from human consequence.

Asian Americans and the Affirmative Action Wars

Liberals have not cornered the public interest lawyering market; they are not the only ideologues implicated in perpetuating inequality. American conservatism, or what's left of it, has a seat at the inequality table, too.

Conservatives have traditionally advocated for fiscal responsibility, free markets, and limited government in social and economic life. But a two-time president and author of *The Art of Deal* has led some of them to cede ground. They are now more open to tariffs and state-sponsored ownership of companies, which is hard to square with free market capitalism, and they have a very generous understanding of presidential power. Maybe they are raging hypocrites, are more diverse than they are credited to be, or have updated their preferences out of expedience. Whatever the reason, such shifts make it hard to neatly cabin a still-unfolding legal conservative project. But a few issues supply some sources of consistency that allow us to talk about advocacy and social inequality: affirmative action, LGBTQ rights, and religion.

Students for Fair Admissions (SFFA) is a nonprofit organization responsible for snuffing out affirmative action in higher education. The group is the creation of Edward Blum, a conservative nonlawyer with a knack for getting cases in front of the Supreme Court. As a *Wall Street Journal* profile put it, "Blum says he is looking for cases in which the law is leveraged to favor one racial or ethnic group over another."[41] But none of SFFA's cases concern favoritism toward whites. This smart strategist appears to have trouble finding such cases (which is hard to believe given current court dockets), doesn't believe white preferences exist (which is consistent with white grievance politics), or only cares about favoritism toward non-whites.[42]

In any event, Blum has compiled an impressive record at the court.

He's suffered some L's, namely the cases of Abigail Fisher, a white woman who graduated at the top of her class, had an average SAT score, and was denied admission into the University of Texas.[43] But he was also behind two cases that successfully hollowed out the Voting Rights Act and, more relevant for our purposes, took Harvard University to court over its affirmative action policies and won.[44]

I'm not here to relitigate affirmative action's desirability or constitutionality. It's a divisive policy issue and conservatives are not the only ones who disapprove of it.[45] Conservative *and* liberal opponents might make two observations. First, they'd look at their perfect child—with sky-high test scores, a stellar GPA from an elite school, and a professionally crafted admissions essay. Then they'd look at the Black, Dominican, or Mexican kid who may have graduated eighth in his class—but from struggling Booker T. Washington High School. After seeing that kid get valet service to Princeton or Yale, it's no surprise why they'd cry foul.

Instead, I'm here to make two points: The first is that the legal controversy that ended affirmative action at the Supreme Court was manufactured by conservatives who strategically constructed test cases and found sympathetic plaintiffs. The second is that some of the appellate cases brought by conservative public interest groups, like those brought by their liberal counterparts, can tap into authentic anxieties about fairness and equality, even when the legal claims range from legitimate to strategically contrived.

A damning fact: After Blum kept losing with his white woman plaintiff, he admitted, "I needed Asian plaintiffs." He made Asian Americans the protagonists in his anti-affirmative action crusade. The crux of the argument in the case against Harvard was that qualified Asian Americans were being denied admission and unqualified Black and Hispanic students got in instead. There were no named Asian American plaintiffs; the suit was filed on behalf of the organization. No Asian American students offered testimony on behalf of SFFA, but some did testify in *support* of affirmative action.

Even if you are a rabid anti-affirmative action opponent, you might find the following set-up problematic: a white legal strategist with no documented history of Asian American advocacy operating on behalf of anonymous Asian Americans on an issue where their views are divided.[46] Read through the most cynical, inequality-viewed lens, a man who spent a chunk of his adult life diluting minority power rebranded himself as a champion of Asian American rights and did so by upending a six-decade-old policy that tried to mitigate a 150-year-plus history of minority educational exclusion.

Whatever his motives were, SFFA prevailed, with the Supreme Court ruling that affirmative action programs designed to improve diversity were unconstitutional. Blum tapped into a long history of Asian Americans being deployed as a "racial wedge" where the "model minority" caricature was weaponized to castigate other racial minorities.[47] In the wake of SFFA's victory, questions remain about their concern about anti-Asian bias. How will they respond to the growing suspicion that Chinese international students constitute national security threats?[48]

Will those who oppose affirmative action keep this same energy if Asian American enrollment increases and potentially displaces whites? Or will they react like the respondents in sociologist Frank Sampson's experiment? Samson found that white Californians championed GPA as the gold standard when they believed they were competing with Black Americans. But when faced with competition from presumably high-performing Asian Americans, their principled stance on academic merit proved conveniently malleable. Suddenly, grades mattered less. (The same thing happened when Jewish students ran circles around their Anglo peers in the early twentieth century, prompting college administrators to redefine merit by downplaying academic performance in favor of subjective qualities like "leadership" and "character.")[49] We may learn at some point whether conservative deployment of anti-Asian bias was a principled stance or unmitigated self-interest.

But if you can muscle past the potential hypocrisy and fix your gaze beyond the opportunism, a legitimate argument about the harms faced by Asian Americans comes into view. The SFFA case is not as straightforward as it seems, notwithstanding its imperfect messenger. To start, we've been having this conversation for almost forty years.

The conservative outlet *Public Interest* covered allegations of anti-Asian discrimination in Ivy Leagues in 1987. In its focus on Brown University, it highlighted how Asian Americans received low nonacademic ratings due to "cultural biases and stereotypes which prevail in the admission office."[50]

This was not that different from the finding in the Harvard case three decades later, where Asian American students scored lower on a subjective "personal rating" that seemed to play into stereotypes of this group as socially awkward, unassimilable foreigners. It's almost as if Black and Latino applicants perform higher on these interpersonal evaluations because they are freestylers and bachata dancers.

In essence, some Asian Americans find themselves caught in a squeeze. On one side, they face the kind of soft subjective assessments that kept high-performing Jewish students out of higher education a century ago. On the other side, elite schools instrumentally give preference to children of alums, donors, and faculty. Asian Americans are less likely to benefit from these legacy preferences due to histories of educational discrimination and the "bamboo ceilings" that some of them face in high-income professions.[51] Black and Latino students are the unfortunate spokespersons for affirmative action, but are we to ignore the experiences Asian Americans have with racial discrimination? Should they just kick rocks?

Since the 1970s, affirmative action has been legally justified through the *diversity rationale*—the idea that racial diversity provides educational benefits to all students, rather than serving as a remedy for past discrimination. The unfortunate reality, long voiced by liberal skeptics of this framework, is that affirmative action was invaluable, but it was also a Band-Aid. It allowed schools to hold on to aspects of their racially exclusionary character while they strutted around as equity focused.[52]

The legal challenge brought on behalf of Asian Americans—many of whom did not support the litigation—illustrates the complexity of legal inequality. The case emerged from external strategic orchestration rather than internal organic grievance, but it revealed genuine concerns about the unfairness toward Asian American students who were otherwise marginalized in the debate. SFFA forced a necessary reckoning with the limitations of diversity-based approaches and demonstrated how contested advocacy can expose real inequities even when deployed for political ends.

Faith vs. Rights:
Religious Liberty in the Age of LGBTQ Inequality

The clash between LGBTQ rights and First Amendment principles represents another area where conservative public interest organizations manufactured a dispute that raised deep, conflicting questions about equality. The Alliance Defending Freedom (ADF) is behind this one. It has been described as "the largest legal force of the religious right."[53] It boasts a network of almost 5,000 attorneys and has funneled 1,800 law students through its Blackstone Legal Fellowship, which equips them to assume leadership positions and "shape the future of law and culture across the globe."[54] They have reported more than $200 million in pro-bono-dedicated time, and in 2022, the organization received nearly 6,300 requests for legal help. Much of the demand comes from clergy, churches, religious organizations, pro-life pregnancy centers, and family-owned businesses.

ADF drew first blood on local antidiscrimination laws in the 2018 decision *Masterpiece Cakeshop, Ltd. v. Colorado Civil Rights Commission*. In that case, baker Jack Phillips refused to create a custom cake for a gay couple, citing his religious beliefs. The couple filed a civil rights complaint accusing the baker of violating a state law that prohibited businesses from discriminating on the basis of sexual orientation. Phillips lost in all his local and state hearings on the issue, but the ADF successfully argued on his behalf at the Supreme Court. LGBTQ-friendly Justice Anthony Kennedy ruled that Colorado's handling of the case demonstrated a hostility to religion.

In 2023, ADF returned for more. They represented Lorie Smith, a web designer who believed making websites for same-sex couples violated her Christian faith. Smith argued that Colorado's antidiscrimination law would force her to either violate her religious beliefs by serving same-sex couples or avoid the wedding website business entirely. In *303 Creative LLC v. Elenis*, the court went further than it had in *Masterpiece Cakeshop* and ruled that Colorado (or any state, for that matter) could not use its antidiscrimination laws to force artists to make expressive messages with which they disagree.

For liberals, *303 Creative* harkened back to the nasty days (i.e., the 1960s) when bigots tried to use the First Amendment to hold on for dear life to segregation. The ruling, in their view, could theoretically allow neo-bigots to discriminate based on race, sex, national origin, and religion. For conservatives, the case wasn't about refusing service based on identity (e.g., because one is gay or lesbian); it was about prohibiting states from forcing people to create a specific message in violation of the First Amendment. Once again, we see how the same set of facts can tell radically different stories depending on who's doing the telling.

What makes this clash of interpretations more complex is that the underlying controversy arose under questionable circumstances. There are two stories here.

The first story involves the facts of the Smith case. Shortly before the Supreme Court issued its decision, journalist Melissa Gira Grant made a TMZ-like discovery: The gay couple that supposedly made the request, "Mike and Stewart" did not exist. Stewart was a real person but had no knowledge of the request, denied making it, and was married to a woman. "It looks like Smith and her attorneys have, perhaps unwittingly, invented a gay couple in need of a wedding website," Grant wrote.[55] If this view is correct, a conservative Supreme Court that makes its fair share of errors relaxed procedural requirements and welcomed the ADF-fabricated case.[56] ADF, in turn, brought this case of "phantom gays" imposing faux harm on an innocent Christian to reach its desired ideological result.

A less scandalous, more scholarly, but still troubling story exists. This one focuses on the reality that whether the couple was real or not, it probably would not have been material to the outcome of the case, considering the composition of the Supreme Court and case law that allows people to challenge laws when they face a "credible threat" of punishment.[57] All it would take is one complaint against Smith, and boom, she's potentially subject to investigation by Colorado. Nevertheless, the case still involved the issuance of a major legal precedent based on an entirely hypothetical scenario that was partially engineered by conservative litigation entrepreneurs and will likely deepen the divide between First Amendment principles and antidiscrimination norms.

In five years, the court went from prohibiting discrimination on the basis of identity to allowing it as long as it is done artistically and with some pizazz. In *Masterpiece Cakeshop*, the Supreme Court assured the public that First Amendment protections "do not allow business owners and other actors in the economy and in society to deny protected persons equal access to goods and services under a neutral and generally applicable public accommodations law."[58]

In *303 Creative*, the Court reneged. It made an exception for "expressive services" like website designing, which it reasoned was different from making a widget. A website, they said, is speech. And forcing someone to design one for a same-sex wedding crosses the First Amendment line, even if it means gay couples can't get their wedding website. It's hard not to see this as an opening salvo. Legal writer Joe Patrice described the inequality concern: "There's nothing limiting a future plaintiff's 'expression' to something artistic. . . . This is how an incremental litigation strategy works! They started with the baker, now it's the web designer. Tomorrow it'll be a tailor. Or a theater venue. Or the lunch counter chef whose cuisine is her art. Subway already employs 'sandwich artists,' after all."[59]

Between *Masterpiece Cakeshop* and *303 Creative*, the Supreme Court welcomed two new members. Both are conservative (Justices Brett Kavanaugh and Amy Coney Barrett), and one received substantial speaking fees for multiple ADF events (Barrett).[60] It's hard not to believe that ADF didn't read the room, saw an opportunity, and pounced like most attorneys would. This strategic timing demonstrates how impact litigation can expose underlying tensions, regardless of whether the immediate case is contrived.

Beyond the legal maneuvering, real people are affected. Being denied services because of who you are inflicts genuine harm on LGBTQ individuals and perpetuates exclusion. Gay men receiving hostile treatment at gyms, lesbians subjected to discriminatory dress codes at nightclubs, or transgender people denied haircuts all face the same fundamental indignity of being told they don't belong. At the same time, it can be a challenge for liberals to understand the deep moral convictions some people hold. This disconnect may reflect liberalism's growing secularity, with more liberals identifying as atheists or having no religious affiliation.[61]

303 Creative demonstrates that a population of people believe that laws are applied in ways that are unfair to people of faith. People may disagree with this view, but it still represents a genuine concern about religious liberty. Of course, it remains to be seen whether these religious liberty protections will prove equally robust when invoked by progressive religious institutions—say, Catholic colleges defending DEI programs as expressions of their faith or churches providing sanctuary to immigrants.[62] These clashes between constitutional principles and antidiscrimination norms show how legal advocacy can reveal genuine conflicts about equality and whose rights deserve protection in a diverse democracy.

SOME OF THE MOST IMPORTANT legal issues of the day are more complicated than liberal hacks, conservative mouthpieces, and gavel-wielding activist judges of all stripes suggest—even if the court's increasingly blunt use of power can obscure that nuance. Not everyone wants to hear this because it acknowledges nuance that some would prefer to avoid; it also raises the possibility of conceding points to the other side.

In my experience, boosters, critics, and outsiders to the American legal system sometimes think it is some kind of machine where lawyers feed disputes and nice, clean, equal results can be churned out. In easy, straightforward cases, this is possible. However, in some high-stakes disputes, courts adjudicate between competing claims about harm and are compelled to make a tragic choice. The outcome can be an unsatisfying compromise or a decision that might worsen the circumstances faced by a social group.[63] Ultimately, the cool, clinical language of the law cannot hide the fact that our legal system is often an orderly way to manage inequality rather than eliminate it—and this might be because it is unwilling or incapable.

Conclusion

For the Record

I F IT WERE UP TO ME, this book would not have a conclusion. In serious nonfiction, conclusions are sometimes long-winded ways of saying "the end," weak attempts to provide closure, or redundant recaps.

But I also understand why this book needs a positive normative vision. At this point, a critical reader like you might say something like, "Complaining is easy, but what does he affirmatively want?" Current and future lawyers may want to know, in earnest, how to think about some of the real structural challenges presented in this book. And general readers may want to know what to do with this harsh appraisal.

I began the book by noting my focus on nonlawyers and lawyers, and I'll end by doing the same. My aim is to be as specific and as practical as possible.

What Can Non-Lawyers Do?

Readers who will never become lawyers but who have some kind of commitment to combating inequality have a few options. Most broadly, they can take aim at the four corners of the legal profession this book engages: law schools, large law firms, government attorneys, and public interest lawyers. I offer these suggestions in a somewhat ecumenical spirit—recognizing that readers may come from different ideological backgrounds.

Law Schools

This book has shown you how the first year of law school is a unique space where certain seeds of inequality are planted while the professional identities of students are cultivated. For general readers surprised by the reality that these courses are inadequately broaching the world's inequalities, the levers for change are limited. Scholars are fiercely protective of their academic freedom, and law schools, especially private ones, operate with considerable autonomy from public input.[1]

One approach that has successfully changed legal education is supporting student groups that advocate for a more socially relevant pedagogy. The conservative Federalist Society, which plays a significant role in determining which conservative judges are appointed to the bench, originated from students' frustration with the lack of conservative perspectives in law school. Meanwhile, critical race theory grew out of the legal left's frustration with the inadequate attention given to race, class, and gender.[2] Supporting organizations that are trying to rethink legal education—whether through donations, mentorship, or amplifying marginalized voices—represents one of the few viable paths for non-lawyers to influence legal education from the outside.

Law Firms

The strategies for addressing law firms' complicity in the reproduction of inequality are simpler.

One low-stakes option is to support investigative journalism and watchdog organizations that document problematic corporate legal strategies and disseminate those stories on your social network. Law firms don't like bad press; the drama around Trump's executive orders supplies the best examples. This approach has its limits, however. After all, corporations often hold "beauty contests" that allow firms to compete for their business; someone is always going to do the "dirty work."[3] Nevertheless, public attention can trigger in-fighting and the loss of existing clients. It can also increase the reputational costs of certain kinds of lawyering.[4]

Another, more demanding approach focuses on consumer activism. You could start an outright boycott of companies that employ law firms with dubious ethical records or those that serve problematic interests. Bud Light's $400 million loss after its transgender-themed promotion, and Disney's 1.7 million cancellations after suspending Jimmy Kimmel show that boycotts have teeth, regardless of one's view of the underlying cause. Boycotting may be challenging, however, because some of these companies are unavoidable due to their market dominance. Are you really going to boycott Walmart, especially when it might be the only player in town? Moreover, be aware that you have a certain kind of privilege when you are able to boycott and choose alternatives that are sometimes more expensive.

Organized consumers can hit firms where it hurts: by targeting their paying clients. Some more aggressive, organized tactics sit in ethical gray areas and should be used with intention, caution, and probably legal advice.[5] These include mass filing of legitimate warranty claims; mass cancellation of subscriptions; mass return of inexpensive items that do not meet customer expectations (which can lead to loss of profit through higher processing costs and depreciation of value); mass online shopping cart abandonment (filling carts with items but not making purchases to distort inventory); and mass membership churning (using free sign-up opportunities and ending memberships within the cancellation windows).

In order to succeed in any of these approaches, you would need to build organized movements capable of coordinating thousands of participants; individual or small-group efforts won't create meaningful impact. But if you couple this with clear messaging about the disapproval of law firm strategies, such coordinated action could minimally impact revenue streams used to hire law firms and potentially refigure how corporations and their counsel think about social responsibility.

Government Lawyers

Applying public pressure on prosecutors is somewhat easier than targeting law schools and law firms, but it is no simple task.

The most obvious tactic is to vote. Examples across the country involve prosecutors of different ideological orientations getting the boot because residents were unhappy with how they did their jobs. This includes progressive San Francisco prosecutor Chesa Boudin, who was recalled because of voters' frustration with his handling of crime and quality of life issues. Houston-based Republican DA Devon Anderson was kicked out of office after jailing a sexual assault survivor for a month to ensure her testimony. She also oversaw an office that destroyed up to twenty thousand pieces of potentially exonerating evidence—as if it were some kind of competition.

Research has shown that some places don't have a sufficient supply of candidates, which plays a role in some incumbents going unchallenged.[6] Even when there is some kind of a contest, "prosecutorial elections are historically low-information, low-turnout affairs" that often boil down to chest beating about "conviction rates, a few high-profile cases, and maybe a scandal."[7] So, please vote in that off-cycle election.

Voters could insist that current and prospective candidates show the real cost of what they prosecute, which they often have little incentive to do. They might focus on the expenses incurred by their office, but they won't break down the price of keeping a person in a cage, the cost of food stamps for the family left behind, or the cost of taking care of the kids who end up in foster care.[8] If they were required to provide such information, maybe the public could hold them more accountable, and maybe they'd be more judicious. Transparency should fit well with the cost-benefit analysis that appeals to "smart-on-crime conservatives." It could also be leveraged in service of equality imperatives.[9]

For readers who find data transparency to be an underwhelming request and want something with a little more oomph, we can take it there. Almost thirty years ago, Paul Butler advocated for the use of *jury nullification*. This occurs when a juror deliberately rejects evidence of guilt and refuses to apply the law to "send a message about some social issue that is larger than the case itself." They may also nullify because the result dictated by law is contrary to the juror's "sense of justice, morality, or fairness."[10]

Here is what it looks like. Say you're on a jury and the evidence shows that someone was braiding hair without a cosmetology license. (A Black woman in Texas was arrested for this and the libertarians at the Institute of Justice have dedicated their time to addressing this issue.)[11] She is technically guilty. But you know or learned through the trial that braiding hair is a skill passed down through generations in Black communities, and that licensing requirements are just barriers that keep people from earning a living. So you vote not guilty even though she technically broke the law.

Courts generally disapprove of the practice because they see it as a violation of the juror's oath. But one can nullify anyway; there is not much courts can do about it as long as a juror chooses to nullify without announcing it to the world. Courts generally respect jury independence by not prying into jurors' minds or punishing them for their verdicts, absent some clear evidence of prejudicial influence.[12] Criminal juries must have unanimous decisions; if one juror "holds out" (a hung jury), the judge will declare a mistrial. The prosecutor may still retry the case, but that may mean expending more public resources. It also means they're restarting the proceedings with the defense counsel's awareness of their trial strategy and weaknesses.

Butler suggested that Black jurors hearing nonviolent drug possession cases should use the jury nullification power. In his view, because we had a racially biased War on Drugs, jury nullification was an appropriate "Black Power" antidote. Interestingly, jury nullification has roots in Anglo-American history and finds support among some legal conservatives. Libertarian journalist Damon Root has suggested that jury nullification has a "historical pedigree that should impress constitutional originalists." He notes how Founding Father James Wilson made a similar point in his 1791 lecture when he said, "whoever would be obliged to obey a constitutional law, is *justified* in refusing to obey an unconstitutional act of the legislature."[13] Libertarian legal scholar Ilya Somin has argued that jury nullification is a critical "counterweight to the enormous discretionary power already wielded by government officials."[14]

Informed readers put on juries may want to nullify when they have strong suspicions of foul play in prosecutions, particularly when serving on the jury for some nonviolent offenses. As a second or alternative step, they might take a cue from the Fully Informed Jury Association, an organization that focuses on spreading legal literacy around the right to nullify. Such messaging is protected under free speech principles if it's general and not directed at a specific juror or designed to influence an outcome in a legal case (which would be criminal jury tampering).[15]

Widespread jury nullification (or suspicion of it) could potentially weaken prosecutors' advantage in plea bargaining, make them more considerate in what they charge, and shift discriminatory enforcement patterns. But there's always the prospect of backlash; nullification could be used as a justification to discriminate in jury selection. It could be deployed by biased jurors who want biased outcomes, or it could lead to jury instructions being altered to require jurors to be more transparent about their nullification practices (or lie about them). It's high risk–high reward.

The civil counterparts to prosecutors, municipal lawyers, occupy a distinctive place in American society. They have a legal duty to their client—the city or county—but they are also public servants who are accountable to the residents whose taxes fund their office.

One approach general readers could take to influence municipal lawyers is to politicize the position and exercise power through the ballot box. Residents would demand that incumbent leaders and candidates for top positions in these offices offer articulable policy platforms on how their legal department will handle legitimate civil rights claims brought against local governments. This is an easier task in jurisdictions like Los Angeles and Houston that elect these attorneys. In cities like New York and Philadelphia, where the leader is designated by elected officials, pressure would need to be applied to the people doing the appointing.

These municipal head honchos should be able to answer variants of these questions, and more: What philosophy will guide you in determining legitimate versus frivolous civil rights cases? Is zealous advocacy appropriate when residents have valid complaints? How do you think about the balance between limiting the municipality's legal liability, adhering to the spirit of civil rights laws, and being morally obligated to right government-caused harms? How will you direct government lawyers to handle these competing priorities? Assuming they don't use boilerplate political language, their responses should be revealing. If they can't answer these questions to the concerned reader's satisfaction, they should feel electoral pain.

And don't let elected officials claim they can't control municipal lawyers. The ethical rules say they represent the city through their duly authorized agents (mayors and legislators). Those officials determine legal objectives and control their budgets. It's time for all of them to be better.[16]

Public Interest Lawyers

Here is a counterintuitive reality: Public interest organizations are arguably the hardest wing of the legal profession for the public to shape. In appellate advocacy, organizations often have ideological missions that are unlikely to change. There's little you can do, for example, to prevent an abortion rights group from advocating for pro-choice jurisprudence, and you're going to have a hard time stopping a religious organization from bringing cases that try to enshrine prayer in public schools. The concerned citizen might highlight the problematic aspects of appellate organizations in their social networks, support countermobilization, or donate to groups that take an opposing view, of course.

Many of the shortcomings of organizations that provide direct services are tied to funding. Donations are an easy solution to counteract this, but if we're being honest, funding is and will always be a perennial problem. Nevertheless, one point of attack could be advocating for increased attorney licensing fees (which are already used in some jurisdictions to pay for legal services). For more than sixty years, the Supreme Court has said such fees are okay as long as they are reasonably incurred for the purpose of "improving the quality of the legal service available to the people of the State."[17] Grassroots advocacy might focus on the state legislatures that set these fees and state supreme courts that regulate the practice of law. It's a privilege to practice law, and lawyers should pay their fair share.

Another option is for general readers to press legislators, bar officials, and state supreme courts to link high-stakes litigation to funding for legal aid. Many states have a "complex litigation program" that identifies cases requiring exceptional court resources. The programs vary by state, but hallmarks include novel interpretations of business statutes, cases involving state securities laws, business licensing agreements disputes, and lots of other rich people stuff. In Connecticut, the statutory fee for such cases is $335, and in California, it is $550.[18] One could imagine upping the fees for this kind of special treatment, with the additional revenue being directed to legal aid organizations through existing state funding mechanisms. These moves are most likely to affect people who can afford the fees (which minimizes but doesn't extinguish the possibility of unintended consequences for poor people).[19] The details, mechanisms, and challenges may vary by state, but the basic principle is straightforward: Make those who benefit most from the legal system help fund access for those who benefit least.

What Can Lawyers Do?

Government Lawyers

Students who care about inequality and are on the road to the DA's office must take a sober view of things. The chief DA is an elected position, so politics can shape the work. Depending on the demographics of the jurisdiction, working at the DA's office may well mean there is a strong possibility that you will play a role in exacerbating race and class disparities. When it comes to earning promotions, you should be aware that a host of factors go into evaluating prosecutors.

Trial skills and an ability to manage a high caseload or complex cases are important, but wins, losses, and plea bargains matter as well. Don't forget that careerism is a hell of a drug.

For future and current prosecutors, I suggest mixing introspection and disruption. These tactics will make you uncomfortable. Some might involve mild versions of occupational self-sabotage or outright job suicide. This work isn't easy.

Prosecutors already have ethical duties and office policies, but sanctions for violating them are rare. Setting your own ethical redlines—beyond what the rules require—can be morally anchoring and advance equality imperatives. For example, a prospective prosecutor might say, I will not 1) abuse the power of bail against poor people who pose no risk of violence; 2) needlessly delay trial in ways that would violate speedy trial rights and cause people to languish in jail; 3) disregard police perjury even if it benefits their case; 4) exploit identity in different parts of criminal adjudication (e.g., race in jury selection or immigration status in plea bargaining); or 5) engage in many other unconstitutional practices that prosecutors have been accused of and are not necessary to do the work. And to the extent this feels superfluous, these red lines would include prespecified strategies you would use to avoid such behavior if certain contexts allow it.

These kinds of ethical red lines may be harder for current prosecutors to establish since they lack some of the objectivity that distance provides. Given daily job pressures, they might dismiss this as unrealistic; critics might argue that these prosecutors are compromised and unable to engage in such line drawing. But for some of these attorneys, their insider knowledge of harmful practices could help them craft more targeted and effective ethical boundaries.

Whether you are newly minted or have been practicing for a while, there should be a process of deeper introspection—periodic "ethical check-ins" that require you to be intellectually honest in your assessments about how you are implicated in inequality, notwithstanding your professional commitments. This might include reviewing your own cases to identify problematic patterns in prosecutorial decision-making and going to therapy (which most lawyers should undertake).

Disruption is tricker because of professional ethics rules and office policies. But some tactics could simultaneously undermine business as usual in inequality-exacerbating DA offices while still complying with the exhortation that prosecutors "do justice." For example, prosecutors have a constitutional and ethical duty to disclose all evidence that could help the defense counsel and undermine their own case. Some prosecutors regularly breach this duty and violations are hard for defense attorneys to detect.[20] The inequality-sensitive prosecutor might understand their disclosure obligations expansively and furnish all relevant information that could exculpate a defendant without a defense attorney's request.

Such prosecutors could offer more favorable plea bargains, recommend probation over incarceration more regularly than their colleagues, and insist on high standards when using informants. They might become technicality-seeking lawyers when scrutinizing the conduct of arresting and investigative officers and select some skeptics of law enforcement when they are paneling a jury. They may avoid being sticklers when overworked and under-resourced defense attorneys make good-faith procedural errors.

These actions would be subject to pressures from police, crime victims, and community residents who want retribution as well as workplace cultures that prioritize wins. But these tactics—which are mostly within prosecutors' discretion and avoid ethical violations—can potentially disrupt prosecutorial spaces where punitiveness is the norm.

Municipal lawyers represent cities/counties and most of the agencies and departments therein, which makes recommendations for them partially distinct. If you are one of these attorneys, you have a legal duty to the municipality. That means advocating for the city/county, even when those interests may not align with the well-being of its residents.

Still, some of the suggestions offered for prosecutors apply here. You may benefit from creating a list of ethical dealbreakers regarding unjust practices. These might include not withholding evidence from plaintiffs in civil rights lawsuits (as one prominent office was accused of),[21] not swindling poor unrepresented plaintiffs to secure favorable outcomes, not ignoring municipal misconduct, and not providing counsel to city officials in a manner that helps them evade accountability.

Municipal lawyers are uniquely positioned to address social and legal inequality. On the compliance side, you may engage in regular audits of local practices and policies to identify problems before they rise to the level of legal dispute. At the settlement phase, you might advocate for quick resolution in cases where the locality was clearly at fault and encourage the inclusion of provisions or robust oversight mechanisms that will prevent future civil rights violations. These may not turn over the apple cart, but they might begin to change the existing order of things.

Big Law

If you are a prospective or current Big Law attorney with deeply held concerns about inequality, you have tough choices to make and issues to consider.

The first set of suggestions concerns intellectual honesty about your goals and what you tell yourself about your practice. If you want to make boatloads of money and become a partner, skip the next two paragraphs.

In some instances, people legitimately need to work in Big Law for a few years to pay off loans. If that is true for you, be careful of the golden handcuffs that lock people into law firm practice. Sometimes, these are discretionary lifestyle choices that people bootstrap themselves into (e.g., expensive mortgages, luxury cars). But you may also encounter legitimate non-negotiables for which you might get more sympathy (e.g., elder care costs, daycare/school education). Such expenses can make off-boarding to lesser-paying jobs more difficult. Underneath these financial motivations are deeper issues.

Consider some ritualistic scripts students tell themselves about

Big Law practice. They might highlight a firm's pro bono initiatives, which can be crude marketing tools and are often subordinated when they conflict with work from paying clients (which there is a lot of). "Working within the system to change it" is another justification. I'm sympathetic to this since these important spaces can't just be abdicated by people with concerns about equality. However, this view can overestimate junior attorneys' authority and underestimate how profit-driven clients and law firm partners can resist reform when it conflicts with profit motives. Sometimes, these "change agents" are branded as "difficult" in ways that can be career-ruining.[22]

With these considerations in mind, the advice I can give prospective Big Law attorneys is three-fold.

First, when considering practice groups, conduct due diligence on some of the firm's most contentious matters. Law firms are complex organizations with some practice groups that may be more socially harmful than others. After determining problematic clients or practice groups, and ideally avoiding them, establish some ethical deal breakers in advance. These might be tied to industry-based harms that you believe are socially intolerable (e.g., no matters involving the fossil fuel industry or debt buyers) or specific issues you personally abhor (e.g., no sexual harassment claims, no cases involving facial recognition).

This is all with the caveat that firms will not let junior attorneys reject all work they find problematic. These strategies won't eliminate the moral detachment that legal training creates—a lawyer could avoid fossil fuel work but still reproduce inequality in transportation law. But being conscious about where your talents get deployed and which harms you're willing to enable is better than operating on autopilot.

One way Big Law attorneys can mitigate social inequalities is through *political tithing*. Much like religious tithing, which involves giving 10 percent of your income to a religious institution, this secular form of giving focuses on donating a regular, percentage-based amount to organizations that share the your beliefs and policy preferences. Political scientist Christina Greer, who coined the term, believes that it is imperative for people to donate to social justice organizations that are "doing the work" when we cannot or do not.[23]

As of this writing, the Cravath pay scale, which sets the market, is $225,000 per year for first-year associates. An associate might allocate 5 percent (about $11,000) or 10 percent (about $22,000) of their income to organizations or causes that align with their equality concerns. If they wanted to scale up, they might find like-minded attorneys, inside or outside of the firm, and form a legal *giving circle*—the cooperative pooling of resources for charitable purposes. Such a collective could increase individual accountability and foster communities of like-minded, equality-concerned Big Law attorneys that we know exist.[24]

There are many options for such individual or collective giving. They include the underfunded public interest organizations and electoral races described earlier in this conclusion. Donations could also go to a range of entities that appeal to people across the ideological spectrum: deportation defense funds, tenants' unions, veterans' rights organizations, child advocacy attorneys focused on special education, domestic violence services, organizations focused on protecting tribal lands, faith-based service providers, government surveillance projects, and rural legal aid.

Donations are a serious demonstration of political commitments, but if they are just a conscience-cleaning exercise of check-writing, then they can resemble a form of offsetting not that different from the environmental type discussed in this book. This is why donations and pro bono work should be accompanied by the interpersonal work that comes with social change—e.g., building real relationships with organizers, leveraging firm resources for broader benefit where appropriate, and showing up in solidarity—some of which time-strapped attorneys already do.[25]

Public Interest Lawyering

Public interest lawyers are unlikely culprits in inequality, partly because they are the lawyers who toil the hardest to address that problem.

For incoming attorneys, there's no way to fully grasp the experience of clients, but at a bare minimum, I'd suggest trying to get a sense of their daily travails, whether it be budgeting for a week based on the federal poverty guidelines, navigating the paratransit system that clients with disabilities use, visiting the food pantries that some of them rely on, or sitting in one of the many waiting rooms that drain poor people of their time. Realizing you have the privileged ability to opt out of all of this might provide you with more perspective about the less-than-obvious barriers facing clients and the kind of assumptions attorneys might have about them. It could also become the start of your search for deeper self-knowledge.

Accordingly, as a new attorney, you might ask yourself, and answer in writing: How do I understand the social distance between me and my clients? What makes me qualified for the job? What is the history of the community I'm serving, and what have relevant *local* experts (e.g., activists, local scholars, and policy wonks) identified as the major issues facing them? Considering my future practice group, how would I define what constitutes an emergency? How do I think racism, sexism, ableism, and language bias play a role in the delivery of legal services?

Answers to these questions, among others, might be more revealing and valuable if you share them with trustworthy individuals (e.g., former clinical supervisors, fellow attorneys from diverse backgrounds, social workers in your practice area, and community organizers). This is a process that requires vulnerability, but it pales in comparison to the vulnerability many of your future clients experience.

Current attorneys should engage in introspection that is tied to accountability partners. The questions you ask yourselves would similarly focus on social distance and assumptions you have about your clients, as well as other client dynamics. These might include: What kind of clients am I more skeptical of, and which ones do I find to be automatically credible? Which kind of clients do I find to be most difficult? Considering the time constraints in this world, what does cutting corners look like, and which type of clients does such triaging impact? Are there any systemic issues I now understand to be unfair but that are ultimately inevitable or not worth fighting?

The social, economic, and political limitations public interest attorneys face are what they are, but this kind of self-examination could nudge them toward more equitable representation within the bounds of those constraints.

Law Students and Legal Educators

Reform-curious legal educators should be reminded that we are part of a vocation that has long-professed ideas about intellectual curiosity, social justice, and equality under the law. Nevertheless, our field has not fully responded to longstanding appeals to incorporate legally relevant discussions about social inequality into our teaching. Now a great deal of scholarship can make this possible; this book cites countless examples. Pick them up and engage; that's what being a lawyer and a scholar is about.

Professors can get a good-enough grasp on new subject matter areas to write scholarly articles, obtain summer funding from their institutions, and apply for large grants for new projects; I can't tell you how many colleagues I have across the country who have become experts in artificial intelligence, crypto, and NFTs overnight. Getting generally familiarized with scholarship on race, poverty, sex, immigration, disability, libertarianism, and conservatism is no small task, but it is doable and should be the price of teaching certain courses in the law school curriculum. Of course, how you implement what you discover will also vary depending on your school, but the COVID-19 pandemic provides an unfortunate and recent example of how we adapt and even consider a hard reset.

Law students themselves can be important catalysts for change in legal education. As a student, you have the capacity to transform some of the conversations happening inside your law school. Reformation is not easy or costless. It involves some risk-taking and additional labor. You can raise relevant questions that fill areas overlooked by the professor, challenge taken-for-granted assumptions raised by your classmates, and support student colleagues who sometimes make these interventions but are isolated in their intellectual bravery.

To be sure, it is fine to go to school and simply be a student; social change doesn't rest on your individual shoulders. I worry, unfortunately, that curricular change will not come willingly or without the kind of pressure that students are well positioned to exert. We all have a part to play if we want to be in the game.

THESE RECOMMENDATIONS ARE limited in what they can accomplish. The professional detachment that pervades our legal system runs deeper than any single book can heal. This is a legal machinery that has been centuries in the making, and it is vaster than any of our imaginations. But perfection is impossible and it shouldn't be the executioner of better. I've tried to outline things that are urgent and, in many instances, achievable within existing constraints.

This legal profession, notwithstanding its failures, has birthed extraordinary transformations. Though it originally sanctioned slavery, it ultimately dismantled it. It secured women's access to credit and employment—things that were hardly assured sixty years ago. It developed the frameworks that guaranteed people with disabilities access to education and public accommodations. It has established principles for organizing society that, while imperfectly applied, continue to create pathways toward justice.

The profession produced me as well—not as a triumph of bootstrap meritocracy, but as a witness positioned to see the full spectrum of the legal system's contradictions. With my own practicing lawyer eyes, I've seen the indescribable joy radiating from a client's face upon learning that Medicaid would cover a life-saving surgery that bureaucrats had initially denied. I've studied civil rights cases in close detail—the high-profile victories and the under-the-radar wins that looked impossible when they were happening and in hindsight. The profession and lessons learned in zip code 10457 provided me with the tools to recognize both the law's harmful patterns and its potential for justice. I'm convinced that the brilliance the profession has inherited and developed can better mold the American experiment. But it requires lawyers to be more sober about how their expertise shapes human consequences.

Acknowledgments

Scores of people made this book possible through friendship, intellectual companionship, and love.

First, I want to thank my parents—for giving me life, for their sacrifices, and for their unwavering belief in me. And my brother Larry, who gave me tough love, street smarts, and the confidence to trust my instincts. These pages wouldn't exist without the three of them.

I'm grateful to my agent, Lisa Adams, who helped shape multiple versions of the proposal and helped me hash out ideas and logistics. My editor, Dan Gerstle, has been fantastic, deeply patient and understanding. He was one of the first non-lawyers to really get what I was doing. Dan offered immensely helpful editorial advice on substance, length, and style—lessons that will stay with me beyond this book. I'm grateful to both of them, as well as Zeba Arora and Rebecca Rider for helping bring this project to a successful finish.

At Northwestern, I found a community of scholars who recognized my talent before I did. Thank you to Celeste Watkins-Hayes, Dorothy Roberts, John Márquez, and Dylan Penningroth. RIP to Richard Iton—you're deeply missed.

While I was a graduate student at Penn, John Jackson and Deborah Thomas played the roles of sherpa, teacher, and mentor. I'm so lucky to now call them colleagues.

This project grew during my time at Berkeley and the American Bar Foundation, where I matured as a scholar. I owe my intellectual identity to the communities in both places—starting with my dissertation committee: Ula Taylor, Charles Henry, Sandra Smith, Leigh Raiford, Ian Haney-López, and Jonathan Simon, and extending to Bertrall Ross, Melissa Murray, Russell Robinson, Kathy Abrams, Leti Volpp, Amanda Tyler, KT Albiston, Cal Morrill, Bob Nelson, Anne O'Connell, Terry Halliday, John Hagan, Susan Shapiro, Fred Smith, Bernadette Atuahene, Ajay Mehotra, Chris Schmidt, Traci Burch, and Beth Mertz. RIP to Lauren Edelman, who pushed me to think big, and to Chris Edley, who helped create the conditions for me to become a law professor.

After law school, I bounced between Sidley, Legal Aid DC, and Columbia Law. I'm grateful to those who sharpened my legal mind: Jeff Green, Daron Watts, Kwaku Akowuah, Jonathan Levy, Chinh Le, Dave Pozen, Jessica Bulman-Pozen, Jeremy Kessler, Bert Huang, Pat Williams, Kendall Thomas, Jamal Greene, Olatunde Johnson, and Danny Richman.

If people knew how generous my colleagues at Penn are, they'd be envious. Many helped me workshop this book and its ideas. Special thanks to Dean Ted Ruger, who supported me with time, research assistance, and encouragement. Dean Sophia Lee picked up the baton and carved out time from her decanal duties to put on her scholarly hat and offer thoughtful feedback. Thanks also to Regina Austin, Dorothy Roberts, Karen Tani, Sally Gordon, Lou Rulli, Liz Pollman, Serena Meyeri, Lisa Fairfax, Cara McClellan, Dave Hoffman, Mitch Berman, Jill Fisch, Tess Wilkinson-Ryan, Anita Allen, Wendell Pritchett, Kate Shaw, Jon Klick, Allison Hoffman, Jean Galbraith, Colleen Shanahan, Sandy Mayson, Jasmine Harris, Angus Corbett, and Seth Kreimer.

I spent a year at Princeton at the University Center for Human Values. That year was crucial, and provided space to make substantial developments to the book. I'm grateful for the intellectual generosity of those who engaged my work, particularly Melissa Lane, Kim Scheppele, Steve Macedo, Daniel Fryer, Rachel Lopez, Tae-Yeoun Keum, and Shatema Threadcraft.

Several folks participated in manuscript workshops across the country and provided no-holds-barred feedback. They helped me avoid costly errors, pushed me to be more precise, pointed me to literature and cases I hadn't known, challenged me to slow down, insisted I pump up the volume, and—most importantly—encouraged me to be myself. I'm indebted to Dorothy Roberts, Regina Austin, Jamillah Bowman Williams, Julian Hill, Osamudia James, Jennifer Fernández, Brittany Farr, Charlton Copeland, James Forman, Nicole Van Cleve, Amna Akbar, Bernadette Atuahene, LaToya Baldwin Clark, Alexander Arnold, Mehrsa Baradaran, Mugambi Jouet, Aya Gruber, Guy Charles, Sasha Natapoff, Steven Cody, Steve Koh, Zohra Ahmed, Aziza Ahmed, Felipe Cole, Jamelia Morgan, Bob Nelson, Eve Ewing, Reuben Miller, Laura Beth Nielsen, Darrell Miller, Jonathan Masur, Beth Mertz, Dave Pozen, Jamal Greene, Jeremy Kessler, Susan Sturm, Kellen Funk, Kerrel Murray, Tanya Hernández, Emma Kaufman, Dorothy Lund, Bert Huang, and Dori Pavel. Scott Cummings and Benjamin Barton also provided immensely helpful feedback and provocations.

I'm also thankful to colleagues at the law schools of Temple, Vanderbilt, Washington University in St. Louis, and Indiana University Bloomington for providing the space to workshop parts of the manuscript. More colleagues lent their expertise by reading portions of the project and/or chatting with me about it. Thanks to Cathie Struve, Maureen Carroll, Deborah Archer, Jane Baron, Alexis Hoag-Fordjour, Deborah Widiss, Daniel Fryer, Michael Livermore, Evelyn Rangel-Medina, Franita Tolson, Akofa Tsiagbe, K-Sue Park, Steve Koh, Luis Fuentes-Rohwer, Eve Primus, Danny Richman, Shelley Welton, Norm Spaulding, Trevor Gardner, Aziz Huq, Lee Fennell, Josh Sellers, Gina-Gail Fletcher, Veronica Root Martinez, Hajin Kim, Rachel Sachs, Lauren Ouziel, and Shirin Bakhshay. Over the years several research assistants have been helpful. Thanks to Erica Rodarte, Abigail Kasdin, Camilla Samuelson, and Yasmine Seghir.

I wrapped up this book while visiting at Harvard Law School and conversations with colleagues there about first-year teaching and the profession helped crystallize my thinking. Thanks to Noah Feldman, Bruce Mann, John Goldberg, Sandy Levinson, Martha Minow, Molly Brady, Anna Lvovsky, David Wilkins, Randy Kennedy, Jill Lepore, Ken Mack, Michael Klarman, Andrew Crespo, Christopher Lewis, and Dick Fallon (RIP).

To a broader circle of family and friends: Jane, Lealah, Tamiko, Gina, Greg, Karen, Trevor, Reuben, Tim, Guy, Aileen, and all my family and friends back in the Bronx, Philadelphia, Chicago, LA, the Bay Area, and DC that are too numerous to name. Big ups.

Finally, to the family I've created: Jasmine—my partner in every sense of the word—editor, therapist, nerve-calmer, cheerleader, voice of reason, and source of life and intellectual wisdom. You make my life better in ways that defy description. To my daughter Lucille—you bring joy and purpose beyond measure. Your strength and curiosity inspire me every day. From me, you will always be met with open arms and unconditional care. Finally, to Clyde, born a few weeks before this manuscript was submitted. You arrived into a complicated world; know that you are loved in it, supported, and never alone.

Notes

INTRODUCTION

1. David Hope and Julian Limberg, "The Economic Consequences of Major Tax Cuts for the Rich," *Socio-Economic Review* 20, no. 2 (April 2022): 539–59.
2. Arya Sundaram, "4-Year-Old Migrant Girl, Other Kids Go to Court in NYC with No Lawyer: 'The Cruelty Is Apparent,'" *Gothamist*, April 22, 2025.
3. World Population Review, "Domestic Violence by State 2025," accessed August 6, 2025.
4. Deborah N. Archer, *Dividing Lines: How Transportation Infrastructure Reinforces Racial Inequality* (W. W. Norton, 2025); Mitchell Duneier, *Ghetto: The Invention of a Place, the History of an Idea* (Farrar, Straus and Giroux, 2017).
5. Peter L'Official, *Urban Legends: The South Bronx in Representation and Ruin* (Harvard University Press, 2020), 25.
6. Randol Contreras, *The Stickup Kids: Race, Drugs, Violence, and the American Dream* (University of California Press, 2012).
7. Margaret F. Brinig and Nicole Stelle Garnett, *Lost Classroom, Lost Community: Catholic Schools' Importance in Urban America* (University of Chicago Press, 2016).
8. Chin Jou, *Supersizing Urban America: How Inner Cities Got Fast Food with Government Help* (University of Chicago Press, 2017).
9. Adam Bonica and Maya Sen, *The Judicial Tug of War: How Lawyers, Politicians, and Ideological Incentives Shape the American Judiciary* (Cambridge University Press, 2021), 12.
10. American Bar Association, "Demographics," Profile of the Legal Profession 2024, accessed August 6, 2025; "The Status of Black Representation in American Law School Faculty," *The Journal of Blacks in Higher Education*, December 16, 2024.
11. Jeanne Theoharis, "Martin Luther King and the 'Polite' Racism of White Liberals," *Washington Post*, January 17, 2020; Jim Lindgren, "Law Faculty Diversity: Successes and Failures," *Washington Post*, March 21, 2015; Ian Haney-López, *Dog Whistle Politics: How Coded Racial Appeals Have Reinvented Racism and Wrecked the Middle Class* (Oxford University Press, 2014).
12. Benjamin H. Barton, *The Credentialed Court: Inside the Cloistered, Elite World of American Justice* (Encounter Books, 2022).
13. Emily Birnbaum and Bill Allison, "Supreme Court Justices Are Richer Than 90% of Americans," *Bloomberg*, April 20, 2023.

14. Compare Lee Epstein and Mitu Gulati, "A Century of Business in the Supreme Court, 1920–2020," *Minnesota Law Review Headnotes* 107 (2022): 49–74, with Jonathan H. Adler, *Business and the Roberts Court* (Oxford University Press, 2016).
15. Karen M. Tani, "Curation, Narration, Erasure: Power and Possibility at the U.S. Supreme Court," *Harvard Law Review* 138, no. 1 (November 2024); AT&T Mobility LLC v. Concepcion, 563 U.S. 333 (2011); Am. Express Co. v. Italian Colors Rest., 570 U.S. 228 (2013); Epic Sys. Corp. v. Lewis, 138 S. Ct. 1612 (2018); TransUnion LLC v. Ramirez, 594 U.S. 413 (2021); Janus v. Am. Fed'n of State, Cnty., & Mun. Emps., Council 31, 585 U.S. 924 (2018); Citizens United v. FEC, 558 U.S. 310 (2010).
16. John G. Roberts, Jr., "2006 Chief Justice's Year-End Report on the Federal Judiciary," Supreme Court of the United States (January 1, 2007), 1.
17. James V. Grimaldi et al., "131 Federal Judges Broke the Law by Hearing Cases Where They Had a Financial Interest," *Wall Street Journal*, September 28, 2021.
18. Lara Bazelon and James Forman, "Aim Lower: Liberals Have Lost the Supreme Court for a Generation," *Intelligencer* (*New York Magazine*), July 5, 2023.
19. Milan Markovic, "The Law Professor Pipeline," *Temple Law Review* 92, no 4 (June 2020): 813–35.
20. Eric J. Segall and Adam Feldman, "The Elite Teaching the Elite: Who Gets Hired by the Top Law Schools?," *Journal of Legal Education* 68, no. 3 (2019): 614, 619.
21. Markovic, "Law Professor Pipeline," 817.
22. Richard H. Sander, "Class in American Legal Education," *Denver University Law Review* 88 (2011): 631, 632.
23. Regina Austin, "Resistance Tactics for Tokens," *Harvard Blackletter Law Journal* 3 (1986): 52–56.
24. Ezra Rosser, "On Becoming 'Professor': A Semi-Serious Look in the Mirror," *Florida State University Law Review* 36, no. 2 (2009): 215, 221.
25. Elizabeth Mertz, *The Language of Law School: Learning to "Think Like a Lawyer"* (Oxford University Press, 2007).
26. "HSBC to Pay $1.9bn in US Money-Laundering Penalties," *BBC News*, December 11, 2012; Kalyeena Makortoff et al., "HSBC Faces Questions over Disclosure of Alleged Money-Laundering to Monitors," *Guardian*, July 28, 2021.
27. On the legal education front, there are at least three omissions. I do not discuss clinical education, which provides students with hands-on experience and allows them to provide legal services to people who might otherwise not be able to afford representation. Clinical programs vary widely by school, are optional, and, depending on the school, often enroll a minority of students. Legal Research and Writing (LRW) courses, which often occur over two semesters, are required and teach students how to navigate legal databases and communicate legal content clearly, among many other important skills. The variation within the course across schools, resource differences, and the unfortunate undervaluation of this important course make it hard to draw distillable lessons from. I also do not cover LLM programs, which provide specialized training and/or American education to international students who typically have experienced their foundational legal training in other countries. On the practice side, my account does not fully cover solo and small-firm practitioners, who constitute the plurality of lawyers and occupy a complicated space in the profession. Like public interest lawyers, they provide access to justice in a system that overwhelmingly favors wealth, assisting ordinary people in disputes over work, housing, and consumer rights. But like Big Law,

their services are often inaccessible to the poorest. They also represent smaller-scale corporate interests that can reproduce localized social and economic harms. Because their work is so diffuse, the precise dynamics are harder to capture, and they do not receive separate treatment here.

CHAPTER 1: LEGAL BOOTCAMP

1. Jakki Petzold, "How Many Law Students Are Following in Their Lawyer Parent's Footsteps?," *Law School Survey of Student Engagement*, February 24, 2021, https://perma.cc/QK2Z-DMW7.
2. Jennifer M. Morton, *Moving Up Without Losing Your Way: The Ethical Costs of Upward Mobility* (Princeton University Press, 2019); Anthony Abraham Jack, *The Privileged Poor: How Elite Colleges Are Failing Disadvantaged Students* (Harvard University Press, 2019).
3. See Lani Guinier et al., *Becoming Gentlemen: Women, Law School, and Institutional Change* (Beacon Press, 1997). On race, see Wendy Leo Moore, *Reproducing Racism: White Space, Elite Law Schools, and Racial Inequality* (Rowman and Littlefield Publishers, 2007).
4. See e.g., Debra Moss Curtis, "Attorney Discipline Nationwide: A Comparative Analysis of Process and Statistics," *Journal of the Legal Profession* 35, no. 2 (Spring 2011): 209–337.
5. Jakki Petzold, "How Much Time Do Law Students Spend Preparing for Class?," *Law School Survey of Student Engagement*, January 16, 2019, https://perma.cc/47SY-T53A.
6. One professor asked students, on a final exam, to pretend that they were lawyers for Kansas, and defend segregation in *Brown*. See Joe Patrice, "This Is One of The Dumbest Law School Exams Ever ... But at Least It's Also Racist," *Above the Law*, May 21, 2018.
7. Some professors, including myself, have modified the Socratic method due to concerns about student anxiety, and some have abandoned it outright, but it is still considered a "signature method" of law school teaching.
8. Kathryne M. Young, *How to Be Sort of Happy in Law School* (Tantor and Blackstone Publishing, 2021) (sociology); Kennon M. Sheldon and Lawrence S. Krieger, "Does Legal Education Have Undermining Effects on Law Students? Evaluating Changes in Motivation, Values, and Well-Being," *Behavioral Sciences and the Law* 22, no. 2 (2004): 261–86 (psychology); Sharon Dolovich, "Making Docile Lawyers: An Essay on the Pacification of Law Students," *Harvard Law Review* 111, no. 7 (May 1998): 2027–44 (student perspective); Phyllis W. Beck and David Burns, "Anxiety and Depression in Law Students: Cognitive Intervention," *Journal of Legal Education* 30, no. 3 (1979): 270–90 (law and psychiatry).
9. CUNY School of Law, "About Us," accessed August 27, 2025.
10. Eric M. Eisenberg, "Ambiguity as Strategy in Organizational Communication," *Communication Monographs* 51, no. 3 (1984): 227, 231.
11. Rule 301, "Objectives of Program of Legal Education," in *ABA Standards and Rules of Procedure for Approval of Law Schools* (2022–2023), 17, https://law.wm.edu/currentstudents/2022-2023-aba-standards-and-rules-of-procedure-for-approval-of-law-schools-chapter-3.pdf (emphasis added).
12. James M. Anderson and Paul Heaton, "How Much Difference Does the Lawyer Make? The Effect of Defense Counsel on Murder Case Outcomes," *Yale Law Journal* 122 (2012): 154–217.

13. Organizations like the National Legal Aid and Defender Association and some bar associations have put forth "performance guidelines" but they are advisory.
14. This includes public defenders as well as attorneys who are privately contracted or appointed by courts to represent people who can't afford a lawyer.
15. Jeffrey L. Kirchmeier, "Drink, Drugs, and Drowsiness: The Constitutional Right to Effective Assistance of Counsel and the *Strickland* Prejudice Requirement," *Nebraska Law Review* 75, no. 3 (2014): 425–75.
16. Ken Armstrong, "What Can You Do with a Drunken Lawyer?" *Marshall Project*, December 10, 2014.
17. Lisa G. Lerman and Philip G. Schrag, *Ethical Problems in the Practice of Law* (Wolters Kluwer, 2020), 58; Mike W. Martin, "Professional and Ordinary Morality: A Reply to Freedman," *Ethics* 91, no. 44 (July 1981): 631–33.
18. Quattrone Center for the Fair Administration of Justice, *Hidden Hazards: Prosecutorial Misconduct Claims in Pennsylvania, 2000–2016* (Penn Carey Law School, University of Pennsylvania, 2021); Samuel R. Gross and Michael Shaffer, *Exonerations in the United States, 1989–2012* (National Registry of Exonerations, 2012).
19. Lara A. Bazelon, "Hard Lessons: The Role of Law Schools in Addressing Prosecutorial Misconduct," *Berkeley Journal of Criminal Law* 16, no. 2 (Fall 2011): 391, 403; Stephanos Bibas, "Plea Bargaining Outside the Shadow of Trial," *Harvard Law Review* 117 (June 2004): 2463, 2470–76. On prosecutorial misconduct see Angela J. Davis, *Arbitrary Justice: The Power of the American Prosecutor* (Oxford University Press, 2007); Bruce A. Green, "Regulating Prosecutors' Courtroom Misconduct," *Loyola University Chicago Law Journal* 50 (2019): 101.
20. Mark Curriden, "The Lawyers of Watergate: How a Third-Rate Burglary Provoked New Standards for Lawyer Ethics," *ABA Journal* 98, no. 6 (June 2012): 36–43. Hayden notes that there was already change in the works, but Watergate sped things up.
21. Thomas L. Shaffer, "Legal Ethics After Babel," *Capitol University Law Review* 19 (1990): 989–1007.
22. Shaffer, "Legal Ethics After Babel," 991.
23. Deborah L. Rhode, "Ethics by the Pervasive Method," *Journal of Legal Education* 42, no. 1 (March 1992): 31–56.
24. Rhode, "Ethics by Pervasive Method," 32.
25. Paul T. Hayden, "Putting Ethics to the (National Standardized) Test: Tracing the Origins of the MPRE," *Fordham Law Review* 71, no. 4 (March 2003): 1299–1337.
26. Frederica Perera and Kari Nadeau, "Climate Change, Fossil-Fuel Pollution, and Children's Health," *New England Journal of Medicine* 386, no. 24 (June 16, 2022): 2303–14.
27. Catherine Rocchi and Camila Bustos, "Lawyers Exacerbate the Climate Crisis: Here's How We Can Help," *American Bar Association*, August 28, 2022.
28. Steven Vaughan, "Existential Ethics: Thinking Hard About Lawyer Responsibility for Clients' Environmental Harms," *Current Legal Problems* 76, no. 1 (2023): 1, 3.
29. Vaughan, "Existential Ethics," 3; David Luban and W. Bradley Wendel, "Philosophical Legal Ethics: An Affectionate History," *Georgetown Journal of Legal Ethics* 30, no. 3 (Summer 2017): 337–64; William H. Simon, "The Ideology of Advocacy: Procedural Justice and Professional Ethics," *Wisconsin Law Review* (1978): 29–144.
30. Etienne C. Toussaint, "The Purpose of Legal Education," *California Law Review* 3, no. 1 (March 4, 2023): 1, 6 (offering a different take on the purpose issue and describing how it has been debated for decades).

31. American Bar Association, "2025 Report for the ABA Task Force for American Democracy," ABA Task Force for American Democracy, September 10, 2025; Mike Scarcella, "US Conservative, Democratic Lawyers Urge Bondi to Defend Lawyers and Firms," *Reuters*, March 27, 2025.
32. Some have written about this, though it is confined to the "best" law professors and not the typical ones. See Gerald F. Hess and Michael Hunter Schwartz, *What the Best Law Teachers Do* (Harvard University Press, 2013).
33. Sanford Levinson, "Taking Law Seriously: Reflections on 'Thinking Like a Lawyer,'" *Stanford Law Review* 30, no. 5 (1978): 1071.
34. Karl Nickerson Llewellyn, *The Bramble Bush: The Classic Lectures on the Law and Law School* (1930/2008), 107.
35. Elizabeth Mertz, *The Language of Law School: Learning to "Think Like a Lawyer"* (Oxford University Press, 2007), 134; James R. Elkins, "Thinking Like a Lawyer: Second Thoughts," *Mercer Law Review* 47, no. 2 (March 1996): 511, 522.
36. Shaun Ossei-Owusu, "Criminal Legal Education," *American Criminal Law Review* 58 (Spring 2021): 413–28.
37. Luc Cohen, "Who Is Danielle Sassoon, the Prosecutor Who Stood Up to Trump's DOJ over Eric Adams' Case?," *Reuters*, February 14, 2025.
38. Kate Berry, *How Judicial Elections Impact Criminal Cases* (Brennan Center for Justice, 2015).
39. See e.g., Jeffrey J. Rachlinski and Andrew J. Wistrich, "Benevolent Sexism in Judges," *San Diego Law Review* 58, no. 101 (2021): 101–41; Tarika Daftary-Kapur et al., "Jury Decision-Making Biases and Methods to Counter Them," *Legal and Criminological Psychology* 15, no. 1 (February 2010): 133–54; Samuel R. Sommers and Phoebe C. Ellsworth, "White Juror Bias, An Investigation of Prejudice Against Black Defendants in the American Courtroom," *Psychology, Public Policy, and Law* 7, no. 1 (2001): 201–9.
40. Karen Sloan, "Major US Law Firms Call on Law Schools to Condemn 'Antisemitism, Islamophobia,'" *Reuters*, November 2, 2023.
41. But with high school book publishers sanitizing the former by calling enslaved people "workers" and the overall erasure of Indigenous Peoples' history from K–college, I might be wrong. See Manny Fernandez and Christine Hauser, "Texas Mother Teaches Textbook Company a Lesson on Accuracy," *New York Times*, October 5, 2015.
42. K-Sue Park, "The History Wars and Property Law: Conquest and Slavery as Foundational to the Field," *Yale Law Journal* 131, no. 4 (February 2022): 1062–1384.
43. Elkins, "Thinking Like a Lawyer," 528.
44. Elkins, "Thinking Like a Lawyer," 515.
45. Evan Mandery, "The First Casualty in the War Against Elite Universities," *Politico Magazine*, June 2, 2025.
46. Tess Wilkinson-Ryan and Jonathan Baron, "Moral Judgment and Moral Heuristics in Breach of Contract," *Journal of Empirical Legal Studies* 6, no. 2 (2009): 405, 409; Michael Welch, *Scapegoats of September 11th: Hate Crimes and State Crimes in the War on Terror* (Rutgers University Press, 2006); Ange-Marie Hancock, *The Politics of Disgust: The Public Identity of the Welfare Queen* (NYU Press, 2004); Eric A. Posner, "Law and the Emotions," *Georgetown Law Journal* 89, no. 6 (2001): 1977–2012; Susan Bandes, *The Passions of Law* (NYU Press, 2000).
47. Mertz, *Language of Law School*; Susan Sturm and Lani Guinier, "The Law School

Matrix: Reforming Legal Education in a Culture of Competition and Conformity," *Vanderbilt Law Review* 60 (2007): 515, 531.
48. This is not inevitable. Students have to affirmatively seek out such courses after 1L, their school has to offer them, and the schools have to have capable personnel.
49. Rebecca Leppert and Katherine Schaeffer, "8 Facts About Americans with Disabilities," *Pew Research Center*, July 24, 2023.
50. Meera E. Deo, *Unequal Profession: Race and Gender in Legal Academia* (Stanford University Press, 2019).

ASSEMBLY #1

1. The boundaries and distinctions are quite complicated and subject to dispute in the states for at least a century. For a helpful primer, see Hanoch Dagan and Benjamin C. Zipursky, "Introduction: The Distinction Between Private Law and Public Law" in *Research Handbook of Private Law Theory* (Edward Elgar Publishing, 2020).
2. The first part of the book proceeds thematically through the core first-year law curriculum. My account draws primarily on casebooks that frame the educational landscape, law review articles from experts who critique how the field is taught, and qualitative studies of legal education. As for the casebooks themselves, a few clarifications are in order. I focused on books based on their widespread adoption (gleaned from conversations with colleagues in each field and publishing representatives) and on their pedagogical orientation (e.g., selecting books known for taking more doctrinal, conservative, or critical perspectives). My list of casebooks isn't exhaustive, and some push against the generalizations I make about the field or its themes. I point out some divergences where it feels useful, but I don't try to list every exception—a task that would quickly descend into inside baseball, add little for general readers, and consume more space than I can spare. That conversation is better left for scholarly articles. My readings began after law school, when I purchased older editions on the cheap. Faculty status later provided access to current online versions, allowing me to track how the books have evolved. At times, a single book's deeper engagement with an issue cast the omissions in others into sharper relief; in that sense, I learned much from all of the books. Importantly, some professors teach against the casebook by supplementing it heavily or treating it as something to argue with. But if a book works by being resisted, it says something about it and the field it represents—whose voices count, what ends up at the margins, and much more. To the authors whose books are discussed here— and those left out—no offense is intended. The point isn't whether a book is "good" or "bad" in the classroom. It's how casebooks train future lawyers by addressing or ignoring questions of inequality. For contracts, I read: Randy E. Barnett and Nathan B. Oman, *Contracts: Cases and Doctrine* (Aspen, 2021); John Dawson et al., *Contracts, Cases and Comments* (Foundation Press, 2019); E. Allan Farnsworth et al., *Cases and Materials on Contracts* (Foundation Press, 2019); Deborah Post et al., *Contracting Law* (Carolina Academic Press, 2023); Robert S. Summers et al., *Contract and Related Obligation: Theory, Doctrine, and Practice* (West Academic Publishing, 2021). For torts, I examined Richard A. Epstein and Catherine M. Sharkey, *Cases and Materials on Torts* (Aspen Publishing, 2024); Ward Farnsworth, Mark F. Grady, et al., *Torts: Cases and Questions* (Aspen Publishing, 2019); Marc A. Franklin et al., *Tort Law and Alternatives: Cases and Materials* (Foundation Press, 2021); John C. P. Goldberg et al., *Tort Law: Responsibilities and Redress* (Aspen Publishing, 2023); John Fabian Witt, Karen

Tani, et al., *Torts: Cases, Principles, and Institutions* (CALI eLangdell® Press, 2020). For property, I examined Jesse Dukeminier et al., *Property* (Aspen Publishing, 2022); Thomas W. Merrill et al., *Property: Principles and Policies* (Foundation Press, 2022); Kali Murray et al., *Integrating Spaces: Property Law and Race* (Aspen Publishing, 2023); Joseph William Singer et al., *Property Law: Rules, Policies & Practices* (Aspen Publishing, 2021); John G. Sprankling and Raymond R. Coletta, *Property: A Contemporary Approach* (West Academic Publishing, 2021). In criminal law, I focused on the following books: Bennett Capers et al., *Criminal Law: A Critical Approach* (Foundation Press, 2023); Joshua Dressler and Stephen Garvey, *Criminal Law: Cases and Materials* (West Academic Publishing, 2019); Sanford H. Kadish et al., *Criminal Law and Its Processes: Cases and Materials* (Aspen Publishing, 2022); John Kaplan et al., *Criminal Law: Cases and Materials* (Aspen, 2021); Cynthia Lee and Angela Harris, *Criminal Law: Cases and Materials* (West Academic Publishing, 2019); Paul H. Robinson et al., *Criminal Law: Case Studies & Controversies* (Aspen Publishing, 2020). Con law books included: Erwin Chemerinsky, *Constitutional Law* (Aspen Publishing, 2023); Jesse H. Choper et al., *Constitutional Law: Cases, Comments & Questions* (West Academic Publishing, 2023); Noah R. Feldman and Kathleen M. Sullivan, *Constitutional Law* (Foundation Press, 2022); Michael Stokes Paulsen et al., *The Constitution of the United States* (Foundation Press, 2022); Geoffrey R. Stone et al., *Constitutional Law* (Aspen Publishing, 2023); Jonathan D. Varat et al., *Constitutional Law: Cases and Materials* (Foundation Press, 2021). And for civil procedure, I consulted Barbara Allen Babcock et al., *Civil Procedure: Cases and Problems* (Aspen Publishing, 2021); Jack H. Friedenthal et al., *Civil Procedure: Cases and Materials* (West Academic Publishing, 2022); Joseph W. Glannon et al., *Civil Procedure: A Coursebook* (Aspen Publishing, 2021); A. Benjamin Spencer., *Civil Procedure: A Contemporary Approach* (West Academic Publishing, 2021); Stephen N. Subrin et al., *Civil Procedure: Doctrine, Practice, and Context* (Aspen Publishing, 2024); Stephen C. Yeazell et al., *Civil Procedure* (Aspen Publishing, 2022).
3. Jonathan Baron and Ilana Ritov, "Reference Points and Omission Bias," *Organizational Behavior and Human Decision Processes* 59, no. 3 (February 1994): 475–98.
4. Peter Singer, *Practical Ethics* (Cambridge University Press, 2011), 181.
5. Adam Bonica et al., "The Legal Academy's Ideological Uniformity," *Journal of Legal Studies* 47, no. 1 (2018): 1–43. Of course, one could be one or all those things and self-identify or be categorized as "liberal." For a controversial take that suggests that law faculty are *too* left leaning and obsessive in their focus on identity, see Ilya Shapiro, *Lawless: The Miseducation of America's Elites* (Broadside Books, 2025).

CHAPTER 2: MANUFACTURED CONSENT AND CONTRACTUAL INEQUALITY

1. Danielle Kie Hart, "Contract Law Now—Reality Meets Legal Fictions," *University of Baltimore Law Review* 41, no. 1 (Fall 2011): 1–81.
2. Jonathan A. Obar and Anne Oeldorf-Hirsch, "The Biggest Lie on the Internet: Ignoring the Privacy Policies and Terms of Service Policies of Social Networking Services," *Information, Communication and Society* 23, no. 1 (2020): 128–47.
3. David Dayen, "Tech Companies' Big Reveal: Hardly Anyone Files Arbitration Claims," *American Prospect*, November 26, 2019.
4. Deepak Gupta and Lina M. Khan, "Arbitration as Wealth Transfer," *Yale Law Review and Policy Review* 35 (2017): 499–520.

5. Gupta and Khan, "Arbitration as Wealth Transfer," 507.
6. Restatement (Second) of Contracts § 157 (American Law Institute, 1981).
7. Omri Ben-Shahar, "The Myth of the 'Opportunity to Read' in Contract Law," *European Review of Contract Law* (ERCL) 5, no. 1 (2009): 1–28.
8. Lochner v. New York, 198 U.S. 45 (1905).
9. Robert J. Miller, "History Commentary—Indian Treaties as Contracts," *Columbia Magazine* 20, no. 1 (Spring 2006).
10. Cherokee Nation v. Georgia, 30 U.S. (5 Pet., 1831) 1.
11. See Noah Zatz, "A Law and Political Economy Approach to Race, Gender, and Power in Contracts," in *Integrating Doctrine and Diversity: Inclusion and Equity in the Law School Classroom*, by Nicole Dyszlewski et al. (Carolina Academic Press, 2021); Erik Encarnacion, "Section 1981 as Contract Law," *Virginia Law Review*, forthcoming).
12. Lendol Calder, *Financing the American Dream: A Cultural History of Consumer Credit* (Princeton University Press, 2001), 162.
13. Amy Dru Stanley, *From Bondage to Contract: Wage Labor, Marriage, and the Market in the Age of Slave Emancipation* (Cambridge University Press, 1998).
14. Evelyn Atkinson, "Slaves, Coolies, and Shareholders: Corporations Claim the Fourteenth Amendment," *Journal of the Civil War Era* 10, no. 1 (2020): 63, 67.
15. Steven W. Bender, "Consumer Protection for Latinos: Overcoming Language Fraud and English-Only in the Marketplace," *American University Law Review* 45 (1996): 1027–1109.
16. Álvaro José Corral, "Raids at Work: Latinx Immigrant Labor Precarity and the Spectacle of ICE Worksite Enforcement Raids," *Political Research Quarterly* 76, no. 3 (2023): 1537.
17. Corral, "Raids at Work," 1537.
18. This statistic is likely overinclusive in that it captures people aged five and over but underinclusive in that it focuses only on people who do not speak English as their primary language and who speak English "less than very well." Sweta Haldar et al., "Overview of Health Coverage and Care for Individuals with Limited English Proficiency," *KKF*, July 7, 2023; Sahana Mukherjee and Mark Hugo Lopez, "How Americans Feel about Making English the Official Language of the U.S." Pew Research Center, March 17, 2025.
19. The Supreme Court has interpreted discrimination on the basis of language as falling within prohibitions based on national origin, which is covered in Title VI and VII of the Civil Rights Act of 1964, the Equal Credit Opportunity Act, the Fair Housing Act, and Section 1557 of the Affordable Care Act.
20. United States Government Accountability Office (GAO), "Consumer Finance: Factors Affecting the Financial Literacy of Individuals with Limited English Proficiency," GAO-1-518, (May 2010), 1 (emphasis added).
21. GAO, "Factors Affecting Financial Literacy," 1.
22. David A. Hoffman and Anton Strezhnev, "Leases as Forms," *Journal of Empirical Legal Studies* 19, no. 1 (March 2022): 90, 123; Meirav Furth-Matzkin, "On the Unexpected Use of Unenforceable Contract Terms: Evidence from the Residential Rental Market," *Journal of Legal Analysis* 9, no. 1 (2017): 1–49.
23. Ihna Mangundayao et al., "More Than $3 Billion in Stolen Wages Recovered for Workers Between 2017 and 2020," Economic Policy Institute, December 22, 2021.
24. Llezlie L. Green, "Wage Theft in Lawless Courts," *California Law Review* 107 (August 2019): 1303–44.

25. When linguistic minorities do appear, they are often filtered through another lens. See e.g., Orcilla v. Big Sur, Inc., 244 Cal. App. 4th 982 (2016) (unconscionability); Morales v. Sun Constructors, Inc. 541 F.3d 218 (2008) (objective theory of assent); Martinez-Gonzalez v. Elkhorn Packing Co. 25 F.4th 613 (2022) (arbitration).
26. John P. Dawson et al., *Contracts: Cases and Comments* (Foundation Press, 2019). 785.
27. Odorizzi v. Bloomfield School District, 54 Cal. Rptr. 533 (1966).
28. Board of Governors of the Federal Reserve System et al., "Interagency Statement on Elder Financial Exploitation," press release, December 4, 2024; See Daniel E. Ho et al., "Mandatory Retirement and Age, Race, and Gender Diversity of University Faculties," *Annual Law and Economics Review* 23, no. 1 (Spring 2021): 100–36.
29. United States Census Bureau, "By 2030, All Baby Boomers Will Be Age 65 or Older: 2020 Census Will Help Policymakers Prepare for the Incoming Wave of Aging Boomers," December 10, 2019.
30. US Census Bureau, "By 2030, All Baby Boomers."
31. Hila Keren, "The Unbearable Narrowness of Undue Influence," in *Research Handbook on the Philosophy of Contract Law*, eds. Mindy Chen-Wishart and Prince Saprai (Edward Elgar Publishing, 2025), 415–30; Reece v. Wells Fargo Bank, N.A., 2019 WL 2612745 (Cal.Ct.App. June 26, 2019); Moore v. Moore, 56 Kan. App. 2d 301 (2018).
32. Keren, "Unbearable Narrowness," 14; Ben Chen, "Elder Financial Abuse: Capacity Law and Economics," *Cornell Law Review* 106 (November 13, 2021): 1457–1538.
33. Seymour H. Moskowitz, "Reflecting Reality: Adding Elder Abuse and Neglect to Legal Education," *Loyola Law Review* 47 (2001): 191.
34. Hall v. Ochs, 817 F.2d 920 (1st Cir. 1987); Seth F. Kreimer, "Releases, Redress, and Police Misconduct: Reflections on Agreements to Waive Civil Rights Actions in Exchange for Dismissal of Criminal Charges," *University of Pennsylvania Law Review* 136, no. 3 (1988): 851–940.
35. Todd J. Behme, "Hispanic Group May Seek Raid Inquiry," *Statemen Journal*, August 4, 1989, 7.
36. Newton v. Rumery 480 U.S. 386 (1987). See e.g., Robert E. Scott & William J. Stuntz, "Plea Bargaining as Social Contract," *Yale Law Journal* 101 (1992): 1909–68.
37. Reliford v. United Parcel Service, 2008 WL 4865987 (N.D. Ill. July 8, 2008).
38. Austin Instrument, Inc. v. Loral Corp., 29 N.Y.2d 124 (1971).
39. Muriel Morisey, "Teaching *Williams v. Walker-Thomas Furniture Co.*," *Temple Political and Civil Rights Law Review* 3 (1993): 102–3; See Brittany Farr, "The Other *Walker-Thomas*: Reading Race in Contracts" (*NYU Law Review*, forthcoming,); Dylan C. Penningroth, "Race in Contract Law," *University of Pennsylvania Law Review* 170, no. 5 (2022): 1199–1301.
40. Duncan Kennedy, "The Bitter Ironies of *Williams v. Walker-Thomas Furniture Co.* in the First Year Law School Curriculum," *Buffalo Law Review* 71, no. 2 (2023): 225–88.
41. Jacob Hale Russell, "Unconscionability's Greatly Exaggerated Death," *UC Davis Law Review* 53 (2019): 965–1026.
42. Tess Wilkinson-Ryan and Jonathan Baron, "Moral Judgment and Moral Heuristics in Breach of Contract," *Journal of Empirical Legal Studies* 6, no. 2 (2009): 405–23.
43. Paul D. Carrington, "Unconscionable Lawyers," *Georgia State Law Review* 19, no. 2 (2002): 361, 362.
44. Carrington, "Unconscionable Lawyers," 361, 362.

CHAPTER 3: INJURIOUS MATTERS

1. Thomas C. Grey, "Accidental Torts," *Vanderbilt Law Review* 54, no. 3 (2001): 1225, 1232.
2. Centers for Disease Control and Prevention, "Intimate Partner Violence Prevention: About Intimate Partner Violence," May 16, 2024.
3. Thompson v. Thompson, 218 US 611, 618–619 (1910).
4. Reva B. Siegel, "'The Rule of Love': Wife Beating as Prerogative and Privacy," *Yale Law Journal* 106 (June 1996): 2117–2207.
5. Elizabeth Katz, "Judicial Patriarchy and Domestic Violence: A Challenge to the Conventional Family Privacy Narrative," *William and Mary Law Journal of Race, Gender, and Social Justice* 21, no. 2 (2015): 379–471.
6. Martha Chamallas and Jennifer B. Wriggins, *The Measure of Injury: Race, Gender, and Tort Law* (NYU Press, 2010), 87.
7. Historically the common law doctrines of chastisement, coverture, and spousal immunity immunized batterers from tort liability. Camille Carey, "Domestic Violence Torts: Righting a Civil Wrong," *Kansas Law Review* 62 (2014): 695, 696. Today, statutes of limitations and the fact that DV is not covered by insurance policies help shield abusers from civil accountability. Chamallas and Wriggins, *Measure of Injury*, 3.
8. See Carey, "Domestic Violence Torts," 709.
9. Public officials do come up, but typically not in this constitutional tort capacity. See, e.g., Tarasoff v. Regents of the University of California, 17 Cal. 3d 425 (1976); Riss v. City of New York 240 N.E.2d 860 (1968).
10. See Kendall Morton et al., "50 Shades of Government Immunity: Complications with Bringing Civil Rights Claims Under State Laws." Institute for Justice, January 25, 2022.
11. John Fabian Witt, *The Accidental Republic: Crippled Workingmen, Destitute Widows, and the Remaking of American Law* (Harvard University Press, 2004), 2.
12. Witt, *Accidental Republic*, 2.
13. Witt, *Accidental Republic*, 44.
14. Nate Holdren, *Injury Impoverished: Workplace Accidents, Capitalism, and Law in the Progressive Era* (Cambridge University Press, 2020).
15. Witt, *Accidental Republic*, 44.
16. Barbara Young Welke, *Recasting American Liberty: Gender, Race, Law, and the Railroad Revolution, 1865–1920* (Cambridge University Press, 2001), 83.
17. William G. Thomas, *Lawyering for the Railroad: Business, Law, and Power in the New South* (LSU Press, 1999), 75.
18. Welke, *Recasting American Liberty*, 105–12.
19. Thomas, *Lawyering for the Railroad*, 64.
20. Tom Baker, "Blood Money, New Money, and the Moral Economy of Tort Law in Action," *Law and Society Review* 35, no. 2 (2001): 275–319.
21. John Fabian Witt and Karen M. Tani, *Torts: Cases, Principles, and Institutions* (CALI eLangdell, 2020), 234.
22. Regina Austin, "The Insurance Classification Controversy," *University of Pennsylvania Law Review* 131, no. 3 (January 1983): 517–83.
23. Jeff Larson et al., "How We Examined Racial Discrimination in Auto Insurance Prices," *ProPublica*, April 5, 2017.
24. Deborah S. Hellman, "Is Actuarially Fair Insurance Pricing Actually Fair?: A Case Study in Insuring Battered Women," *Harvard Civil Rights–Civil Liberties Law Review* 32, no. 2 (1997): 355, 358.

25. Kimberly A. Yuracko and Ronen Avraham, "Valuing Black Lives: A Constitutional Challenge to the Use of Race-Based Tables in Calculating Tort Damages," *California Law Review* 106, no. 2 (April 2018): 325–72.
26. G.M.M. ex rel. Hernandez-Adams v. Kimpson, 116 F. Supp. 3d 126, 140 (E.D.N.Y. 2015).
27. Alejandra Ayotitla and Ross Pesek, "Valuing the Lives of Plaintiffs of Color in Tort Law: A Critique of the Use of Race-Based Data in Damage Award Calculations," *Nebraska Law Review Bulletin*, August 27, 2023, 1–28.
28. Frank M. McClellan, "The Dark Side of Tort Reform: Searching for Racial Justice," *Rutgers Law Review* 48 (1996): 761, 784.
29. Emily Gottlieb et al., "'Tort Reform' and Racial Prejudice: A Troublesome Connection" (Center for Justice and Democracy, 2004).
30. Carl Bogus, *Why Lawsuits Are Good for America: Disciplined Democracy* (NYU Press, 2001), 34, 35.
31. Michael I. Krauss and Robert A. Levy, "Can Tort Reform and Federalism Coexist?," *Cato Institute: Policy Analysis*, no. 514 (April 14, 2004): 1–31; Bernard S. Black et al., *Medical Malpractice Litigation: How It Works—Why Tort Reform Hasn't Helped* (Cato Institute, 2021).
32. John C. P. Goldberg et al., *Tort Law: Responsibilities and Redress* (Aspen Publishing, 2021), 40.

CHAPTER 4: PROPERTY, OWNERSHIP, AND INJUSTICE

1. Mica Doctoroff et al., *Civil Asset Forfeiture: Profiting from California's Most Vulnerable* (ACLU, 2016).
2. Child Care Law Center, "2016 Annual Report," accessed October 7, 2025, https://www.childcarelaw.org/wp-content/uploads/2022/03/Child-Care-Law-Center-Annual-Report-2016.pdf; see also Catherine Albiston et al., "Cutting Child Care Out from Under Californians," policy brief (Berkeley Center on Health, Economic and Family Security, 2010).
3. There is also intellectual property, which refers to creations of the mind (e.g., trademarks, patents, and inventions).
4. D. Benjamin Barros, "Home as a Legal Concept," *Santa Clara Law Review* 46, no. 2 (2006): 255–57.
5. Lee Anne Fennell, "Co-Location, Co-Location, Co-Location: Land Use and Housing Priorities Reimagined," *Vermont Law Review* 39 (2015): 925, 933.
6. The US Department of Housing and Urban Development, "The 2023 Annual Homelessness Assessment Report (AHAR) to Congress" (Office of Community Planning and Development, 2023), 2–4.
7. Jeremy Waldron, "Homelessness and the Issue of Freedom," *UCLA Law Review* 39 (1991): 295.
8. City of Grants Pass v. Johnson, 603 U.S. 520 (2024).
9. Gregg Colburn and Clayton Page Aldern, *Homelessness Is a Housing Problem: How Structural Factors Explain U.S. Patterns* (University of California Press, 2022).
10. Timothy M. Mulvaney and Joseph William Singer, "Essential Property," *Minnesota Law Review* 107, no. 2 (2022): 605, 634. This might include developers who may or may not be inclined to be build affordable housing, eviction-hungry, gentrify-loving landlords, and financial institutions who have lending practices that can make getting a home hard or losing one easy.

11. Jane B. Baron, "The 'No Property' Problem: Understanding Poverty by Understanding Wealth," *Michigan Law Review* 102, no. 6 (2004):1000, 1004.
12. Waldron, "Homelessness and the Issue of Freedom," 314.
13. J. Peter Byrne, "Two Cheers for Gentrification," *Howard Law Journal* 46, no. 3 (2003): 405, 408; John Joe Schlichtman et al., *Gentrifier* (University of Toronto Press, 2017).
14. Tom Slater, "The Eviction of Critical Perspectives from Gentrification Research," *International Journal of Urban and Regional Research* 30, no. 4 (December 2006): 737–57.
15. Davarian L. Baldwin, *In the Shadow of the Ivory Tower: How Universities Are Plundering Our Cities* (Bold Type Books, 2021).
16. National Low Income Housing Coalition, "Gentrification and Neighborhood Revitalization: What's the Difference?" April 5, 2019.
17. Ayobami Laniyonu, "Assessing the Impact of Gentrification on Eviction: A Spatial Modeling Approach," *Harvard Civil Rights–Civil Liberties Law Review* 54 (2019): 741, 742; Tejada v. Littlecity Realty LLC, 308 F. Supp. 3d 724 (E.D.N.Y. 2018).
18. See Friends of McMillan Park v. DC Zoning Comm'n, 149 A.3d 1027 (DC 2016); Crenshaw Subway Coal. v. City of Los Angeles, 291 Cal. Rptr. 3d 90 (Ct. App. 2022).
19. Joshua Akers and Eric Seymour, "Instrumental Exploitation: Predatory Property Relations at City's End," *Geoforum* 91 (May 2018): 127–40; Erin McElroy and Alex Werth, "Deracinated Dispossessions: On the Foreclosures of 'Gentrification' in Oakland, CA," *Antipode* 51, no. 3 (2019):878–98.
20. Schlichtman et al. *Gentrifier*; Monique Taylor, *Harlem Between Heaven and Hell* (University of Minnesota Press, 2002); Mary Pattillo, *Black on the Block: The Politics of Race and Class in the City* (University of Chicago Press, 2010).
21. Jacob Anbinder, "The Pandemic Disproved Urban Progressives' Theory About Gentrification," *The Atlantic*, January 2, 2021.
22. E. J. Antoni, "Home Prices: From American Dream to American Nightmare," Heritage Foundation, October 23, 2023; Caitlin Young et al., "Rethinking Homeownership as 'the American Dream,'" *Urban Institute*, June 26, 2023.
23. Thomas W. Merrill et al., *Property: Principles and Policies* (Foundation Press, 2022), 567.
24. James Grimmelmann, "Raze and Rebuild the Property Course," *Law and Political Economy Project*, November 2, 2018.
25. James Grimmelmann, "Real + Imaginary = Complex: Toward a Better Property Course," *Journal of Legal Education* 66, no. 4 (2017): 930, 934; Robert H. Sitkoff and Max M. Schanzenbach, "Jurisdictional Competition for Trust Funds: An Empirical Analysis of Perpetuities and Taxes," *Yale Law Journal* 115 (2005): 356, 370–76.
26. See generally, Katharina Pistor, *The Code of Capital: How the Law Creates Wealth and Inequality* (Princeton University Press, 2019).
27. The figure is disputed but it is in the trillions. See Cerulli Associates, "U.S. High-Net-Worth and Ultra-High-Net-Worth Markets 2024," Cerulli.com, accessed August 11, 2025.
28. Brooke Harrington, *Capital Without Borders: Wealth Managers and the One Percent* (Harvard University Press, 2016), 219–20.
29. Jack H. L. Whiteley, "Perpetuities in an Unequal Age," *Northwestern University Law Review* 117, no. 6 (2023): 1477, 1483.
30. Holland and Knight, "International Private Client Group," accessed August 11, 2025; Holland and Knight, "Private Wealth Services," accessed August 11, 2025.
31. Proskauer, "Expertise, Experience, Discretion—Generation to Generation," accessed

August 11, 2025; White and Case, "Private Wealth and Family Offices," accessed August 11, 2025.
32. Wendell E. Pritchett, "The 'Public Menace' of Blight: Urban Renewal and the Private Uses of Eminent Domain," *Yale Law and Policy Review* 21, no. 1 (2003): 1–52.
33. Technically, there is a third category, *administrative forfeiture*, which is when an agency seizes assets, and no one files a claim to contest the taking.
34. John Malcolm, "Civil Asset Forfeiture: When Good Intentions Go Awry," *Heritage Foundation*, July 22, 2016.
35. Lisa Knepper et al., *Policing for Profit: The Abuse of Civil Asset Forfeiture*, 3rd ed. (Institute for Justice, 2020), 6.
36. Federal Deposit Insurance Corporation, *2023 FDIC National Survey of Unbanked and Underbanked Households* (pdf) (FDIC, 2023), 38.
37. United States v. McClellan, 44 F.4th 200, 211 (4th Cir. 2022).
38. Comptroller General, *Asset Forfeiture—A Seldom Used Tool in Combatting Drug Trafficking* (US Government Accountability Office, 1981), 5.
39. For a helpful training manual that provides insights into the complication, see, Louis S. Rulli, *Training Manual: Civil Forfeiture of Private Property Under the Pennsylvania Controlled Substances Forfeitures Act* (Rulli, 2017).
40. Michael van den Berg, "Proposing a Transactional Approach to Civil Forfeiture Reform," *University of Pennsylvania Law Review* 163 (2015), 867, 868.
41. Knepper et al., *Policing for Profit*, 6.
42. Knepper et al., *Policing for Profit*, 30.
43. Dick Carpenter et al., "The Complex Process of Civil Forfeiture," *CrimRxiv*, February 21, 2022.
44. Bobby Allyn, "DA Krasner: Philadelphians Whose Property Was Wrongly Seized Should Be Reimbursed," *WHYY Philadelphia*, April 25, 2019.
45. Ryan Briggs, "Inside the Philadelphia DA's Side Hustle—Selling Seized Homes to Speculators and Cops," *WHYY Philadelphia*, December 10, 2018.
46. Sourovelis v. City of Philadelphia, 515 F. Supp. 3d 343 (E.D. Pa. 2021); Louis S. Rulli, "Seizing Family Homes from the Innocent: Can the Eighth Amendment Protect Minorities and the Poor from Excessive Punishment in Civil Forfeiture?," *University of Pennsylvania Journal of Constitutional Law* 19, no. 5 (2017): 1111–68.
47. Nick Sibilla, "Maryland Dairy Farmer Beats the IRS, Will Recover Nearly $30,000 Seized Through Civil Forfeiture," *Forbes*, June 29, 2016.
48. Eric Boehm, "FBI Seized $86 Million from People Not Suspected of Any Crime. A Federal Court Will Decide if That's Legal," *Reason*, December 6, 2023; Snitko v. United States, 90 F.4th 1250, 1257 (9th Cir. 2024).
49. See e.g., Hudson v. City of Sunrise, 237 So. 3d 1031 (4th DCA 2018); Velez v. Miami—Dade Cty. Police Dep't, 934 So. 2d 1162 (Fla. 2006).
50. Culley v. Marshall, 601 US 377 (2024) (addressing post-seizure hearings, not the substance of forfeiture); Ilya Somin, "Supreme Court Issues Flawed Ruling in Asset Forfeiture Case," *Reason*, May 9, 2024.
51. Bernadette Atuahene and Timothy R. Hodge, "Stategraft," *Southern California Law Review* 91, no. 2 (2018): 263, 265.
52. Harmelin v. Michigan, 501 US 957, 978 (1991). See also Harjo v. City of Albuquerque, 326 F. Supp. 3d 1145, 1151 (D.N.M. 2018).
53. Leonard v. Texas, 580 US 1178 (2017).

54. Stephanie Holmes Didwania, "Asset Forfeiture and Inequality," *Stanford Law Review* 77, no. 1 (January 2025): 159–234; Ilya Somin, "America's Weak Property Rights Are Harming Those Most in Need," *The Atlantic*, March 24, 2020.
55. See e.g., Southern Burlington County NAACP v. Mt. Laurel, 67 N.J. 151 (1975).
56. Economic Policy Institute, "Child Care Costs in the United States," accessed August 11, 2025.
57. ReadyNation, "$122 Billion: The Growing, Annual Cost of the Infant-Toddler Child Care Crisis," Council for a Strong America, February 2, 2023.
58. People should be cautious when using this term because it stigmatizes family, friend, and neighbor care and reifies the idea that licensed care is the best care. See Shelby Brunson, "Please Stop Using the Phrase 'Child Care Desert,'" *National Women's Law Center*, August 3, 2023.
59. Child Care Aware of America, *Demanding Change: Repairing our Child Care System* (2022), 7.
60. Ann M. Cibulskis and Marsha Ritzdorf, *Zoning for Child Care* (American Planning Association, 1989); American Planning Association, *Policy Implementation Statement on Child Care* (1987); American Society of Public Administration, *Policy Statement on Child Care* (1986), cited in Marsha Ritzdorf, "A Feminist Analysis of Gender and Residential Zoning in the United States," *Women and the Environment*, vol 13, *Human Behavior and Environment*, eds. Altman and Churchman (Springer, 1994).
61. See Annie Nakao, "Day Care Dilemma," *SFGate*, May 8, 1996.
62. Noah M. Kazis, "Fair Housing for A Non-Sexist City," *Harvard Law Review* 134, no. 5 (March 2021): 1683, 1711.
63. Susan Marie Connor, "Zoning and Matters of Age: Tots, Teens, and Seniors," *Probate and Property* 19, no.1 (January/February 2005): 61–66.
64. Karen Lehrman and Jana Pace, "Day-Care Regulation: Serving Children or Bureaucrats?," *Cato Institute*, September 25, 1985.
65. Marsha Ritzdorf, "A Feminist Analysis of Gender and Residential Zoning in the United States," In *Women and the Environment*, eds. Irwin Altman and Arza Churchman, HUBE, vol. 13 (Springer, 1994), 269.
66. Kazis, "Fair Housing," 1711; Alexis Stephens, "Philly Moms May Soon Have Fewer Childcare Options," *Next City*, November 12, 2014.
67. Anika Singh Lemar, "The Role of States in Liberalizing Land Use Regulations," *North Carolina Law Review* 97, no. 2 (2019): 293–353; Kendra Hurley, "How to Fix Crumbling Child Care Infrastructure," *Bloomberg*, April 25, 2023.

ASSEMBLY #2

1. Jesse Wegman, "The Crisis in Teaching Constitutional Law," *New York Times*, February 26, 2024. (Driver's comments were about con law, but they apply broadly).

CHAPTER 5: TEXTBOOK INJUSTICE

1. Shaun Ossei-Owusu, "Making Penal Bureaucrats," *Inquest*, August 23, 2021; Shaun Ossei-Owusu, "Criminal Legal Education," *American Criminal Law Review* 58 (Spring 2021): 413–28.
2. Peter Moskos, *Cop in the Hood: My Year Policing Baltimore's Eastern District* (Princeton University Press, 2009), 57.
3. Criminal procedure is often split into two separate classes—Investigations and Adjudication.

4. To the extent that producing "bar-ready" or "practice-ready" attorneys is a law school's objective, the bifurcation of criminal law and procedure (and sometimes trifurcation) raises efficiency issues. After all, the bar exam squeezes criminal law and criminal procedure into a single twenty-five-question section, while law schools stretch the same material across two or three courses. Meanwhile, subjects like torts, property, and contracts get the same twenty-five questions on the bar but usually take just one course. The NextGen Bar Examination, which will be administered in July 2026, attempts to address some of this siloing.
5. Gary Peller, "Criminal Law, Race, and the Ideology of Bias: Transcending the Critical Tools of the Sixties," *Tulane Law Review* 67, no. 6 (1993): 2331, 2232 (emphasis added).
6. It could come up in questions about defenses. See Stephen J. Morse, "The Twilight of Welfare Criminology: A Reply to Judge Bazelon," *Southern California Law Review* 49, no. 6 (1976): 1247–68; Michele Estrin Gilman, "The Poverty Defense," *University of Richmond Law Review* 47, no. 2 (January 2013): 495–554.
7. Franklin E. Zimring, "Is There a Remedy for the Irrelevance of Academic Criminal Law?," *Journal of Legal Education* 64, no. 1 (2014): 5–15.
8. Ronald F. Wright and Kay L. Levine, "The Cure for Young Prosecutors' Syndrome," *Arizona Law Review* 56 (2014): 1065, 1125.
9. Wright and Levine, "Cure for Young Prosecutors' Syndrome," 1065, 1125.
10. Kathryne M. Young, *How to Be Sort of Happy in Law School* (Stanford University Press, 2018), 235.
11. Riaz Tejani, *Law Mart: Justice, Access, and For-Profit Law Schools* (Stanford University Press, 2017).
12. Gerald P. López, "Training Future Lawyers to Work with the Politically and Socially Subordinated: Anti-Generic Legal Education," *West Virginia Law Review* 91, no. 2 (1989): 305, 326.
13. United States v. Cole, 622 F. Supp. 2d 632, 637 (N.D. Ohio 2008).
14. First Step Alliance, "What We Can Learn from Norway's Prison System: Rehabilitation and Recidivism," First Step Alliance, January 3, 2022. See Jamiles Lartey, "Fish Tanks, Plants and Podcast Studios—Some States Try a New Approach to Incarceration," The Marshall Project, April 19, 2025.
15. Francis A. Allen, *The Decline of the Rehabilitative Ideal: Penal Policy and Social Purpose* (Yale University Press, 1981).
16. Robert Blecker, "Haven or Hell? Inside Lorton Central Prison: Experiences of Punishment Justified," *Stanford Law Review* 42, no. 5 (1990): 1149–1249.
17. Erin Cox et al, "Maryland Governor Pardons 175,000 Marijuana Convictions in Sweeping Order," *Washington Post*, June 17, 2024.
18. Georg Rusche and Otto Kirchheimer, *Punishment and Social Structure* (Columbia University Press, 1939).
19. Ruth Wilson Gilmore, *Golden Gulag: Prisons, Surplus, Crisis, and Opposition in Globalizing California* (University of California Press, 2007).
20. John M. Eason, *Big House on the Prairie: Rise of the Rural Ghetto and Prison Proliferation* (University of Chicago Press, 2017).
21. Katherine Beckett and Bruce Western, "Governing Social Marginality: Welfare, Incarceration, and the Transformation of State Policy," *Punishment and Society* 3, no. 1 (2001): 43–59; Loïc Wacquant, *Punishing the Poor: The Neoliberal Government of Social Insecurity* (Duke University Press, 2009); Joe Soss, et al., *Disciplining the Poor: Neoliberal Paternalism and the Persistent Power of Race* (University of Chicago Press, 2011).

22. Kelly Lytle Hernández, *City of Inmates: Conquest, Rebellion, and the Rise of Human Caging in Los Angeles, 1771–1965* (University of North Carolina Press, 2018); Michelle Alexander, *The New Jim Crow: Mass Incarceration in the Age of Colorblindness* (New Press, 2012); Mae M. Ngai, *Impossible Subjects: Illegal Aliens and the Making of Modern America* (Princeton University Press, 2004); Douglas A. Blackmon, *Slavery by Another Name: The Re-enslavement of Black Americans from the Civil War to World War II* (Vintage, 2009).
23. Leslie J. Reagan, *When Abortion Was a Crime: Women, Medicine, and Law in the United States, 1867–1973* (University of California Press, 1997); Jolynn Dellinger and Stephanie Pell, "Bodies of Evidence: The Criminalization of Abortion and Surveillance of Women in a Post-Dobbs World," *Duke Journal of Constitutional Law and Public Policy* 19, no. 1 (2024): 1–108; Dobbs v. Jackson Women's Health Organization, 597 US 215 (2022).
24. Caitlin Killian, *Failing Moms: Social Condemnation and Criminalization of Mothers* (Polity, 2023); Dorothy E. Roberts, "Motherhood and Crime," *Iowa Law Review* 79 (1993): 95–141.
25. Mariame Kaba and Andrea J. Ritchie, *No More Police: A Case for Abolition* (New Press, 2022); Amna A. Akbar, "An Abolitionist Horizon for (Police) Reform," *California Law Review* 108, no. 6 (2020): 1781–1846; Angela Y. Davis, *Are Prisons Obsolete?* (Seven Stories Press, 2003).
26. Federal Bureau of Investigation, "Expanded Homicide Data Table 6: Murder—Race, Sex, and Ethnicity of Victim by Race, Sex and Ethnicity of Offender" (US Department of Justice, 2019).
27. Eric Martínez and Kevin Tobia, "What Do Law Professors Believe About Law and the Legal Academy?," *Georgetown Law Journal* 112 (2023): 111, 174; Thomas Ward Frampton, "The Dangerous Few: Taking Seriously Prison Abolition and Its Skeptics," *Harvard Law Review* 135, no. 8 (2022): 2013–52.
28. Aya Gruber, *Feminist War on Crime: The Unexpected Role of Women's Liberation in Mass Incarceration* (University of California Press, 2020); Clare McGlynn, "Challenging Anti-Carceral Feminism: Criminalisation, Justice and Continuum Thinking," *Women's Studies International Forum* 93 (2022): 102614.
29. Alice Ristroph, "The Curriculum of the Carceral State," *Columbia Law Review* 120 (2020): 1631, 1664.
30. Ristroph, "Curriculum of the Carceral State," 1667–68.
31. Ristroph, "Curriculum of the Carceral State," 1668.
32. Jeannie Suk Gersen, "The Socratic Method in the Age of Trauma," *Harvard Law Review* 130, no. 9 (October 2017): 2320–47.
33. Federal Bureau of Investigation, "Crime in the United States 2019: Table 42, Arrests by Sex" (US Department of Justice, 2020).
34. Naiymah Sanchez, "Street-Based Sex Workers and the Revolving Door of Incarceration," ACLU of Pennsylvania, December 13, 2022.
35. Anna Lvovsky, *Vice Patrol: Cops, Courts, and the Struggle over Urban Gay Life Before Stonewall* (University of Chicago Press, 2021); J. Kelly Strader and Lindsey Hay, "Lewd Stings: Extending *Lawrence v. Texas* to Discriminatory Enforcement," *American Criminal Law Review* 56, no. 2 (2019): 465–509.
36. Human Rights Watch, "Sex Workers at Risk: Condoms as Evidence of Prostitution in Four US Cities," July 2012, 75; United States Department of Justice, Civil Rights Division, "Investigation of the New Orleans Police Department" (March 16, 2011), 10.

37. Some of these include George Santos (R-NY), Chris Collins (R-NY), Chaka Fattah (D-PA), Bob Menendez (D-NJ), Steve Stockman (R-TX), Duncan Hunter (R-CA).
38. Scott Zamost and Contessa Brewer, "Inside the Mind of Criminals: How to Brazenly Steal $100 Billion from Medicare and Medicaid," CNBC, March 9, 2023.
39. Doug Bailey, "Insurance Fraud Epidemic Continues; Drives up Operational, Consumer Costs," *Insurance Newsnet*, March 5, 2024.
40. Tanya Basu, "Timeline: A History Of GM's Ignition Switch Defect," NPR, March 21, 2014.
41. Sally Q. Yates, *Individual Accountability for Corporate Wrongdoing*, memorandum, (US Department of Justice, September 9, 2015).
42. Russell Mokhiber, "Critics Rip GM Deferred Prosecution Agreement in Engine Switch Case," *Common Dreams*, September 17, 2015.
43. Rebecca Ruiz, "Woman Cleared in Death Caused by GM's Faulty Ignition Switch," *New York Times*, November 24, 2014.
44. Bill Chappell, "How Bad Is Boeing's 2024 So Far? Here's a Timeline," NPR, March 20, 2024.
45. Joel Rose, "'Cozy' Relationship Between Boeing and the US Draws Scrutiny Amid 737 Max 9 Mess," NPR, January 19, 2024.
46. Harrington v. Purdue Pharma L. P., 144 S. Ct. 2071 (2024.)
47. Barry Meier, "Origins of an Epidemic: Purdue Pharma Knew Its Opioids Were Widely Abused," *New York Times*, May 29, 2018.
48. US Department of Justice, "Opioid Manufacturer Purdue Pharma Pleads Guilty to Fraud and Kickback Conspiracies," press release, November 24, 2020.
49. Emma Ockerman, "Opioid Execs Who Bribed Doctors with Strip-Club Visits Just Got Their Convictions Partly Overturned," *Vice*, November 27, 2019.
50. Esme Murphy, "Behind Bars: Denny Hecker's Life in Prison," CBS Minnesota, May 15, 2011.

CHAPTER 6: THE ULTIMATE CON JOB?

1. Jack M. Balkin, *Constitutional Redemption: Political Faith in an Unjust World* (Harvard University Press, 2011); Sanford Levinson, *Constitutional Faith* (Princeton University Press, 1988); Thomas C. Grey, "The Constitution as Scripture," *Stanford Law Review* 37, no. 1 (1984): 1–25; Edward S. Corwin, "The Worship of the Constitution," *Constitutional Review* 4 (January 1920): 3.
2. Aziz Rana, *The Constitutional Bind: How Americans Came to Idolize a Document That Fails Them* (University of Chicago Press, 2024); Mary Anne Franks, *The Cult of the Constitution* (Stanford University Press, 2020).
3. Elie Mystal, *Allow Me to Retort: A Black Guy's Guide to the Constitution* (New Press, 2022), 2; see also Paul Gowder, "Ameliorative Constitutionalism," *University of Pennsylvania Law Review* 173, no. 7 (June 2025): 2037–80.
4. See, e.g., Joseph Fishkin and William E. Forbath, *The Anti-Oligarchy Constitution: Reconstructing the Economic Foundations of American Democracy* (Harvard University Press, 2022); Dorothy E. Roberts, "Abolition Constitutionalism," *Harvard Law Review* 133, no. 1 (November 2019).
5. See, e.g., San Antonio Independent School District v. Rodriguez, 411 US 1 (1973); Oliphant v. Suquamish Indian Tribe, 435 US 191 (1978); City of Cleburne v. Cleburne Living Center, Inc., 473 US 432 (1985); McCleskey v. Kemp, 481 US 279 (1987).

6. Frankel v. Regents of Univ. of California, 2024 WL 3811250 (C.D. Cal. Aug. 13, 2024); Sharon Zhang, "Pro-Palestine Activists Win $100K Settlement from University of Maryland," *Truthout*, August 7, 2025.
7. Religion does come in some related and slightly different contexts. See Trump v. Hawaii, 585 US ___ (2018); Masterpiece Cakeshop, Ltd. v. Colorado Civil Rights Commission, 584 US 617 (2018), City of Boerne v. Flores, 521 US 507 (1997).
8. Sahar F. Aziz, "Security and Technology: Rethinking National Security," *Texas A&M Law Review* 2, no. 4 (2015): 791, 795.
9. Korematsu v. United States, 323 US 214 (1944).
10. Trump v. Hawaii; Jessica A. Clarke, "Explicit Bias," *Northwestern University Law Review* 113, no. 3 (2018): 505–86.
11. David M. Drucker, "Congress Began Ceding Power to Presidents Long Before Trump," *Bloomberg*, March 26, 2025.
12. Aziz Huq and Tom Ginsburg, "How to Lose a Constitutional Democracy," *UCLA Law Review* 65, no. 1 (2018): 78–169; Mark Tushnet, "Constitutional Hardball," *John Marshall Law Review* 37, no. 2 (Winter 2004): 523–54.
13. Daniel Immerwahr, *How to Hide an Empire: A History of the Greater United States* (Farrar, Straus and Giroux, 2019).
14. Philip P. Frickey, "Adjudication and Its Discontents: Coherence and Conciliation in Federal Indian Law," *Harvard Law Review* 110, no. 6 (1997): 1754, 1765.
15. Gregory Ablavsky, "The Savage Constitution," *Duke Law Journal* 63, no. 5 (2014): 999–1090.
16. US Const. art. I, § 1.
17. US Const. art. II, § 2. Lone Wolf v. Hitchcock 187 US 553 (1903) (ruling that Congress unilaterally repeal treaties with Native Tribes).
18. US Const. art. VI, § [TK], cl. 2; US Const. art. I, § 2, cl. 3.
19. National Congress of American Indians, *Becoming Visible: A Landscape Analysis of State Efforts to Provide Native American Education for All* (NCAI, October 2019).
20. Sarah B. Shear et al., "Manifesting Destiny: Re/presentations of Indigenous Peoples in K-12 U.S. History Standards." *Theory and Research in Social Education* 43, no. 1 (2015): 68–101.
21. Adam Jortner, "The Empty Continent: Cartography, Pedagogy, and Native American History," in *Why You Can't Teach United States History without American Indians*, ed. Susan Sleeper-Smith et al. (University of North Carolina Press, 2015), 78, 81.
22. James M. Grijalva, "Compared When? Teaching Indian Law in the Standard Curriculum," *North Dakota Law Review* 82, no. 3 (2006): 697, 700.
23. "The State of Indian Law at ABA-Accredited Law Schools" (National Native American Bar Association, April 2021).
24. Grijalva, "Compared When?," 708.
25. Meera E. Deo, "Better Than Bipoc," *Minnesota Journal of Law and Inequity* 41, no. 1 (2023): 71–132.
26. Addie C. Rolnick, "Indigenous Subjects," *Yale Law Journal* 131 (2022): 2562–758; Matthew L.M. Fletcher, "The Original Understanding of the Political Status of Indian Tribes, *St. John's Law Review* 82, no. 1 (Winter 2008): 153–82.
27. Elizabeth A. Reese, "The Other American Law," *Stanford Law Review* 73, no. 3 (March 2021): 555–636; Wenona T. Singel, "The First Federalists," *Drake Law Review* 62, no. 3 (2014): 775–856.

28. Sandy Grande, "Competing Moral Visions: At the Crossroads of Democracy and Sovereignty," in *Red Pedagogy: Native American Social and Political Thought* (Rowman and Littlefield, 2015), 50.
29. "Colonialism," Cornell Law School, Legal Information Institute: Wex, accessed August 12, 2025.
30. Maggie Blackhawk, "The Constitution of American Colonialism," *Harvard Law Review* 137, no. 1 (2023): 3–5.
31. Blackhawk, "Constitution of American Colonialism," 2–3.
32. Sasha Abramsky, "Trump's 2025 Foreign Policy Plan: Make Colonialism Great Again," *The Nation*, January 3, 2025; Karen DeYoung and Cate Brown, "Gaza Postwar Plan Envisions 'Voluntary' Relocation Of Entire Population," *Washington Post*, September 2, 2025.
33. US Const. art. IV, § 3.
34. Stuart Banner, *Possessing the Pacific: Land, Settlers, and Indigenous People from Australia to Alaska* (Harvard University Press, 2007), 291.
35. Banner, *Possessing the Pacific*, 311.
36. Juliana Hu Pegues, *Space-Time Colonialism: Alaska's Indigenous and Asian Entanglements* (University of North Carolina Press, 2021).
37. Terrence Cole, "Jim Crow in Alaska: The Passage of the Alaska Equal Rights Act of 1945," *Western Historical Quarterly*, 23, no. 4 (November 1992): 429–49.
38. Claire Stremple, "Alaska Lawmakers Support Push to Investigate, Document Forced Assimilation in Boarding Schools," *Alaska Beacon*, May 13, 2024.
39. Daniel B. Rice, "Territorial Annexation as a 'Great Power,'" *Duke Law Journal* 64, no. 4 (2015): 717–69.
40. Joint Resolution of Apology to Native Hawaiians, Pub. L. No. 103–150, 107 Stat. 1510 (1993).
41. United States v. Vaello Madero, 596 US 159, 180–189 (2022) (emphasis added).
42. Stephen Vladeck, *The Shadow Docket: How the Supreme Court Uses Stealth Rulings to Amass Power and Undermine the Republic* (Basic Books, 2023).
43. Laura Kalman, *Abe Fortas: A Biography* (Yale University Press, 1990), 72.
44. Mitchell N. Berman and Kevin Toh, "Pluralistic Nonoriginalism and the Combinability Problem," *Texas Law Review* 91, no. 7 (2013):1739, 1749.
45. Philip Bobbitt, *Constitutional Fate: Theory of the Constitution* (Oxford University Press, 1983); David E. Pozen and Adam M. Samaha, "Anti-Modalities," *Michigan Law Review* 119, no. 4 (2021): 729–96.
46. Philip Bobbitt, *Constitutional Interpretation* (Blackwell, 1991), 22.
47. Pozen and Samaha, "Anti-Modalities," 12; Richard H. Fallon, Jr., "A Constructivist Coherence Theory of Constitutional Interpretation," *Harvard Law Review* 100, no. 6 (April 1987): 1189–1286; Andrew M. Siegel, "Constitutional Theory, Constitutional Culture," *University of Pennsylvania Journal of Constitutional Law* 18, no. 4 (2016): 1067, 1083. See Eugene Volokh et al., "The Second Amendment as Teaching Tool in Constitutional Law Classes," *Journal of Legal Education* 48 (1998): 591; Paul F. Campos et al., *Against the Law* (Duke University Press, 1996), 142; Akhil Reed Amar, "In Praise of Bobbitt," *Texas Law Review* 72, no. 7 (June 1994):1703–6.
48. Pozen and Samaha, "Anti-Modalities," 729–96.
49. On this point, see Leah Litman, *Lawless: How the Supreme Court Runs on Conservative Grievance, Fringe Theories, and Bad Vibes* (Atria/One Signal Publishers, 2025).

50. Linda Greenhouse, "Ruth Bader Ginsburg, Supreme Court's Feminist Icon, Is Dead at 87," *New York Times*, Sept. 18, 2020.
51. Patricia Tevington, "Growing Share of Americans See the Supreme Court as 'Friendly' Toward Religion," Pew Research Center, November 30, 2022.
52. Gonzales v. Carhart, 550 US 124, 159 (2007).
53. Nolan McCarty, *Polarization: What Everyone Needs to Know* (Oxford University Press, 2019).
54. Erwin Chemerinsky, *We the People: A Progressive Reading of the Constitution for the Twenty-First Century* (Picador, 2018); David A. Strauss, *The Living Constitution* (Oxford University Press, 2010); and Larry D. Kramer, *The People Themselves: Popular Constitutionalism and Judicial Review* (Oxford University Press, 2004).
55. There are different waves of originalism, camps, and internal debates about what it should prioritize. See Robert G. Natelson, "Answering the Latest Anti-Originalism Narrative," *Law and Liberty*, September 25, 2025; Randy E. Barnett and Lawrence B. Solum, "Originalism After Dobbs Bruen, and Kennedy: The Role of History and Tradition," *Northwestern University Law Review* 118, no. 2 (2023): 433–94; Keith E. Whittington, "Originalism: A Critical Introduction," *Fordham Law Review* 82, no. 2 (2013): 375–410.
56. Saul Cornell, "Why the Right's Mythical Version of the Past Dominates When It Comes to Legal 'History,'" *Slate*, May 14, 2024; Amanda Hollis-Brusky, *Ideas with Consequences: The Federalist Society and the Conservative Counterrevolution* (Oxford University Press, 2015)
57. Adam Bonica et al., "The Legal Academy's Ideological Uniformity," *Journal of Legal Studies* 47, no. 1 (2018): 1–43.
58. Jesse Wegman, "The Crisis in Teaching Constitutional Law," *New York Times*, February 26, 2024.
59. William Baude, "Is Originalism Our Law?," *Columbia Law Review* 115 (2015): 2349–2408.
60. Angie Gou, "'Cherry-Picked' History: Reva Siegel on 'Living Originalism' in *Dobbs*," *SCOTUSblog*, August 4, 2022.
61. Guy-Uriel E. Charles and Luis Fuentes-Rohwer, "Race, Originalism, and Skepticism," *University of Pennsylvania Journal of Constitutional Law* 25, no. 5 (2024): 1241; Serena Mayeri, "The Critical Role of History after Dobbs," *Journal of American Constitutional History* 2, no. 1 (2024): 171–273.
62. Michael C. Dorf, "Equal Protection Incorporation," *Virginia Law Review* 88 (2002): 951, 959; Jamal Greene, "Fourteenth Amendment Originalism," *Maryland Law Review* 71, no. 4 (2012):978–1014.
63. Orville Vernon Burton and Armand Derfner, *Justice Deferred: Race and the Supreme Court* (Belknap Press, 2021); Adam Cohen, *Supreme Inequality: The Supreme Court's Fifty-Year Battle for a More Unjust America* (Penguin Press, 2020); Ian Millhiser, *Injustices: The Supreme Court's History of Comforting the Comfortable and Afflicting the Afflicted* (Nation Books, 2015); Girardeau A. Spann, *Race Against the Court: The Supreme Court and Minorities in Contemporary America* (NYU Press, 1993).
64. Rana, *The Constitutional Bind*; Erwin Chemerinsky, *No Democracy Lasts Forever: How the Constitution Threatens the United States* (Liveright, 2024); Ryan D. Doerfler and Samuel Moyn, "The Constitution Is Broken and Should Not Be Reclaimed," *New York Times*, August 19, 2022; Louis Michael Seidman, *On Constitutional Disobedience* (Oxford University Press, 2012).

CHAPTER 7: CIVIL PROCEDURE AND THE ARCHITECTURE OF INEQUALITY

1. National Center for State Courts, "Data for Court Professionals," accessed August 13, 2025. Much of what we call "state courts" (including my own shorthand here) are in fact local courts. See Justin Weinstein-Tull, "The Structures of Local Courts," *Texas Law Review* 98, no. 4 (2020): 743–810.
2. Northwestern Pritzker School of Law, Bar Passage Disclosure Report, 2025, accessed October 7, 2025, https://wwws.law.northwestern.edu/admissions/disclosures/documents/bar-passage.pdf; DePaul University College of Law, ABA Consumer Bar Passage Report, 2025, accessed October 7, 2025, https://law.depaul.edu/about/Documents/2025%20Consumer%20Bar%20Admission.pdf; Loyola University Chicago School of Law, Bar Passage Disclosure, 2025, accessed September 28, 2025, https://www.luc.edu/media/lucedu/law/bar-passage.pdf; and University of Chicago Law School, Consumer Bar Passage Report, 2025, accessed September 28, 2025, https://www.law.uchicago.edu/sites/default/files/2025-02/UChicago_Law-2025-Bar_Passage.pdf.
3. Comparative approaches that juxtapose a few state and federal rules could provide students with a more comprehensive view of procedural diversity, get them to think more critically about the pros and cons of states' different approaches to procedural issues, prepare them for multijurisdictional practice, and potentially give them better forum selection skills (e.g., which states might be more favorable for the clients).
4. One book, which is lead-authored by a former public defender, stands out for its engagement on issues. See Barbara Allen Babcock et al., *Civil Procedure: Cases and Problems* (Aspen Publishing, 2021).
5. Federal Rules of Civil Procedure, Rule 4, Summons (Fed. R. Civ. P. 4(c)(3)); Federal Rules of Appellate Procedure, Rule 24, Proceeding in Forma Pauperis (Fed. R. App. P. 24); US Code Title 28, Judiciary and Judicial Procedure Section 1915 (28 USC § 1915).
6. Kate Andrias, "Separations of Wealth: Inequality and the Erosion of Checks and Balances," *University of Pennsylvania Journal of Constitutional Law* 18, no. 2 (2015): 419–504, 492.
7. Merritt E. McAlister, "White-Collar Courts," *Vanderbilt Law Review* 76, no. 4 (2023): 1161.
8. Stephen B. Burbank and Sean Farhang, *Rights and Retrenchment: The Counterrevolution Against Federal Litigation* (Cambridge University Press, 2017), 67.
9. Patricia W. Hatamyar Moore, "The Anti-Plaintiff Pending Amendments to the Federal Rules of Civil Procedure and the Pro-Defendant Composition of the Federal Rulemaking Committees," *University of Cincinnati Law Review* 83, no. 4 (2015): 1087.
10. Brooke D. Coleman, "One Percent Procedure," *Washington Law Review* 91, no. 3 (2016): 1005, 1067.
11. Andrew Hammond, "Pleading Poverty in Federal Court," *Yale Law Review* 128 (2019): 1478, 1527, 1530.
12. Maureen Carroll, "Civil Procedure and Economic Inequality," *DePaul Law Review* 69, no. 2 (2020): 269, 270–72.
13. Carroll, "Civil Procedure and Economic Inequality," 269, 270–72.
14. McAlister, "White-Collar Courts,"1155.
15. Richard M. Re, "Equal Right to the Poor," *University of Chicago Law Review* 84, no. 3 (2017): 1149, 1151.

16. John MacArthur Maguire, "Poverty and Civil Litigation," *Harvard Law Review* 36, no. 4 (1923): 361, 362.
17. Helen Hershkoff, "Poverty Law and Civil Procedure: Rethinking the First-Year Course," *Fordham Urban Law Journal* 34, no. 4 (2007): 1325, 1326.
18. William B. Rubenstein, "The Concept of Equality in Civil Procedure," *Cardozo Law Review* 23, no. 5 (2002): 1865, 1873–74.
19. Hershkoff, "Poverty Law and Civil Procedure," 1336; Rubenstein, "Concept of Equality"; Frank I. Michelman, "The Supreme Court and Litigation Access Fees: The Right to Protect One's Rights—Part I 1973," *Duke Law Journal* 1974 (1974): 1153, 1163.
20. Hammond, "Pleading Poverty in Federal Court," 148; See generally Brooke Coleman et al., *A Guide to Civil Procedure: Integrating Critical Legal Perspectives* (NYU Press, 2022).
21. Colleen F. Shanahan et al., "The Institutional Mismatch of State Civil Courts," *Columbia Law Review* 122, no. 5 (June 2022): 1471, 1473.
22. Hannah Lieberman, "Uncivil Procedure: How State Court Proceedings Perpetuate Inequality," *Yale Law and Policy Review* 35, no. 1 (2016): 257, 264.
23. Adrian Gottshall, "Solving Sewer Service: Fighting Fraud with Technology," *Arkansas Law Review* 70, no. 4 (2018): 813.
24. Human Rights Watch, "Rubber Stamp Justice: US Courts, Debt Buying Corporations, and the Poor" (January 20, 2016), 38.
25. Human Rights Watch, "Rubber Stamp Justice," 39.
26. Sara Sternberg Greene and Kristen M. Renberg, "Judging Without a J.D.," *Columbia Law Review* 122 (2022): 1287, 1341.
27. Greene and Renberg, "Judging Without a J.D.," 1287, 1341.
28. Norman W. Spaulding, "The Ideal and the Actual in Procedural Due Process," *UC Law Constitutional Quarterly* 48, no. 2 (Winter 2021): 261, 292.
29. Pamela K. Bookman and Colleen F. Shanahan, "A Tale of Two Civil Procedures," *Columbia Law Review* 122, no. 5 (2022): 1183, 1237.
30. Elizabeth Pollman, "The Supreme Court and the Pro-Business Paradox," *Harvard Law Review* 135, no. 1 (2021): 220, 225.
31. Kiobel v. Royal Dutch Petroleum Co., 569 US 108 (2013); Nestle USA, Inc. v. Doe, 593 US 628 (2021). See also Jesner v. Arab Bank, PLC, 584 US 241 (2018).
32. These include subject matter jurisdiction, personal jurisdiction, and forum non conveniens.
33. Bell Atl. Corp. v. Twombly, 550 US 544 (2007).
34. Thom Weidlich, "Wall Street Banks Benefit from Tougher Suit Standards in U.S.," *Bloomberg*, September 8, 2010.
35. Comcast Corp. v. Behrend, 569 US 27 (2013); Wal-Mart v. Dukes, 564 US 338 (2011).
36. Epic Sys. Corp. v. Lewis, 584 US 497 (2018).
37. Debra Lyn Bassett, "The Forum Game," *North Carolina Law Review* 84, no. 2 (2006): 333, 350.
38. Bassett, "The Forum Game," 344.
39. This is assuming the company sold, marketed, and serviced its products there. See Ford Motor Co. v. Montana Eighth Judicial District, 592 US 351 (2021).
40. Helen Hershkoff and Luke Norris, "The Oligarchic Courthouse: Jurisdiction, Corporate Power, and Democratic Decline," *Michigan Law Review* 122, no. 1 (2023): 1–54.

41. Cara Reichard, "Keeping Litigation at Home: The Role of States in Preventing Unjust Choice of Forum," *Yale Law Journal* 129, no. 3 (2020): 866, 878–80.
42. Yoder v. Heinold Commodities, Inc., 630 F. Supp. 756, 759 (E.D. Va. 1986); Reichard, "Keeping Litigation at Home," 880.
43. Economic Policy Institute, "Unlawful: How the Supreme Court Has Undermined Workers' Right to Act Collectively" (2019).
44. Hershkoff and Norris, "The Oligarchic Courthouse," 21; Zachary D. Clopton and Alexandra D. Lahav, "Fraudulent Removal," *Harvard Law Review* 135 (2021): 87, 95; Theodore Eisenberg and Trevor W. Morrison, "Overlooked in the Tort Reform Debate: The Growth of Erroneous Removal," *Journal of Empirical Legal Studies* 2, no. 3 (November 2005): 551–76.
45. Edward A. Purcell, Jr., *Brandeis and the Progressive Constitution: Erie, the Judicial Power, and the Politics of the Federal Courts in Twentieth-Century America* (Yale University Press, 2000), 66.
46. David Freeman Engstrom and Jonah B. Gelbach, "Legal Tech, Civil Procedure, and the Future of Adversarialism," *University of Pennsylvania Law Review* 169, no. 4 (2021): 1001–99.
47. Family Code §6309 (concerning discovery in domestic violence cases; California); Superior Court of the District of Columbia, Civil Division, *Small Claims and Conciliation Branch Information Handbook* (rev. May 2015); Claire Johnson Raba, "Forfeiting Due Process: How Adjudicative Reform Fails Property Owners," *Fordham University Urban Law Journal* 51, no. 2 (2023): 299.

PRELIMINARY HEARING

1. Julie Turkewitz, "Helping Poor Defendants Post Bail in Backlogged Bronx," *New York Times*, January 23, 2014; Ray Rivera, "Bronx Courts Trim Big Backlog with Outside Judge at the Helm," *New York Times*, August 30, 2013.
2. Vianna Davila, "How Ken Paxton Is Stretching the Boundaries of Consumer Protection Laws to Pursue Political Targets," *Texas Tribune*, May 30, 2024.
3. Coleman et al. v. Newsom et al., No. 24-3707, 2024 WL 5629534 (9th Cir. Apr. 15, 2025); Brown et al. v. Plata et al., 563 US 493 (2011).

CHAPTER 8: THE POWER TO CHOOSE

1. Jordan Moss, "Burning Questions," *City Limits* 36, no. 1, (April 2012) 17–18.
2. Moss, "Burning Questions," 20.
3. Moss, "Burning Questions," 20.
4. Daniel C. Richman, "Accounting for Prosecutors," in *Prosecutors and Democracy: A Cross-National Study*, ed. Máximo Langer and David Alan Sklansky (Cambridge University Press, 2017), 40–75.
5. Jeffrey Bellin, "The Power of Prosecutors," *New York University Law Review* 94, no. 2 (2019): 171, 191.
6. Anna Roberts, "Dismissals as Justice," *Alabama Law Review* 69, no. 2 (2017): 327, 330.
7. Reflective Democracy Campaign, "Tipping the Scales: Challengers Take on the Old Boys' Club of Elected Prosecutors," Women Donors Network, October 2019, 1.
8. Reflective Democracy Campaign, "Tipping the Scales," 2.
9. Kate Stohr and Deirdra Funcheon, "Fusion: Few Things Whiter Than America's

Prosecutors—America's Prosecutor Problem," *Clean Up City of St. Augustine, Florida* (blog), December 29, 2016.
10. Katherine J. Bies et al., "Stuck in the '70s: The Demographics of California Prosecutors," Stanford Criminal Justice Center, July 2015, 10, 14.
11. I. India Thusi, "The Pathological Whiteness of Prosecution," *California Law Review* 110 (June 2022): 795–872.
12. Angela J. Davis, *Arbitrary Justice: The Power of the American Prosecutor* (Oxford University Press, 2007), 63.
13. Davis, *Arbitrary Justice*, 63.
14. Adam M. Gershowitz, "The Prosecutor Vacancy Crisis," *Brigham Young University Law Review* 50, no. 2 (2024): 355–430.
15. Gershowitz, "Prosecutor Vacancy Crisis," 355–430.
16. Ronald F. Wright and Kay L. Levine, "The Cure for Young Prosecutors' Syndrome," *Arizona Law Review* 56, no. 4 (2014): 1065–1128. But see Emma Harrington et al., "Prediction Errors, Incarceration, and Violent Crime: Evidence from Linking Prosecutor Surveys to Court Records," *American Economic Journal: Economic Policy*, conditionally accepted, May 14, 2025.
17. Gershowitz, "Prosecutor Vacancy Crisis," 355–430.
18. David Keenan et al., "The Myth of Prosecutorial Accountability After Connick v. Thompson: Why Existing Professional Responsibility Measures Cannot Protect Against Prosecutorial Misconduct," *Yale Law Journal Online* 121, no. 203 (October 25, 2011).
19. A. Rafik Mohamed and Erik D. Fritsvold, *Dorm Room Dealers: Drugs and the Privileges of Race and Class* (Lynne Rienner Publishers, 2010).
20. Robin Conley, *Confronting the Death Penalty: How Language Influences Jurors in Capital Cases* (Oxford University Press, 2015), 150.
21. Jamelia N. Morgan, "Rethinking Disorderly Conduct," *California Law Review* 109, no. 5 (October 2021): 1637–1702.
22. Kate Levine, "Who Shouldn't Prosecute the Police," *Iowa Law Review* 101, no. 4 (May 2016): 1447–96.
23. Alexandra Natapoff, "Misdemeanor Declination: A Theory of Internal Separation of Powers," *Texas Law Review* 102, no. 5 (2024): 937, 946. In the state felony context, declination rates are approximately 25 percent.
24. Even I have had police officers search my testicles for nonexistent drugs. Andrew Gelman et al., "An Analysis of the New York City Police Department's 'Stop-and-Frisk' Policy in the Context of Claims of Racial Bias," *Journal of the American Statistical Association* 102, no. 479 (2007): 813–23.
25. Vera Institute of Justice, "Race and Prosecution in Manhattan: Research Summary," July 2014, 1–10; But see Besiki Luka Kutateladze, "Tracing Charge Trajectories: A Study of the Influence of Race in Charge Changes at Case Screening, Arraignment, and Disposition," *Criminology* 56, no. 1 (2018): 123–53.
26. Christopher Robertson et al., "Race and Class: A Randomized Experiment with Prosecutors," *Journal of Empirical Legal Studies* 16, no. 4 (December 2019): 807–47.
27. See Alex Chohlas-Wood et al., "Blind Justice: Algorithmically Masking Race in Charging Decisions," *AIES '21: Proceedings of the 2021 AAAI/ACM Conference on AI, Ethics, and Society* (2021): 35, 40–43. The authors caution these findings may not apply elsewhere.

28. Hannah Shaffer, "Prosecutors, Race, and the Criminal Pipeline," *University of Chicago Law Review* 90, no. 7 (2023): 1889.
29. Grady Bridges and J.J. Prescott, "Prosecutor Transparency Project: Racial Disparities Study (Washtenaw County, Michigan)," (December 2023, draft), http://dx.doi.org/10.2139/ssrn.4680695.
30. "Racial Disparities in the Arkansas Criminal Justice System Research Project, Report of Research Findings" (August 28–29, 2015); Arkansas Code Title 5. Criminal Offenses § 5-41-202. "Unlawful Act Regarding Computers."
31. Criminal Justice Policy Program, *Racial Disparities in the Massachusetts Criminal System* (Harvard Law School, 2020).
32. Jawjeong Wu, "Racial/Ethnic Discrimination and Prosecution: A Meta-Analysis," *Criminal Justice and Behavior* 43, no. 4 (2016).
33. Lauren Gase, "Racial Disparities in Prosecutorial Outcomes," University of Denver, Colorado Evaluation and Action Lab (November 2021); Vera Institute, "Race and Prosecution in Manhattan," 5.
34. Taja-Nia Y. Henderson and Jamila Jefferson-Jones, "#livingwhileblack: Blackness as Nuisance," *American University Law Review* 69, no. 3 (2020): 863–914.
35. Traci Schlesinger, "Racial Disparities in Pretrial Diversion: An Analysis of Outcomes Among Men Charged with Felonies and Processed in State Courts," *American Society of Criminology* 3, no. 3 (April 30, 2013): 210–38.
36. Carlos Berdejó, "Criminalizing Race: Racial Disparities in Plea-Bargaining," *Boston College Law Review* 59, no. 4 (2018): 1187–1250.
37. Carlos Berdejó et al. "The 'Distance Traveled': Investigating the Downstream Consequences of Charge Reductions for Disparities in Incarceration," *Justice Quarterly* 36, no. 7 (2019): 1229–57; Christi Metcalfe and Ted G. Chiricos, "Race, Plea, and Charge Reduction: An Assessment of Racial Disparities in the Plea Process," *Justice Quarterly* 35, no. 2 (2018): 1–31; Besiki L. Kutateladze et al., "Opening Pandora's Box: How Does Defendant Race Influence Plea Bargaining?," *Justice Quarterly* 33, no. 3 (April 2016): 398–426.
38. Gase, "Racial Disparities in Prosecutorial Outcomes."
39. Strauder v. West Virginia, 100 US 303 (1880).
40. Berkeley Law Death Penalty Clinic, *Whitewashing the Jury Box: How California Perpetuates the Discriminatory Exclusion of Black and Latinx Jurors* (Berkeley Law, 2020), v.
41. Kiana Cox, "Most Black Americans Believe U.S. Institutions Were Designed to Hold Black People Back," Pew Research Center, June 15, 2024.
42. Berkeley Law Death Penalty Clinic, *Whitewashing the Jury Box*, vi.
43. Equal Justice Initiative, "Who Is Responsible for Discrimination?," in *Race and the Jury: Illegal Discrimination in Jury Selection* (2021).
44. Hernandez v. New York, 500 US 352 (1991).
45. People v. Robinson, 454 P.3d 229, 231 (2019).
46. People v. Arredondo, 21 Cal. App. 5th 493, 504 (2018).
47. State v. Kirk, 157 Idaho 809 (Ct. App. 2014).
48. State v. Ibarra-Erives, 23 Wash. App. 2d 596 (2022)
49. State v. Rogan 984 P.2d 1231 (1999).
50. State v. Monday, 171 Wash. 2d 667, 678, (2011) (citing State v. Dhaliwal, 150 Wash.2d 559, 583) (2003).
51. Wright and Levine, "Cure for Young Prosecutors' Syndrome," 1065, 1125.

52. Laurie L. Levenson, "The Problem with Cynical Prosecutor's Syndrome: Rethinking a Prosecutor's Role in Post-Conviction Cases," *Berkeley Journal of Criminal Law* 20, no. 2 (Fall 2015): 335–98.
53. Kathryne M. Young and Jessica Pearlman, "Racial Disparities in Lifer Parole Outcomes: The Hidden Role of Professional Evaluations," *Law and Social Inquiry* 47, no. 3 (2022): 783–820.
54. Cynthia Godsoe and Maybell Romero, "Prosecutorial Mutiny," *American Criminal Law Review* 60, no. 4 (2023): 1403–30; Han Li, "Bay Area District Attorney Recall Campaigns Have Been Led by Asian Americans. Why?," *San Francisco Standard*, August 16, 2023.

CHAPTER 9: MUNICIPAL MATTERS

1. "Document: Class Action Complaint and Demand for Jury Trial" (June 1, 2022), Disability Rights New York v. City of New York (US District Court, Southern District of New York) (No. 1:22-CV-04493), Civil Rights Litigation Clearinghouse, 8.
2. "Document: Fourth Amended Complaint" (August 9, 2007), Frame v. City of Arlington (US District Court, North District of Texas) (No: 4:05-cv-00470-Y), 7.
3. Brief of the National League of Cities and 76 California Cities, Barden v. City of Sacramento, 292 F.3d 1073 (9th Cir. 2002).
4. New York City Law Department, "Office Overview," Office of the Corporation Counsel, NYC.gov, accessed August 15, 2025; American Bar Association, Model Rules of Professional Conduct, Rule 1.13: Organization as Client, accessed August 15, 2025.
5. Heather Cherone, "Final Tally: Chicago Taxpayers Spent at Least $107.5M to Resolve Police Misconduct Lawsuits in 2024, Analysis Finds," WTTW, February 10, 2025.
6. Alan Feuer, "The Lawyers Protecting the N.Y.P.D. Play Hardball. Judges Are Calling Them Out," *New York Times*, September 12, 2018.
7. Report of Plaintiffs' Expert Dr. Jeffrey Fagan, Jaenean Ligon, et al., v. City of New York, et al., 2012 WL 8282311 (S.D.N.Y.).
8. Ligon v. City of New York, 925 F. Supp. 2d 478, 493 (S.D.N.Y. 2013).
9. Ligon v. City of New York at 494.
10. Floyd v. City of New York, 959 F. Supp. 2d 540 (S.D.N.Y. 2013).
11. Peter Morales, "Sheriff Joe Arpaio, Arizona's 'Bull' Connor," *Guardian*, July 19, 2012.
12. Joe Hagan, "The Long, Lawless Ride of Sheriff Joe Arpaio," *Rolling Stone*, August 2, 2012; Jesse Taylor, "Sheriff Joe Arpaio—'Tent City' Concentration Camp," YouTube, uploaded June 1, 2012.
13. Manuel De Jesus Ortega Melendres, et al., v. Joseph M. ARPAIO, et al., 2012 WL 3793134 (D.Ariz.).
14. Ray Stern, "Sheriff Joe Arpaio's Office Commits Worst Racial Profiling in U.S. History, Concludes DOJ Investigation," *Phoenix New Times*, December 15, 2011.
15. Stern, "Sheriff Arpaio's Office Commits Worst Racial Profiling."
16. Melendres v. Arpaio, 989 F. Supp. 2d 822 (D. Ariz. 2013).
17. United States v. Cnty. of Maricopa, Arizona, 889 F.3d 648, (9th Cir. 2018).
18. Jacques Billeaud, "Taxpayers in Metro Phoenix Still Footing the Bill for Joe Arpaio's Immigration Crackdowns," *AP News*, May 19, 2025.
19. Emma Tucker, "New Jersey County Agrees on Landmark $10 Million Settlement to Black Man Paralyzed After Police Encounter," CNN, May 15, 2022.

20. Monica Davey and Mitch Smith, "Justice Officials to Investigate Chicago Police Department After Laquan McDonald Case," *New York Times*, December 6, 2015.
21. Margo Schlanger, "Inmate Litigation," *Harvard Law Review* 116, no. 6 (April 2003): 1555, 1681.
22. Police Scorecard, "We Evaluated Policing in San Diego City and County. Here's What We Found," accessed August 15, 2025.
23. K.J.P. v. Cnty. of San Diego, 621 F. Supp. 3d 1097, 1111 (S.D. Cal. 2022). This officer would separately cost the city millions because of settlements involving a dozen *other* lawsuits for assault; Greg Moran, "San Diego Settles In-Custody Death Case for $12M After Judge Threw Out Previous Award," Lexipol Media Group: Police 1, January 23, 2023.
24. K.J.P. v. Cnty. of San Diego, 2016 WL 7385620, at 3–4 (S.D. Cal. Apr. 29, 2016).
25. Moore v. Moore, 2019 WL 6683171, at 1 (N.D. Ohio Dec. 6, 2019); Jon Schuppe, "Rogue East Cleveland Cops Framed Dozens of Drug Suspects," NBC News, March 17, 2017; "Charges Against 40 Defendants Arrested by Corrupt East Cleveland Officers to Be Dropped," Cleveland 19 News, December 13, 2016.
26. Barnes v. City of El Paso, 2023 US Dist. Lexis 169485 (W.D. Tex. Sept. 21, 2023).
27. Jamelia N. Morgan, "Policing Under Disability Law," *Stanford Law Review* 73 (June 2021): 1401, 1404.
28. David Lohr, "Police Allegedly Beat Pearl Pearson for Disobeying Orders He Could Not Hear," *Huffington Post*, January 15, 2014.
29. Talila A. Lewis, "Police Brutality and Deaf People," ACLU: News and Commentary, March 21, 2014.
30. USAFacts, "What Is the State of American Hearing?" December 20, 2023.
31. Kelly McAnnany and Aditi Kothekar Shah, "With Their Own Hands: A Community Lawyering Approach to Improving Law Enforcement Practices in the Deaf Community," *Valparaiso University Law Review* 45, no. 3 (2011): 875, 878.
32. Williams v. City of New York, 121 F. Supp. 3d 354, 359 (S.D.N.Y. 2015).
33. Am. Council of the Blind of New York, Inc. v. City of New York, 579 F. Supp. 3d 539, FN3, 545 (S.D.N.Y. 2021).
34. Am. Council of Blind of Metro. Chicago v. City of Chicago, 667 F. Supp. 3d 767, 770 (N.D. Ill. 2023).
35. Am. Council of Blind of Metro. Chicago at 770–771, 783.
36. Am. Council of Blind of Metro. Chicago at 770n4.
37. Am. Council of the Blind of New York v. City of New York at 221.
38. Am. Council of Blind of Metro. Chicago at 776.
39. Am. Council of Blind of Metro. Chicago at 777.
40. Mozhgon Rajaee et al., "Socioeconomic and Racial Disparities of Sidewalk Quality in a Traditional Rust Belt City," *SSM—Population Health* 16 (December 2021): 100975.
41. Robinson v. California, 370 US 660 (1962).
42. Jones v. City of Los Angeles, 444 F.3d 1118 (9th Cir. 2006), vacated, 505 F.3d 1006 (9th Cir. 2007).
43. Parker v. Municipal Judge of City of Las Vegas, 83 Nev. 214, 216 (1967).
44. Pottinger v. City of Miami, 810 F. Supp. 1551, 1564 (S.D. Fla. 1992).
45. Jones v. City of Los Angeles 1118, 1122 (9th Cir. 2006).
46. Jones v. City of Los Angeles (9th Cir. 2006) at 1127.

47. It also argued that if they were prosecuted and there were no shelters available, they would have the criminal law defense of necessity that would prevent a conviction.
48. The Jones decision was vacated by settlement and the Pottinger case was settled and ended with a consent decree.
49. Martin v. City of Boise, 920 F.3d 584 (9th Cir. 2019).
50. City of Grants Pass v. Johnson, 144 S. Ct. 2202 (2024).
51. Ben A. McJunkin, "The Negative Right to Shelter," *California Law Review* 111 (2023): 127, 163–74.
52. City of Grants Pass, Oregon v. Johnson, 603 US 520, 530 (2024).
53. Adam Shanks, "SF No Longer Requires Offers of Shelter Before Clearing Encampments," *San Francisco Examiner*, August 5, 2024.
54. Susan Du, "Public Housing Tenant Challenging MPHA's Right to Evict Without a Rental License," *Minnesota Star Tribune*, April 15, 2023.
55. Du, "Public Housing Tenant Challenging Right to Evict."
56. Marable v. City of Minneapolis, No. A19-1558, 2020 WL 2312940, at *2 (Minn. Ct. App. May 11, 2020).
57. Faiza Mahamud, "Mpls. Council OKs $150K Settlement for Tenant Who Said City Failed to Enforce Code Violations in Public Housing," *Minnesota Star Tribune*, June 17, 2022.
58. Mayo Clinic, "Lead Poisoning," Mayo Clinic: Diseases and Conditions, accessed August 15, 2025.
59. US Department of Justice, "Manhattan U.S. Attorney Announces Settlement with NYCHA and NYC to Fundamentally Reform NYCHA Through the Appointment of a Federal Monitor and the Payment by NYC of $1.2 Billion of Additional Capital Money over the Next Five Years," United States Attorney's Office, Southern District of New York, June 11, 2018.
60. Luis Ferré-Sadurní, "Little Decline in Number of Children in Public Housing with High Lead Levels, Report Says," *New York Times*, August 30, 2018.
61. Paige v. New York City Hous. Auth., 2018 WL 1226024, at 2 (S.D.N.Y. Mar. 9, 2018).
62. The City-Wide Council of Presidents v. The New York City Housing Authority, No. 100283/18, 2018 WL 1911926, at 7 (N.Y. Sup. Ct. Apr. 23, 2018).

A SOBER VIEW OF BIG LAW

1. Robert L. Nelson, *Partners with Power: The Social Transformation of the Large Law Firm* (University of California Press, 1988), 1.
2. This refers to equity partners. Nonequity partners do not have this stake.
3. Leigh Joines, "Napping Pods: One Firm's Solution for Tired Lawyers," Law.com: The American Lawyer, May 16, 2017.
4. Michael Asimow, "Embodiment of Evil: Law Firms in the Movies," *UCLA Law Review* 48 (2001): 1339, 1344–47.
5. John Bliss, "From Idealists to Hired Guns? An Empirical Analysis of 'Public Interest Drift' in Law School," *UC Davis Law Review* 51, no. 5 (2018): 1973–2032.
6. Randall Kennedy, *Sellout: The Politics of Racial Betrayal* (Knopf Doubleday, 2009), 192–94.
7. Richard Wasserstrom, "Lawyers as Professionals: Some Moral Issues," *Human Rights* 5, no. 1 (Fall 1975): 5–6.

CHAPTER 10: TRANSACTIONAL VIOLENCE

1. Noam Scheiber, "Why Big Law Firms Aren't Standing Together Against Trump's Assault," *New York Times*, April 19, 2025.
2. Emily Stewart, "What Is Private Equity, and Why Is It Killing Everything You Love?," *Vox*, January 6, 2020.
3. Jamie Lutz and Caitlin Welsh, "Foreign Purchases of U.S. Agricultural Land: Facts, Figures, and an Assessment of Real Threats," *Critical Questions* (blog), Center for Strategic and International Studies, September 8, 2021.
4. Anirban Sen, "Kirkland & Ellis Tops M&A Legal Adviser Rankings for First Time," *Reuters*, January 3, 2024.
5. Lucas Boschelli et al., "Conglomerates at the Court: The Political Consequences of Mergers & Acquisitions," *Research and Politics* 11, no. 3 (September 2024): 1; John M. de Figueiredo and Brian Kelleher Richter, "Advancing the Empirical Research on Lobbying," *Annual Review of Political Science* 17 (2014): 163–85; Bo Cowgill et al., "Political Power and Market Power," Working Paper No. 33255 (National Bureau of Economic Research, December 2024): 1.
6. "The Lawyers Behind AT&T's Time Warner Offer," *Bloomberg Law News*, October 24, 2016.
7. Megan Brenan, "Low Satisfaction With Gov't Regulation of Businesses," Gallup, February 7, 2022.
8. George W. Dent, "Business Lawyers as Enterprise Architects," *Business Lawyer* 64, no. 2 (2009): 279–328.
9. Elisabeth de Fontenay, "Law Firm Selection and the Value of Transactional Lawyering," *Journal of Corporation Law* 41, no. 2 (2015): 393–429; Steven L. Schwarcz, "Explaining the Value of Transactional Lawyering," *Stanford Journal of Law, Business and Finance* 12 (2007): 486–535.
10. Cathy Hwang, "Value Creation by Transactional Associates," *Fordham Law Review* 88, no. 5 (2020): 1649–63.
11. Cecilia Kang and Mike Isaac, "U.S. and States Say Facebook Illegally Crushed Competition," *New York Times*, December 9, 2020.
12. Gustavo Grullón et al., "Are US Industries Becoming More Concentrated?," *Review of Finance* 23, no. 4 (2019): 697–743.
13. Christopher R. Leslie, "Banking Deserts, Structural Racism, and Merger Law," *Minnesota Law Review* 108 (2023): 699–704.
14. Vitaly M. Bord, "Bank Consolidation and Financial Inclusion: The Adverse Effects of Bank Mergers on Depositors" (unpublished manuscript, 2017), 1–89.
15. Mehrsa Baradaran, *How the Other Half Banks: Exclusion, Exploitation, and the Threat to Democracy* (Harvard University Press, 2015).
16. Mary Hendrickson et al., "The Food System: Concentration and Its Impacts," Family Farm Action Alliance (November 19, 2020), 9.
17. "The Economic Cost of Food Monopolies: The Dirty Dairy Racket," Food and Water Watch (January 2023).
18. Hannah Andrew, "Addressing Consolidation in Agriculture: USDA's Response to President Biden's Directive to Promote Competition in the American Economy," issue brief, Center for Agriculture and Food Systems, Vermont Law and Graduate School, July 2022, 2.

19. Siddharth Cavale and Jessica DiNapoli, "What Walmart May Gain from FTC's Kroger-Albertsons Lawsuit," *Reuters*, February 28, 2024.
20. Adam Schrader and A. L. Lee, "Biden Targets Mergers, Housing Rental Fees and Food Prices That 'Drive Up Costs,'" *UPI*, July 19, 2023.
21. Rahul Mukherjee et al., "How the 'Big Five' Airlines Came to Dominate the Skies," *Axios*, December 8, 2023; Scott McCartney, "Why an American Airlines Monopoly Works for Charlotte," *Wall Street Journal*, February 21, 2018.
22. Zack Cooper et al., "Do Higher-Priced Hospitals Deliver Higher-Quality Care?," Working Paper No. 29809 (National Bureau of Economic Research, February 2022), 2.
23. Jodi L. Liu et al., *Environmental Scan on Consolidation Trends and Impacts in Health Care Markets* (RAND Corporation, 2022), 11.
24. Nia Johnson, "Harnessing Intersecting Political Alliances to Achieve Medicaid Expansion" (unpublished manuscript, July 2024).
25. Zachary Levinson et al., "Ten Things to Know About Consolidation in Health Care Provider Markets," KFF, April 19, 2024.
26. Kenneth M. Johnson and Daniel T. Lichter, "Growing Racial Diversity in Rural America: Results from the 2020 Census," University of New Hampshire Carsey School of Public Policy, May 25, 2022; Tracey Farrigan, "Nonmetro Poverty Rates Remain Higher Than Metro," *Economic Research Service*, February 26, 2024.
27. "Rural Hospitals at Risk: Cuts to Medicaid Would Further Threaten Access," American Hospital Association, accessed August 18, 2025.
28. Caitlin Carroll et al., "Hospital Survival in Rural Markets: Closures, Mergers, and Profitability," *Health Affairs* 42, no. 4 (April 2023): 498–507.
29. Nancy D. Beaulieu et al., "Changes in Quality of Care After Hospital Mergers and Acquisitions," *New England Journal of Medicine* 382, no. 1 (January 2020): 51–59. (highlighting benefits of mergers).
30. Carroll et al., "Hospital Survival in Rural Markets."
31. Paula Chatterjee, "Causes and Consequences of Rural Hospital Closures," *Journal of Hospital Medicine* 17, no. 11 (November 2022): 938–99.
32. Tony Leys, "As a Baby Bust Hits Rural Areas, Hospital Labor and Delivery Wards Are Closing Down," NPR, July 15, 2024.
33. H. Joanna Jiang et al., "Quality of Care Before and After Mergers and Acquisitions of Rural Hospitals," *JAMA Network Open* 4, no. 9 (Sept. 1, 2021): e2124662.
34. Levinson, "Ten Things to Know"; James P. Waters, et al., "Are There Any Benefits to Hospital Consolidation?," *American Journal of Surgery* 238 (2024): 115754.
35. Elena Andreyeva et al., "The Corporatization of Independent Hospitals," *Journal of Political Economy Microeconomics* 2, no. 3 (2024): 602–63.
36. Brent D. Fulton, "Health Care Market Concentration Trends in the United States: Evidence and Policy Responses," *Health Affairs* 36, no. 9 (September 1, 2017): 1530–38.
37. Joanne Kenen, "Getting the Facts on Hospital Mergers and Acquisitions," Association of Health Care Journalists, September 30, 2014.
38. David B. Burmeister, "Understanding the Wide-Reaching Impact of Healthcare Merger and Acquisition Activity," *International Journal of Health Policy and Management* 12, no. 1 (November 26, 2023): 1–4.
39. Kara Harnett, "M&A, Private Equity Deals Likely to Keep Law Firms Busy: Survey," *Modern Healthcare* 54, no 4 (April 8, 2024).

40. Tom Huddleston Jr., "Pair of Health Care Deals Give Am Law Firms Shot in Arm," *Am Law Daily*, June 24, 2013.
41. Moe Tkacik, "Workers Blow the Whistle on Mass Death," *In These Times*, August 3, 2020.
42. Karen Bouffard and Joel Kurth, "Dirty, Missing Instruments Plague DMC Surgeries," *Detroit News*, August 25, 2016.
43. Karen Bouffard, "Delay in Care, Including Deaths, Blamed on DMC Staffing Levels; Probe Requested," *Detroit News*, April 26, 2022.
44. John J. D'Andrea et al. "Drinker Biddle Advises Mission Health on $1.5B Hospital Merger with HCA Healthcare," Faegre Drinker Biddle & Reath LLP (February 1, 2019).
45. Mark A. Hall, "Mission Hospital's Financial Performance Under HCA," working draft (Wake Forest University, Health Law and Policy Program, April 23, 2024).
46. Hall, "Mission Hospital's Financial Performance."
47. North Carolina State Health Plan for Teachers and State Employees et al. *Hospital Executive Compensation: A Decade of Growing Wage Inequity Across Nonprofit Hospitals* (2023), 10.
48. Neil Cotiaux, "Confused Mission Health Patients Want Answers About Surprise Fee," *Carolina Public Press*, February 10, 2020.
49. Mark Barrett, "Mission Criticized on Staff Shortages, Patient Care," *Mountain Xpress*, February 12, 2020.
50. Barrett, "Mission Criticized on Staff Shortages."
51. North Carolina State Health Plan, *Hospital Executive Compensation*, 11.
52. Mehrsa Baradaran, *The Quiet Coup Neoliberalism and the Looting of America* (W. W. Norton, 2024).

CHAPTER 11: ENVIRONMENTAL DEGRADATION IN THE REGULATORY WILD WEST

1. Susan Dudley, "Milestones in the Evolution of the Administrative State," *Daedalus* 150, no. 3 (July 2021), 33–34.
2. Victor Fleischer, "Regulatory Arbitrage" SSRN Electronic Journal 89, no. 2 (March 2010): 1567212, ultimately published as *Texas Law Review* 89 (2010): 227.
3. John W. Bagby and Nizan G. Packin, "RegTech and Predictive Lawmaking: Closing the RegLag Between Prospective Regulated Activity and Regulation," *Michigan Business and Entrepreneurial Law Review* 10, no. 2 (January 2021): 127–77.
4. C. K. Gourdet et al., "A Baseline Understanding of State Laws Governing E-Cigarettes," *Tobacco Control* 23, no. 3 (July 2014): 37–40.
5. Katie Thomas and Sheila Kaplan, "E-Cigarettes Went Unchecked in 10 Years of Federal Inaction," *New York Times*, October 14, 2019.
6. Teresa W. Wang et al., "Tobacco Product Use and Associated Factors Among Middle and High School Students—United States, 2019," *Morbidity and Mortality Weekly Report, Surveillance Summaries* 68, no. 12 (2019): 1–22.
7. Sara Merken, "U.S. Law Firm Partner Pay Hits New Highs, with Deal Lawyers in the Lead," *Reuters*, October 19, 2022.
8. Ethical rules do prohibit an attorney from offering privileged information that they obtained while in government, but that prohibition is much narrower than expertise former government workers can provide law firms. See American Bar Association,

"Rule 1.11: Special Conflicts of Interest for Former and Current Government Officers and Employees," in *Model Rules of Professional Conduct*, accessed August 19, 2025.
9. Devlin Barrett, "Eric Holder: U.S. May Need to Sue to Enforce Gay Marriage Ruling," *Wall Street Journal*, July 5, 2015.
10. Jeff Sommer, "How 2 Labor Dept. Rules Can Undermine Your Retirement Plans," *New York Times*, August 21, 2020.
11. Jamila Trindle, "Another Scalia Vexes Regulators," *Wall Street Journal*, October 2, 2012.
12. This issue could be its own book. For a few takes, see Michael P. Vandenbergh et al., "The New Revolving Door," 70 *Case Western Reserve Law Review* 70, no. 4 (2020): 1121–49; Wentong Zheng, "The Revolving Door," *Notre Dame Law Review* 90, no. 3 (2015): 1265–1308; David Zaring, "Against Being Against the Revolving Door," *University of Illinois Law Review* 2013, no. 2 (2013): 507–49.
13. US Environmental Protection Agency, "Inventory of U.S. Greenhouse Gas Emissions and Sinks: 1990–2022," April 2024, accessed August 19, 2025.
14. Rob Nixon, *Slow Violence and the Environmentalism of the Poor* (Harvard University Press, 2013), 2.
15. Rights and Resources Initiative, "State of Indigenous Peoples', Local Communities', and Afro-Descendant Peoples' Carbon Rights in Tropical and Subtropical Lands and Forests," policy brief, McGill University, November 2024.
16. "Emissions and Carbon Trading," Clifford Chance LLP, accessed September 20, 2025.
17. Dentons, "Jeffrey C. Fort," accessed September 20, 2025.
18. Akin Gump Strauss Hauer & Feld LLP, "Carbon Offsets," accessed August 19, 2025.
19. Alastair Marsh, "Companies Keep Climate Goals Secret as 'Green Hushing' Takes Off," *Bloomberg Law*, October 17, 2022.
20. "Carbon Trading and Investment," Clifford Chance LLP, accessed August 19, 2025.
21. World Bank, "Journey into the Congo Basin—The Lungs of Africa and Beating Heart of the World," October 24, 2022.
22. Adam Hochschild, *King Leopold's Ghost: A Story of Greed, Terror, and Heroism in Colonial Africa* (Houghton Mifflin, 1999).
23. Gleb Raygorodetsky, "Indigenous Peoples Defend Earth's Biodiversity—But They're in Danger," *National Geographic*, November 16, 2018.
24. Lucas Chancel, "Climate Change and the Global Inequality of Carbon Emissions, 1990–2020," World Inequality Lab, October 2021.
25. Louise Boyle, "COP26: Carbon Offsetting 'a New Form of Colonialism,' Says Indigenous Leader," *The Independent*, November 4, 2021.
26. Patrick Greenfield, "The 'Carbon Pirates' Preying on Amazon's Indigenous Communities," *Guardian*, January 21, 2023); Human Rights Watch, "Carbon Offsetting's Casualties: Violations of Chong Indigenous Peoples' Rights in Cambodia's Southern Cardamom REDD+ Project," February 28, 2024.
27. Heidi Bachram, "Climate Fraud and Carbon Colonialism: The New Trade in Greenhouse Gases," *Capitalism Nature Socialism* 15, no. 4 (December 2004): 5–20.
28. "Dentons Helps Cambodia Monetize Sustainable Environmental Practices," Dentons, November 14, 2013.
29. Human Rights Watch, "Carbon Offsetting's Casualties."
30. Latham & Watkins LLP, "Latham Advises on Landmark Forest Protection Funding in the Amazon," September 25, 2024; Latham & Watkins LLP, "Latham Advises on Landmark Forest Carbon Credit Agreements," December 8, 2023.

31. Anthony Boadle, "Indigenous Groups in Brazil: We Were Not Consulted on Carbon Credits," *Reuters*, October 14, 2024.
32. The C technically stands for *consent*, or the ability of communities to veto, but the group refers to the C as being for *consultation*, which is a lower threshold. See Anthony Boadle (Reuters), "Associações indígenas e organizações divulgam carta contra o desrespeito do governo do Pará em projetos de crédito de carbono" (Indigenous Associations and Organizations Release Letter Against the Pará Government's Disrespect for Carbon Credit Projects), Comissào Pastoral da Terra (CPT), October 8, 2024.
33. Anthony Boadle, "Brazil State to Consult Indigenous People on Carbon Credits Sale," *Reuters*, October 15, 2024.
34. Ann Danaiya Usher, "Growing Frustration Among Indigenous Leaders with Forest Carbon Scheme LEAF," *Development Today*, November 3, 2022.
35. Carla Ruas, "'World's Largest' Carbon Credit Deal in the Amazon Faces Bumpy Road Ahead," *Mongabay*, October 9, 2024. Firms like Clifford Chance and Freshfields connect to slavery and British imperialism. Sullivan and Cromwell served as counsel to United Fruit Company and helped it develop one-sided contracts in Latin America that were "legendary" and "mastered the exquisite art of squeezing concessions out of weak countries." Lawyers at that firm also played a role in a coup to unseat Guatemala's democratically elected president to protect the company's interest in the region. See Stephen Kinzer, *The Brothers: John Foster Dulles, Allen Dulles, and Their Secret World War* (Times Books, 2013), 148; Simon Lock, "Law Firms' Past Links to Slavery and Imperialism Unearthed," *Law.com*, June 19, 2020.
36. Manuel Pastor et al., "Up in the Air: Revisiting Equity Dimensions of California's Cap-and-Trade System," University of Southern California Equity Research Institute (ERI)/USCDornsife, February 1, 2022; Lara J. Cushing et al., "A Preliminary Environmental Equity Assessment of California's Cap-and-Trade Program," USC ERI/USCDornsife, September 14, 2016; for a different take, see Danae Hernandez-Cortes and Kyle C. Meng, "Do Environmental Markets Cause Environmental Injustice? Evidence from California's Carbon Market," Working Paper 27205 (National Bureau of Economic Research, November 2022).
37. Lara Cushing et al., "Carbon Trading, Co-Pollutants, and Environmental Equity: Evidence from California's Cap-And-Trade Program (2011–2015)," *PLOS Medicine* 15, no. 7 (July 2018): e1002604.
38. Timothy Q. Donaghy et al., "Fossil Fuel Racism in the United States: How Phasing Out Coal, Oil, and Gas Can Protect Communities," *Energy Research and Social Science* 100, no. 2 (June 2024): 103104; Food and Water Watch, "Cap and Trade: More Pollution for the Poor and People of Color," issue brief, November 2019. But see Hernandez-Cortes, and Meng, "Do Environmental Markets Cause Environmental Injustice?" (which finds that California's cap-and-trade program narrowed environmental justice gaps in local air pollution concentrations between disadvantaged and other communities).
39. Lynne L. Dallas, "Short-Termism, the Financial Crisis, and Corporate Governance," *Journal of Corporation Law* 37, no. 2 (2012): 264–363.
40. Katharina Pistor, *The Code of Capital: How the Law Creates Wealth and Inequality* (Princeton University Press, 2019).
41. Patrick Greenfield, "Revealed: More Than 90% of Rainforest Carbon Offsets by Biggest Certifier Are Worthless, Analysis Shows," *The Guardian*, January 18, 2023.
42. Patrick Greenfield, "CEO of Biggest Carbon Credit Certifier to Resign After Claims

Offsets Worthless," *Guardian,* May 23, 2023; Patrick Greenfield, "Biggest Carbon Credit Certifier to Replace Its Rainforest Offsets Scheme," *Guardian,* March 10, 2023; Cynthia Giles and Cary Coglianese, "Auditors Can't Save Carbon Offsets," *Science* 389, no. 6756 (2025): 107.
43. This is the problem of additionality. Put simply, offsets were purchased for renewable energy projects that were already cheaper than coal or gas in most countries and/or were backed by government subsidies. See Akshat Rathi et al., "Junk Carbon Offsets Are What Make These Big Companies 'Carbon Neutral,' " *Bloomberg,* November 21, 2022.
44. Heidi Blake, "The Great Cash-for-Carbon Hustle," *New Yorker,* October 16, 2023.
45. Grayson Badgley et al., "Systematic Over-Crediting in California's Forest Carbon Offsets Program," *Global Change Biology* 28, no. 4 (2022): 1433–45.
46. Jared Stapp et al., "Little Evidence of Management Change in California's Forest Offset Program," *Communications Earth and Environment* 4, no. 1 (September 21, 2023): 1–10; Shane R. Coffield et al., "Using Remote Sensing to Quantify the Additional Climate Benefits of California Forest Carbon Offset Projects," *Global Change Biology* 28, no. 22 (2022): 6789–6806; Raphael Calel et al., "Do Carbon Offsets Offset Carbon?," *American Economic Journal: Applied Economics* 17, no. 1 (2025): 1–40.
47. Halley I. Townsend and Alexander S. Holtan, "CFTC, DOJ and SEC Announce First Coordinated Action Aimed at Voluntary Carbon Market Fraud," Holland and Knight Alert, October 8, 2024.
48. Indictment, United States v. Newcombe et al., No. 24-cr-567 (D. Colo. Oct. 2024), Indictment, 17–18.
49. Verra, "Verra Cancels 5 Million Overissued Credits Linked to C-Quest Capital," press release, October 17, 2024.
50. Akin Gump, "Carbon Offsets," accessed August 28, 2025; "2023 Environmental Sustainability Report," Latham and Watkins LLP, accessed August 19, 2025; Norton Rose Fulbright, "Norton Rose Fulbright Leads Sustainability-Driven Carbon Credit Financing in Africa," press release, April 2022; Latham and Watkins LLP, "Jean-Philippe Brisson," accessed August 28, 2025.
51. Ari Aisen and Michael Franken, "Bank Credit During the 2008 Financial Crisis: A Cross-Country Comparison," IMF Working Paper No. 10/47, February 2010; Renae Merle, "A Guide to the Financial Crisis—10 Years Later," *Washington Post,* September 10, 2018.
52. Chapman and Masie, "Carbon Offsets All They're Cracked Up to Be?"

CHAPTER 12: LITIGATING LABOR

1. Ellen Berrey et al., *Rights on Trial: How Workplace Discrimination Law Perpetuates Inequality* (Chicago University Press, 2017).
2. Berrey et al., *Rights on Trial,* 127.
3. Rebecca Rainey, "Inadequate Labor Department Resources Stymie Enforcement Efforts," *Bloomberg,* November 7, 2023.
4. Randy J. Kozel and David Rosenberg, "Solving the Nuisance-Value Settlement Problem: Mandatory Summary Judgment," *Virginia Law Review* 90, no. 7 (2004):1849–1907.
5. Cynthia L. Eastlund, "Economic Rationality and Union Avoidance: Misunderstanding the National Labor Relations Act," *Texas Law Review* 71 (1993): 921, 927.
6. Vivia Chen, "Class Action Killers: Paul Hastings," *American Lawyer,* January 1, 2010.
7. "Class and Collective Actions," Proskauer Rose LLP, accessed June 22, 2025 (emphasis added).

8. In 2017, Wal-Mart changed its name to Walmart.
9. Wal-Mart Stores, Inc. v. Dukes, 564 US 338, 371 (2011).
10. Bryce Covert, "Nearly Two Decades Ago, Women Across the Country Sued Walmart for Discrimination. They're Not Done Fighting," *Time*, May 9, 2019.
11. Dahlia Lithwick, "Class Dismissed: The Supreme Court Decides That the Women of Wal-Mart Can't Have Their Day in Court," *Slate*, June 20, 2011.
12. Some of these firms include Skadden, Orrick, Arnold and Porter, Seyfarth, and even my old firm Sidley Austin.
13. Lee Epstein et al., "How Business Fares in the Supreme Court," *Minnesota Law Review* 97 (2013): 1431–72.
14. *Wal-Mart Stores, Inc.*, 350.
15. Alix Valenti, "Class Actions Ten Years After *Wal-Mart Stores, Inc. v. Dukes*: Difficult But Not Impossible," *Atlantic Law Journal* 24 (2022): 2, 27 (detailing studies describing the decline in class action certifications, class action lawsuits, and settlement figures post-*Dukes*).
16. Stephanie Bornstein and Joseph M. Sellers, "The Legacy of *Wal-Mart v. Dukes* and the Administrative Response," *ABA Journal of Labor and Employment Law* 37 (2023): 289, 292.
17. Richard Thompson Ford, "Discounting Discrimination: *Dukes v. Wal-Mart* Proves That Yesterday's Civil Rights Laws Can't Keep Up with Today's Economy," *Harvard Law and Policy Review* 5, no. 1 (2011): 69, 78.
18. See e.g., US Equal Employment Opportunity Commission, "Walmart, Inc. to Pay $20 Million to Settle EEOC Nationwide Hiring Discrimination Case," September 10, 2020; Michael Sainato, "Walmart Facing Gender Discrimination Lawsuits from Female Employees," *Guardian*, February 18, 2019.
19. Ihna Mangundayao et al., "More Than $3 Billion in Stolen Wages Recovered for Workers Between 2017 and 2020," Economic Policy Institute, December 22, 2021.
20. Martha Ross et al., "A Closer Look at Low-Wage Workers Across the Country," *Brookings*, March 2020.
21. David Cooper and Teresa Kroeger, "Employers Steal Billions from Workers' Paychecks Each Year: Survey Data Show Millions of Workers Are Paid Less Than the Minimum Wage, at Significant Cost to Taxpayers and State Economies," Economic Policy Institute, May 10, 2017.
22. Grace Elletson, "MVP: Duane Morris' Gerald L. Maatman Jr.," *Law360*, February 14, 2025.
23. Crook v. PJ Operations, LLC, No. CV 5:21-321-KKC, 2024 WL 1048136 (E.D. Ky. Mar. 11, 2024).
24. Noah Smith, "Uber Better Not Be the Future of Work," *Bloomberg*, March 8, 2018.
25. Ehret v. Uber Technologies, Inc., 68 F.Supp.3d 1121 (2014).
26. Charlotte S. Alexander, "Misclassification and Antidiscrimination: An Empirical Analysis," *Minnesota Law Review* 101 (2017): 907, 910.
27. David Weil, "Lots of Employees Get Misclassified as Contractors. Here's Why It Matters," *Harvard Business Review*, July 5, 2017.
28. Dynamex Operations W. v. Superior Ct., 4 Cal. 5th 903, 917, 416 P.3d 1, 8 (2018)
29. California Trucking Association v. Bonta, 723 F. Supp. 3d 920 (S.D. Cal. Mar. 15, 2024); Olson v. California, 104 F.4th 66 (9th Cir. 2024).
30. Veena Dubal, "The New Racial Wage Code," *Harvard Law and Policy Review* 15 (2021):

511, 516–517; Faiz Siddiqui and Nitasha Tiku, "Uber and Lyft Used Sneaky Tactics to Avoid Making Drivers Employees in California, Voters Say. Now, They're Going National," *Washington Post*, November 17, 2020.
31. Economic Policy Institute, "Union Workers Are Paid 11.2% More and Have Greater Access to Health Insurance and Paid Sick Days Than Their Nonunion Counterparts," press release, August 25, 2020.
32. Josh Bivens et al., "Unions Promote Racial Equity," Economic Policy Institute Fact Sheet, July 31, 2023; Aurelia Glass, "How Labor Unions Help Reduce the Pay Gap for Disabled Workers," Center for American Progress, December 6, 2023.
33. Justin McCarthy, "U.S. Approval of Labor Unions at Highest Point Since 1965," Gallup, August 30, 2022.
34. Alexander Saxton, *The Indispensable Enemy: Labor and the Anti-Chinese Movement in California* (University of California Press, 1971).
35. Teamsters v. United States, 431 US 324 (1977); James B. Jacobs, *Mobsters, Unions, and Feds: The Mafia and the American Labor Movement* (New York University Press, 2006).
36. Ian Kullgren, "Why Didn't Unions Stop Sexual Harassment?," *Politico*, November 14, 2017.
37. "Union Bucking," *Oxford Reference* (online), accessed June 22, 2025.
38. "Union Avoidance," Barnes and Thornburg LLP, accessed October 10, 2025 (emphasis added).
39. Robert Michael Smith, *From Blackjacks to Briefcases: A History of Commercialized Strikebreaking and Unionbusting in the United States* (Ohio University Press, 2003), 102.
40. Committee on Education and Labor, Subcommittee on Labor-Management Relations, *The Forgotten Law: Disclosure of Consultant and Employer Activity Under the LMRDA*, vol. 4 (US GPO, 1985).
41. Celine McNicholas et al., "Unlawful: U.S. Employers Are Charged with Violating Federal Law in 41.5% of All Union Election Campaigns," Economic Policy Institute, December 11, 2019.
42. Aída Chávez, "Attorneys from Union-Busting Law Firms Are Throwing Support Behind Joe Biden," *Intercept*, January 31, 2020.
43. Alex N. Press, "Duke University Is Trying to Turn Back Time on Graduate Worker Unions," *Jacobin*, March 9, 2023; Daniel Moattar, "University of Chicago Grad Students, After Being Told Their Labor Union Election Was Irregular, Vote Anyway," *In These Times*, October 17, 2017.
44. Emily Steinlight and Amy C. Offner, "Faculty Should Not Participate in Penn's Antiunion Campaigns," *The Daily Pennsylvanian*, August 31, 2023.
45. Peter Perl, "The Battle of the Airport Hilton," *Washington Post Magazine*, April 6, 1997.
46. John Logan, "Consultants, Lawyers, and the 'Union Free' Movement in the USA Since the 1970s," *Industrial Relations Journal* 33, no.3 (2002), 209.
47. Steve Ellman, "Labor Pains," Law.com, May 31, 2001.
48. Kevin T. Dugan, "Big Law Firms Are Donating Pro Bono Hours to Block Unions at Legal Nonprofits Where Their Partners Are Board Members," *Business Insider*, June 7, 2021.
49. Shannon, "In Kansas, 'ACLU' Apparently Stands for 'Another Corporate Lackey Unmasked,'" *United Media Guild*, September 1, 2020.
50. Nicole S. Cohen and Greig de Peuter, *New Media Unions: Organizing Digital Journalists* (Routledge, 2020), 44.

51. Andrew McCormick, "A Law Firm in the Trenches Against Media Unions," *Columbia Journalism Review*, December 13, 2018.
52. Reid Cherlin et al., "The 50 Most Powerful People in Washington," *GQ*, January 18, 2012.
53. Cherlin et al., "The 50 Most Powerful People."
54. Rachel Sherman, *Class Acts: Service and Inequality in Luxury Hotels* (University of California Press, 2007); Oxfam Canada, "Tourism's Dirty Secret: The Exploitation of Hotel Housekeepers," October 2017, 12.
55. Oxfam Canada, "Tourism's Dirty Secret," 11.
56. CP Anchorage Hotel 2 d/b/a Hilton Anchorage & Unite Here! Loc. 878, Afl-Cio, 371 NLRB No. 151 (Sept. 29, 2022).
57. National Labor Relations Act, 29 USC. § 158(a)(1); § 158(a)(5) (2020).
58. CP Anchorage Hotel 2, LLC v. National Labor Relations Board., 98 F.4th 314 (DC Cir. 2024).
59. Securities and Exchange Commission v. Jarkesy, 603 US ___ (2024); Consumer Financial Protection Bureau v. Community Financial Services Association of America, Ltd., 601 US 416 (2024); Loper Bright Enterprises v. Raimondo, 603 US 369 (2024); Starbucks Corp. v. McKinney, 602 US ___ (2024).

INTAKE

1. Association of American Law Schools, *Before the JD: Undergraduate Views on Law School* (Gallup, 2018), 43.
2. David Goldberg, *Black Firefighters and the FDNY: The Struggle for Jobs, Justice, and Equity in New York City* (University of North Carolina Press, 2020) (describing racial exclusion in New York City's fire department); Roscoe C. Scarborough, "Risk a Lot to Save a Lot: How Firefighters Decide Whose Life Matters," *Sociological Forum* 32, no. S1 (December 2017): 1073–92 (sociologist-firefighter describing the tension between the egalitarian nature of public service and the reality of prejudiced individuals).
3. As one scholar notes, "As university employees, we are implicated, for example, by working in and drawing a wage from institutions that burden students with debt (a difficult contradiction with which we must tarry)." Remi Joseph-Salisbury and Laura Connelly, *Anti-Racist Scholar-Activism* (Manchester University Press, 2021), 198.
4. Kentucky Department of Education, "Minimum Salary Schedule for Certified Staff," Office of Career and Technical Education, accessed September 30, 2025.
5. Kentucky Department of Public Advocacy, "Public Defender Attorney Positions," (2024), accessed September 30, 2025.
6. Frank Bruni, "The Horror of Smug Liberals," *New York Times*, March 18, 2017.
7. Verna Williams, "Public Interest Attorneys Are Key to Preserving Voting Rights," Law360, May 17, 2024.
8. Catherine R. Albiston and Laura Beth Nielsen, "Funding the Cause: How Public Interest Law Organizations Fund Their Activities and Why It Matters for Social Change," *Law and Social Inquiry* 39, no.1 (Winter 2014): 80.
9. Alan K. Chen and Scott Cummings, *Public Interest Lawyering: A Contemporary Perspective* (Aspen Publishing, 2014). See also Steven M. Teles, *The Rise of the Conservative Legal Movement: The Battle for Control of the Law* (Princeton University Press, 2008); Ann Southworth, *Lawyers of the Right: Professionalizing the Conservative Coalition* (University of Chicago Press, 2008).

CHAPTER 13: HOW WE GOT HERE

1. This pattern pervades American social policy: welfare programs that provide barely subsistence-level benefits with time limits rather than addressing poverty's root causes; healthcare systems that offer piecemeal coverage tied to employment or disability status while avoiding universal care; and education funding through Title I supplements that maintain rather than challenge property tax-based inequalities.
2. I have written about this extensively and it is the subject of a separate book. See e.g., Shaun Ossei-Owusu, "The Sixth Amendment Façade: The Racial Evolution of the Right to Counsel," *University of Pennsylvania Law Review* 167, no. 5 (2019): 1161–1239; Shaun Ossei-Owusu, "Civil vs. Criminal Legal Aid," *Southern California Law Review* 94 (2021): 1561–1617. This is the topic of my forthcoming book with Princeton University Press.
3. Shira A. Scheindlin, "Legal Services-Past and Present," *Cornell Law Review* 59, no. 5 (1974): 967.
4. Ange-Marie Hancock, *The Politics of Disgust: The Public Identity of the Welfare Queen* (New York University Press, 2004).
5. Strickland v. Washington, 466 US 668 (1984).
6. Muniz v. Smith, 647 F.3d 619 (6th Cir. 2011).
7. Mayfield v. Woodford, 270 F.3d 915, 940-941 (9th Cir. 2001). The court did not find ineffectiveness on issues of guilt but did on sentencing issues; Sara Catania, "A Killer Job," *LAWeekly*, January 23, 2002.
8. David Luban, "Taking Out the Adversary: The Assault on Progressive Public Interest Lawyers," *California Law Review* 91, no. 1 (2003): 209–46; Philip Hamburger, *Purchasing Submission: Conditions, Power, and Freedom* (Harvard University Press, 2021).
9. Luban, "Taking Out the Adversary," 224.
10. Michael T. Taussig, *Defacement: Public Secrecy and the Labor of the Negative* (Stanford University Press, 1999)
11. Maryland Pro Bono Resource Center, *Jenny Egan, Esq.*, accessed 2024.
12. Cara McClellan, *Our Girls, Our Future: Investing in Opportunity and Reducing Reliance on the Criminal Justice System in Baltimore* (LDF Thurgood Marshall Institute, 2018).
13. Jacob Brogan, "'The 'How Does a Public Defender Work?' Transcript," *Slate*, May 23, 2017.
14. Brogan, "'How Does a Public Defender Work?'"
15. *Minor Crimes, Massive Waste: The Terrible Toll of America's Broken Misdemeanor Courts* (National Association of Criminal Defense Lawyers, 2009), 39.
16. Tina Peng, "I'm a Public Defender. It's Impossible for Me to Do a Good Job Representing My Clients," *Washington Post*, September 3, 2015 (emphasis added).
17. Eve Brensike Primus, "Culture as a Structural Problem in Indigent Defense," *Minnesota Law Review* 100 (2016): 1769, 1771.
18. Primus, "Culture as a Structural Problem," 1776.
19. Primus, "Culture as a Structural Problem," 1776.
20. Jonathan A. Rapping, "Directing the Winds of Change: Using Organizational Culture to Reform Indigent Defense," *Loyola Journal of Public Interest Law* 9 (2008): 177, 191.
21. Alexandra Natapoff, "Speechless: The Silencing of Criminal Defendants," *New York Law Review* 80, no. 5 (2005): 1449, 1474.
22. Kate Taylor, *System Overload: The Costs of Under-Resourcing Public Defense* (Justice Policy Institute, July 2011).
23. Matthew Clair, *Privilege and Punishment: How Race and Class Matter in Criminal Court*

(Princeton University Press, 2020); Nicole Gonzalez Van Cleve, *Crook County: Racism and Injustice in America's Largest Criminal Court* (Stanford University Press, 2017).
24. Clair, *Privilege and Punishment*, 13.
25. Zohra Ahmed, "Bargaining for Abolition," *Fordham Law Review* 90, no. 5 (2022): 1953, 1958.
26. Legal Services Corporation. "The Justice Gap: The Report," accessed August 21, 2025.
27. Corey S. Shdaimah, *Negotiating Justice: Progressive Lawyering, Low-Income Clients, and the Quest for Social Change* (New York University Press, 2009), 151–52.
28. Marc Feldman, "Political Lessons: Legal Services for the Poor," *Georgetown Law Journal* 83 (1995): 1529, 1552–53.
29. Carol Ruth Silver, "The Imminent Failure of Legal Services for the Poor: Why and How to Limit Caseload," *Journal of Urban Law* 46 (1969): 217.
30. Diana Calais, "Ethical Violations Resulting from Excessive Workloads in Legal Aid Offices: Who Should Bear the Responsibility for Preventing Them?," *Loyola University Chicago Law Journal* 16, no. 3 (Spring 1985): 589, 594–95.
31. Shdaimah, *Negotiating Justice*, 149; Tina Lee, *Catching a Case: Inequality and Fear in New York City's Child Welfare System* (Rutgers University Press, 2016), 168.
32. Michael B. Katz, *The Undeserving Poor: America's Enduring Confrontation with Poverty* (Oxford University Press, 2013).
33. Jay Doran and Beth Leonard, "The Power of Story: How Legal Aid Narratives Affect Perceptions of Poverty," *Seattle Journal for Social Justice* 15, no. 2 (2016): 333, 348.
34. Doran and Leonard, "The Power of Story," 353.

CHAPTER 14: POWER, PREJUDICE, AND PATERNALISM IN THE PINK GHETTO

1. Andrea Estes, "Rachael Rollins Retreats from Attack on 'Overwhelmingly Privileged' Public Defenders After Strong Backlash," *Boston Globe*, May 7, 2020.
2. Rashaan Hall, "Uncomfortable Truths," ACLU, accessed August 21, 2025; Ashley Nellis, *The Color of Justice: Racial and Ethnic Disparity in State Prisons* (The Sentencing Project, 2021), 5.
3. Black Public Defender Association, "BPDA Statement on Remarks Made by Suffolk County District Attorney Rachael Rollins," May 12, 2020.
4. They were right on the ethical front; Rollins resigned almost three years later after being investigated for other forms of misconduct. Jullian Harris-Calvin, Premal Dharia, "The Suffolk County DA's Attack on Public Defenders Was Misguided," *The Appeal*, May 22, 2020.
5. Alexis Hoag, "Black on Black Representation," *New York University Law Review* 96 (November 2021):1493, 1525.
6. Sandra Simkins, "The 'Pink Ghettos' of Public Interest Law: An Open Secret," *Buffalo Law Review* 68, no. 3 (2020): 857, 878–79.
7. Simkins, "The 'Pink Ghettos,'" 857, 878–79; But see Robert Nelson et al., *After the JD III: Third Results from a National Study of Legal Careers* (American Bar Association and NALP Foundation for Law Career Research and Education, 2022), which notes some movement for lawyers in this setting.
8. Felice Batlan, *Women and Justice for the Poor: A History of Legal Aid, 1863–1945* (Cambridge University Press, 2015).
9. American Bar Association, *2023: Profile of the Legal Profession* (ABA, November 2023).

10. National Association for Law Placement, *The Demographics of Jobs from 1991–2021* (NALP, March 2023).
11. Cynthia F. Epstein and Hella Winston, "The Salience of Gender in the Choice of Law Careers in the Public Interest," *Buffalo Journal of Gender, Law and Social Policy* 18 (2009): 21–41; Pamela A. Wilkins, "Stories That Kill: Masculinity and Capital Prosecutors' Closing Arguments," *Cleveland State Law Review* 71, no. 4 (2023): 1147, 1159; Ann C. McGinley, "Masculine Law Firms," *FIU Law Review* 8 (2013): 423–46.
12. Lee Norton et al., "Burnout and Compassion Fatigue: What Lawyers Need to Know," *UMKC Law Review* 84, no. 4 (2016): 987, 997.
13. National Association for Law Placement, *NALP's Public Service Attorney Salary Survey Shows Pay Remains Lowest at Civil Legal Services Organizations* (NALP, 2024).
14. National Association for Law Placement, *2023 Associate Salary Survey* (NALP, 2023).
15. Simpkins, "The 'Pink Ghettos,'" 882.
16. Epstein and Winston, "The Salience of Gender," 38; Robert L. Nelson, *The Making of Lawyers' Careers: Inequality and Opportunity in the American Legal Profession* (University of Chicago Press, 2023).
17. Averil Y. Clarke, *Inequalities of Love: College-Educated Black Women and the Barriers to Romance and Family* (Duke University Press, 2011). See also Corina Boar and Danial Lashkari, "Occupational Choice and the Intergenerational Mobility of Welfare." Working Paper No. w29381 (National Bureau of Economic Research, 2021), which describes how parental income allows children to pursue jobs with lower pay but higher non-monetary rewards.
18. Sandra Simkins, "Public Interest Burnout: Seven Factors That Increase the Risk," *DePaul Journal for Social Justice* 17, no. 1 (2023): 1, 2.
19. Andrew P. Levin and Scott Greisberg, "Vicarious Trauma in Attorneys," *Pace Law Review* 24, no. 1 (Fall 2003): 245, 248–49.
20. Atinuke O. Adediran, "Nonprofit Board Composition," *Ohio State Law Journal* 83 (2022): 357, 388.
21. US Code, 42 USC. § 2996f(c).
22. Adediran, "Nonprofit Board Composition," 405.
23. Adediran, "Nonprofit Board Composition," 402; Paul E. Lee and Mary M. Lee, "Reflections from the Bottom of the Well: Racial Bias in the Provision of Legal Services to the Poor," *Clearinghouse Review* 27 (Special Issue 1993): 311, 315–16.
24. Adediran, "Nonprofit Board Composition," 399.
25. Atinuke O. Adediran, "Racial Allies," *Fordham Law Review* 90, no. 5 (2022): 2151, 2174.
26. Adediran, "Racial Allies," 2188; Christopher Ingraham, "Three Quarters of Whites Don't Have Any Non-White Friends," *Washington Post*, August 25, 2014.
27. Adediran, "Racial Allies," 2189.
28. Adediran, "Racial Allies," 2200.
29. Jamelia N. Morgan, "Reflections on Representing Incarcerated People with Disabilities: Ableism in Prison Reform Litigation," *Denver Law Review* 96, no. 4 (2019): 973, 986.
30. Morgan, "Representing Incarcerated People with Disabilities," 980.
31. Morgan, "Representing Incarcerated People with Disabilities," 986, 980, 987.
32. Shaun Ossei-Owusu, "The New Penal Bureaucrats," *University of Pennsylvania Law Review* 170, no. 6 (June 2022): 1389, 1418; Danielle M. Romain Dagenhardt, "Observing Gender and Race Discourses in Probation Review Hearings," *Feminist Criminology* 15, no. 4 (2020): 492, 501.

33. Ossei-Owusu, "New Penal Bureaucrats," 1419; M. J. Gathings and Kylie Parrotta, "The Use of Gendered Narratives in the Courtroom: Constructing an Identity Worthy of Leniency," *Journal of Contemporary Ethnography* 42, no. 6 (2013). 668, 675, 679.
34. Eva S. Nilsen, "The Criminal Defense Lawyer's Reliance on Bias and Prejudice," *Georgetown Journal of Legal Ethics* 8 (Fall 1994): 1, 44.
35. Abbe Smith, "Defending Defending: The Case for Unmitigated Zeal on Behalf of People Who Do Terrible Things," *Hofstra Law Review* 28, no. 4 (2000): 925, 953.
36. Nilsen, "Criminal Defense Lawyer's Reliance," 1.
37. Nilsen, "Criminal Defense Lawyer's Reliance," 10. Professional conduct rules prohibit lawyers from discrimination based on race, gender, and other categories, but exclude "legitimate advice or advocacy"—a loophole that could cover such tactical exploitation. American Bar Association, "Model Rules of Professional Conduct, Rule8.4(g)," accessed August 22, 2025; Nicole Gonzalez Van Cleve, *Crook County: Racism and Injustice in America's Largest Criminal Court* (Stanford University Press, 2017), 104–20; Matthew Clair, *Privilege and Punishment: How Race and Class Matter in Criminal Court* (Princeton University Press, 2020).
38. For a view that opposes Smith's, see Anthony V. Alfieri, "Defending Racial Violence," *Columbia Law Review* 95, no. 5 (1995): 1301–42.
39. Theodore Eisenberg and Sheri Lynn Johnson, "Implicit Racial Attitudes of Death Penalty Lawyers," *DePaul Law Review* 53, no. 4 (2003): 1539–45.
40. Eisenberg and Johnson, "Implicit Racial Attitudes," 1540.
41. Vanessa A. Edkins, "Defense Attorney Plea Recommendations and Client Race: Does Zealous Representation Apply Equally to All?," *Law and Human Behavior* 35, no. 5 (2011): 413–25.
42. Van Cleve, *Crook County*, 158. Clair, *Privilege and Punishment*, 141.
43. Kristin Henning, "Race, Paternalism, and the Right to Counsel," *American Criminal Law Review* 54 (2017): 649–94.
44. L. Song Richardson and Phillip Atiba Goff, "Implicit Racial Bias in Public Defender Triage," *Yale Law Journal* 122 (2013): 2626–49.
45. Henning, "Race, Paternalism," 667–79.
46. Henning, "Race, Paternalism," 671.
47. Henning, "Race, Paternalism," 671.
48. Henning, "Race, Paternalism," 674.
49. Jerry Kang and Mahzarin R. Banaji, "Fair Measures: A Behavioral Realist Revision of 'Affirmative Action,'" *California Law Review* 94, no. 4 (2006): 1063, 1072.

CHAPTER 15: HIGH-LEVEL IMPACT LITIGATION AND INEQUALITY

1. Lilie Chouliaraki, *Wronged: The Weaponization of Victimhood* (Columbia University Press, 2024).
2. David Cole, "Defending Speech We Hate," American Civil Liberties Union, February 20, 2024.
3. Bryan Marquard, "John W. Roberts, Who Led the State ACLU in Protecting Free-Speech and Abortion Rights, Dies at 89," *Boston Globe*, May 26, 2024.
4. American Civil Liberties Union, "Shall We Defend Free Speech for Nazis in America?" (October 1934), 2 (emphasis added).
5. Mary Anne Franks, *The Cult of the Constitution* (Stanford University Press, 2019), 156.

6. American Civil Liberties Union of Virginia, "Why We Represented the Alt-Right in Charlottesville," August 28, 2017.
7. A smug point that, in isolation, could be read as ignoring the ways the First Amendment has failed to protect Black Lives Matter (BLM) protestors and ignores the international aspects of the movement that are not subject to American law. Michael Powell, "Once a Bastion of Free Speech, the A.C.L.U. Faces an Identity Crisis," *New York Times*, September 28, 2021.
8. Richard Delgado and Jean Stefancic, *Must We Defend Nazis? Why the First Amendment Should Not Protect Hate Speech and White Supremacy* (New York University Press, 2018), 114.
9. Franks, *The Cult of the Constitution*, 156.
10. Powell, "Once a Bastion."
11. The only exceptions apply to federal crimes, such as abetting terrorism, and intellectual property violations, like failing to take down copyrighted materials after being notified.
12. Cory Doctorow, "Wanna Make Big Tech Monopolies Even Worse? Kill Section 230," Electronic Frontier Foundation, May 24, 2024; Jason Kelley, "Section 230 Is Good, Actually," Electronic Frontier Foundation, December 3, 2020.
13. Brief of Scholars of Civil Rights and Social Justice as *Amici Curiae* in Support of Respondent, 10, 15, Gonzalez v. Google LLC, 598 US 617 (2023).
14. Brief of Scholars of Civil Rights and Social Justice at 11.
15. Andrew Gilden, "The Queer Limits of Revenge Porn Laws," *Boston College Law Review* 64, no. 4 (2023): 801, 861.
16. Danielle Keats Citron, *Hate Crimes in Cyberspace* (Harvard University Press, 2014), 12.
17. See, for example, the definition for cyberharassment in the Rhode Island General Assembly Laws Ann. § 11-52-4.2 and in the New Jersey Statutes. Ann. § 2C:33-4.1.
18. Pew Research Center, "The State of Online Harassment," January 13, 2021.
19. Carafano v. Metrosplash.com, Inc., 339 F.3d 1119, 1121 (9th Cir. 2003).
20. Herrick v. Grindr, LLC, 306 F. Supp. 3d 579, 585 (S.D.N.Y. 2018), aff'd, 765 F. App'x 586 (2d Cir. 2019). Carrie Goldberg, "Herrick v. Grindr: Why Section 230 of the Communications Decency Act Must Be Fixed," *Lawfare*, August 14, 2019.
21. EFF filed a brief in this case supporting Grindr.
22. Rachel Weiner, "College Student Who Hosted Racist 'Swatting' Group Is Sentenced to 33 Months," *Washington Post*, March 15, 2021.
23. Ali Breland, "Alt-Right Trolls Are Trying to Sabotage Black Lives Matter Chatrooms," *Mother Jones*, June 8, 2020.
24. Anemona Hartocollis, "After Writing an Anti-Israel Letter, Harvard Students Are Doxxed," *New York Times*, October 18, 2023.
25. Anti-Defamation League (ADL), "Online Hate and Harassment: The American Experience 2023," accessed August 22, 2025; ADL, "Doxing Should Be Illegal. Reporting Extremists Should Not," January 15, 2021.
26. Decca Muldowney, "Info Wars: Inside the Left's Online Efforts to Out White Supremacists," *Propublica*, October 30, 2017.
27. ADL, "Doxing Should Be Illegal."
28. Pengfei Zhang and Kara Curtis, "The Special Interest Politics of Online Intermediary Liability," unpublished paper, (School of Economic, Political, and Policy Science, University of Texas at Dallas, March 2024), 1–37.
29. New York State Rifle and Pistol Association Inc. v. Bruen, 597 US 1 (2022).

30. McDonald v. City of Chicago, 561 US 742 (2010); District of Columbia v. Heller, 554 US 570 (2008).
31. 597 US 1 (2022).
32. See e.g., Matthew Guariglia, *Police and the Empire City: Race and the Origins of Modern Policing in New York* (Duke University Press, 2023); Clarence Taylor, *Fight the Power: African Americans and the Long History of Police Brutality in New York City* (New York University Press, 2021); Floyd, et al. v. City of New York, et al., 959 F. Supp. 2d 540 (S.D.N.Y. 2013).
33. Bruen, 12–13 (2022).
34. "Brief of the Black Attorneys of Legal Aid, The Bronx Defenders, Brooklyn Defender Services, et al. as *Amici Curiae* in Support of Petitioners," 7, New York State Rifle & Pistol Ass'n, Inc. v. Bruen, 597 US 1 (2022).
35. Avinash Samarth et al., "Second Class," *Inquest*, November 5, 2021.
36. Elie Mystal, "Why Are Public Defenders Backing a Major Assault on Gun Control?," *The Nation*, July 26, 2021.
37. Mitchell L Doucette et al., "Impact of Changes to Concealed-Carry Weapons Laws on Fatal and Nonfatal Violent Crime, 1980–2019," *American Journal of Epidemiology* 192, no. 3 (2023): 342–55; John J. Donohue et al., "Right-to-Carry Laws and Violent Crime: A Comprehensive Assessment Using Panel Data and a State-Level Synthetic Control Analysis," *Journal of Empirical Legal Studies* 16 (2019): 198–247.
38. Michael Sigel, *The Impact of State-Level Firearms Laws on Homicide Rates by Race/Ethnicity* (National Criminal Justice Reference Service, 2020).
39. Shannon Schumacher, et al., "Americans' Experiences with Gun-Related Violence, Injuries, And Deaths," KFF, April 11, 2023.
40. Marissa Edmund, "Guns and Violence Against Women," *Center for American Progress*, January 5, 2022.
41. Douglas Belkin, "The Man Behind the Push to End Affirmative Action," *Wall Street Journal*, June 29, 2023.
42. Juliet Hooker, *Black Grief/White Grievance: The Politics of Loss* (Princeton University Press, 2023); Ashley Jardina, *White Identity Politics* (Cambridge University Press, 2019).
43. Fisher v. University of Texas at Austin, 579 US 365 (2016); Fisher v. University of Texas at Austin, 570 US 297 (2013).
44. Shelby County v. Holder, 570 US 529 (2013); Northwest Austin Municipal Utility District No. One v. Holder, 557 US 193 (2009).
45. Prew Research Center, "More Americans Disapprove Than Approve of Colleges Considering Race, Ethnicity in Admissions Decisions," June 8, 2023.
46. Niel G. Ruiz et al., "Asian Americans Hold Mixed Views Around Affirmative Action," Pew Research Center, June 8, 2023.
47. Jerry Kang, "Asians Used, Asians Lose: Strict Scrutiny from Internment to SFFA," *California Law Review* 113 (June 2025): 979–96; Vinay Harpalani, "Asian Americans, Racial Stereotypes, and Elite University Admissions," *Boston University Law Review* 102, no. 1 (2022): 233–326; Claire Jean Kim, "The Racial Triangulation of Asian Americans," *Politics and Society* 27, no. 1 (1999): 105–38.
48. Lavender Au, "Chinese Students Feel a Familiar Chill in America," *Atlantic*, July 2, 2025; Helen Gao, "Clash of Civilizations: The Confusion of Being a Chinese Student in America," *Atlantic*, December 12, 2011.
49. Frank L. Samson, "Multiple-Group Threat and Malleable White Attitudes Towards

Academic Merit," *Du Bois Review Social Science Research on Race* 10, no. 1 (Spring 2013): 233–60.
50. John Bunzel and Jeffrey Au, "Diversity or Discrimination? Asian Americans in College," *Public Interest* 87 (Spring 1987): 59.
51. Jane Hyun, *Breaking the Bamboo Ceiling: Career Strategies for Asians* (Harper Business, 2006); Ling-chi Wang, "*Lau v. Nichols*: The Right of Limited-English-Speaking Students," *Amerasia Journal* 2, no. 2 (1974): 16–45.
52. Derrick Bell, "Diversity's Distractions," *Columbia Law Review* 103, no. 6 (2003): 1622–33; Osamudia R. James, "White Like Me: The Negative Impact of the Diversity Rationale on White Identity Formation," *New York University Law Review* 89, no. 2 (May 2014): 425–512; Regents of the University of California v. Bakke, 438 US 265 (1978).
53. Erik Eckholm, "Legal Alliance Gains Host of Court Victories for Conservative Christian Movement," *New York Times*, May 11, 2014.
54. Alliance Defending Freedom, "Alan Sears, Founder," accessed August 26, 2025.
55. Melissa Gira Grant, "The Mysterious Case of the Fake Gay Marriage Website, the Real Straight Man, and the Supreme Court," *The New Republic*, June 29, 2023.
56. Ryan Gabrielson, "It's a Fact: Supreme Court Errors Aren't Hard to Find," *ProPublica*, October 17, 2017.
57. Richard M. Re, "Does the Discourse on *303 Creative* Portend a Standing Realignment?," *Notre Dame Law Review Reflection* 99, no. 1 (2023): 67–92.
58. Masterpiece Cakeshop v. Colorado Civil Rights Commission, 584 US 617 (2018).
59. Joe Patrice, "The Supreme Court Is Lying to You About This Web Designer Opinion," *Above the Law*, June 30, 2023.
60. Emma Brown and Jon Swaine, "Amy Coney Barrett, Supreme Court Nominee, Spoke at Program Founded to Inspire a 'Distinctly Christian Worldview in Every Area of Law,'" *Washington Post*, September 27, 2020.
61. Pew Research Center, "Religious 'Nones' in America: Who They Are and What They Believe," January 24, 2024; but see Gregory A. Smith et al., "Decline of Christianity in the U.S. Has Slowed, May Have Leveled Off," Pew Research Center, February 26, 2025 (showing that it has slowed).
62. Josh Moody and Sara Weissman, "Religious Freedom as a Defense for DEI?," *Inside Higher Ed*, March 13, 2025; Sophie Hills et al., "Is Sanctuary Covered by the First Amendment?," *Christian Science Monitor*, January 30, 2025.
63. Guido Calabresi and Philip Bobbitt, *Tragic Choices: The Conflicts Society Confronts in the Allocation of Tragically Scarce Resources* (W. W. Norton, 1978).

CONCLUSION

1. The weaponization of Title VI and threats to tax endowments may change this reality.
2. Shaun Ossei-Owusu, "The New Penal Bureaucrats," *University of Pennsylvania Law Review* 170, no. 6 (2022): 1389–1449.
3. David B. Wilkins, "Do Clients Have Ethical Obligations to Lawyers? Some Lessons from the Diversity Wars," *Georgetown Journal of Legal Ethics* 11 (1998): 855, 884.
4. Erin Mulvane et al., "The Law Firms That Appeased Trump—And Angered Their Clients," *The Wall Street Journal*, June 1, 2025.
5. Either because they may violate contractual agreements or terms of service, make the life of workers harder, or, if they came across the desk of the wrong prosecutor, might be interpreted as harassment. See e.g., Title 18 of Pennsylvania's Statutes: 18 Pa. C.S. § 2709.

6. Carissa Byrne Hessick and Michael Morse, "Picking Prosecutors," *Iowa Law Review* 105 (2020): 1545–90.
7. Bidish Sarma, "Using Deterrence Theory to Promote Prosecutorial Accountability," *Lewis and Clark Law Review* 21, no. 3 (2017): 573, 592; Stephanos Bibas, "Prosecutorial Regulation Versus Prosecutorial Accountability," *University of Pennsylvania Law Review* 157, no. 4 (April 2009): 959, 961.
8. Russell M. Gold, "Promoting Democracy in Prosecution," *Washington Law Review* 86 (2011): 69, 82.
9. David S. Abrams, "The Imprisoner's Dilemma: A Cost-Benefit Approach to Incarceration," *Iowa Law Review* 98, no. 3 (March 2013): 905–69; Darryl K. Brown, "Cost-Benefit Analysis in Criminal Law," *California Law Review* 92, no. 2 (2004): 323, 325.
10. Bryan A. Garner, "Jury Nullification," in *Black's Law Dictionary*, 11th ed. (Thomson Reuters, 2019).
11. Editorial Board, Texan of the Year, "Isis Brantley Fought to Make Texas Understand Black Hair," *Dallas Morning News* (December 29, 2023); Angela C Erickson, "Barriers to Braiding: How Job-Killing Licensing Laws Tangle Natural Hair Care in Needless Red Tape," Institute for Justice, July 2016.
12. Federal Rules of Evidence. Rule 606(b).
13. Damon Root, "The Originalist Case for Jury Nullification," *Reason*, January 19, 2018.
14. Ilya Somin, "Does Jury Nullification Undermine the Rule of Law?," *Volokh Conspiracy* (podcast), *Reason*, January 17, 2018.
15. United States v. Heicklen, 858 F. Supp. 2d 256 (S.D.N.Y. 2012).
16. American Bar Association, Model Rules of Professional Conduct: Rule 1.2: Scope and Representation and Allocation of Authority Between Client and Lawyer, accessed August 26, 2025; Model Rules of Professional Conduct: Rule 1.13: Organization as Client, accessed August 26, 2025.
17. Keller v. State Bar of California, 496 US 1, 14 (1990); Lathrop v. Donohue, 367 US 820, 843, (1961).
18. Connecticut General Statues, § 52-259; California Government Code § 70616.
19. These suggestions would be subject to specific rules on a state's authority to tax and spend, would require waivers where necessary, and aim to avoid excessiveness that could trigger unconstitutional takings claims.
20. Jon B. Gould et al., "Mapping the Path of *Brady* Violations: Typologies, Causes and Consequences in Erroneous Conviction Cases," *Syracuse Law Review* 71 (2021): 1061–1119.
21. Alan Feuer, "The Lawyers Protecting the N.Y.P.D. Play Hardball. Judges Are Calling Them Out," *New York Times*, September 12, 2018,
22. Marina Zaloznaya and Laura Beth Nielsen, "Mechanisms and Consequences of Professional Marginality: The Case of Poverty Lawyers Revisited," *Law and Social Inquiry* 36, no. 4 (Fall 2011): 919–944.
23. Christina Greer, "Political Tithing," *New York Amsterdam News*, June 2, 2017.
24. John Bliss, "From Idealists to Hired Guns? An Empirical Analysis of 'Public Interest Drift' in Law School," *University of California, Davis, Law Review* 51 (2018): 2017–32;' David B. Wilkins, "Doing Well by Doing Good—The Role of Public Service in the Careers of Black Corporate Lawyers," *Houston Law Review* 41 (2004): 1–91.
25. Dean Spade, *Mutual Aid: Building Solidarity During This Crisis* (Verso, 2020).

Index

Page numbers after 362 refer to notes.

ableism, 197–98, 209–12, 317–18
abolitionism, police and prison, 117–18
abortion, 46, 117, 141–44
absolute prosecutorial immunity, 182
acceptance, in contract formation, 59
accessible pedestrian signals (APS), 212
accidental harm, 80–82
accomplice liability, 119
actuarial fairness, 84–85
Adediran, Tinu, 316
Adegbile, Debo, 218
admission of wrongdoing, settling without, 205, 207
affirmative action, 7, 12, 17–18, 28, 145, 147, 334–38
airline industry, M&As in, 237
Akin Gump, 263
Alaska, 137–38
Alaska Airlines, 123
Albertson, 236–37
Alliance Defending Freedom (ADF), 294, 338–41
American Bar Association (ABA), 36–41, 44
American Bar Foundation, 12, 268
American Center for Law and Justice (ACLJ), 294
American Civil Liberties Union (ACLU), 18, 79, 90, 283, 325–27, 330
American Council for the Blind, 211–12
American Hospital Association, 239
Americans with Disabilities Act (ADA), 195, 199, 210, 211

Anderson, Candice, 122–23
Anderson, Devon, 346
AppalReD, 294
appellate review, 152, 349
arbitration, 56–57, 162–64
Arkansas, 188
Arlington, Tex., 198, 199
Arpaio, Joe, 204
Asian Americans, 62–63, 206, 335–38
associates, Big Law, 224–25
AT&T, 233
attorney licensing fees, 349–50
audits, by municipal attorneys, 353
authorization cards, 282

bail decisions, 185
Ballis, Jon, 233
banking industry, M&As in, 236
Barbalho, Helder, 261
Barnes, Anna, 208–9
Barnes and Thornburg, 281
bar readiness, 43, 47–48, 114, 152
Barrett, Amy Coney, 340
Barshay, Scott, 230
battery, 74
Bayonet Constitution, 138
Bell Atlantic, 161–62
bias, 29, 44–45, 47, 312, 319–22
Biden, Joe, 237, 248, 257, 264
Big Law (large corporate law firms), 223–28
  basic firm structure, 224
  burdens of working for, 224–25

Big Law (*continued*)
  combating inequality involving, 344–45, 353–55
  compensation in, 181, 314
  cynical view of, 225–27
  government agencies and, 252–53
  inequality as structural imperative at, 17
  litigation by, 268–87
  professional responsibility at, 40
  regulatory work by, 247–67
  role of, in global economy, 223–24
  romantic view of, 227–28
  transactional work by, 229–46
  types of work in, 22–23
bilingual jurors, 191
Black Lives Matter (BLM) protests, 329, 404
Black people
  as affirmative action spokespeople, 335–37
  criminalization of race, 116
  freedom of contract for, 61
  gentrification's impact on, 89, 90
  gun possession for, 331
  implicit bias against, 320, 322
  in legal education, 5, 8, 9
  likelihood of prosecution of, 187
  predatory lending targeting, 2
  prosecutorial discretion's impact on, 187–91
  selective enforcement against, 16
Black Public Defender Association, 311
Blackstone Legal Fellowship, 338
Black Sunday, 176–77
Blum, Edward, 334–36
Boeing, 737 Max crashes for, 123–24
Bogus, Carl, 87
Boudin, Chesa, 346
boycotts, 345
Brady, Philip, 261
Brazil, 260–62
breach, in contract law, 59, 66, 70
Bronx (New York City), 5–6, 8, 54–55, 109, 169–70, 174–77, 198, 199, 203, 331
Bronx Defenders, 169–70, 332, 333
Bronx effect, 86–87
Brown vs. Board of Education, 31–33, 365
Bud Light, 345
burglary, 120
burnout, 315
business compulsion, 68–69
Butler, Paul, 346, 347

California, 190–93, 255–57, 262, 264, 278–79, 350
California Rural Legal Assistance, 301
California Trucking Association, 278
Cambodia, 260
Canary Mission, 329
cannabis possession, 115–16
cap-and-trade programs, 257
Carafano, Christianne, 328–29
carbon offsetting, 249–50, 254–67
  additionality problem, 396
  benefits of, 256
  discursive power of Big Law, 258–59
  failure rate in, 264
  financial crisis of 2008 and, 265–67
  fraud by C-Quest Capital, 264–65
  in Global South, 259–63
  markets for, 255–56
  phantom credits in, 263–64
  regulatory lag, 257–58
  slow violence of, 256–65
  stewards of land that host, 257
care giving, 314–15
casebooks, 28–29, 368
caseloads, direct service, 303–5, 307–8
cash, carrying, 100–101
Castile, Philando, 332
Castro, Fany Kuiru, 260
Center for Family Representation (CFR), 283
Chamber of Commerce, 275
change of control provisions, 234–35
charging decisions, 178–80, 184–88
Cherokee Nation, 60–61
Chicago, Ill., 202, 205, 211–12
child care shortage, 91, 92, 103–6, 376
Chinese Exclusion Act (1882), 280
Choctaw Nation, 135
Chong people, 260
civil asset forfeiture, 90, 92, 99–103
civil procedure, 16, 149–66
  bias as topic in, 44–45
  corporate interests in, 160–65
  everyday applications of, 149
  focus of, 107, 151–54
  in local and state courts, 157–60
  mechanical nature of learning, 149–50
  municipal attorneys' use of, 207–9
  omission of issues of poverty in, 154–57

resource-based disparities in impact, 150–51
silent endorsement of, 108
structural failures in, 165–66
in workplace litigation, 271, 275–76
civil rights
constitutional torts and, 77–79
contested advocacy to undermine, 17–18
contract law and, 61–62, 68
digital, 327–30
in employment law, 268–69, 273–76
impact litigation on, 338–41
mass incarceration and, 113
municipal defenses for violations of, 170–71, 195, 198, 206–7, 218–19
public interest attorneys' work on, 292, 298
Civil Rights Act (1866), 61
Class Action Fairness Act (2005), 86
class action lawsuits, 162, 275–77, 302
class inequality, 1, 10–14, 89, 90, 102–3, 110, 112–13, 116, 117, 125, 180
classroom engagement, 31–34
Clean Water Act, 248
climate change, 253–56, 262, 266–67
clinical education, 364
Clinton, Bill, 293
closing statements, 191
coded capital, 263
Code of Federal Regulations, 250
cold calling, 31–34
collateralized debt obligations, 266
Colombian Amazon, 260
colonialism, 133–40
Comcast, 162
Commerce Department, 226
Committee for Public Counsel Services (CPCS), 310–11
complaint, 151
compliance, 250
compliance markets, 255–56
concealed carry laws, 332
concurrent ownership, 93
Congo Basin, 259
consent, in contract law, 56–58, 61
consideration, 59
Constitution, US, 111, 127–30, 133–40
Fifteenth Amendment, 128
Fifth Amendment, 112
First Amendment, 127, 130–32, 171, 297, 325–30, 338–41

Fourteenth Amendment, 128, 147
Fourth Amendment, 111–12, 297
Property/Territory Clause, 137–40
Second Amendment, 330, 331, 333
Sixth Amendment, 297–98
Supremacy Clause, 134
Treaty Clause, 134, 138
constitutional decision-making, 141–45
constitutional interpretation, 140–47
constitutional law, 127–48
on Alaska's statehood, 137–38
Americans' understanding of, 127–28
assumptions in, 132–33
colonialism as topic in, 133–40
core topics, 107, 131–32
on exclusionary origins of Constitution, 128–30
historically selective and politically evasive approach to, 147–48
influence of politics on, 140–47
living constitutionalism vs. originalism debate in, 145–47
modalities of interpretation and decision-making, 141–45
morality in, 46
omissions from curricula, 130–31, 147–48
silent endorsement of, 108
constitutional torts, 77–79
consumer activism, 345
consumer credit contracts, 61–62
consumer fraud, 162
consumer protection laws, 171
consumers, predatory M&As and, 235–45
contested advocacy, legal inequality as, 17–18, 186, 338
contingency lawyers, 272
contract formation, 59
contract law, 54–71
Big Law firms in, 225
consent in, 56–58
focus of, 51
freedom of contract in, 59–64
lopsided economic arrangements in, 55–56, 70–71
policing the bargain in, 66–70
on predatory contracting, 54–55
presumption of understanding in, 64–66
sidelining of relevant issues in, 58

contracts
  forum selection provisions in, 163
  for sale of land, 93
  transactional work on, 231
coordinated consumer activism, 345
corporate lawyers
  inequality as structural imperative for, 17
  on public interest boards, 316
corporations
  advantages for, in regulatory cases, 248–49, 251–53
  benefits of consolidation for, 240
  civil procedure that benefits, 150, 154–55, 160–65
  costs of workplace litigation for, 273
  employment discrimination defense for, 268–69
  right to representation, 246
Costco, 275
covenants not to sue, 56–57, 68
Covington and Burling, 253
Cozen O'Connor, 282
C-Quest Capital, 264–65
criminal act, 118
criminal forfeiture, 100
criminal justice system, 109, 113–14, 117–18, 179–80
criminal law, 109–26; *See also* public defenders
  crimes focused on in, 118–21
  cruel realities of, 109
  defined, 111
  focus of, 107
  influence of politics on, 43–44
  in law education and on bar exams, 377
  prosecutors, 170, 174–94
  on purposes of punishment, 114–18
  selective attention in, 109–11, 125–26
  selective enforcement in, 16
  separation of criminal procedure and, 111–13
  silent endorsement of system in, 108
  structural critiques in, 113–14, 117–18
  white-collar crime in, 121–25
criminal negligence, 176–77
criminal procedure, 111–13, 130, 352, 377
critical race theory, 344
Cuba, 139
cultural factors, in prosecutorial decisions, 180–81

cultural fluency, of law students, 27–28
culture wars, 248–49
cyberharassment, 328–29

damages calculation, 74, 84–86
Davis, Margaret, 101–2
debt collection, 159
declination, 187–88
decontextualization, 3–4, 14, 73–74, 80–82, 88, 129
defamation, 74
default judgments, 159
defense attorneys, implicit bias of, 320
defense of necessity, 390
defense to contract enforceability, 59
deferred judgments, 190
delaying union formation, 282
democracy, 132–33, 136, 140, 165, 227
Denver, Colo., 189, 190
Department of Education, 248
Department of Justice (DOJ), 79, 120, 123, 132, 202, 218, 264
Department of Labor (DOL), 272–73, 281
deservingness, clients', 308–9
detached mastery, 47, 244
deterrence, punishment for, 114–15
Detroit Medical Center (DMC), 241
devil's advocates, 42
direct legal services, 310–22
  care work in, 314
  combating inequality in, 349–50
  exploiting prejudice in, 317–19
  impact litigation vs., 323, 324
  implicit bias of attorneys, 319–22
  occupational segregation in, 313–15
  racial dynamics in, 310–11, 315–17
  resource constraints in, 322
  role of attorneys, 311–13
disabilities, people with, 19, 28, 100, 195–200, 209–12, 317–18
disclosure regulations, 281–82, 352
discovery, 151
discrimination
  in employment, 268–69, 273–76
  gender-based, 274–76, 287, 294
  language-based, 2, 180–81, 191, 370
  prohibitions of, 2, 403
  racial, 190–91, 202–5, 320–21, 334–38
  in unions, 280

discursive power, legal inequality as, 16, 18, 63–64, 87, 106, 136, 184, 204–5, 207, 258–59
dismissals, 151, 189
Disney, 345
displacement, due to gentrification, 96, 97
distributive justice, tort reform and, 86–88
district attorneys (DAs), 178, 350–51
distrust, in legal system, 191
diversity rationale, for affirmative action, 337
doctrinal arguments, 142
domestic violence, 2, 74–77, 332–34, 372
DoorDash, 278
Doran, Jay, 308
doxing, 329–30
due diligence, 245, 354
Dukes, Betty, 274–76
duress, 59, 67–68
"duty to rescue" laws, 52
Dynamex, 278–79

East Cleveland, Ohio, 207–8
e-cigarettes, 252
economic inequality, 55–56, 70–71, 150–51, 155–57, 183–85, 238, 269–73, 283
economics, intersection of law and, 8–9, 45
effective representation, 36–37
Egan, Jenny, 303
election law, 130
Electronic Frontier Foundation (EFF), 327–30
eligibility restrictions, legal aid, 306–7
El Paso, Texas, 208–9
embezzlement, 120–21
Emergent, 260–61
eminent domain, 99
emotional arguments, 143, 144
emotional detachment, 46–47, 194
empathy, for clients, 355–56
employment discrimination defense, 268–69, 273–76
employment litigation, 268–69, 271–79, 286–87
Environmental Protection Agency (EPA), 248
environmental regulatory work, 8, 48, 249, 254–67
equality
 as aspiration, 1, 2, 18, 309
 competing visions of, 186

disagreements about, in impact litigation, 324–25, 341–42
equipage, 156–57
equity partners, 390
ethical arguments, 142
ethical check-ins, prosecutors', 351–52
ethical redlines, 351–53
ethics, 29
evidence, 42, 192–93
evidence law, 112
executive directors (EDs), 316, 317

failure to train lawsuits, 208–9
false imprisonment, 74
federal bureaucracy, 247–49, 252–53
federal courts, 150–57, 404
Federal Deposit Insurance Corporation (FDIC), 248
federal funding, for legal aid, 301–2, 316
federal government attorneys, 171–72
Federal Indian Law courses, 134–35
federalism, 131
Federalist Society, 344
federal judges, 11, 154
Federal Rules of Civil Procedure, 151, 152
Federal Trade Commission (FTC), 253, 257
Feinberg, Ken, 85
felony charges, 188, 190, 298
filing fees, federal court, 155
financial abuse, 67
financial crisis (2008), 94, 265–67
fire-related deaths, 174–77
Fisher, Abigail, 335
fixation, 91, 97–99, 118–21
Flint water disaster, 171
Floyd, George, 44
Food and Drug Administration (FDA), 250, 252
food industry, 236–37
foreseeability, 244
Fortas, Abe, 141
forum-limiting techniques, 163
forum selection, 162–63
fossil fuel industry, 40
fragmentation, of legal work, 233–35, 244
fraud, 59, 65, 122, 264–65
freedom of contract, 59–64
frivolous lawsuits, 201, 273
Fully Informed Jury Association, 348

fundamentalist arguments, 143, 144
fundraising, legal aid, 308–9

gender-based discrimination, 274–76, 287, 294
gender disparities
  in constitutional law, 128
  in contract law, 61–62
  in criminal law, 120
  in damages calculations, 85
  in direct service work, 312
  disability leave for giving birth, 196
  in insurance markets, 83
  occupational segregation and, 313–15
  in property law, 91, 103–6
  prosecutorial decisions reinforcing, 185
  in prosecutors' offices, 180
  in punishment, 117
  in salary, 274–75
gender stereotypes, strategic use of, 318
general counsel, 233, 234
general deterrence, 114–15
general litigation, 269
General Motors, 122–23
gentrification, 95–97, 197
Gershowitz, Adam, 181
ghettos, defined, 313
Gibson Dunn, 241, 253
gig workers, 278–79
Ginsburg, Ruth Bader, 143
giving circles, 355
global economy, Big Law in, 223–24
Global South, 257, 259–63
Goldtooth, Tom, 259–60
Gonzales v. Carhart, 144
Google, 57
Gorsuch, Neil, 139–40
government attorneys, 169–73
  aspects of work by, 169–71
  combating of inequalities by, 346–53
  at federal level, 171–72
  legal inequality by design for, 17
  at local level, 172–73
  municipal, 195–219
  prosecutors, 174–94
  at state level, 171
government officials, torts against, 77–80
grading, law school, 34
Great Depression, 247–48

green hushing, 258
Greer, Christina, 354
Grindr, 329
Guam, 139–40
Guerrero, Yocasta, 284–86
gun policy, 145, 330–34

harm, 72–73, 324–25, 341–42
Harris, Jasmine, 197
Hart–Scott–Rodino (HSR) filings, 234
Harvard University, 335–37
Hawai'i, Kingdom of, 138–39
HCA Healthcare, 241–43
healthcare M&As, 232, 237–43
health insurance, 238
hearing disabilities, people with, 210–11
Hee, Sung, 284–86
Hernandez-Adams, Niki, 85
Herrick, Matthew, 329
Hilton, 284–86
hired-gun transactional work, 244
historical arguments, 141
Holder, Eric, 253
Holland and Knight, 99
home, social significance of, 93
home-based childcare, 104–6
homelessness, 90, 93–94, 97, 119, 213–18
homicide, 118–19, 122–25, 332–33
horizontal forum shopping, 162
hotel industry, 284–86
housekeeping workers, 284–86
housing code violations, 215–16
housing insecurity, 93–94, 213–18

immigrants
  access to home ownership for, 89
  assertion of contractual rights by, 64–65
  class actions representing, 17
  criminalization of, 116
  exclusion of, from unions, 280
  with limited English proficiency, 64–66
  Obama-era deportation of, 293
  punishment of, 116–17
  undocumented, 17, 64, 302
Immigration and Customs Enforcement (ICE), 64, 117
impact litigation, 295, 323–42
  on affirmative action, 334–38
  direct legal services vs., 323, 324

disagreements over inequality in, 324–25, 341–42
on free speech rights, 325–30
goals of, 323–24
on gun policy, 330–34
on LGBTQ rights and religious liberty, 338–41
implicit bias, 312, 319–22
imposter syndrome, 28
incapacitation, punishment for, 114, 115
incapacity defense, 59
incomplete offenses, 119
incremental litigation strategy, 340
independent contractors, 251, 277–79
Indigenous Peoples, 257, 259–63, 367; See also Native Americans
individual coercion, 68
industry consolidation, 233, 235
ineffective assistance of counsel, 299–301
informants, 179
Ingram, Xavier, 205
in-house counsel, 233, 234
initial public offering (IPO), 231
inmate litigation, 205–6
Instacart, 278
Institute for Justice, 79
Insular Cases, 139–40
insurance markets, 82–84, 238
Insys Therapeutics, 124–25
intake attorney, 187
intellectual property, 373
intentional torts, 74–75, 77
interests in land, 93
international finance, 231
Islamophobia, 45

January 6th Capitol insurrection, 44
Jenner and Block, 227
Jet Blue, 237
Johnson, Robert, 177
Jones Day, 283, 284
Jordan, Michael, 294
judges, 11, 154, 159, 179; See also Supreme Court, US
judicial activism, 147
Judicial Hellholes report (Tort Reform Foundation), 87
judicial review, 131
Judiciary Act (1789), 155

jurisdiction, 151
jury nullification, 346–48
jury selection, 190–91
justiciability doctrines, 132
juvenile justice system, 320–22

Kalākaua, David, 138
Kapoor, John, 125
Kavanaugh, Brett, 340
Kennedy, Anthony, 144, 338
Kingdom of Hawai'i, 138–39
Kirkland and Ellis, 233
Kroger, 236–37

labor law, 271, 279–87
Labor-Management Reporting and Disclosure Act (LMRDA), 281
landlords, charges in fire-related deaths for, 175–76
landlord-tenant relationships, 93
land use, 93
language-based discrimination, 2, 180–81, 191, 370
language choices, prosecutors', 184, 192
larceny, 120
Latham and Watkins, 260–61
Latinos, 64–65, 89, 90, 188–91, 204, 331, 335–37
law, defined, 14
law professors
 class position of, 95
 combating of inequality by, 49, 357
 compensation for, 11
 discursive power of, 63–64
 influence of, on curricula, 35–36
 "liberal," 52, 369
 limitations on knowledge of, 135
 on purpose of law school, 41–50
law school, 27–50, 364
 civil procedure curricula, 149–66
 combating legal inequalities in, 344, 357–58
 constitutional law curricula, 127–48
 contract law curricula, 54–71
 criminal law curricula, 109–26
 government lawyering through lens of, 170
 law professors on purpose of, 41–50
 not endorsing existing system in, 107–8
 omissions from curricula, 51–53
 orientation, 28–29

law school (*continued*)
  overall purpose of, 35–41
  property law curricula, 89–106
  socialization of law students, 29–30
  student groups that are trying to rethink, 344
  tort law curricula, 72–88
  undergraduate education vs., 30–34
lead paint, 216–18
Learned Hand formula, 79
legal aid attorneys and organizations, 296, 298–99, 301–2, 305–9, 313–17, 320, 323, 350
Legal Aid Society of the District of Columbia, 170, 197, 291
legal conclusions, reaching, 42
legal education, *See* law school
legal ethics, 37–39, 170–71
legal inequalities; *See also* strategies for combating legal inequalities
  causes of, 2–4
  as contested advocacy, 17–18, 186, 338
  by design, 17, 18, 162, 185, 279
  as discursive power, 16, 18, 63–64, 87, 106, 136, 184, 204–5, 207, 258–59
  examples of, 1–2
  groups impacted by, 14–15
  overview of six types, 14–19
  for prosecutors, 183–87
  as reflection of societal hierarchies, 15–16, 18, 31, 83–84, 106, 110, 125, 129, 159, 183–84, 270, 292, 302, 312, 315
  as selective enforcement, 16, 18, 174–77, 184–85
  as structural imperative, 17, 18, 107–8, 113–14, 117–18, 185–86, 199–200, 204, 232, 243–45, 319
legal reasoning, privileged, 129–30
Legal Research and Writing (LRW) courses, 364
Legal Services Corporation (LSC), 306
legislators, mass incarceration and, 179
legitimate forms of constitutional argument (modalities), 141–42
Leonard, Beth, 308
Levine, Kate, 185
LGBTQ individuals, 19, 28, 120, 170, 328, 338–41

LGBTQ+ panic defense, 318
liability, for government officials, 79–80
liberal orthodoxy, 52, 147, 293, 294, 298, 341, 369
licensing fees, 349–50
Liebman, Wilma, 280
Liliʻuokalani, Queen, 138
limited English proficiency (LEP), individuals with, 2, 64–66, 370
line prosecutors, 178, 187, 193
litigation, 23, 268–87
  civil procedures curricula on, 151
  employment, 268–69, 271–79
  expenses incident to, 156–57
  general, 269
  impact, 323–42
  involving company vs. individual, 269–70
  labor law, 279–86
  merit of claim in, 149
  misconceptions about, 268
  regulatory work and, 249, 250
  transactional work vs., 230
  workplace, 268–87
Littler Mendelson, 282, 285
living constitutionalism, 129, 145–48
LLM programs, 364
local courts, 150, 157–60, 383
local governments, 169–73, 261–62
Lochner v. New York, 60
logrolling, 143
Los Angeles, Calif., 192–93, 198, 199, 214
Lowering Emissions by Accelerating Forest Finance (LEAF) Coalition, 260–61
low-income households, 2, 150, 154–57, 159–60, 232, 236, 262, 293; *See also* poverty
Lyft, 278

Maatman, Gerald, 277
Macquarie, 259
mandatory arbitration clauses, 163–64
Marable, Stacey, 215–16
Maricopa County Attorney's Office, 203–4
Massachusetts, 189
mass incarceration, 38, 113, 178–80, 293
mass negligence, 122–23
mass pardons, 115–16
Masterpiece Cakeshop, Ltd. v. Colorado Civil Rights Commission, 338–40

Masterson, Chase, 328–29
Matchmaker, 328–29
maternity leave, 196
Mayfield v. Woodford, 400
McDonald, Laquan, 205
McKinley, William, 138
McMillan v. the City of New York, 85
Medicaid, 238, 239, 241, 291
Medicare, 241, 278
mental health issues, people with, 196
mental states, 118
mergers and acquisitions (M&As), 23, 232–45
  airline industry, 237
  banking industry, 236
  consumer impact of predatory, 235–45
  corporate influence on politics after, 233
  food industry, 236–37
  fragmentation of work on, 233–35
  healthcare system, 237–43
  inequality as structural imperative in, 243–45
#MeToo movement, 328
Miami, Fla., 213–14, 303
Michigan, 188
middle class, legal assistance for, 306–7
minimum wage, 276–77
Minneapolis Public Housing Authority (MPHA), 215–16
misdemeanors, 119, 125–26, 187–88, 190, 303
Mission Health, 242–43
modification, contract, 62
moral detachment, 126, 145, 148, 150–51, 177–78, 230, 232–35, 287, 325, 354
morality, 37–38, 46
mortgages, 93
Multistate Professional Responsibility Examination (MPRE), 39–40
municipal attorneys, 173, 195–219
  city functions relying on, 200
  combating of inequality by, 348–49, 352–53
  defense of ableism by, 209–12
  disability rights and, 195–200, 209–12
  homelessness and housing insecurity issues, 213–18
  in local civil rights conflicts, 218–19
  police misconduct issues, 200–209
  sidewalk accessibility issues, 198–200
  zealous advocacy by, 199–200
Musk, Elon, 250

NAACP Legal Defense Fund (NAACP-LDF), 324
Natapoff, Alexandra, 304–5
National Association for Criminal Defense Lawyers (NACDL), 333
National Grocers Association, 236
National Labor Relations Act (NLRA), 279
National Labor Relations Board (NLRB), 250, 279, 282, 285–87
National Legal Aid and Defender Association, 366
national security law, 131
Native Americans, 45, 60–61, 133–36; *See also specific nations*
Navajo Nation, 135
Nazis, free speech rights of, 325–26, 330
negligence doctrine, 74, 80–82
Nestlé, 161
Newcombe, Kenneth, 264, 265
New Deal, 296, 297
New York City Housing Authority (NYCHA), 216–18
New York City Law Department, 188, 189, 201–3, 211, 219
New York Magazine, 283
New York Police Department (NYPD), 202–3, 219, 330–31
New York State Rifle & Pistol Association v. Bruen, 330–33
Nixon, Richard, 39, 104
nonstarters (non-modalities), 142
North Carolina, 188
Northwestern University, 7–8, 10, 153

Oath of Professionalism, 29
Obama, Barack, 123–24, 253, 280, 293
Objectives of Program of Legal Education (ABA Rule 301), 36–41
objective theory of assent, 70
Occupational Safety and Health Administration (OSHA), 248
occupational segregation, 313–15
offer, in contract, 59
Ogletree Deakins, 277, 283

Oklahoma County, 210
Olson, Ted, 275
O'Melveny and Myers, 279
One Big Beautiful Bill Act, 117, 238–39
opening statements, 191
Operation Clean Halls, 203
opioid crisis, 124–25
orientation, law school, 28–29
originalism, 129, 145–48, 382
outside counsel, 233–34
OxyContin, 124

Papa John's, 276–77
Parker, Jashawn, 175–77
parole, 193
partisan arguments, 143–44
partners, Big Law, 224
Paul, Weiss, 226, 230
Paul Hastings, 274
Pearson, Pearl, 210
Peng, Tina, 304
performance, in contract law, 59
personal property, 92
phantom credits, 263–64
Philippines, 139–40
Philips, Jack, 338
Phounsy, Lucky, 206
pink collar jobs, 313
pink ghetto, 313
Planned Parenthood v. Casey, 144
plea bargains, 178, 179, 189–90, 304
Pledge of Allegiance, 127
police
    accountability for, 15
    civil asset forfeiture to, 90, 99–103
    disposal of unhoused people's property by, 213–14
    go-to charges used by, 110
    gun ownership and shootings by, 332
    mass incarceration and, 179
    misconduct charges for, 185–86
    municipal attorneys' defense of, 200–210
    people with disabilities and, 210–11
    prosecutors and, 187–88
    striking jurors for contact with, 191
policing the bargain, 66–70
policy arguments, 142–43
political status, of Native Americans, 135
political tithing, 354–55

politics
    Big Law and, 223
    constitutional law and, 132, 140–48
    corporate influence on, 233
    criminal law and, 43–44
    gentrification and, 96–97
    of lawyers who expand/erode rights, 20–21
    of public interest attorneys, 293, 294
Politics and Prose bookstore, 283–84
politics of wealth defense, 99
popularity arguments, 143, 144
Postmates, 278
poverty, 5–6, 8, 239; *See also* housing insecurity; low-income households
poverty law, 291, 296–99, 314, 315
power relations, 12, 21, 73–74, 326–27
predatory lending, 2, 54–55
preemptory strikes, 190–91
prejudice, exploiting, 312, 317–19
prejudiced outcome, Strickland standard on, 300
presumption of understanding, 64–66
pretrial diversion, 189
prices, M&As and, 236–38, 240, 242
Primus, Eve, 304
private equity, 231
private law, 51, 107
privileged information, 393
professional responsibility, 39–41, 182, 201, 244
professional skills development, 46–47
property law, 89–106
    applications of, in San Francisco Bay Area, 89–92
    civil asset forfeiture in, 99–103
    core areas in, 92–93
    defined, 51
    gentrification in, 95–97
    homelessness/housing insecurity in, 93–94
    RAP in, 97–99
    selective attention in, 91–92, 106
    zoning and child care shortage, 103–6
prosecutorial discretion, 177
prosecutorial misconduct, 182
prosecutorial process, 187–93
prosecutors, 173–94
    of Bronx fire-related deaths, 174–77
    of carbon offsetting industry, 264–65

civic good and mass incarceration by, 178–80
combating of inequality by, 193–94, 346–48, 350–52
in criminal justice system, 179–80
immunity and accountability for, 182
legal ethics vs. morality in work of, 38
political influence on, 44
release-dismissal agreements by, 68
resource constraints on offices of, 181
role of, 178
selective enforcement by, 16, 174–77
six dimensions of legal inequalities for, 183–87
trade-offs inherent for, 186–87
unrepresentative leadership of, 180–81
prosecutor vacancy, 181
Proskauer Rose, 99, 274, 282, 283
prudential arguments, 142
public defenders, 36, 269, 296, 298–305, 310–11, 313, 318–22
public interest work, 291–95
author's experience in, 291
combating inequality in, 349–50, 355–57
compensation for, 292
criticizing attorneys in, 291–95
cynical view of Big Law in, 226
direct legal services, 310–22
government attorneys in, 169–70
impact litigation, 323–42
involving companies vs. individuals, 270
liberal orthodoxy wound up in, 293
murky definitional boundaries of, 293–95
sacrifices made by attorneys in, 292–93
structural constraints of, 296–309
public law, 51, 107
public secrets, 303
Puerto Rico, 139–40
punishment, 110, 114–18, 178
Purdue Pharma, 124

Quinn Emanuel, 277

racial discrimination, 190–91, 202–5, 320–21, 334–38
racial disparities, 83–86, 100, 112, 116, 128, 180, 188–93, 206, 262, 331
racialization, of Native Americans, 135

racial minorities, 28; *See also specific groups*
complicity of, in legal inequalities, 208
property problems for, 89–90
at public interest organizations, 317
Section 230 protections for, 327–28
racial representation, 8–10, 180–81, 310–12, 315–17
racial stereotypes, 139–40, 318
racist rhetoric, by prosecutors, 192
railroad torts, 81–82
rape, 119–20
Rapping, Jonathan, 304
reading, law school, 30–31
Reagan, Ronald, 301
real estate projects, 231
real property, 92
reform prosecutors, 193–94
regulatory arbitrage, 251
regulatory lag (RegLag), 251–52, 257–58
regulatory work, 22–23, 247–67
on carbon offsetting, 254–67
corporate advantage in, 251–53
environmental, 249, 254–67
impact of, on society, 251
misconceptions about, 268
and role of federal bureaucracy, 247–49
role of regulatory lawyers, 249
specialization in, 250–51
by transactional attorneys or litigators, 250
union avoidance as, 282
rehabilitation, punishment for, 115
release-dismissal agreements, 68
relevant but forbidden forms of constitutional argument (anti-modalities), 142–45
religious liberty, 338–41
remedies for breach, 59, 62
removal, in procedural process, 164
repossession, 62
representation in leadership, 180–81, 310–12, 315–17
restraining orders, 333–34
retainer fee, 272
retribution, punishment for, 114–16
robbery, 120
Roberts, John, 10, 11, 143
Roe v. Wade, 46, 143–44, 294
role differentiation, 228

Rollins, Rachel, 310–11, 401
Rucker, Jeannette, 203
rule against perpetuities (RAP), 97–99
rural areas, 232, 236, 238–40
Russian Empire, 137

Safe Drinking Water Act, 248
San Diego County, Calif., 206, 389
San Francisco Bay Area, Calif., 89–92
Scalia, Antonin, 102, 275
Scalia, Eugene, 253
secret ballot election, for union, 282
Section 230 protections for online platforms, 327–30
Section 1983 police brutality claims, 202–3, 208–9
Securities and Exchange Commission (SEC), 248
selective attention, 91–106, 109–26
selective enforcement, 16, 18, 174–77, 184–85
selectivity, 91–92, 99–103, 147–48
self-defense, 111, 119, 330–31
self-representation, 158
sentencing recommendations, 183–84
separation of powers, 131
September 11th Victim Compensation Fund, 85
settlements, 205–7, 273, 353
sewer service, 159
sexual harassment, 17, 280, 284, 328–29
sex work, 117, 119, 120
Shell, 161
sidewalk accessibility, 198–200
Sidley Austin, 224–25, 269
Skadden Foundation, 294
Slate magazine, 283
slavery, 45, 297, 367
slow violence, 256–57
small businesses, 161
small-firm practitioners, 364–65
Smith, Lorie, 338–40
social hierarchies, legal inequalities reflecting, 15–16, 18
  in civil procedure, 159
  in constitutional law, 129
  in criminal law, 110, 125
  in direct legal services, 312, 315
  in property law, 106

  for prosecutors, 183–84
  in public interest law, 292, 302
  in Socratic cold calling, 31
  in tort law, 83–84
  in workplace litigation, 270
socialization, 3, 4, 29–30, 55–56, 144
social policies, 323–24, 400
Social Security Administration (SSA), 248
social welfare, 270, 297
society, impact of regulatory work on, 251, 266–67
Socratic method, 31–34, 365
solo legal practitioners, 364–65
Sotomayor, Sonia, 10
South Pole (firm), 263–64
sovereign wealth funds, 259
Space X, 286
Spanish-American War, 139
Spanish Empire, 139–40
specialization, in regulatory work, 250–51
specific deterrence, 115
Spirit Airlines, 237
Starbucks, 282, 286
state attorneys general (AGs), 171, 172
state courts, 150, 152–54, 157–60, 383
state violence, 77–80, 130, 305
statute of limitations, 207–8
Steele, Jason, 264–65
stereotypes, reinforcing, 317–19
Stern, Mark Joseph, 283
stop-and-frisk policy, 188, 203, 331, 386
strategies for combating legal inequalities, 343–58
  at Big Law firms, 344–45, 353–55
  for government attorneys, 346–53
  at law schools, 344, 357–58
  for lawyers, 350–58
  for non-lawyers, 343–50
  for prosecutors, 193–94
  for public interest attorneys, 349–50, 355–57
Strickland v. Washington, 299–301
structural arguments, 142
structural constraints on public interest work, 296–309
  and history of poverty law, 296–99
  legal aid attorneys on, 305–9
  legal disparities exacerbated by, 309
  public defenders on, 302–5

Index | 421

restrictions on legal aid attorneys who receive federal funding, 301–2
Strickland standard and, 299–301
structural imperative, legal inequality as, 17, 18
and critiques of criminal justice system, 113–14, 117–18
failures in civil procedure and, 165–66
in M&As, 232, 243–45
for municipal attorneys, 199–200, 204
for prosecutors, 185–86
in strategic use of prejudice, 319
and teaching without endorsing system, 107–8
student debt, 399
Students for Fair Admissions (SFFA), 294, 334–38
Subsys, 124
summary judgment, 152
summons, 151
Supreme Court, US
  on absolute prosecutorial immunity, 182
  on affirmative action, 335, 336
  on asset forfeiture, 102
  on attorney licensing fees, 350
  on California prison system, 171
  on class action suits, 275
  constitutional interpretation by, 128–29, 132–33, 140–47
  on gun ownership, 330, 333
  in history of poverty law, 297, 298
  on ineffective assistance of counsel, 300–301
  influence of, on civil procedure, 154
  Insular Cases, 139–40
  on jury exclusion, 190, 191
  lack of diversity on, 9–11
  on LGBTQ rights and religious liberty, 338–40
  on NLRB, 286
  on opioid crisis, 124
  pro-business jurisprudence by, 161–62
  on unhoused people in public, 94, 213–15

Tani, Karen, 197
tax avoidance strategies, 98, 251
Teamsters Union, 280
Tenet Healthcare Corporation, 241

"Tent City," Maricopa County, 204
termination, threat, 285–86
textual arguments, 141
theft, 120–21
thinking like a lawyer, 41–46
Thomas, Clarence, 10, 102, 331
Thompson v. Thompson, 75–77
303 Creative LLC v. Eleni, 338–41
Time Warner, 233
tip theft, 277
title, 93
Title IX, 248
tokenism, 316
tort, defined, 72
tortfeasor, 72
tort law, 72–88
  damages calculation, 84–86
  domestic violence in, 74–77
  everyday experiences involving, 72–73
  focus of, 51
  inequality in insurance markets, 82–84
  negligence doctrine, 80–82
  obscuring power relations in, 73–74
  state violence in, 77–80
  stripping of context in curriculum on, 88
tort reform, 74, 82, 86–88
Trader Joe's, 286
transactional work, 22, 229–46
  business compulsion cases in, 68–69
  fragmentation in, 229–30, 233–35
  mergers and acquisitions, 232–45
  misconceptions about, 268
  by municipal attorneys, 219
  regulatory work and, 249, 250
  response to critique of, 246
  types of, 230–31
transferred intent, 113
treaties, with Native Nations, 60–61
trespass, doctrine of, 94
trial
  procedural rules for, 152
  prosecutorial discretion in, 192
Trump, Donald, 20, 44, 132, 136, 144, 171–72, 223, 225–26, 230, 233, 248, 250, 257, 286, 344

Uber, 251, 277–79
unconscionability doctrine, 59, 69–71
unconstitutional takings claims, 407

underdevelopment, 92, 103–6
undergraduate education, law school vs., 30–34
understatement of corporate interests, in civil procedure, 160–65
undocumented immigrants, 17, 64, 302
undue influence doctrine, 67
union busting, 279–84
United Fruit Company, 395
United States v. Rahimi, 333–34
Unite the Right rally, 326, 330
University of California, Berkeley, 12, 28, 89, 90, 114, 170, 196–97, 215, 226, 268, 327
University of Pennsylvania, 13–14, 20, 96, 170, 181
unreasonably deficient performance, 300

Vanguard Health Systems, 241
Verra, 263, 265
vertical forum shopping, 162–63
veto power, community, 395
voluntary markets for carbon, 255
voting, 346, 348–49

wage theft, 66, 271, 276–79
Walmart, 162, 274–76
Wal-Mart v. Dukes, 274–77, 287
War on Poverty, 296, 298–99
Washington, DC, 197–98
Watergate scandal, 39, 366
wealth transfer, 98–99
Weil, David, 278

White and Case, 99
white-collar crime, 120–25
Whitman-Walker, 170
Whole Foods, 286
Wilcox, Gwynne, 286
Williams v. Walker-Thomas Furniture Co., 69
WilmerHale, 227
Winston and Strawn, 283
Wisconsin, 190
Women's Law Project, 294
worker misclassification, 251, 277–79
working-class individuals, 19, 306–7
working conditions, 286–87
workplace litigation
    employment, 268–69, 271–79
    impact of, on working conditions, 286–87
    labor law, 279–86

Ynfante, Ana, 284–86

zealous advocacy
    corporate lawyers use of civil procedure for, 165
    by direct services attorneys, 312
    and erosion of union power, 284–86
    exploiting prejudice for, 317–19
    by municipal attorneys, 199–200, 219
    by prosecutors, 180–81
    by unconscionable lawyers, 71
    in workplace litigation, 270, 286, 287
Zimbabwe, 263–64
zoning, 91, 92, 96, 103–6